WHAT'S IN THE BIBLE

WHAT'S IN THE BIBLE

A ONE-VOLUME GUIDEBOOK TO GOD'S WORD

■ ■ ■

R. C. Sproul
AND
Robert Wolgemuth

THOMAS NELSON
Since 1798

NASHVILLE   DALLAS   MEXICO CITY   RIO DE JANEIRO   BEIJING

Published by W Publishing Group, a Division of Thomas Nelson, Inc., P.O. Box 141000, Nashville, Tennessee, 37214.

Library of Congress Cataloging-in-Publication Data

Sproul, R. C. (Robert Charles), 1939–
    What's in the Bible : the story of God through time & eternity / R. C. Sproul, Robert Wolgemuth.
        p. cm.
    ISBN-10: 0-8499-4460-0
    ISBN-13: 978-0-8499-4460-4
    1. Bible—Introductions. I. Wolgemuth, Robert, 1948– II. Title.

BS475.3 .S67 2001
22.6'1—dc21   00–053394
                                                                              CIP

Printed in the United States of America
07 QW 6

To James Montgomery Boice . . .
A faithful expositor of the whole counsel of God.
—R. C. SPROUL

∾◦∾

To the Adventure Sunday school class of
First Presbyterian Church, Nashville, Tennessee . . .
*We spent sixteen years digging into the wonder and truth
of God's Word together, and it changed us all.*
—ROBERT WOLGEMUTH

CONTENTS

ACKNOWLEDGMENTS

Over the years there were people who introduced us to the truth of the Holy Bible. And there were those who poured into us a love for its wonder and power. These people include grandparents, parents, teachers, professors, theologians and philosophers (past and present), pastors, colleagues, friends, and family members. We thank them with all our hearts for introducing us to the Book that changed us forever.

We have both taught overviews of Holy Scripture, and we're thankful to our friends at W Publishing Group for coming up with the idea of this book—the blended viewpoints of two men with diverse backgrounds and experiences, yet two men with like-minded faith.

Thanks to Vesta Sproul and Bobbie Wolgemuth, who have gotten used to the necessary solitude of their writing husbands. They are truly godly women who have loved us, supported us, and thoroughly edited our work.

Robert Barnes and R. C. Sproul Jr. contributed their editorial skills to early renditions of the manuscript. Our thanks to them both.

When the manuscript for this book was complete, we sent it to five people and asked them to tell us what they thought of it—a minister, a physician, a businessman, a homemaker, and a neighbor. Their input was wonderfully valuable and we thank them: Mark DeVries, Randall Loy, Regina Sentell, Yolanda Tabuchi, and especially Daniel Wolgemuth.

Finally, thanks to you for choosing to spend a few hours with us. Our hope and prayer is that this book will be helpful to you in your own walk with God.

—R. C. Sproul and Robert Wolgemuth

INTRODUCTION

The Bible can look like quite an ominous tome—sixty-six different books, penned by forty-five writers over a period of time spanning fifteen hundred years, and packed into a single volume of almost two thousand pages. Like we said, "ominous."

Because it's been around for so long, nearly everyone knows something *about* the Bible, but very few people actually *know* it in its entirety. As history's all-time best-selling book, nearly everyone owns a copy, but most of these copies have never been read as a whole. Maybe this describes the Bible on your shelf.

In church or school, you have heard sermons and lectures that apply meaning to specific passages. You probably have even read or studied books that illuminate particular biblical texts. Yet you may never have looked at the Bible as a single book to read from cover to cover.

In 1992, best-selling author and renowned theologian Dr. R. C. Sproul recorded fifty-five messages on audio- and videotape. The series was entitled *Dust to Glory.* The purpose of the project was to help people learn to understand the entire Bible with a new sense of appreciation . . . from a theologian's perspective.

And, in 1995, best-selling author and businessman Robert Wolgemuth recorded sixty lessons on audiotape for his Sunday school class. The series was entitled *Adventures Through the Bible.* The purpose of this series was to help people learn to understand the entire Bible with a new sense of appreciation . . . from a layman's perspective.

Then, in 2000, R. C. and Robert took their shared vision and created this book. As longtime friends, such collaboration between a theologian and a layman made a lot of good sense.

This book is an overview. R. C. and Robert have highlighted the essence of God's voice, activity, and purpose throughout the Old and New Testaments. And they've done their best to deliver this to you in an interesting and thoroughly readable form.

The book is divided into seventeen chapters, which cover major groupings of Bible books. Each chapter is broken down into smaller sections, focusing on a more specific period of time, a pivotal theme, or a major Bible character.

At the close of each chapter you'll find a brief summary so you can look back and get an overview of what you've just read.

You may choose to read *What's in the Bible* from cover to cover, or you may want to study it a section at a time. Either way, R. C. and Robert's hope is that the book will provide you with a road map that will help you to better comprehend the whole of Scripture and to begin—or enhance—your daily walk with its Author, the Sovereign God of the universe.

God bless you.

AUTHORS' PREFACE

HAVE YOU EVER BEEN LOST?

Because you have been lost, you know it's not an enjoyable experience. If you're in your car, you know how it feels when your stomach tightens and your hands grip the steering wheel until your knuckles are white. You're moving down the road but you have no idea where you are.

Over the years, we both (R. C. and Robert) have experienced this very uncomfortable thing. Of course, the stress of the situation has been intensified when we've been late for a meeting or when our wives have been in the car with us and encouraged us (begged us) to stop and ask for directions.

Being lost is no fun at all.

In the late eighties, I (Robert) was in Phoenix on a business trip. Because I had the evening free, I decided to visit one of Arizona's largest shopping malls. Once inside the mall I walked straight to the big colorful lighted box that had the word *Directory* plainly printed on the top. I was looking for a bookstore and knew this was the best way to find it.

Scanning the list of stores, I found the one I was looking for—in the blue section of the mall. Based on the size of the store on the map, I knew I was in for a treat . . . a nice *big* bookstore.

All I needed to do was to get from where I was to where the store was. But I had a problem. Someone had peeled the "You Are Here" sticker off the face of the Directory. I knew where I was going but I had no idea where I was.

Frustrated and muttering under my breath, I started walking the mall, hoping to accidentally stumble across my bookstore. As I said, being lost is no fun at all.

THE BIBLE

If we were to scan the faces of the many people who regularly attend church—almost fifty million of them in the United States alone—we would find lots of "lost" people.

Now we're not necessarily talking about people who are lost because they have no personal faith. We're referring to those people who are unsuccessfully trying to keep up with the reading of the Scripture and the context of the sermon. But, because they don't have an understanding of the whole story of the Bible, their faces are telling us that they're wandering the corridors of biblical illiteracy, hoping to bump into something they recognize . . . like trying to find the illusive bookstore in the blue section of the Phoenix Mall.

Maybe this lost person is you?

If so, we think you're in for a treat. We have written this book to help you find your way—directions to help you get "un-lost" in the sometimes confusing maze of historical records, poetry, prophecy, and stories that make up the Holy Bible.

BUT WHY? . . . WHAT'S THE POINT?

"Okay," you might be saying, "I admit it. I'm the one with the blank look in church. When the minister refers to 'the Patriarchs' or 'the Exile' or 'the Incarnation' or 'the messianic secret,' I really don't understand what he's talking about. But what difference does it make? Why do I need to know any more about the Bible than I already know?"

That's a good question because if you don't know why you need to know more, although this book may be interesting to read, it's probably going to be a waste of your time.

First, we have a confession to make. There was a time in our lives when we felt just like this. We knew that our ministers, our professors, and the authors of some of the books on our shelves knew all about the Bible. And as long as they knew, we really didn't need to know.

So, what changed our minds? Why did we decide to get to know the whole Bible for ourselves? Here are some of the reasons. Maybe they'll be helpful for you.

THE BEST-SELLING BOOK OF ALL TIME

When a book reaches the *New York Times* Bestseller List, authors and publishers celebrate. In order to reach this list—depending on what other titles are there and how well they're selling—a book usually sells around 100,000 copies. And when a particular book sits on that list for a long time, sales may reach a million copies.

On a very rare occasion, a book reaches multiple millions in sales. When it does, nearly everyone knows about it. You'll overhear people at lunch chatting about it. Book reviewers of every stripe will write about this book. Teachers, professional speakers, writers, and ministers will quote from this book. When millions of copies of a book are sold, it cannot be overlooked.

From the time of the scribes in the first century—tediously duplicating copies of the original biblical manuscripts by hand—until the present day, where we can log on to a Web site and download an entire book in seconds, billions of copies of the Bible have been distributed. Yes, we said "billions."

Not only has the Bible been printed and distributed millions of times, it has been printed *millions* of millions of times.

The sheer fact of this massive distribution of a single book should at least raise our level of interest, if for no reason other than mere curiosity.

THE MARTYRS

We know this sounds preposterous, but down through the centuries, people were willing to sacrifice everything—even their own lives and the lives of their children—rather than deny the truth of the Bible. Imagine being able to avoid burning at a stake or having your family ripped apart by lions simply by saying that the whole Bible is not truth. Not only did these heroes refuse to deny the perfection of the Scripture, they dared to stand nose to nose with those who denied its infallibility. It was the combination of these two steadfast positions that cost so many so much.

For example, one of the pivotal truths of the Christian faith that these brave people surely believed is found in both the Old and New Testaments: The just shall live by faith.

This is a straightforward statement. There should be no confusion about its meaning. Being right in God's eyes—"just-ness"—only comes by faith. It does not come by way of anything we can do apart from confession and complete trust in God's work of grace in Jesus Christ. No other effort on our part is sufficient.

Now suppose that some evening while you were scanning the available

channels on your television you came across a preacher. He was looking directly into the camera and unabashedly declaring that if you sent a check to him,
he would have the power to forgive your sin. And then he posted a price list.
The greater the sin the more you had to pay to be forgiven. He declared that
as God's emissary he had the right to strike this deal with you.

You'd probably come out of your chair in utter shock and disbelief. We can
imagine you might even call your spouse in from the other room and tell them
what you had heard. If you have any understanding of the Bible at all, you'd be
thoroughly scandalized by this horrific claim.

Well, listen to this.

In the early sixteenth century, during the reign of Pope Leo X, a man by the
name of Tetzel published a list of indulgences. This was literally a pay-as-you-sin
price list. For example, Tetzel claimed that if you committed fornication, you
could be forgiven by dropping an extra nine shillings into the offering plate. If
you killed a commoner, paying seven shillings and a sixpence could erase the
consequences of your crime. If you murdered your wife or your parents, the cost
was ten shillings and a sixpence. Anyone, including a priest, could keep a mistress
in exchange for the same price. Once you paid this fee, you were declared clean.

In the face of this incredible fund-raising scam, using the Bible as their only
authority, courageous people stepped forward and challenged this practice.
What gave them the right to challenge it? Who or what was their witness? It
was the Bible, pure and simple.

These staunch believers distributed a list of twenty truths, called "Certain
Principles Founded upon the Truth of God's Word." Truth by truth, the activities of a corrupt church were exposed by this list. (Number 14 was "A man is
justified by faith, without works, freely by grace, not of ourselves.")

And for this, people were dragged from their homes and given an opportunity to apologize and recant—or lose their lives. Hundreds chose execution.
The Bible's accuracy was not to be questioned, no matter what the cost.

Again, remember that these people—let's call them saints—were willing to
lose everything because of something they believed: The Bible, God's Word, is
truth.

We believe that getting to know more about a book that people were willing to die for is a very good idea.

GOD

As you will see in the pages that follow, the Bible is the source of information about God, the Sovereign and Holy Creator of the universe. No other book gives us more information about Him than Scripture.

"But why is this important?" you might ask.

Our culture is fascinated with entrepreneurs and leaders. Almost every day there's a story in the newspaper about Bill Gates, the founder of Microsoft, or Jack Welch, the CEO of General Electric. Who are these people? What are they like? How did they get to be so powerful?

From the first time we peeked into a microscope to the last time we went for an evening walk under a crystal sky, we have been filled with wonder. Who made all of this? What is He like? What does He do with all His power?

Beginning with the dust of creation and concluding with His promise of our joining Him in heaven's glory, the Bible tells us about God. It tells of His creativity and His sustaining might, His judgment and His mercy, His holiness and His grace, our rebellion and His redemptive plan.

Why *wouldn't* we want to read the story about this One?

WHAT THE BIBLE SAYS ABOUT ITSELF

One of the most interesting features of the Bible is what it says about itself. Here are a few examples. Notice how many of these characteristics speak to Scripture's impact on us, the readers.

> *All Scripture is given by inspiration of God,*
> *and is profitable for doctrine, for reproof,*
> *for correction, for instruction in righteousness,*
> *that the man of God may be complete,*
> *thoroughly equipped for every good work.* (2 Timothy 3:16–17)

Doctrine

The Bible is truth. Like any authoritative document, the Scripture is unequivocal about good and evil, right and wrong. And with the skill of a master teacher, through historical accounts and parables, the Bible skillfully connects with those of us who read it.

Reproof

When we were youngsters, our mothers used to get our attention by loudly calling our names. From any location in our homes, we could hear that voice and know we were in for a serious bout with reality. Throughout its pages, the Bible does the same thing. As powerfully as our mothers' voices, the Scripture calls our names. "Listen up," it says. "I'm talking to you." That's reproof.

Correction

Once our mothers had our attention and we were in their presence, they made it painfully clear what we had done to deserve this interruption to our complacency or disobedience. The Bible does this as well. It clearly spells out the nature of our infractions—often through the real-life examples of folks just like us—and the predictable consequences.

Instruction in Righteousness

Once the Bible has our attention and has clarified the truth of our failure and its aftereffect, then the Scripture tells us what to do—how to act, how to speak, how to think.

A Harvest of Right Living

> *Your word I have hidden in my heart,*
> *That I might not sin against You.* (Psalm 119:11)

Time and time again the men and women of the Bible found themselves steeped in self-inflicted trouble. We all can relate. So what can be done about this? The Scripture encourages us to take its truth and plant it into our hearts like seeds. The crop will be a harvest of right acting, right speaking, and right thinking. Sheer force and discipline cannot achieve these things. They are by-products—the Bible calls them "fruit"—of having planted good seed. God's Word is good seed.

Lost and Found

Your word is a lamp to my feet
And a light to my path. (Psalm 119:105)

The Bible keeps us from stumbling, from falling, and from getting lost. If you have ever tried to walk on an unfamiliar trail in the dark of night, you know what comfort there is in having a working flashlight. Without it you're sure to get in trouble. God's Word is exactly that—a wonderfully reliable light source to keep us on the right track. The Bible is light.

Who wouldn't want to understand the Bible and experience all of these things?

DECADES OF "AHAS"

Both of us (R. C. and Robert) have stood before groups of people, large and small. We have done this hundreds of times from coast to coast and around the world. We have had the privilege of opening the Bible and talking about the integrity of its message. And, as we have looked out into the audience, we have seen the lights go on—the unmistakable "ahas" on people's faces. We readily admit that our communication prowess has nothing to do with this dawning look of understanding. God—through His Holy Spirit—changes people through the power of His Word. We have seen this happen in many people. And we have experienced this ourselves.

There's just *something* about the Bible that compels people . . . and changes them.

෴

And so, because we believe that the Bible is worth knowing about, we have written this book. If you have spent a lifetime in church, we hope there will be things that will be helpful to you in gaining the larger picture of Scripture. And if you're a beginner, we believe that you'll find this book to be extremely helpful in gaining a new and deeper understanding of God's story.

ONE MORE THING . . .

When a book is written by more than one writer, sometimes there's confusion as to who is doing the speaking. So we have decided to write the remainder of this book using only R. C.'s voice throughout. Even though many of the illustrations are Robert's, it was our decision to tuck all the words into one writer's pen. This way there should be no confusion as to who is "talking."

This book is, in every sense, a collaboration between two friends. And our goal is to have you join us as our companion in this adventure of gaining a deeper understanding of what's in the Bible.

Welcome.

WHAT'S IN THE BIBLE

CHAPTER ONE

CREATION AND BLESSING

- **Creation**
- The Image of God
- The Fall
- The Covenant with Abraham
- Patriarchal Blessing

IN THE BEGINNING

If you have seen the start of a race at a track meet, you know what happens just before the runners sprint from their starting blocks. The official raises a small pistol in the air and shouts the following words: "Runners to your mark" . . . "set" . . . and then he squeezes the trigger, sending the athletes on their way. Every race has a beginning. It's exactly the same with everything we know to be—all of creation.

> *In the beginning God created the heavens and the earth.* (Genesis 1:1)

This is perhaps the most important, and the most controversial, sentence of the entire Bible. There was a time when there was nothing—no creation, no life, no earth, no solar systems, no universe—and then, suddenly, like the gun starting a race, there was action, life . . . something.

The word *Genesis* means "beginning, a starting point in time." What it underscores is that life has a starting place, a critical element in a biblical world-view. From the instant of creation, life became linear, not cyclical. We are not, as the nineteenth-century philosopher Friedrich Nietzche claimed in his "myth of eternal recurrence," caught in an endless cycle like a scratched record, clicking back to the previous groove and playing the same thing over and over again. And because we're not caught in an incessant replaying of the same tune, as with the irrational idea of reincarnation, life has direction and meaning. And mankind's existence has purpose. He is charged with ultimate responsibility for his own thoughts and actions, unable to escape the ultimate excuse of simply reliving life as a victim of his ancestors.

In his novel *The Sun Also Rises,* Ernest Hemingway picked up this pagan notion. The sun rises and sets and rises and sets . . . with no discernible beginning or end to the orbit of human history. If this were true, it would naturally lead to the position that there is no specific starting place and no purposeful end to our lives. We would be, in a cosmic sense, running around in circles.

Contrary to this thought, even contemporary theories of evolution affirm that there was a beginning—a time when things were not and a time when things were. Of course, these theories hold that by blind chance, all matter in the universe gathered into a single point and then exploded, leaving us with swirls of matter that would eventually condense into suns and planets and all living things.

These theorists have more faith than I do. To believe that all of this took place with no Creator, no grand designer, and no one shouting, "Runners to your mark," takes a great deal of confidence in pure speculation. In fact, scientists' own law of inertia makes a case against them. Even Captain Von Trapp in *The Sound of Music* knew better than this when he crooned, "Nothing comes from nothing . . . nothing ever could."

The presupposition that "things at rest tend to stay at rest" begs the case against this sleeping nothingness suddenly and without notice coming together to create something: and not *just* something. Nothingness exploded, spontaneously formed light, billions of galaxies, the Grand Tetons, alligators, and eyelashes. Although they would not like to be given this distinction, these are people of *great* faith.

GOD

The opening sentence in Holy Scripture also tells us that there was Someone Whose voice was heard throughout the vast emptiness: "Runners to your mark."

The Bible does not simply say, "In the beginning . . . ," but God's Word makes it clear that in the beginning, *God* was. He was not the result of His own conception, He was clearly separate and apart from it. God is eternal. He has no beginning and no end. He was not created; He was the Creator.

When our children were small, sometimes they would argue with my decisions, especially those decisions that affected them. Sometimes, after my unsuccessful attempts to build my case, I would simply say, "It's going to be this way, just because it *is*."

This is not an argument for the existence of God that I'm fond of making, but the fact of the Creation and the reality of the Creator are true just because they are. Given the alternatives to these truths—like the "Big Bang" or natural selection—my sincere hope is that you will simply come to the point of believing that God is and that He was the Creator . . . just *because*. For there to be a beginning, there must be something or someone who has the very power of being itself first to start the cosmic process in motion.

> God is eternal. He has no beginning and no end. He was not created; He was the Creator.

CREATED

In the beginning God did something. We're not told of a static existence of Divinity, but of a God in action: God doing something. And what He did here is the most fantastic work that has ever been done, work that will never be done again.

You and I use the word *create* to describe what entrepreneurs do with businesses, what architects do with buildings, or what artists do with painting or music. Actually, my closest friends know that I dabble in some of the arts myself—especially painting and music. Over the years I have read about the ways great men and women have used these mediums to communicate and express themselves and their ideas. I have been completely taken with their brilliance. When I get out tubes of paint—and don't forget, I'm a rank amateur—and face a clean, white canvas, I feel like a kid playing in the mud.

But, even though some would call what the world's great artists do with their paints—even what I do—"creative," it's not truly that at all, not in the Genesis sense of the creative acts of God. All I am doing is taking what already exists and rearranging it into something different. This is not true creativity but mediated creativity. The biblical view of creation is more startling than this.

The biblical concept of God's creativity presents an act of creation where there is no medium except the sound of Someone's voice. It's not as though God came down with His palette and began to mix and paint and draw. There was no paint. There were no brushes. There was not even a blank canvas. There was only endless emptiness.

In fact, this is the reason why we theologians use a special phrase to talk about God's creative works: *ex nihilo*. These words, literally meaning "out of nothing," explain that there was no preexistent matter that God used to create. All of His art, that which we know as tangible and intangible reality, did not come from rearranging anything, it came from scratch.

No amount of study that describes those things that are going on around us can account for creation *ex nihilo*. This act goes beyond the natural, into the supernatural realm. This act takes us above and beyond the theater of nature, to the beginning of nature, to the Author of nature and His creation out of nothing.

> The biblical concept of God's creativity presents an act of creation where there is no medium except the sound of Someone's voice.

Much to our chagrin, the Bible does not give us a scientific description of how He did this work, the specific times, or how many watts of power were needed. The only thing we are told is that creation happened by the power of God's spoken word. Saint Augustine called this simply, the divine imperative or fiat—not to be confused with a small Italian automobile.

Thoughtful and convincing arguments among Bible scholars swirl around the exact amount of time God used in creation. Were the six "days" of creation a form of poetry and symbolism, or were they literally twenty-four-hour days? I certainly encourage you to join me in the exploration of this issue. However, as I have done with my students over the years, I find that it is always dangerous to shout where God has whispered. Either way, the Bible is crystal-clear as to the "Who" of creation, and ultimately that will have to be enough.

In the beginning, God created. These are foundational words of Scripture because they point us to right thinking. God is the all-powerful, all-wise Creator of the universe. This is the beginning of our journey.

- Creation
- **The Image of God**
- The Fall
- The Covenant with Abraham
- Patriarchal Blessing

Almost as soon as she could speak, Darby, one of my granddaughters, began learning the answers to questions from the Children's Catechism. When I would ask Darby, "Who made you?" she would smile and say, "God did."

But my favorite question to ask her—and I think her favorite one to answer, given the sparkle in her eyes—was the one that speaks of God's ultimate purpose in creating humanity.

"Darby," I would ask our precious little girl, "why did God make you?"

"Fo His gwowy," she would respond.

Underdeveloped pronunciation skills, brilliant theology—I hope she never, never forgets this.

God created the animals, the birds, the fish, the brilliantly colored vegetation and the earth teeming with His creation. But God looked down and saw that none of these creations bore His image. Even though He pronounced all of these creations "good," none of them were made in His likeness. So God created a special being, with a unique capacity to be like Him. This extraordinary work of creation would have the ability to reflect God's glory. He would have the ability to display His character. Although mankind could not be exactly *like* God, there would be points of analogy, enabling mankind to have a special understanding of God and, amazing though it may seem, please Him by loving and worshiping Him.

When we read the Scriptures, we are reading a book that is unfolding on every page a divine purpose for your existence and for mine . . . for His glory.

With this foundational idea in place, let's look at the story of how God created mankind.

> *Then God said, "Let Us make man in Our image, according to Our likeness;*
> *let them have dominion over the fish of the sea, over the birds of the air,*
> *and over the cattle, over all the earth and over every*
> *creeping thing that creeps on the earth." (Genesis 1:26)*

Just as with Genesis 1:1, we see God in action as a Creator with a purpose. Within the Godhead—Father, Son, and Holy Spirit—there is a conversation, an agreement, a plan. None of this came about by accident. The origin of mankind was founded through the ordered, intelligent decision by a supernatural Being Who has a supremely well-conceived purpose for everything He does.

Even among some well-intentioned scholars, this truth is often overlooked, downplayed, or ignored. But if we want to understand the basics of Scripture, we must understand that God's plan for everything He created is not accidental; it is thoroughly intentional. We are not left with the option to see any single part of human existence as the result of chance. As Albert Einstein noted, "God does not play dice."

> We were created intelligent, moral creatures, and it's from this place of favor that we fell.

With all other creatures, God simply spoke them into being. But with mankind we see tantalizing details and puzzling phrases, all revealing something of God's purpose for us—creatures made in His image.

Of course, we cannot think as God thinks, with omniscience and absolute certitude. So what does it mean to be made in the image of God? Well, to be created by this design means that we are able to participate in this incredible phenomenon called thinking, reflecting, deciding, learning, feeling, and knowing.

We are also gifted with a moral sense—truly knowing right from wrong. You cannot speak of the "fall" of mankind (as we will discuss later) without granting that there was somewhere to fall from. We were created intelligent, moral creatures, and it's from this place of favor that we fell.

Another reflection of the image of God is mankind's capacity for relationship. The Sovereign God is three persons—Father, Son, and Holy Spirit—Who enjoy perfect communication, flawless empathy, and unfettered relationship. We mirror that capacity to be in relationship with one another, to magnify the reflection of God's glory through our mutual love for others, especially the holy relationship of marriage.

We have been made for that which is sacred and holy, in His image, to fulfill the purposes of God . . . "for His gwowy."

- Creation
- The Image of God
- **The Fall**
- The Covenant with Abraham
- Patriarchal Blessing

"It was a dark and stormy night . . ." So wrote the ever-aspiring novelist Snoopy sitting atop his doghouse in the "Peanuts" comic strip.

So far in the Bible, everything had been pronounced "good." Even when God saw that Adam was lonely—a not-good thing—He created a woman to be Adam's companion—a good thing.

But as soon as we get to the opening of the third chapter of Genesis, there is, like Snoopy's black and threatening skies, something ominous going on. These words prepare us for an interruption in the bliss this first man and woman were experiencing in the Garden of Eden.

> *Now the serpent was more cunning than any beast of the field*
> *which the LORD God had made.* (Genesis 3:1a)

Adam and Eve had never encountered the idea of something sly. But in this creature, there was nothing but guile. And his sinister cleverness was revealed from the first words he spoke:

> *Has God indeed said, "You shall not eat of*
> *every tree of the garden?"* (Genesis 3:1b)

"What is so clever about the serpent's question?" you may ask. Eve knew that God had not said that. Her response, in fact, made it clear that she knew what God had actually said.

> *We may eat the fruit of the trees of the garden;*
> *but of the fruit of the tree which is in the midst of the garden, God has said,*
> *"You shall not eat it, nor shall you touch it, lest you die."* (Genesis 3:2b–3)

Eve had successfully defended the character of God. But here was the subtle power of the serpent's thinly veiled suggestion, asked in the form of a question. He implied that if God places one thing out of bounds, if He says, "No," at any point of your liberty, if God gives laws, then He might as well take away all your freedom. If you don't have unfettered free reign over everything, then you're no more than a slave.

Satan had come to Eve, "innocently" concerned that God had not given Adam and Eve a balanced diet of all the fruit of the garden. Eve had successfully defended God's Word. But the serpent said to the woman,

> *You will not surely die. For God knows that in the day you eat of it*
> *your eyes will be opened, and you will be like God,*
> *knowing good and evil.* (Genesis 3:4b–5)

Now the subtlety drops. A direct assault on the truth of God is launched, flatly contradicting the words of God. Of course, Eve could have reminded Satan that she was *already* like God, having been made in His image and in His likeness. But she knew that this was not what the serpent was referring to. What Satan was saying was that Eve could destroy the wall separating creature and Creator. She could do away with the chasm-like distance between mankind and God, knowing everything God knows.

The tension in this moment and Eve's struggle to obey are played out on almost every page of Scripture from this point forward. Who will rule, God or man? Will mankind seek autonomy or will he submit to the authority of God? Will man serve God or will he pursue personal power, selfish purposes, and sensual desires? Whose word will prevail?

Like you and me, Eve was challenged to live out her days under God's law or face death for a false freedom, the only kind of freedom Satan can offer. Unfortunately, Eve failed the test for very familiar reasons.

> *So when the woman saw that the tree was good for food,*
> *that it was pleasant to the eyes,*
> *and a tree desirable to make one wise, she took of its fruit and ate.*
> *She also gave to her husband with her, and he ate.*
> *Then the eyes of both of them were opened,*
> *and they knew that they were naked; and they sewed fig leaves together*
> *and made themselves coverings.* (Genesis 3:6–7)

Adam and Eve were created to run to the presence of God, to enjoy Him. But when they violated God's Law, they received more knowledge than they bargained for—they discovered that they were naked little creatures, still far less when compared to a Holy God. And this drove them to shame. As God moved through the Garden in the cool of the evening, instead of running to Him with joy, they fled into the bushes like frightened animals.

Because of their disobedience, Adam and Eve became fugitives from even the gaze of God. We have been running ever since.

> The tension in this moment and Eve's struggle to obey are played out on almost every page of Scripture from this point forward.

In his book *Knowing God*, Dr. J. I. Packer reminds us that the theme of all Sacred Scripture is redemption. Here is the first of myriad examples. The history of man's relationship to his heavenly Father is not one of him chasing after God. No, the accounts in the Bible, the stories of history, and the reality of today are filled with the miracle of God pursuing His creatures. God stoops to clothe our nakedness. He soothes our embarrassments and pain. He covers our guilt and restores us to our position as His image-bearers and vice-regents. God takes the first step.

We love Him because He first loved us. (1 John 4:19)

We only have the desire and capacity to love God because of His love for us. Our love for Him is the only appropriate response to His aggressive pursuit after our fall. This is the amazing story we will see repeatedly throughout the Bible.

- Creation
- The Image of God
- The Fall
- **The Covenant with Abraham**
- Patriarchal Blessing

Some have said that the Old Testament is the autobiography of God, not His entire life, of course, for He is eternal, having neither a beginning nor an end. However, it would be accurate to say that the first thirty-nine books of the Bible provide us with a thin slice of God's story.

And without question, the most important character in this narrative is Abraham, the father of God's chosen people, the Jews. So significant was the life of this man that two thousand years after we are first introduced to him, Mary, the soon-to-be mother of Jesus Christ, mentions his name. In fact, as she accepted the overwhelming duty and privilege of being the mother of the Savior, Mary summarized two millennia of God's faithfulness to her people, comparing her call from God to that of her obedient ancestor Abraham.

> *He has helped His servant Israel,*
> *In remembrance of His mercy,*
> *As He spoke to our fathers,*
> *To Abraham and to his seed forever.* (Luke 1:54–55)

Even Zacharias, the father of John the Baptist, was inspired by the Holy Spirit to say:

[God has promised] to perform the mercy promised to our fathers
And to remember His holy covenant,
The oath which He swore to our father Abraham. (Luke 1:72–73)

Have you ever felt a strong compelling to do something you have never done before? If you're married, you remember the moment when you believed, without a shadow of doubt, that this person was to be your life's companion. So you did something you had never done before—you promised your life to another person.

If you have ever picked up your family and moved, changed careers, started a business on a shoestring, or given away a large amount of money, you have felt this compelling impulse—some would refer to this as a "call"—to go for it. Sometimes you take action on this call with the support of your friends. And occasionally you move ahead over their protests.

"You're doing what?" they might say.

But you are not dissuaded. You've felt a call.

Although we have no record of how his friends received the news, that must have been the case with Abraham almost four thousand years ago. Can't you picture this prosperous man telling his friends and neighbors that he was pulling up stakes and moving to a place he had never heard of? And can you imagine him announcing this to his family?

And not only was Abraham's urge to make a change something he *felt* or even something he *believed*, Scripture tells us that this was a call he *heard*. Can you imagine waking up to the sound of God's voice?

Now the LORD had said to Abram:
"Get out of your country,
From your family
And from your father's house,
To a land that I will show you.
I will make you a great nation;
I will bless you
And make your name great;
And you shall be a blessing.

> *I will bless those who bless you,*
> *And I will curse him who curses you;*
> *And in you all the families of the earth shall be blessed."* (Genesis 12:1–3)

But when God spoke to Abraham it was more than just a call. For this message wasn't only a challenge to a man regarding his life and his future, it was a promise from the One who was doing the calling—a two-way deal. The Bible refers to this special kind of announcement as a *covenant*. It's like a contract, spelling out the roles and responsibilities of *both* parties:

COVENANT

Whereas, the undersigned, Abraham, will leave his homeland and move to an unknown destination. And, whereas, the undersigned Sovereign God will bless and make great the name of the undersigned Abraham.

God

Abraham

And, as God often did with the recipients of these covenants throughout Scripture, He repeated this promise to Abraham. In these reaffirmations, God answered Abraham's most difficult question: "How do I know You will do these things?"

> *The word of the LORD came to Abram in a vision, saying,*
> *"Do not be afraid, Abram. I am your shield,*
> *your exceedingly great reward."* (Genesis 15:1)

> *When Abram was ninety-nine years old,*
> *the LORD appeared to Abram and said to him,*
> *"I am Almighty God; walk before Me and be blameless.*
> *And I will make My covenant between Me and you,*
> *and will multiply you exceedingly."* (Genesis 17:1–2)

The Almighty took an oath. He swore upon His own life that whatever He promised, He would fulfill. Talk about a promise Abraham could count on.

There are three separate components to God's covenant with Abraham:

1. *The gift of land.* During Abraham's life, the only piece of land he owned was called Machpellah (modern-day Hebron), which was his burial plot. But God pledged to him "a land which I will show you"—the Promised Land.

2. *The father of a great nation.* Certainly when Abraham heard this, he pictured lots of children filling his tent. Over the next two thousand years, Abraham's offspring would ultimately number in the millions, but God gave Abraham and Sarah only one son.

3. *All the nations of the earth will be blessed.* Never in his lifetime could Abraham have conceived of God's redemptive plan to save the world through his descendant Jesus Christ.

God's covenant promises are not about the worthiness of the recipient. They are not even about the immediate evidence of God's pledge. Covenants are always about the faithfulness of the One making the promise. They are trustworthy and sure.

- Creation
- The Image of God
- The Fall
- The Covenant with Abraham
- **Patriarchal Blessing**

You'll remember that, at a moment in time, God lifted His starter's pistol, squeezed the trigger, and time began. From the time of the covenant with Abraham, the format of the race changed to a relay race. God handed the baton—His blessing—to Abraham. Abraham passed it to Isaac, his son. Finally, Isaac passed the baton of God's blessing to his son Jacob. These three runners are often called the Patriarchs.

The Patriarchs had authority over their extended families as well as over their entire nomadic tribes. They not only gave traveling directions to their people, these men also set the religious course, designating by example—and sometimes unpopular commands—which Deity their people would reverence. It is from this superintendence that the Bible often refers to the Lord as the God of Abraham, Isaac, and Jacob. As God's appointed leaders, these were the ones to decide who was to be worshiped from the myriad of gods.

Having created this cultural structure, God accommodated Himself by dealing primarily with these men as He revealed Himself to mankind. It was through His covenant promises to the Patriarchs, and their oaths of allegiance to Him, that God's relationship with mankind was defined. And the blessings of this covenant flowed through these leaders who passed the duties and responsibilities of keeping their portion of the covenant with God to the next generation.

As we have seen, God initially promised Abraham land, a family that would grow to be a nation inheriting the land, and blessings that would flow through him to the world. In the custom of the day, the inheritance normally would be given to the firstborn son. This man would receive the lion's share of his father's possessions. When Abraham was giving his inheritance to his descendants, the primary assets to be dispensed were not his tents, his animals, or his treasures. No, the chief item was the anointing God had given to him.

And it came to pass, after the death of Abraham,
that God blessed his son Isaac. (Genesis 25:11a)

Abraham's descendants became the recipients of God's covenant blessing. Incredibly, as children of God, this blessing continues its flow through us to our own children. And it comes to us not simply because we ask, but because God chooses to do so.

As we have said, in the tradition of these people, the largest portion of a man's inheritance was usually given to his firstborn son. However, throughout history, God has always taken the liberty to accomplish His purposes in His own way. Witness the fact that neither Isaac nor Jacob were their father's firstborn.

Abraham's firstborn son, Ishmael, was not through Sarah, but through Hagar, Sarah's maid. Ishmael was not to be the inheritor of the blessing. God insisted that the blessing be given to Isaac and so it was. And from this, the book of Genesis overflows with intrigue and conflict as the rich benefits of Abraham's covenant inheritance are decided.

From Isaac's wife, Rebecca, came twin boys. The firstborn was Esau. But, just as was the case with Ishmael, it was not God's plan to bless him with his father's covenant inheritance. And even though Jacob and his deceiving mother conspired and lied in order to wrest the blessing from the ancient and blind Isaac, it was still God's plan for Jacob to succeed his father as the next patriarch.

The old proverb "God can make a straight lick with a crooked stick" doesn't begin to explain what happens here.

> Throughout history, God has always taken the liberty to accomplish His purposes in His own way.

The question I have been asked, perhaps more frequently than any other—in fact, the question I have asked myself since coming to faith many decades ago—is, "How could God let this happen?" "How could God allow this scheming, lying, thieving, undeserving son to get the blessing?"

The answer may not be completely satisfying to the honest seeker, but it's the unvarnished truth. Jacob was chosen by God to receive the blessing. And whether we like it or not, whether we agree with it or not, whether we think it's fair or not, God *always* gets His way.

> *When Rebecca also had conceived by one man, even by our father Isaac*
> *(for the children not yet being born, nor having done any good or evil,*
> *that the purpose of God according to election might stand,*
> *not of works but of Him who calls),*
> *it was said to her, "The older shall serve the younger."*
> *As it is written, "Jacob I have loved, but Esau I have hated."*
> *What shall we say then?*
> *Is there unrighteousness with God? Certainly not!*
> *For He says to Moses,*
> *"I will have mercy on whomever I will have mercy,*
> *and I will have compassion on whomever I will have compassion."*
> *So then it is not of him who wills, nor of him who runs,*
> *but of God who shows mercy.* (Romans 9:10b–16)

This is a hard saying, but it is the only one that makes sense of why God would use the worst of sinners to perform His most glorious deeds. The prevailing question is not why God would choose some and not others, but rather why the Holy One would choose anyone at all.

Long after Jacob deceived his father, Isaac, thinking he had stolen the blessing, Jacob found himself in a physical duel with a special emissary from God.

> *Then Jacob was left alone;*
> *and a Man wrestled with him until the breaking of day.*
> *Now when He saw that He did not prevail against [Jacob],*
> *[the Man] touched the socket of his hip;*
> *and the socket of Jacob's hip was out of joint as He wrestled with him.*
> *And [the Man] said, "Let Me go, for the day breaks."*
> *But [Jacob] said, "I will not let You go unless You bless me!"*
> *So [the Man] said to him, "What is your name?"*
> *He said, "Jacob."*
> *And [the Man] said, "Your name shall no longer be called Jacob, but Israel;*
> *for you have struggled with God and with men, and have prevailed." . . .*
> *So Jacob called the name of the place Peniel: "For I have seen*
> *God face to face, and my life is preserved." (Genesis 32:24–30)*

Even though Jacob had been chosen to receive the blessing, he was not exempt from conflict and the pain of self-examination. Years before, Isaac, his blind father, had asked a lying Jacob his name. "I am Esau, your firstborn," Jacob had said.

Now, another Man asks the blessing-seeking Jacob the same question. This time he tells the truth: "I am Jacob."

A number of years ago, Dr. Ravi Zacharias helped me to see the importance of this moment in Jacob's life. The first time Jacob sought the blessing, he lied his way into receiving the covenant promise. This time, Jacob was a changed man. When the Man asked Jacob his name, he did not say "Esau." Perhaps this was the first time he had told the truth, the whole truth, so help him God . . . about himself.

To illustrate that Jacob had truly been converted, he didn't run away. In fact, Jacob—blessed again, with a new name to go with it, Israel—went to meet his estranged brother, Esau. He fell on his face before his brother, begged his forgiveness, and was wonderfully reconciled.

The Patriarchs were not chosen by God because of their flawless perfection. As I have said, they were chosen . . . just *because*. And as they carried the baton of blessing from generation to generation, the Patriarchs' stories are filled with repeated sinfulness, painful contrition, God's outrageous compassion, and unencumbered forgiveness.

So begins the narrative of Holy Scripture: a perfect Creator, an image-bearing but fallen mankind, a promise-making God, and a generation-to-generation blessing sealed by the free gift of redemption.

SUMMARY

■ CREATION

There was a time when there was nothing—no creation, no life, no earth, no solar systems, no universe—and then, suddenly, like the gun starting a race, there was action, life . . . something. The word *Genesis* means "beginning, a starting point in time." What it underscores is that life has a starting place. From the instant of creation, life became linear, not cyclical.

Even contemporary theories of evolution affirm that there was a beginning—a time when things were not and a time when things were. Of course these theories hold that by blind chance, all matter in the universe gathered into a single point and then exploded, leaving us with swirls of matter that would eventually condense into suns and planets and all living things. These theorists have more faith than I do.

> The prevailing question is not why God would choose some and not others, but rather why the Holy One would choose anyone at all.

The opening sentence in Holy Scripture also tells us that there was Someone Whose voice was heard throughout the vast emptiness: "Runners to your mark." The Bible does not simply say "in the beginning," but the Bible makes it clear that in the beginning, *God* was. He was not the result of His own conception; He was clearly separate and apart from it. God is eternal. He has no beginning and no end. He was not created. He was the Creator.

This is not an argument for the existence of God that I'm fond of making, but the fact of the Creation and the reality of the Creator are true just because they are. Given the alternatives to these truths, you will simply come to the point of believing that God is and was the Creator . . . just *because*. For there to be a beginning, there must be something or someone who has the very power of being itself first to start the cosmic process in motion.

■ THE IMAGE OF GOD

God created the animals, the birds, the fish, the brilliantly colored vegetation and the earth teeming with His creation. But God looked down and saw that none of these creations bore His image. Even though He pronounced all of these creations "good," none of them were made in His likeness. So God created a special being, with a unique capacity to be like Him. This extraordinary work of creation would have the ability to reflect God's glory. He would have the ability to display His character. Although mankind could not be exactly *like* God, there would be points of analogy, enabling mankind to have a special understanding of God and, amazing though it may seem, please Him by loving and worshiping Him.

To be created by this design means that we are able to participate in this incredible phenomenon called thinking, reflecting, deciding, learning, feeling, and knowing. We are also gifted with a moral sense—truly knowing right from wrong. You cannot speak of the "fall" of mankind without granting that there was somewhere to fall from. We were created intelligent, moral creatures, and it's from this place of favor that we fell.

Another reflection of the image of God is mankind's capacity for relationship. The Sovereign God is three persons—Father, Son, and Holy Spirit—who enjoy perfect communication, flawless empathy, and unfettered relationship. We mirror that capacity to be in relationship with one another, to magnify the reflection of God's glory through our mutual love for others, especially the holy relationship of marriage.

■ THE FALL

The tension in the conversation between the serpent and Eve is played out on almost every page of Scripture from this point forward. Who will rule: God or man? Will mankind seek autonomy or will he submit to the authority of God? Will man serve God or will he pursue personal power, selfish purposes, and sensual desires? Whose word will prevail?

Like you and me, Eve was challenged to live out her days under God's Law or face death for a false freedom, the only kind of freedom Satan can offer. Unfortunately, Eve failed the test for very familiar reasons.

Adam and Eve were made to run to the presence of God, to enjoy Him. But because of their disobedience, Adam and Eve became fugitives from even the gaze of God. We have been running ever since.

The history of man's relationship to his heavenly Father is not one of his chasing after God. No, the accounts in the Bible, the stories of history, and the reality of today are filled with the miracle of God pursuing His creatures as they flee. God stoops to clothe our nakedness. He soothes our embarrassments and pain. He covers our guilt and restores us to our position as His image-bearers and vice-regents. God takes the first step.

■ THE COVENANT WITH ABRAHAM

God visited a man named Abraham almost four thousand years ago. He told Abraham to pull up stakes and move to a place he had never heard of. And not only was Abraham's urge to make a change something he *felt* or even something he *believed*, but Scripture tells us that this was a call he *heard*.

And when God spoke to Abraham it was more than just a call, it was a two-way deal. The Bible refers to this special kind of announcement as a *covenant*. It's like a contract, spelling out the roles and responsibilities of *both* parties: a person and God. The Almighty took an oath. He swore upon His own life that whatever He promised, He would fulfill.

There are three separate components to God's covenant with Abraham: (1) the gift of land; (2) the father of a great nation; and (3) all the nations of the earth would be blessed.

■ PATRIARCHAL BLESSING

Abraham, Isaac, and Jacob were Israel's first leaders—we call them the Patriarchs. God dealt primarily with these men as He revealed Himself to the people. It was through His covenant promises to the Patriarchs, and their oaths of allegiance to Him, that God's relationship with mankind was defined. And the blessings of this covenant flowed through these leaders, who passed the duties and responsibilities of keeping their portion of the covenant with God to the next generation.

CHAPTER TWO

RELEASE FROM CAPTIVITY

- Moses and the Exodus
- The Passover

How did Jacob's family become a nation? In God's providence, it would take a shepherd boy becoming a mighty prince, and a prince becoming a lowly shepherd. Like bookends separated by more than three centuries, Joseph and Moses helped to establish, preserve, and lead Israel.

JOSEPH

Number eleven of Jacob's twelve sons, Joseph's life began as a shepherd boy. As the firstborn son of his beloved wife, Rachel, his father foolishly singled him out by giving him a special, multicolored long-sleeved cloak. But his ten older brothers, seething with jealousy over their father's special treatment of their little brother, made plans for his demise. Throwing him into a pit

> Like bookends separated by more than three centuries, Joseph and Moses helped to establish, preserve, and lead Israel.

to die, then spilling blood on his coat to present to their father, seemed like a perfect scheme.

> *We shall say, "Some wild beast has devoured him."* (Genesis 37:20b)

But passing Midianite traders traveling to Egypt provided a more economically rewarding scenario. So Joseph was sold like a common slave.

Once in Egypt, Joseph was sold again, this time to the household of Potiphar, captain of Pharaoh's guard. The young Hebrew found favor with his master. However, more treachery befell Joseph as Potiphar's wife falsely accused him of attempted rape and Joseph was thrown in prison.

> But the LORD was with Joseph [in prison] and showed him mercy,
> and He gave him favor in the sight of the keeper of the prison.
> And the keeper of the prison committed to Joseph's hand
> all the prisoners who were in the prison;
> whatever they did there, it was his doing . . . And whatever
> he did, the LORD made it prosper. (Genesis 39:21–23b)

Through almost ten years of imprisonment, God demonstrated His sovereignty by preparing Joseph to bring about great blessing, both for this lowly shepherd boy and for His people. While in prison Joseph interpreted Pharaoh's dream and was finally released. He outlined a strategy for guiding Egypt through a devastating famine and was given the helm as the prince of the land.

Because of Joseph's obedience and his forgiveness of his undeserving brothers, God brought the entire family of Israel, now numbering in the hundreds of thousands, from Canaan to Egypt. Here, because of Joseph's leadership, the Hebrews were treated as guests.

Near his death, at the end of Genesis, Joseph's father, Jacob, surveyed the children with which God had blessed him. Filled with gratitude, he called his sons together to grant them his last will and testament. When it was time to deliver the covenant blessing, not only did Jacob bypass Reuben, the oldest son, but he passed the blessing to Judah, his *fourth* son:

> Judah, you are he whom your brothers shall praise;
> Your hand shall be on the neck of your enemies;
> Your father's children shall bow down before you . . .
> The scepter shall not depart from Judah. (Genesis 49:8, 10a)

Several years later, when Joseph died, he gathered his surviving and still-fearful siblings together and gave them a clinic on providence and perspective:

Then his brothers also went and fell down before his face,
and they said, "Behold, we are your servants."
Joseph said to them, "Do not be afraid,
for am I in the place of God?
But as for you, you meant evil against me;
but God meant it for good, in order to bring it about as it is this day,
to save many people alive." (Genesis 50:18–20)

What Joseph did not know was that it would be four hundred years before his family would be released from Egypt and the Exodus would occur. And it would be many generations before God would raise up a new covenant leader to guide His people from what had become their dreadful captivity into the Promised Land.

This Egyptian enslavement of Abraham's descendants is the point of transition from the history of the Patriarchs to the most important redemptive act in the Old Testament: the Exodus and the giving of the Law on Mount Sinai.

The biblical record is replete with details of God's covenant family up to this point, but between the end of the book of Genesis and the beginning of Moses' record of the Exodus, we learn very little of the individuals God used to bless His people.

> This threat to the political stability of the Egyptians turned into years of oppression, slavery, and eventually wholesale genocide for the Hebrews.

What we do know is that the Hebrews were in the land of Goshen, enjoying prosperity under the Hyksos dynasty. But, when his successor, Thutmose, came to power, the Jews were perceived as a political threat.

Now there arose a new king over Egypt, who did not know Joseph.
And he said to his people,
"Look, the people of the children of Israel are more and mightier than we;
come, let us deal shrewdly with them, lest they multiply,
and it happen, in the event of war, that they also join our enemies
and fight against us, and so go up out of the land." (Exodus 1:8–10)

This threat to the political stability of the Egyptians turned into years of oppression, slavery, and eventually wholesale genocide for the Hebrews. But God miraculously provided a man to lead His people out of Egyptian bondage.

MOSES

The conditions under which the covenant child, Moses, was born were unthinkable. The descendants of Abraham, Isaac, and Jacob, who had been welcomed into Egypt as Pharaoh's special guests, were now being treated like chattel—tangible assets amid the nation's extravagant wealth. The oppression of the Hebrews, God's chosen people, was inconceivable.

1. *The pharaoh appointed taskmasters to rule over the people.* These men had godlike authority over the Hebrews, forcing them to build the houses, the grain silos, and even the pyramids of the burgeoning kingdom.

2. *New orders were given to the taskmasters to make them work harder.* Not only were the Hebrews enslaved and given larger quotas to fill, but eventually the essential building materials were no longer provided for them. They were forced to gather the raw materials themselves. Amazingly, even though they were completely under his rule, the pharaoh continued to be restless about the multiplying Jews, and so he issued a horrific edict.

> Any mother or father can only imagine how difficult it would be to gently lay their child into the river, knowing they would probably never see him again.

3. *Every male Hebrew child was to be killed as soon as he was born.* Hebrew midwives were assigned to "help" the Jewish women give birth, but this was not an act of charity. These midwives may have been announced to the Hebrews as a measure of keeping an accurate record of the number of children being born, but these women were commanded to kill the baby boys.

4. *Every Egyptian was granted the right to shed innocent blood.* The midwives refused to be a part of the slaughter and gave comically flimsy excuses as to why the children of the Hebrews continued to live.

> *And the midwives said to Pharaoh,*
> *"Because the Hebrew women are not like the Egyptian women;*

for they are lively and give birth before
the midwives come to them." (Exodus 1:19)

The pharaoh was forced to take even more heinous steps to successfully eliminate the Hebrew boys. As his final form of oppression, he commanded that all Egyptian citizens take part in killing any sons born to the Hebrews. This systematic elimination of the Jewish people could be considered the first Holocaust.

But when it looked as though there was no hope and God's chosen people would eventually vanish from the face of the earth, He sovereignly intervened in the preservation of one baby boy.

And a man of the house of Levi went and took as wife a daughter of Levi.
So the woman conceived and bore a son.
And when she saw that he was a beautiful child,
she hid him three months.
But when she could no longer hide him,
she took an ark of bulrushes for him,
daubed it with asphalt and pitch, put the child in it,
and laid it in the reeds by the river's bank. (Exodus 2:1–3)

Although we are not granted any details as to how this baby boy's parents must have felt, any mother or father can only imagine how difficult it would be to gently lay their child into the river, knowing they would probably never see him again. But the baby's mother had no choice. If she didn't release him into the river, he would most certainly be murdered by the Egyptians.

Surrounded by legions of protecting angels, the little basket found its way into a small tributary where a group of Egyptian women were bathing. As they peered into the basket, the baby let out a cry heard 'round the world, and the daughter of Pharaoh was touched, as only a woman could be.

And when she opened [the basket],
she saw the child, and behold, the baby wept.
So she had compassion on him, and said,
"This is one of the Hebrews' children." (Exodus 2:6)

Amazingly, the daughter of the man who had called for the wholesale butchering of children was given a heart of compassion. In disobedience to her father's dictates, she rescued the child, gave him a name, and made him her son.

As He would also do centuries later, God's sovereign plan for the redemption of His people would begin with the birth of a baby boy.

Moses—meaning "to draw out of the water"—was raised in the palace as a prince surrounded by the accouterments of royalty. And as a sealing act of a merciful God, Moses' mother, unknown to the Egyptians, was hired to nurse the child. The boy's mother had released him into God's tender hand. And by that same hand, the child was safely given over to her care.

> As He would also do centuries later, God's sovereign plan for the redemption of His people would begin with the birth of a baby boy.

As Prince Moses grew up in the palace, his heart was strangely drawn to the plight of the Hebrews. As an adult, instead of giving blind allegiance to the pagan regime that kept them in bondage, Moses walked among the Jews, secretly mourning their burdens. One day, he came upon an Egyptian, mercilessly beating one of Moses' kinsmen. Filled with rage, he killed the Egyptian and buried the body in the sand (Exodus 2), hoping no one had seen him do this deed.

BREAKING THE LAW

Even though the story of God's people is just beginning, we are already dealing with the ethics of their dilemma. First, they disobeyed the laws of the land in deference to their fidelity to a Holy God.

When the Hebrew midwives refused to murder the children, they were knowingly disobeying civil authority. And when Moses' parents hid their son, their actions were understandable but, according to Egyptian law, also illegal. Generations later, Jesus (Mark 12:17; Luke 20:25) would encourage His followers to "render to Caesar the things that are Caesar's, and to God the things that are God's."

But when "Caesar's" laws are in direct opposition to God's sovereign commands, His people have no choice but to engage in civil disobedience. Far better to face a criminal justice system and receive its penalties, than to willfully transgress God's Law and suffer eternal consequences.

And what of Moses, taking the life of the Egyptian? Certainly, he was right in attempting to protect the Hebrew slave, but his indignation turned to rage. His act of murder seemed quite intentional.

> So [Moses] looked this way and that way,
> and when he saw no one,
> he killed the Egyptian and hid him in the sand. (Exodus 2:12)

Like a conscience-laden youngster making certain his mother isn't looking before raiding the cookie jar, Moses seemed to do what he did on purpose. His mindful decision to kill the Egyptian, and the guilt that surrounded that decision, plagued Moses' conscience. In fact, only one day after doing the deed, he encountered two Hebrews in a fight. When he tried to break it up, one of the men confronted Moses.

> Who made you a prince and a judge over us?
> Do you intend to kill me as you killed the Egyptian? (Exodus 2:14a)

Knowing he had committed a crime, and hearing that Pharaoh intended to prosecute him, Moses became a fugitive from the law, fleeing to Midian, hundreds of miles to the east. There he tended sheep. Moses' banishment from his royal home in Egypt for forty years was punishment for breaking both civil and moral law. The prince had become a lowly shepherd.

No one was more surprised than this broken man tending Jethro's sheep to discover that God was not finished with Moses. In fact, the prince turned shepherd would be chosen to be the liberator of the Hebrews, the mouthpiece of God in delivering the Law, and the one through whom God would establish the nation of Israel. Most important, Moses would become the mediator of the Old Covenant, standing between a Sovereign God and sinful people. Time and time again, we will find Moses pleading his people's case before the Judge, and time and time again, we will see God's gracious mercy issued from the bench. Thus begins the pattern followed by Jesus

Christ, the Incarnate God, pleading His people's case before His Father's throne.

Years later, God spoke through Moses to His people:

> The LORD your God will raise up for you a Prophet like me from your midst, from your brethren. Him you shall hear. (Deuteronomy 18:15)

Centuries later, in the issuing of a new covenant, a Savior is born. And like Moses, His role is that of Mediator between a Holy God and a sinful mankind.

> But Christ came as High Priest of the good things to come,
> with the greater and more perfect tabernacle not made with hands,
> that is, not of this creation.
> Not with the blood of goats and calves,
> but with His own blood He entered the Most Holy Place once for all,
> having obtained eternal redemption.
> For if the blood of bulls and goats and the ashes of a heifer, sprinkling the unclean,
> sanctifies for the purifying of the flesh,
> how much more shall the blood of Christ, who through the eternal Spirit
> offered Himself without spot to God,
> cleanse your conscience from dead works to serve the living God?
> And for this reason [Christ] is the Mediator of the new covenant, by
> means of death, for the redemption of the transgressions under the first covenant,
> that those who are called may receive the promise
> of the eternal inheritance. (Hebrews 9:11–15)

You cannot understand the New Testament without a grasp of the book of Exodus. The story of the New Testament is the record of the new "Moses," Jesus Christ, leading God's people out of their bondage to sin and into the Promised Land of forgiveness and grace. To understand what Jesus was doing in the New Testament requires an understanding of what Moses did in the Old. Augustine said, "The Old Testament is the New concealed, and the New Testament is the Old revealed."

CLOSE ENCOUNTERS WITH A HOLY GOD

If you were to fly at thirty-five thousand feet over the Sierra Nevada mountain range, it might be difficult to tell which mountain peaks are the highest. Perspective at such a distance is sometimes a problem. But, because snow melts more slowly at higher elevations, you can tell which mountains are taller from your airplane window seat by looking for the ones covered with snow.

A survey of the Bible must include an examination of those events that rise above the others—the ones covered with an undeniable presence of the holiness of God. The miracle of creation was clearly one of these landmark events. Joseph's amazing rise to power in Egypt also was certainly an act of the Most High. Another such snowcapped peak was God's call to Moses the shepherd after forty years in Midian.

Because of the desert heat, it wasn't too unusual for a spark from a sheepherder's campfire to ignite a scrub brush, sending a flame skyward. What *was* extremely unusual that day was that the bush, although engulfed in flames, was not consumed. It burned as though it was propelled by some natural—or in this case, supernatural—reservoir of energy. The other extraordinary feature of the bush that would not be depleted was the audible voice that emanated from it. This would have been a spectacular event in the life of any busy person, but imagine the sedentary Moses' shock when such an incredible thing appeared before his very eyes.

To add to the amazing moment, the voice from the bush called Moses' name, and then announced its identity as God Himself.

"I am the God of your father—the God of Abraham,
the God of Isaac, and the God of Jacob."
And Moses hid his face, for he was afraid to look upon God.
And the LORD said,
"I have surely seen the oppression of My people who are in Egypt,
and have heard their cry because of their taskmasters,
for I know their sorrows.
So I have come down to deliver them out of the hand of the Egyptians,

and to bring them up from that land to a good and large land,
to a land flowing with milk and honey." (Exodus 3:6–8a)

Can you feel what Moses must have been feeling? The trauma of seeing the flames and hearing God's voice was tempered with the gratitude and euphoria of knowing that the God of the Patriarchs was about to make His move and free the Hebrews from their captivity.

Moses must have been thinking to himself, *Go for it, Sovereign One. It's about time You intervene with those nasty Egyptians and set my people free.*

Unfortunately for Moses, God had not concluded His speech to the astonished shepherd. Moses' short-lived experience as a spectator was about to come to an abrupt close.

"Come now, therefore, and I will send you to Pharaoh
that you may bring My people, the children of Israel, out of Egypt."
But Moses said to God, "Who am I that I should go to Pharaoh,
and that I should bring the children of Israel out of Egypt? . . .
Indeed, when I come to the children of Israel and say to them,
'The God of your fathers has sent me to you,'
and they say to me, 'What is His name?'
what shall I say to them?"
And God said to Moses,
"I AM WHO I AM . . . Thus you shall say to the children of Israel,
'I AM has sent me to you.'" (Exodus 3:10–11, 13–14)

A discussion between Moses and God ensued, clarifying Moses' understandable fears about facing Pharaoh and demanding the Hebrews' release. Finally satisfied with His directive, Moses traveled back to Egypt with his brother, Aaron, armed with the presence of the Lord God. Facing the most powerful man in the world was going to be a formidable task, but Moses went confidently to Pharaoh packing the covenant promises of a Holy God. The conflagration that ensued could certainly have been billed as the Battle of the Titans, with the freedom of God's chosen people as the prize. However, as the apostle Peter would remind us, God's plan for His people was for them to replace the bondage of their Egyptian taskmasters with a special kind of captivity under the rule of a loving heavenly Father.

> *For this is the will of God,*
> *that by doing good you may put to silence the ignorance of foolish men—*
> *as free, yet not using liberty as a cloak for vice,*
> *but as bondservants of God.* (1 Peter 2:15–16)

But Pharaoh denied Moses' request for the release of the Hebrews. In doing so, he brought upon his nation and his own house curses beyond his wildest dreams. The signs and wonders God performed in Egypt were sent not only to free the Israelites, but also to judge this wicked, arrogant ruler and his godless nation. What followed Pharaoh's hardness of heart was a systematic manifestation of God's mighty power over the elements, the weather, and even over life itself. God's plan was to save His people so that His holy name would be proclaimed over all the earth.

> What followed Pharaoh's hardness of heart was a systematic manifestation of God's mighty power over the elements, the weather, and even over life itself.

There is no period in the Old Testament where miracles are so heavily concentrated. God's methodical humiliation of the gods of Egypt is ablaze with supernatural power. The only other time in redemptive history where miracles are so prevalent is centuries later during the ministry of Jesus Christ.

As He did through His only begotten Son, God underscored His covenant blessing to His people—and to the world—through the miracles Moses orchestrated. God validated the words Moses spoke before the audience of two entire nations, demonstrating for all time that he was an oracle of God. These miracles formed the basis of Moses' prophetic ministry, legitimizing not only what he said to Pharaoh, but all that he would announce to his own people in the years to come on behalf of God.

- Moses and the Exodus
- **The Passover**

Several years ago, I was delivering a series of lectures on the campus of Grove City College in western Pennsylvania. During one of the breaks, I was strolling across the open commons area when a student approached me. After several minutes of small talk, the young man cut straight to the chase.

"Dr. Sproul," he asked, "why do you Christians refer to your conversion experience as 'getting saved'? I don't understand. From what or whom are you getting saved?"

I could tell by the look on his face that his question was sincere. Unlike the trap cynical students sometimes set for visiting lecturers—hired guns from their ivory towers of intellect—this student truly wanted to know.

My mind raced through a sequence of answers. I reviewed the first chapter of Zephaniah where the prophet warns against the Great and Terrible Day of the Lord. And then I thought of the tenth plague—the unquenchable wrath of God revealed in the instantaneous slaughter of thousands of children.

> God's plan is to save His people from His *own* fury.

As a resident of Central Florida, my family and I are no strangers to devastation. Late every summer, our eyes and ears are delicately tuned to the airwaves, listening to weather experts warning our communities of the possibility of impending hurricanes. You have seen the aerial footage of entire cities leveled by these horrifying storms. For us, this is serious business.

But there is no devastation that compares to the destruction that comes as a result of the wrath of a Holy God. To find yourself in its way is to be eternally ravished.

Standing face to face with my inquisitive student friend, it was clear to me that in His mercy, God's plan is to save His people from His *own* fury. I'm not sure if my answer satisfied the young man, but I will never forget the intensity of the moment and the epiphany that followed.

In His grace, God protects His faithful ones from His own judgment. This is the story of the tenth plague, and the Passover.

The tenth plague is announced in the eleventh chapter of Exodus. In this final demonstration of God's willingness to do whatever was necessary to change Pharaoh's heart, He snatched the lives of the Egyptian firstborn and *saved*—there's that word again—the lives of the obedient Hebrews.

> And the LORD said to Moses,
> "I will bring one more plague on Pharaoh and on Egypt.
> Afterward he will let you go from here. When he lets you go,
> he will surely drive you out of here altogether." . . .
> Then Moses said, "Thus says the LORD:
> 'About midnight I will go out into the midst of Egypt;
> and all the firstborn in the land of Egypt shall die,
> from the firstborn of Pharaoh who sits on his throne,
> even to the firstborn of the female servant who is behind the handmill,
> and all the firstborn of the animals.
> Then there shall be a great cry throughout all the land of Egypt,
> such as was not like it before, nor shall be like it again.'" (Exodus 11:1, 4–6)

Moses' instructions to his people were clear and precise. In order to escape they were to take a young and spotless lamb or goat, kill it, and paint its blood on the doorposts and lintels of the entrances to their homes. In the night of terror, God would spare the life of the firstborn of these homes, passing over them when He saw the blood.

Can you imagine the utter chaos of the morning following this experience—devastation and suffering such as the world had never seen? The land of Egypt was strewn with the bodies of men, women, and children. Even the carcasses of dead animals covered the landscape. God's righteous indignation made the fury of a Florida hurricane look like child's play.

But for the Hebrews, there was great relief. At the cost of a spotless lamb, God had provided a way for them to escape His anger.

Even to this day, Jews celebrate this event. When they are preparing to eat the Passover meal, it's the custom of the youngest child in the family to ask the father, "What do these things mean?"

The father explains to all present what each part of the Passover symbolizes.

What is often forgotten in this celebration by Jews and Christians alike is that the Hebrews were saved, not from a pagan and capricious pharaoh, but from the wrath of a Holy God—saved *by* God *from* God. This is a critical thing to understand; one that will grow more important as the Scripture unfolds.

> *But if our unrighteousness demonstrates the righteousness of God,*
> *what shall we say?*
> *Is God unjust who inflicts wrath?* (Romans 3:5)

> *But now the righteousness of God apart from the law is revealed,*
> *being witnessed by the Law and the Prophets,*
> *even the righteousness of God, through faith in Jesus Christ, to all*
> *and on all who believe. For there is no difference;*
> *for all have sinned and fall short of the glory of God,*
> *being justified freely by His grace through the redemption that is in Christ Jesus,*
> *whom God set forth as a propitiation by His blood, through faith,*
> *to demonstrate His righteousness, because in His forbearance God*
> *had passed over the sins that were previously committed.* (Romans 3:21–25)

The New Testament underscores the idea of God's wrath being atoned for us by the blood of His own Son. As in the Old Testament, we see a Holy God, Who is Himself willing to provide a way for us to be saved from His own anger over our sin.

> *The next day John [the Baptist] saw Jesus coming toward him, and said,*
> *"Behold! The Lamb of God who takes away the sin of the world!"* (John 1:29)

John the Baptist, a practicing Jew, knew how his words would be connected to the Passover Lamb in the minds of those who heard his words—the Lamb Whose shed blood would save His people from God's wrath and the judgment that awaits those who do not put their trust in the Savior.

What the blood of the Passover lambs did for a moment, Christ's blood does for all eternity.

The Jews were to always remember the salvation that God had accomplished by bringing the Hebrews out of Egypt. And even today, as Jewish people celebrate Passover, they do not remember "those" whom God redeemed; they celebrate God's provision for "us," identifying God's ongoing work of grace in the lives of all mankind.

God used the elements of the Passover to communicate critical truths about redemption and judgment. He required in the ancient Passover that the bread be unleavened. This flat loaf, baked with no yeast, represented the Hebrews' leaving Egypt in a hurry, before the bread had time to rise. Yeast with its bacterial quality was also a symbol of corruption, so it could not be included in this holy meal.

> What the blood of the Passover lambs did for a moment, Christ's blood does for all eternity.

The wine and bitter herbs in the Passover meal demonstrated the two-edged sword of God's judgment. The herbs reminded the people of the bitterness of being on the wrong side of God's deliverance. But the sweetness of the wine was to remind them of the blessings of God's favor. In a moment, one nation could be freed from slavery and another plundered of both sons and possessions.

Also prescribed during the Passover meal was that traveling clothes be worn, including a belt for holding up the garments, making walking less cumbersome. In addition, provisions and additional clothing could be attached to this belt.

In the gospel accounts, as Christ sat down with His disciples in Jerusalem the night before His execution, the Scriptures say Christ deeply longed to celebrate the Passover with His friends. He gave instructions on how the room and the meal were to be prepared. And as they celebrated this meal in roughly the same way as it had been done for two millennia, Jesus abruptly changed the formula. "This is My body," He said as He broke the bread. "This is My blood, shed for the remission of sins," He declared as He lifted the cup declaring the New Covenant. Now, instead of the blood of a lamb or a goat, *His* blood would be spilled for them.

The disciples were dumbfounded as Christ announced His plan for the ultimate rescue of God's people, forever tying the communion celebration of the Lord's Supper to the Passover, from which it was taken.

And it was a good thing that the disciples wore their traveling clothes to this supper. From that evening on, these men were scattered: first to hide, then to meet the risen Savior. For them, Jesus' admonition to "go, tell, and be," became a way of life.

SUMMARY
■ MOSES AND THE EXODUS

How did Jacob's family become a nation? In God's providence, it would take a shepherd boy becoming a mighty prince, and a prince becoming a lowly shepherd. Like bookends separated by more than three centuries, Joseph and Moses helped to establish, preserve, and lead Israel.

Number eleven of Jacob's twelve sons, Joseph's life began as a shepherd boy. His father foolishly singled him out by giving him a special multicolored, long-sleeved cloak. But his ten older brothers, seething with jealousy over their father's special treatment of their little brother, made plans for his demise. Throwing him into a pit to die, then spilling blood on his coat to present to their father, seemed like a perfect scheme. But passing Midianite traders traveling to Egypt provided a more economically rewarding scenario. So Joseph was sold like a common slave.

But God demonstrated His sovereignty by preparing Joseph to bring about great blessing, both for this lowly shepherd boy and for His people. Because of Joseph's obedience and his forgiveness of his undeserving brothers, God brought the entire family of Israel, now numbering in the hundreds of thousands, from Canaan to Egypt. Here, because of Joseph's leadership, the Hebrews were treated as guests.

The Hebrews enjoyed prosperity under the Hyksos dynasty, but when his successor, Thutmose, came to power, the Jews were perceived as a political threat. This threat to the political stability of the Egyptians turned into years of oppression, slavery, and eventually wholesale genocide for the Hebrews. But God miraculously provided a man to lead His people out of Egyptian bondage.

The conditions under which the covenant child, Moses, was born were unthinkable. The descendants of Abraham, Isaac, and Jacob, who had been welcomed into Egypt as Pharaoh's special guests, were now being treated like chattel—tangible assets amid the nation's extravagant wealth. The oppression of the Hebrews, God's chosen people, was inconceivable.

But when it looked as though there was no hope and God's chosen people would eventually vanish from the face of the earth, He sovereignly intervened in the preservation of one baby boy.

Moses' parents gently laid their child into a basket and then into the river, knowing they would probably never see him again. But the baby's mother had no choice. If she didn't release him into the river, he would most certainly be murdered by the Egyptians.

Surrounded by legions of protecting angels, the little basket found its way into a small tributary where a group of Egyptian women were bathing. As they peered into the basket, the baby let out a cry and the daughter of Pharaoh was touched. Amazingly, the daughter of the man who had called for the wholesale butchering of children was given a heart of compassion. In disobedience to her father's dictates, she rescued the child, gave him a name, and made him her son.

As Prince Moses grew up in the palace, his heart was strangely drawn to the plight of the Hebrews. One day, he came upon an Egyptian mercilessly beating one of Moses' kinsmen. Filled with rage, he killed the Egyptian and buried the body in the sand (Exodus 2), hoping no one had seen him do this deed.

Knowing he had committed a crime, and hearing that Pharaoh intended to prosecute him, Moses became a fugitive from the law, fleeing to Midian, hundreds of miles to the east. There he tended sheep. The prince had become a lowly shepherd.

Because of the desert heat, it wasn't too unusual for a spark from a sheepherder's campfire to ignite a scrub brush, sending a flame skyward. What *was* extremely unusual that day was that the bush, although engulfed in flames, was not consumed. To add to the amazing moment, the voice from the bush called Moses' name, and then announced its identity as God Himself.

A discussion between Moses and God ensued, clarifying Moses' understandable fears about facing Pharaoh and demanding the Hebrews' release. Satisfied with His directive, Moses traveled back to Egypt with his brother, Aaron, armed with the presence of the Lord God. Facing the most powerful man in the world was going to be a formidable task, but Moses went confidently to Pharaoh, packing the covenant promises of a Holy God.

But Pharaoh denied Moses' request for the release of the Hebrews. In doing so, he brought upon his nation and his own house curses beyond his wildest dreams.

■ THE PASSOVER

There is no devastation that compares to the destruction that comes as a result of the wrath of a Holy God. To find yourself in its way is to be eternally ravished. This is the story of the tenth plague, and the Passover.

In this final demonstration of God's willingness to do whatever was necessary to change Pharaoh's heart, He snatched the lives of the Egyptian firstborn and saved the lives of the obedient Hebrews.

Moses' instructions to his people were clear and precise. In order to escape they were to take a young and spotless lamb or goat, kill it, and paint its blood on the doorposts and lintels of the entrances to their homes. In the night of terror, God would spare the life of the firstborn of these homes, passing over them when He saw the blood. At the cost of a spotless lamb, God had provided a way for them to escape His anger.

The New Testament underscores the idea of God's wrath being atoned for us by the blood of His own Son. As in the Old Testament, here we have a Holy God, providing a way Himself for us to be saved from His own anger over our sin.

CHAPTER THREE

THE WILDERNESS

- **The Giving of the Law**
- The Tabernacle
- Leviticus, Numbers, and Deuteronomy
- The Old Testament Sacrificial System

Dr. John Gerstner was one of my seminary professors. He was—and continues to be—one of my greatest mentors in the faith and in my love for a disciplined pursuit of theological truth. I had visited with Dr. Gerstner many times, but on this particular day, I dropped onto a chair with a telltale thud.

My professor and friend knew I was upset.

I explained to him that I was troubled by the shift in our church away from a strong view of the authority of Holy Scripture and toward an evolving accommodation to secularism. "How can this kind of church, committed to relativism and convenient theology, survive?" I asked. In the words of the apostle Paul, "The world has squeezed this church into its mold" (see Romans 12:1–2).

Dr. Gerstner leaned back in his chair. This man was not afraid of tough questions. And although his brow furrowed just a bit, I knew he was ready with an answer.

"R. C.," he began, "we are standing between Migdol and the sea." He recalled the account of the Hebrews, caught in a death vise between the stampeding Egyptians and certain drowning in the water. Then he added, "What we need is for God to send us a Moses who will lift up his hand so that the sea will be separated and we may pass through safely."

John Gerstner was speaking metaphorically, of course. As an orthodox theologian, he did not pray for—nor did he expect—a literal reincarnated Moses to appear. But the rescue that God provided for His people that day on the shores

of the Red Sea has become one of history's great examples of divine intervention and rescue.

Pharaoh was having second thoughts. Sure, he not only had released the
purveyors of the perilous plagues, he had literally driven the troublemakers
out of Egypt. He was happy to see them go. But, soon after the dust on the
horizon had settled from the Hebrews' caravan, Pharaoh remembered how
valuable these slaves had been in his economy. He had second thoughts.

> Now it was told the king of Egypt that the people had fled,
> and the heart of Pharaoh and his servants was turned against the people;
> and they said, "Why have we done this,
> that we have let Israel go from serving us?"
> So he made ready his chariot and took his people with him.
> Also, he took six hundred choice chariots,
> and all the chariots of Egypt with captains over every one of them.
> And the LORD hardened the heart of Pharaoh king of Egypt,
> and he pursued the children of Israel;
> and the children of Israel went out with boldness. (Exodus 14:5–8)

Ironically, God led the people out of Egypt on a southeastern route,
straight into trouble. How could this have happened, since the more logical
journey to the Promised Land would have been northeasterly?

> Oh, the depth of the riches both of the wisdom and knowledge of God! How
> unsearchable are His judgments and His ways past finding out! (Romans 11:33)

From God's perspective, He was preparing a fabulous rescue of His people
against overwhelming odds. Not only was God's sense of direction perfect,
but in His sovereignty, this circuitous route to Canaan provided the opportunity for His miraculous deliverance of the Hebrews and the obliterating
drowning of the Egyptian army. What other "natural" disaster could have
been so perfectly designed?

From Migdol, the armies of Pharaoh approached. Just when they knew that
they had the Hebrews right where they wanted them, God, in the form of a pil-

lar of fire, moved in front of the Egyptian chariots to stop them. Moses raised his hands, and a mighty wind began to blow from the east. Throughout the night, the relentless wind blew and, by morning, there was a dry path through the Red Sea. Moses gave the order and the Hebrews walked through the sea on solid ground.

> Their final thoughts as torrents of waters swallowed them up must have been that the God of the Hebrews simply was not to be defied.

At the right time, God removed the impediment from the Egyptians, allowing them to give chase. They needed no encouragement to close in on the hapless Hebrews. Imagine the scene: hundreds of foot soldiers flanked by six hundred chariots, manned with the best in Pharaoh's army. This sophisticated army is descending on the Israelites—men, women, and children—protected by walls of water, mysteriously suspended on each side of their path through the sea.

As they gave chase, the Egyptians must have been astounded at the water mounted up around them. And their final thoughts as torrents of waters swallowed them up must have been that the God of the Hebrews simply was not to be defied. Not even by the mighty Egyptian army.

I know that some critical scholars have argued that the body of water the Hebrews passed through was not the Red Sea, but the Reed Sea, a swamp with water no deeper than four to six inches. They argue that ordinary tidal forces and a good breeze would make this body of water passable. Fair enough. But I'm reminded of the little boy who was in a Sunday school class taught by a teacher enlightened by the Reed Sea explanation. When the boy's parents asked him what he had learned in Sunday school, he reported, "I learned that God is very big and powerful. He drowned all the armies of Egypt in ankle-deep water."

Even creative scholarship cannot dim the glory of God that flows from the story of the Exodus.

THE TEN COMMANDMENTS

For the next three months, the Hebrews traveled in safety, led by the pillar of cloud by day and the pillar of fire by night. They arrived at the foot of

Mount Sinai, where God was going to consecrate them as a nation and give them His Law.

In the third month after the children of Israel had gone out of the land of Egypt,
on the same day, they came to the Wilderness of Sinai . . .
And Moses went up to God, and the LORD called to him from the mountain, saying,
"Thus you shall say to the house of Jacob, and tell the children of Israel:
'You have seen what I did to the Egyptians, and how I bore you on eagles' wings
and brought you to Myself.
Now therefore, if you will indeed obey My voice and keep My covenant,
then you shall be a special treasure to Me above all people;
for all the earth is Mine.
And you shall be to Me a kingdom of priests and a holy nation.'
These are the words which you shall speak to the children of Israel."
So Moses came and called for the elders of the people,
and laid before them all these words which the LORD commanded him.
Then all the people answered together and said,
"All that the LORD has spoken we will do."
So Moses brought back the words of the people to the LORD. (Exodus 19:1, 3–8)

When we see the context of the presentation of the Ten Commandments, we see that the Law was given as God's plan for redemption. This was not simply a list of dos and don'ts. The Law was a critical part of the covenant God was making with His people.

Three days prior to the giving of the commandments, the people were required to ceremonially cleanse themselves, symbolic of the inner work God required: repentance. And after the Law was received, Moses built an altar, worshiping God through sacrifices. This was symbolic of the salvation that came through the atoning sacrifice of the lamb during the Passover. The Ten Commandments were like a priceless painting delivered to the people, framed by their contrition for sin and humble reverence before God.

The instructions were clear. In fact, God told Moses to tell the people not to touch either the mountain or Moses himself before the giving of the Law, or they would die.

Why would God require this? Why were His commands so harsh?

The answer is this: because of His holiness.

Except for an expletive used by a late well-known sportscaster ("Holy Cow") or the words stamped on the pew Bible in front of our knees at church (Holy Bible), the word *holy* is not a very frequently used word these days.

However, to understand the character of God, "holy" is one of the first things that God needed to teach His people about Himself. We do not treat a Holy God casually. He is not our cosmic bellman. We do not drop in on Him and order Him around when it suits us or when we have a little extra free time.

> The Ten Commandments were like a priceless painting delivered to the people, framed by their contrition for sin and humble reverence before God.

"Is he . . . quite safe?" asked the trembling Susan to Mr. Beaver. She had only heard of Aslan, the godlike lion in C. S. Lewis's *The Lion, the Witch and the Wardrobe*, and she was more than a little frightened.

"Who said anything about safe?" replied Mr. Beaver. "Of course, he isn't safe. But he is good. He's the King, I tell you."

Very good. Definitely not safe. Two apt ways to define God's holiness.

From the time Adam and Eve sinned and God sent an angel with a flaming sword to guard the entrance to the Garden of Eden, man has been separated from the immediate presence of God. This is because of our sinfulness and His holiness.

> *Then it came to pass on the third day, in the morning,*
> *that there were thunderings and lightnings, and a thick cloud on the mountain;*
> *and the sound of the trumpet was very loud,*
> *so that all the people who were in the camp trembled.*
> *And Moses brought the people out of the camp to meet with God,*
> *and they stood at the foot of the mountain.*
> *Now Mount Sinai was completely in smoke,*
> *because the* LORD *descended upon it in fire.*
> *Its smoke ascended like the smoke of a furnace,*
> *and the whole mountain quaked greatly.* (Exodus 19:16–18)

Imagine how Moses must have felt at this moment. God had allowed him into His holy presence, and blessed him with the sole responsibility to deliver the Law to the people. For this prince turned shepherd turned covenant leader, it must have been quite an awesome thing.

Moses descended from the smoke on Mount Sinai and delivered the foundational portion of God's Law to man, the Ten Commandments (Exodus 20:1–17).

1. *I am the* LORD *your God . . . You shall have no other gods before Me.*
2. *You shall not make for yourself a carved image—any likeness or anything that is in heaven above, or that is in the earth beneath, or that is in the water under the earth; you shall not bow down to them nor serve them . . .*
3. *You shall not take the name of the* LORD *your God in vain, for the* LORD *will not hold him guiltless who takes His name in vain.*
4. *Remember the Sabbath day, to keep it holy. Six days you shall labor and do all your work, but the seventh day is the Sabbath of the* LORD *your God . . .*
5. *Honor your father and your mother, that your days may be long upon the land which the* LORD *your God is giving you.*
6. *You shall not murder.*
7. *You shall not commit adultery.*
8. *You shall not steal.*
9. *You shall not bear false witness against your neighbor.*
10. *You shall not covet your neighbor's house; you shall not covet your neighbor's wife, nor his male servant, nor his female servant, nor his ox, nor his donkey, nor anything that is your neighbor's.*

The first four commandments tell the people about a correct relationship with a Holy God. They make it clear that He is to be held in the highest place. The final six commandments form the basis for right human relationships.

What is incredible to me about this moment is the people's response. Once Moses had presented this foundational portion of the Law, they did not shuffle off like Boy Scouts to their pup tents. This was more than campers having just heard a listing of rules from their scoutmaster. The Law was no simple list of suggestions for happy living attached to someone's plastic clipboard.

Now all the people witnessed the thunderings, the lightning flashes,
the sound of the trumpet, and the mountain smoking;
and when the people saw it, they trembled and stood afar off.
Then they said to Moses,
"You speak with us, and we will hear;
but let not God speak with us, lest we die."
And Moses said to the people,
"Do not fear; for God has come to test you, and that His fear
may be before you, so that you may not sin." (Exodus 20:18–20)

One of the most interesting things about these words is that, in the midst of the greatest light show in history, he commanded the people, "Do not fear." These are the identical words spoken to the shepherds on the night the Incarnate Christ was born:

And behold, an angel of the Lord stood before them,
and the glory of the Lord shone around them,
and they were greatly afraid.
Then the angel said to them,
"Do not be afraid, for behold, I bring you good tidings of great joy
which will be to all people.
For there is born to you this day in the city of David a Savior,
who is Christ the Lord." (Luke 2:9–11)

Can you see the similarity of this scene with that of Moses descending from the mountain to deliver the Law?

A great spectacle of light and sound . . . trembling souls . . . a message from God about the fulfillment of His sovereign plan . . . and a "do not be afraid."

And I, if I am lifted up from the earth,
will draw all peoples to Myself. (John 12:32)

These words from Jesus Christ, God Incarnate, are exactly what the Hebrews standing at the foot of the mountain were hearing.

God's holiness fills mankind with awe and wonder. His presence and His message leave no room for doubt. But His love mysteriously invites us to come. His holiness overwhelms us, but His mercy welcomes us.

This was no casual experience for the people of Israel. I'm sure that even the children present at this moment remembered it for the rest of their lives. As old men, their grandchildren must have said to them, "Tell us again, Grandfather. Tell us again what happened when Moses brought the Law to our people."

And then these men would tell their children and grandchildren stories about their personal encounters with the holiness of God.

When we approach God in prayer and worship and are truly aware of His presence, we will surely be overwhelmed by His greatness. And as we cultivate an awe of this Holy God, we will avoid the sin of presumption and vanity that often clouds our experience. God calls His people to approach Him in humility and to worship Him.

The truth about God will make us want to bow before Him. His power and holiness, and our desire to please Him, will naturally compel us to right thinking and obedient living.

Mr. Beaver was right: Very good . . . definitely not safe.

- The Giving of the Law
- **The Tabernacle**
- Leviticus, Numbers, and Deuteronomy
- The Old Testament Sacrificial System

> LORD, *You have been our dwelling place in all generations.*
> *Before the mountains were brought forth,*
> *Or ever You had formed the earth and the world,*
> *Even from everlasting to everlasting,*
> *You are God.* (Psalm 90:1–2)

Most of the psalms were written by King David. However, Moses is credited with penning this one.

It's ironic that Moses refers to God as the people's "dwelling place"—ironic, because under Moses' leadership these people had no homeland and no permanent houses or buildings of any kind. Then why would he call God "our dwelling place"?

Centuries later, in telling us of the coming of Jesus Christ, the Incarnate God, the apostle John wrote:

> *And the Word became flesh and dwelt among us,*
> *and we beheld His glory,*
> *the glory as of the only begotten of the Father,*
> *full of grace and truth.* (John 1:14)

The Word (God's divine expression) became flesh (put skin on) and dwelt (pitched His tent) among us.

So what was Moses referring to when he called God the dwelling place? And what kind of tent was John referring to? Following the delivery of the Law, God told Moses to get in the building business.

> *And let them make Me a sanctuary, that I may dwell among them.*
> *According to all that I show you, that is,*
> *the pattern of the tabernacle and the pattern of all its furnishings,*
> *just so you shall make it.* (Exodus 25:8–9)

God was speaking to Moses. He told him that the people needed a physical place to symbolize His presence in their midst. But, because the Hebrews were on history's longest road trip and the land they were living on did not belong to them, they couldn't actually construct a permanent building.

So God gave them detailed instructions on how to build a huge, mobile church—a portable tent building called the Tabernacle, which they could move from place to place as they traveled.

> The Word (God's divine expression) became flesh (put skin on) and dwelt (pitched His tent) among us.

And when John introduced his people to God in human flesh, he reminded them that this was just like Moses' Tabernacle . . . Jesus Christ was God's dwelling place for everyone to see.

It was not without precedent that God set aside time or space for sacred use. After the Passover, He commanded His people to set aside a day to remember His deeds in Egypt. In the Ten Commandments, He told them to set aside a day for rest and holy worship. Now God instructs Moses and the people in great detail how to build a hallowed space.

> He was not an aloof or absentee magnate; He was an ever-present Sovereign Ruler who "dwelt among them."

The Tabernacle dramatized God's promise to Abraham, Isaac, Jacob, Joseph, and Moses that He would be with them. We are also taught about Christ's redemptive mission through the articles that accompanied the Tabernacle. And through the procedures for tabernacle worship mandated to the people, we understand the need for humility, contrition, and repentance in the presence of a Holy God.

The Tabernacle was a large tent and fenced-in area, encompassing twelve hundred square yards, one quarter the size of a football field. It was divided into three sections: the outer court, the inner court, and a small room called the Holy of Holies. Whenever the Israelites would prepare to move to a new place, they would gather their own tents, and the families of Levi would pack up the Tabernacle for the journey.

When they arrived at a new location, God would instruct them to make camp. The Levites would first set up the Tabernacle, then the others would place their own tents in a circular arrangement according to their family of origin, keeping God's dwelling place at the absolute center. Like other traveling Semitic tribes who would always put their monarch's tent in the middle of their campground, the Tabernacle was placed in the heart of the encampment, demonstrating that God was the King of Israel, worthy of the highest respect. He was not an aloof or absentee magnate; He was an ever-present Sovereign Ruler who "dwelt among them."

Once the Tabernacle was set up, this is how it was to be used:

The Outer Court. This was the large area, bordered by huge linen cloths, suspended on pillars of silverwork, and resting in brass sockets. Anyone could enter this area for the purpose of participating in or observing a sacrifice. The bronze laver was filled with water and was used by Aaron and his sons to wash their hands and feet.

The altar, also located in the outer court, was where animals were sacrificed as a symbol of the people's repentance. The carcasses were burned, the smoke rising in the air as a visible representation of the ascending penitence of the people.

The Inner Court or the Holy Place. This was an actual tent, located at one end of the fenced-in space and taking up less than one-tenth of the entire area. Only those specially ordained could enter this tent. It contained a menorah, a seven-headed golden oil lamp, and an altar used to burn incense. The sweet smell of this incense had the practical effect of covering the smell of burning flesh from the sacrifice, but it also filled the Tabernacle with an invisible but very real reminder of the presence of God.

The Holy of Holies. This small room located inside the inner court contained only one object, the ark of the covenant. The ark was a small, ornate wooden chest overlaid with solid gold. On the lid—also known as the Mercy Seat, symbolizing God's throne—were two winged, angelic creatures. Inside the ark were the two tablets of stone containing the Ten Commandments along with the rod that Aaron carried as he accompanied Moses into the courts of Pharaoh. This room could be entered by only the high priest and then only once a year.

Years later, when the Hebrews finally came to the Promised Land, the pattern of the Tabernacle became the template used in the construction of Solomon's Temple.

After centuries of slavery, helping the Egyptians to build their palaces, homes, and monuments, the Tabernacle became the Hebrews' first building project for their own people. The symbolism of this structure was clear. God was in their midst, dwelling among them. He was to be revered and worshiped with penitent hearts.

In the New Testament, God's home was built again as the Word became flesh—Jesus, the Incarnate God—dwelt among His people.

And now, two millennia later, God is still in the building business. His Tabernacle is our hearts, and we, His children, have the privilege of being His Word made flesh again.

> *For by grace you have been saved through faith,*
> *and that not of yourselves; it is the gift of God,*
> *not of works, lest anyone should boast. For we are His*
> *workmanship, created in Christ Jesus for good works, which God*
> *prepared beforehand that we should walk in them.* (Ephesians 2:8–10)

You and I are God's ongoing building project. And His promise is to finish what He started.

> *Being confident of this very thing,*
> *that He who has begun a good work in you will complete it*
> *until the day of Jesus Christ.* (Philippians 1:6)

It's hard to believe, but God's design of a tent so precisely clarifies His redemptive work in the Bible.

- The Giving of the Law
- The Tabernacle
- **Leviticus, Numbers, and Deuteronomy**
- The Old Testament Sacrificial System

Over the years I have met people who vowed that they were going to read the entire Bible, from Genesis to Revelation. Some start well, finishing off the book of Genesis with a flurry, then successfully making it through the book of Exodus with a sense of accomplishment. But Leviticus stops all but the most committed pupils. Numbers finishes off the rest. For those who make it to Deuteronomy, an instant replay of Exodus awaits them.

So why do these books have such an effect on well-meaning zealots? Certainly, the exhaustive and detailed instructions and regulations dealing with topics such as skin disease, the survey of the land, dietary laws, and guidance in legal situations are the biggest reason. Readers are tempted to simply set all this aside since they believe that most of this fine print has little bearing on their lives.

This may be true, but as much as it may be a struggle to understand books like Leviticus, Numbers, and Deuteronomy, these books are a storehouse of information about how God illustrated to His people His requirements of holiness. These books can also be helpful toward a greater understanding of the person and work of Jesus Christ.

> [Jesus said,] *"Do not think that I came to destroy the Law or the Prophets.*
> *I did not come to destroy but to fulfill."* (Matthew 5:17)

For if He fulfilled the ceremonial law through His perfect life, obedient death, and historic resurrection, then we can surely learn something about Jesus Christ through the study of those laws He completed.

LEVITICUS

The book of Leviticus was an operating manual for the priestly family of Levi. Israel had an elaborate set of rituals, each pointing to a proper understanding of God's holiness. These reminded the Hebrews, as they remind us, that approaching Him without adequate preparation is not only a waste of time, it can be hazardous to one's well-being. It's important to understand that the rites did not, in and of themselves, atone for anything. Instead, they

> These books are a storehouse of information about how God illustrated to His people His requirements of holiness.

pointed the Israelites to faith in God's future grace of sending the great sacrificial Lamb, Jesus Christ, Who would be the final atonement for God's people.

The story of Aaron's two sons, Nadab and Abihu, is a gruesome reminder of God's holiness and the severe requirements of godly leadership. These young priests were experimenting with sacrificial innovations that God had not authorized. On the surface, it looked harmless. But God's response to their cleverness was to kill them instantly.

How could God do this? What kind of God would execute young priests for such an insignificant thing? I can see Aaron running to Moses' tent, demanding to know why God had obliterated his sons.

> *And Moses said to Aaron,*
> *"This is what the LORD spoke, saying:*
> *'By those who come near Me*
> *I must be regarded as holy;*
> *And before all the people*
> *I must be glorified.'"* (Leviticus 10:3)

In this succinct explanation, we find the cardinal crystallization of the essence of worship for all God's people for all time. First, Moses reminded Aaron of the special instructions given to the priests—those who carry the message to the people. Then, Aaron was reminded that from the first offering given by Abel in the Garden of Eden to the descriptions of the worshiping angels in the book of Revelation, God was to be regarded as holy. This is more important than feelings, personal preferences regarding worship style, or other doctrinal issues. God will take extreme measures to ensure that He is held in deepest reverence and His reputation is not tarnished by those in leadership.

Leviticus also challenged God's people with the issue of *personal* holiness.

> *For I am the LORD who brings you up out*
> *of the land of Egypt, to be your God.*
> *You shall therefore be holy,*
> *for I am holy.* (Leviticus 11:45)

Even the introduction of dietary laws delivered a powerful message to the Hebrews: God's people must be different from the world. And this difference must affect every dimension of life.

NUMBERS

The book of Numbers was concerned with taking a census of the families—tribes—of Israel. Reading through these chapters may sound as fascinating as curling up in front of a fireplace on a cold evening with your favorite telephone book. But Numbers reminds us of God's faithful watch-care over every single one of His children. Like an accountant who lies awake at night dreaming about huge sheets of paper covered with tiny little numbers, our Sovereign heavenly Father loves each one of us. There will never be too many "numbers" for Him to care for.

> [Jesus said,] "Are not two sparrows sold for a copper coin?
> And not one of them falls to the ground apart from your Father's will . . .
> Do not fear therefore; you are of more value
> than many sparrows." (Matthew 10:29, 31)

As an aside, tucked inside this book is a very important story, not having anything to do with numbers. In the midst of a severe draught, a huge gathering of carping Jews, longing to be slaves again in Egypt, cornered Moses and Aaron. God commanded Moses to speak to a rock. If he would do this, water would come gushing out, quenching their thirst. But not willing to do something as benign as this before these incorrigible Israelites, Moses disobeyed God and struck the rock with his rod. He was showing off.

God provided water as He had said He would, but He punished Moses for his act of braggadocio by denying him the privilege of ever stepping into the Promised Land during his lifetime.

For years I wondered why God had treated Moses so severely. Wouldn't a slap on the wrist have been a more proportionate punishment for a little grandstanding before the people? Actually, no. Moses learned a painful lesson that day about disobeying the directives of a

> Time and time again throughout Scripture, people dared to share His awesomeness and lost. Every time.

Holy God, especially instructions that are in place to safeguard God's glory. Time and time again throughout Scripture, people dared to share His awesomeness and lost. Every time. Moses disregarded it, and it cost him entrance to the one place he wanted to go: the Promised Land. He learned. Don't challenge God's holiness. Don't step in its way.

DEUTERONOMY

Deuteronomy was the second book of the Law, a reaffirmation of the laws first laid down in Exodus. The prophets used the principles found in

Deuteronomy as the foundation for their legal case against Israel, having broken the covenants God made with them. Deuteronomy was an extremely important book to the writers of the New Testament, who quoted from it more than fifty times as they reminded the Jews of their day how they had not obeyed the Law.

At the close of the book, Moses passed his covenant authority to the great military strategist Joshua. It was Joshua who would lead the Hebrews on their conquest of Canaan. At the end of his life, Moses blessed the twelve tribes, and in a remarkable moment God took him to the top of Mount Nebo. From there God showed Moses the Promised Land and then welcomed him into his eternal rest.

God's holiness and grace are underscored in that moment. He had given His oath that the Jews would reach their homeland. He had blessed Moses with great success but had also denied him the right to enter the land because of his disobedience. But in His mercy, God granted Moses the chance at least to see the territory that was to be his legacy.

- The Giving of the Law
- The Tabernacle
- Leviticus, Numbers, and Deuteronomy
- **The Old Testament Sacrificial System**

Primitive and *obscene* were words I had never associated with God's holiness or the Old Testament technicalities of approaching Him in repentance and worship.

More than thirty years ago, as a professor at the Conwell School of Theology in Philadelphia, I was invited to lecture on the relationship between the Old and New Covenants at a local church. In my presentation, I described how the atonement of Jesus Christ fulfilled the Old Testament sacrificial system.

But something happened that evening that I will never forget; such a thing had not happened before and it has not happened since.

As I spoke concerning Christ and His death on the cross, someone from the audience shouted out, "That's primitive and obscene."

In that moment, hundreds of people froze in their seats, their eyes transfixed on me. I'm certain my face flushed with embarrassment. A relatively young and inexperienced teacher, I mentally scrambled for my next move.

"Would you please repeat that?" I said, secretly hoping the man would keep quiet. I was not that fortunate.

"I said, that's primitive and obscene," he bellowed, even louder than before.

"You're absolutely right," I countered. "It *is* primitive and obscene. I couldn't agree with you more."

> Christ's pardon for us is spelled out in big, bloody letters: YOU ARE FORGIVEN.

The crowd—including the outspoken man—sat stunned in amazement. For the next few minutes I explained.

The reason why I liked the word *primitive* is that when we look at the Old Testament ritual system—people cutting the throats of animals and offering their blood as a sacrifice—it sounds savage and barbaric to us. But something we must understand about Judeo-Christianity is that the faith that has been delivered to us is not an elite religion only understood by a handful of intellectuals.

God's plan is to communicate His message to the simplest, most uncivilized person in the world. So the truth of Christ's atonement for our sin is primitively dramatized in the Old Testament because God's people were primitive. And we still are. Christ's pardon for us is spelled out in big, bloody letters: YOU ARE FORGIVEN.

I went on to tell the man that I also thought his choice of the word *obscene* was excellent. Has there ever in the history of mankind been a more obscene sight than Jesus Christ, the perfect Son of a Holy God, hanging on a cross? And at that moment, Jesus had taken upon Himself the sum total of our sins . . . and nothing is more dark and obscene than this.

Even the heavens became dark, and God Himself turned His back on this disgusting obscenity. Jesus Christ condescended to take upon Himself our filth. And because of that, we can stand guiltless before a Holy God, believing that Christ bore our sin. So instead of God turning away from us, the Father welcomes us to fellowship with Him.

The entire sacrificial system instituted in the Old Testament dramatically portrays the truth of Christ's bearing our sin. This is not a faith for the faint of heart. It is a faith for those who have come face to face with the ugliness of their sin and who are ready to be forgiven, no matter what the cost.

It remains true: The Old Testament is the New concealed, but the New Testament is the Old revealed. The Law does much to help us understand Jesus Christ's sacrifice for His people, and Christ's sacrifice for us makes real what was only a dark shadow during the time of Moses.

God's chosen people were established as a nation by a shepherd boy turned prince and a prince turned lowly shepherd. His kingdom is continued by a sinful and hopeless mankind, welcomed into the throne room of a Holy God as His precious children.

SUMMARY
■ THE GIVING OF THE LAW

The rescue that God provided for His people on the shores of the Red Sea has become one of history's great examples of divine intervention and rescue.

Pharaoh was having second thoughts. Sure, he had not only released the purveyors of the perilous plagues, he had literally driven the troublemakers out of Egypt. He was happy to see them go. But, soon after the dust on the horizon had settled from the Hebrews' caravan, and Pharaoh remembered how valuable these slaves had been in his economy, he had second thoughts.

Ironically, God led the people out of Egypt on a southeastern route, straight into trouble. How could this have happened, since the more logical journey to the Promised Land would have been northeasterly? From God's perspective, He was preparing a glorious rescue of His people against overwhelming odds.

From Migdol, the armies of Pharaoh approached. Just when they knew that they had the Hebrews right where they wanted them, God, in the form of a pillar of fire, moved in front of the Egyptian chariots to stop them. Moses raised his hands, and a mighty wind began to blow from the east. Throughout the night, the relentless wind blew and, by morning, there was a dry path through the Red Sea. Moses gave the order and the Hebrews walked through the sea on solid ground.

At the right time, God removed the impediment from the Egyptians, allowing them to give chase.

The Egyptians must have marveled at the water mounted up around them. And their final thoughts, as torrents of water swallowed them up, must have been that the God of the Hebrews simply was not to be defied. Not even by the mighty Egyptian army.

For the next three months, the Hebrews traveled in safety, led by the pillar of cloud by day and the pillar of fire by night. They arrived at the foot of Mount Sinai, where God was going to consecrate them as a nation and give them His Law.

When we see the context of the presentation of the Ten Commandments, we see that the Law was given as God's plan for redemption. This was not simply a list of dos and don'ts. The Law was a critical part of the covenant God was making with His people.

The first four commandments tell the people about a correct relationship with a Holy God. They make it clear that He is to be held in the highest place. The final six commandments form the basis for right human relationships.

■ THE TABERNACLE

In order to have a place that symbolized God's presence among His people, God gave them detailed instructions on how to build a huge, mobile church— a portable tent building called the Tabernacle, which they could move from place to place as they traveled.

Whenever the Israelites would prepare to move to a new place, they would gather their own tents, and the families of Levi would pack up the Tabernacle for the journey.

When they arrived at a new location, God would instruct them to make camp. The Levites would first set up the Tabernacle, then the others would place their own tents in a circular arrangement according to their family of origin, keeping God's dwelling place at the absolute center. Like other traveling Semitic tribes who would always put their monarch's tent in the middle of their campground, the Tabernacle was placed in the heart of the encampment, demonstrating that God was the King of Israel, worthy of the highest respect. And He was not an aloof or absentee magnate, He was a Sovereign Ruler who "dwelt among them."

Years later, when the Hebrews finally came to the Promised Land, the pattern of the Tabernacle became the template used in the construction of Solomon's Temple.

In the New Testament, God's home was built again as the Word made flesh—Jesus, the Incarnate God—dwelt among His people.

And now, two millennia later, God is still in the building business. His Tabernacle is our hearts and we, His children, have the privilege of being His Word made flesh again. You and I are God's ongoing building project. And His promise is to finish what He started.

■ LEVITICUS, NUMBERS, AND DEUTERONOMY

The book of Leviticus was an operating manual for the priestly family of Levi. Israel had an elaborate set of rituals, each pointing to a proper understanding of God's holiness. These reminded the Hebrews, as they remind us, that approaching Him without intercession and atonement is not only a waste of time, it can be hazardous to our well-being. It's important to understand that the rites did not, in and of themselves, atone for anything. Instead, they pointed the Israelites to faith in God's future grace of sending the great sacrificial Lamb, Jesus Christ, Who would be the final atonement for God's people.

Leviticus also challenged God's people with the issue of *personal* holiness. Even the introduction of dietary laws delivered a powerful message to the Hebrews: God's people must be different from the world. And this difference must affect every dimension of life.

The book of Numbers was concerned with taking a census of the families—tribes—of Israel. Numbers reminds us of God's faithful watch-care over every single one of His children. Like an accountant who lies awake at night dreaming about huge sheets of paper covered with tiny little numbers, our Sovereign heavenly Father loves each one of us. There will never be too many "numbers" for Him to care for.

Deuteronomy was the second book of the Law, a reaffirmation of the laws first laid down in Exodus. The prophets used the principles found in

Deuteronomy as the foundation for their legal case against Israel, having broken the covenants God made with them. Deuteronomy was an extremely important book to the writers of the New Testament, who quoted from it more than fifty times as they reminded the Jews of their day that they had not obeyed the Law.

At the close of the book, Moses passed his covenant authority to the great military strategist Joshua.

■ THE OLD TESTAMENT SACRIFICIAL SYSTEM

God's plan is to communicate His message to the simplest, most uncivilized person in the world. So the truth of Christ's atonement for our sin is primitively dramatized in the Old Testament because God's people were primitive. And we still are. Christ's pardon for us is spelled out in big, bloody letters: YOU ARE FORGIVEN.

The entire sacrificial system instituted in the Old Testament dramatically portrays the truth of Christ's bearing our sin. This is not a faith for the faint of heart. It is a faith for those who have come face to face with the ugliness of their sin and who are ready to be forgiven, no matter what the cost.

God's chosen people were established as a nation by a shepherd boy turned prince and a prince turned lowly shepherd. His kingdom is continued by a sinful and hopeless mankind, welcomed into the throne room of a Holy God as His precious children.

CHAPTER FOUR

THE LAND AND ITS PEOPLE

- Joshua and the Conquest of Canaan
- The Cycle of Judges
- The Monarchy Begins

When was the last time you bumped into a Canaanite down at the grocery store? Have you ever had the chance to work on a business project alongside a Gibeonite? An Amorite? Or how about an Assyrian? Of course not. Why?

Although these nations were once mighty, their kingdoms eventually vanished. But the lowly Israelites—the Jews—have miraculously endured. God's chosen people have survived.

The book of Joshua tells the story of the military conquest of the Promised Land—Canaan. It was the same land God promised to Abraham as he obediently left his homeland of Ur centuries before. Canaan was the land God swore to Moses as he led the Hebrews from captivity in Egypt. But there was a problem. Getting back to the land to possess it meant that someone already living there had to be removed.

When Jacob and his family had accepted Joseph and Pharaoh's invitation to migrate to Egypt, other peoples had eventually taken their places in Canaan. So if the Israelites were to reinhabit the land, someone would have to go. And of course, they wouldn't go easily.

So why does the story of the Old Testament *have* to include all of these military conquests? Why *must* the Jews return to their homeland? Why couldn't God's people find happiness wherever they were? Why couldn't they just live and let live?

During the 1960s, every July the Green Bay Packers started their summer workouts, preparing for the fall football season. And each year Vince Lombardi, the Packer's head coach, would gather his men together in the locker room to begin the process of getting them ready. He would take a football in his hand and hold it high enough for them to see. Once he was certain that each man had focused on what he was showing them, the great Lombardi would speak.

"Gentlemen," he would say with confidence, "*this* is a football . . . am I going too fast?" Knowing how easy it is to forget the basics, Lombardi was comfortable getting right to the point.

> Now the LORD had said to Abram:
> "Get out of your country,
> From your family
> And from your father's house,
> To a land that I will show you.
> I will make you a great nation;
> I will bless you
> And make your name great;
> And you shall be a blessing.
> I will bless those who bless you,
> And I will curse him who curses you;
> And in you all the families of the earth
> shall be blessed." (Genesis 12:1–3)

I have no doubt that as Joshua took the reins of leadership from Moses, he visited this covenant promise. In fact, since he was so successful as a military strategist, I can imagine Joshua regularly standing before his troops, reciting these words. It was simply a reminder to Joshua's army, a reminder of God's binding oath. These inexperienced and fearful men would remember why they were there in the first place.

Like Lombardi, Joshua would lift high the partriarchal promise to his troops. Once he was certain that he had their attention, he would speak: "This is a covenant . . . am I going too fast?"

By the way, if God had made this promise to the father of the Canaanites, or the father of the Gibeonites, the Amorites, or even the powerful Assyrians, the answer to the above question would have been "yes."

But because God's blessing was to fall on the Israelites, you probably *do* have a good friend who is Jewish. Perhaps you are Jewish yourself—a member of this covenant family. God keeps His promises. Come hell or high walls, the conquest of Canaan and the establishment of a nation were going to happen. Those promises were sure.

Joshua was a prominent figure in this occupation. Of the twelve who went, he was one of the two men (the other was Caleb) who had returned on a spy mission for Moses to Canaan with an optimistic report. Ten little men saw giants; two great men of faith saw God. And Joshua continued to display great faith as he led his army against seemingly impossible odds. Joshua and his armies went up against well-fortified cities, sometimes several at once, with inexperienced men and low-quality weaponry.

> With this solemn charge, Joshua began his work. But as always, with the blessings came responsibilities.

It is an obvious miracle every time the relatively tiny forces of Israel win in battle, and it took a man of great faith to lead them into those frightening situations.

> After the death of Moses the servant of the LORD,
> it came to pass that the LORD spoke to Joshua the son of Nun,
> Moses' assistant, saying:
> "Moses My servant is dead. Now therefore, arise, go over this Jordan,
> you and all this people, to the land which I am giving to them—
> the children of Israel.
> Every place that the sole of your foot will tread upon
> I have given you, as I said to Moses.
> From the wilderness and this Lebanon as far as the great river,
> the River Euphrates, all the land of the Hittites,
> and to the Great Sea toward the going down of the sun,
> shall be your territory.
> No man shall be able to stand before you all the days of your life;
> as I was with Moses, so I will be with you.
> I will not leave you nor forsake you.
> Be strong and of good courage,
> for to this people you shall divide as an inheritance

> *the land which I swore to their fathers to give them.*
> *Only be strong and very courageous,*
> *that you may observe to do according to all the law*
> *which Moses My servant commanded you;*
> *do not turn from it to the right hand or to the left,*
> *that you may prosper wherever you go.*
> *This Book of the Law shall not depart from your mouth,*
> *but you shall meditate in it day and night,*
> *that you may observe to do according to all that is written in it.*
> *For then you will make your way prosperous,*
> *and then you will have good success.*
> *Have I not commanded you?*
> *Be strong and of good courage; do not be afraid, nor be dismayed,*
> *for the LORD your God is with you wherever you go."* (Joshua 1:1–9)

"Make no mistake about it," God was saying to Joshua. "I will continue the patriarchal blessing upon this covenant people through you. Stay close to the Book of the Law, Joshua. Think about it, speak about it, and obey it. And I will bless you."

With this solemn charge, Joshua began his work. But as always, with the blessings came responsibilities. In the midst of these affirmations, God made it clear that the requirements of the Law had not been diminished.

Wouldn't it be great if God would make the same promise to you and me? Actually, He *has.*

> *Christ has redeemed us from the curse of the law,*
> *having become a curse for us . . .*
> *that the blessing of Abraham might come upon*
> *the Gentiles in Christ Jesus, that we might receive the promise*
> *of the Spirit through faith.* (Galatians 3:13–14)

"Make no mistake about it," God is also saying to us. "Through your faith in the blood of Jesus Christ, I will pass the covenant blessing I promised to Abraham directly to you, too."

A SURPRISE VISITOR

One of my favorite accounts in the book of Joshua is this scene from chapter five:

> *And it came to pass, when Joshua was by Jericho,*
> *that he lifted his eyes and looked, and behold,*
> *a Man stood opposite him with His sword drawn in His hand.*
> *And Joshua went to Him and said to Him,*
> *"Are You for us or for our adversaries?"*
> *So He said, "No, but as Commander of the army of the LORD I have now come."*
> *And Joshua fell on his face to the earth and worshiped, and said to Him,*
> *"What does my Lord say to His servant?"*
> *Then the Commander of the LORD's army said to Joshua,*
> *"Take your sandal off your foot, for the place where you stand is holy."*
> *And Joshua did so.* (Joshua 5:13–15)

The translators of this passage took some interpretive license, believing that this "Man" was the preincarnate representation of Christ. By capitalizing all the references to this person, those who have passed the original manuscripts down through the centuries have drawn this conclusion. We have no way of proving this, although I tend to agree that this was a possible Christophany (an Old Testament visitation by Jesus Christ). The fact that He did not protest when Joshua fell down and worshiped Him is certainly a strong measure of evidence.

But the thing that I like about this story is not this potential physical revelation of Christ, it's the humor of the encounter.

Joshua had taken stock of his impending battle with the inhabitants of Jericho. He had inventoried his troops and, armed with God's promise, he was ready. But this really big guy showed up. Joshua made a quick mental scan of his roster. No one fit this description. *Who is this?* Joshua said to himself.

So Joshua asked Him straight out—because it must have been too dark to see the color of His uniform—"Are You for us or for our adversaries?"

The Man's answer was hilarious. He said, "No."

In a split second, Joshua must have thought to himself, *I ask Him if He's my ally or my enemy and He says no? "No" is not one of the choices.*

At the height of the Civil War, a newspaper reporter approached Abraham Lincoln. "Mr. Lincoln," asked the man, "do you think God is on the side of the Union or the Confederacy?"

Without a moment's hesitation, President Lincoln replied, "The question is *not* whether God is on *our* side, young man. The question is whether or not we're on *His.*"

This was exactly what the sword-wielding Man said to Joshua. I'm neither on your side *nor* your enemy's side. I'm on God's side. And although He didn't add the following challenge, He certainly could have: "And God's side is exactly where you'd better be as well, Joshua."

All humor aside, however, the Man told Joshua to do the same thing God told Moses to do at the burning bush. "Take off your sandals. You're standing on holy ground."

Once Joshua realized Who this Man was, he didn't bother with his shoes. Instead, he fell on his face, terrorized to be in the presence of a Holy God. From that moment forward, Joshua would remember that the power of his conquests flowed from God alone—the battle was His.

In the battle that followed this supernatural encounter, God's sovereignty was demonstrated as He unleashed His power against Jericho. Once again, the lesson to be learned is crystal-clear. God gave His people, through Joshua, unusual and specific marching orders. In giving them these orders, God assured the Israelites of His presence and imminent victory, but still the orders were to be carried out to crisp perfection. Once receiving God's assurance, Joshua could have told his troops to take leave. "Don't worry about this one," he might have said. "The scoreboard is already set. We will win."

> From that moment forward, Joshua would remember that the power of his conquests flowed from God alone—the battle was His.

No, instead he ordered his army to carry out God's instructions flawlessly. The people marched, the people shouted, the trumpets blew, and the walls of Jericho collapsed.

Taking an answering cue from the Man with the raised sword, I have a question for you. "Was it God's promise or Joshua's obedience that conquered Jericho?"

You're way ahead of me on this one, aren't you? The answer is absolutely, "yes."

ACHAN'S DISOBEDIENCE

In the wake of this spectacular victory, you would think that the Hebrews would never be tempted to disobey God's commands again. Tragically, in the very next chapter, one man did that very thing. And in his disobedience, all the people learned a painful lesson.

Joshua had given the army strict orders regarding the spoils of battle. But when the walls of Jericho fell and the Israelites spread throughout the city, a man named Achan couldn't resist the temptation. Instead of following the rules, he took a beautiful garment, two hundred shekels (about ten pounds) of silver, and a wedge of gold and buried them under his tent.

As a result of Achan's theft, thirty-six fighting men lost their lives in the next battle against the diminutive nation of Ai. Not only that, but once Achan had confessed his transgression to Joshua, his entire family—his wife, his children, even his livestock—was executed before all the people.

This was a shocking display of how God demanded obedience. It was also a demonstration of how resolute He was about His people remaining free from the ravages of greed and avarice. The army of Israel would not be reduced to a band of marauding thieves; they were God's people, taking possession of the land that had been promised to them. They were simply evicting trespassers.

But, one more time, this raises the question: Why was it so necessary to God that the poachers on His land be completely evicted? Why couldn't Israel live peacefully alongside the pagans? Better yet, couldn't some of these unbelievers have been converted—led to join the Hebrews' covenant community?

Apparently God's answer to these questions was a resounding "No." The reason was because *syncretism*—attempts to unify conflicting philosophies—would destroy this young nation. God's people would have been quickly seduced by the advanced nations surrounding them. And God's redemptive purposes would not have been accomplished through an amalgam of assimilated people. So the nations in the way of Israel's reclamation of Canaan had to be purged. Holy devotion to God alone was not negotiable.

Centuries later the apostle Paul would issue the same kind of warning to Christian believers:

> Do not be unequally yoked together with unbelievers.
> For what fellowship has righteousness with lawlessness?
> And what communion has light with darkness?
> And what accord has Christ with Belial?
> Or what part has a believer with an unbeliever? (2 Corinthians 6:14–15)

Though God does not demand that we remain ethnically exclusive in marriage, He does command us to marry and develop binding relationships only within the covenant community. Marriage is not a fitting venue for evangelizing a lost spouse. It's a recipe for disaster.

The question has been asked of me many, many times: "Okay, so the Jews were not to intermarry with pagans, but why was it necessary for them to be destroyed as well?"

With all due compassion and respect, this is the wrong question. The correct query should be: "Why was God so patient with the Israelites? Why didn't He, like someone flicking a housefly off their salad, obliterate the Hebrews? How could He have been so patient . . . and so merciful . . . when, time and time again, they openly disobeyed His commands, defying Him without remorse?"

The answer, although not very satisfying to some, is quite simple. In describing the acts of a Holy God, Scripture is unequivocal about this issue.

> Therefore He has mercy on whom He will,
> and whom He will He hardens . . .
> "Does not the potter have power over the clay,
> from the same lump to make one vessel for honor
> and another for dishonor?" (Romans 9:18, 21)

In his final address to the Israelites, Joshua underscores this theme, reminding the people that it is only by God's sovereign choice that they have been the recipients of His blessing. He warned them about taking this covenant blessing for granted.

> *You cannot serve the LORD,*
> *for He is a holy God.*
> *He is a jealous God;*
> *He will not forgive your transgressions nor your sins.*
> *If you forsake the LORD and serve foreign gods,*
> *then He will turn and do you harm and consume you,*
> *after He has done you good.* (Joshua 24:19b–20)

In the generations that were to follow, Israel went through many cycles of sin and repentance. Eventually, after reaching the Promised Land, the Hebrews did suffer the covenant punishment God predicted would happen if they strayed from Him. However, even the mighty Assyrians didn't prevail as God restored His people to their homeland once more.

- Joshua and the Conquest of Canaan
- **The Cycle of Judges**
- The Monarchy Begins

During one of the summers between college semesters, I worked as a counselor in a Jewish boys' camp. I was zealous to communicate the Scriptures to the campers but was understandably restricted as to how much I could say.

So, each night I would read stories from the book of Judges to the boys in my cabin. Gathering around my bunk or sitting on the edge of their cots, these youngsters sat in rapt attention to my reading of these accounts from Scripture.

This was before the proliferation of videos depicting biblical accounts, but that was all right. My dramatic and spellbinding readings of these stories would have made even the best Hollywood animators green with envy.

Although Judges covers 350 years of Jewish history, the book itself is relatively brief. Under the inspiration of the Holy Spirit, the author of the book concentrated on the information he believed was most important. This is, of course, true in all the historical narratives: Joshua, Judges, 1 and 2 Kings, 1 and 2 Samuel, 1 and 2 Chronicles, Ezra, Nehemiah, and Esther. So what we have here is Jewish history . . . in concentrated form.

In these books, certain details are left in and others are not mentioned in order to construct a literary work with a purpose. This was not ordinary history; it was history that was edited to teach proper theology, politics, ethics, and to address other critical issues that were concurrent with the writing of the history.

Judges describes a transitional period of Jewish history where Israel existed as a loose confederation of city-states. Between the time of Joshua's death (1405 B.C.) and the coronation of King Saul (1050 B.C.), the nation of Israel had no single leader. During this time,

> Even when good judges reigned, the people's character and conduct were contemptible.

instead of one king ruling the entire nation, there were many autonomous civil groups, united primarily by a common heritage and mutual religious concerns and led by individuals called judges.

Now these were not judges in a Western civilization sense. They did not wear black robes and smack their gavels demanding silence in their courtrooms. No, they were leaders, appointed and empowered by the Holy Spirit to deliver Israel from their enemies and to exercise priestly duties (Samuel), military leadership (Samson), or administrative skills (Deborah).

Like other significant figures in Scripture, the character of these judges ran the gamut from great (Gideon) to seriously flawed (Samson). One of the most successful judges of all was Deborah, the woman who shamed her male counterparts by serving with such authority that they begged her to lead their troops into battle.

Even when good judges reigned, the people's character and conduct were contemptible.

> *Then the children of Israel did evil in the sight of the LORD,*
> *and served the Baals; and they forsook the LORD God of their fathers,*
> *who had brought them out of the land of Egypt;*

and they followed other gods from among the gods
of the people who were all around them,
and they bowed down to them;
and they provoked the LORD to anger. (Judges 2:11–12)

This is a grim recapitulation of the history of this time. These same people had promised Joshua that they would obey God and not worship other idols. And God had promised that if Israel violated the terms of His covenant with them, He would allow them to experience great suffering. Guess who kept His promise?

And the anger of the LORD was hot against Israel.
So He delivered them into the hands of plunderers who despoiled them;
and He sold them into the hands of their enemies all around,
so that they could no longer stand before their enemies.
Wherever they went out, the hand of the LORD was against them for calamity,
as the LORD had said, and as the LORD had sworn to them.
And they were greatly distressed. (Judges 2:14–15)

HE WINS . . . EITHER WAY

From the time I was a boy, I have loved the Pittsburgh Steelers. The names of the great ones—Bleier, Harris, Bradshaw, Greene, Swann, Lambert—will be forever etched in my memory. And over the years I have noticed something about the great football teams. They can win games if they have a spectacular offense *or* a powerful defense. They don't have to possess both. Games can be won by scoring lots of points or by keeping the other team from scoring. Either way, football teams with great offenses or brutal defenses win games.

Throughout history, God has promised blessings and cursings, prosperity and calamity. The consistent thing, however, is that either way, God is glorified. Whether the people choose to obey or foolishly fall into sin, His holiness remains perfectly intact. His sovereignty is never threatened. Either way, God wins . . . although for His people, it is always less painful for Him to be glorified because they are obedient.

And mankind's sinfulness always becomes a laboratory for God's relentless grace.

> *The LORD raised up judges who delivered them*
> *out of the hand of those who plundered them.*
> *Yet they would not listen to their judges,*
> *but they played the harlot with other gods,*
> *and bowed down to them.*
> *They turned quickly from the way in which their fathers walked,*
> *in obeying the commandments of the LORD;*
> *they did not do so.*
> *And when the LORD raised up judges for them,*
> *the LORD was with the judge and delivered them out of the hand of their*
> *enemies all the days of the judge;*
> *for the LORD was moved to pity by their groaning*
> *because of those who oppressed them and harassed them.*
> *And it came to pass, when the judge was dead,*
> *that they reverted and behaved more corruptly than their fathers,*
> *by following other gods, to serve them and bow down to them.*
> *They did not cease from their own doings*
> *nor from their stubborn way.* (Judges 2:16–19)

The book of Judges provides us with a great gallery to view how God's mercy is sure, the implications of "He will never leave us or forsake us." Though we are faithless at times, God remains faithful to discipline those whom He loves.

Like a loving and trustworthy Father, God used the natural consequences of disobedience plus His supernatural judgment to bring about the covenant sanctions against Israel when they willfully transgressed His Law. And do you remember God's orders to

> Sin always produces more pain than the suffering God allows, so He was not slow in causing Israel to suffer.

Joshua's armies against syncretism—that attempt to blend inharmonious philosophies with their neighbors?

Well, His warnings were not without grounds. During the time of the judges, the Hebrews' greatest sin was that of idolatry, finding more attractive gods next door—keeping up with the Joneses . . . or the Philistines, the Canaanites, the Sidonians, or the Hivites.

The reason why a loving earthly father disciplines his children is because, as painful as the punishment may be, nothing is *more* painful than the consequence of the infraction. Sin always produces more pain than the suffering God allows, so He was not slow in causing Israel to suffer. It was well worth their pain if it would lead them back to righteousness.

GIDEON

One of the greatest stories in Judges—at least by the account of my campers in those late-night story times—was the one about Gideon. He was one of the godly judges who was addressed one day by an angel of the Lord: "The LORD is with you, you mighty man of valor!"

Can you imagine such a greeting from an emissary of the Sovereign God— and to a common man like Gideon, a simple farmer and not a military man? Not one to shy away from confrontation, Gideon replied:

> *O my lord, if the LORD is with us,*
> *why then has all this happened to us?*
> *And where are all His miracles which our fathers told us about, saying,*
> *"Did not the LORD bring us up from Egypt?"*
> *But now the LORD has forsaken us*
> *and delivered us into the hands of the Midianites.* (Judges 6:13)

How many times do mortals ask these questions? Perhaps you're facing something like this right now.

The angel of the Lord responded by assuring Gideon that He would prevail—the same thing God promises to you and me right now. And don't forget, God was saying this to a desperately inexperienced soldier from a tiny Jewish tribe. So Gideon was obedient and followed the Lord's amazing instructions—reducing his army of 32,000 troops to 300 . . . against a Midianite army of at least 100,000 men. God awakened Gideon in the middle of the night and sent him and the Israelite army on a surprise attack. And because God had sovereignly prepared the Midianites for defeat by sending a rumor of conquest at the hands of a tumbling barley loaf, they fled like frightened children.

The story of God's empowerment of a weak man from a small town with a miniature army and a rumor spread among a mighty army is told to demonstrate that crucial to Israel's success would be to always remember the "salvation of the LORD" (2 Chronicles 20:17). With Him, victory is never a numbers game; it is always an adventure into the consequences of obedience. And He expects to get the glory.

> And the LORD said to Gideon,
> "The people who are with you are too many for Me
> to give the Midianites into their hands,
> lest Israel claim glory for itself against Me,
> saying, 'My own hand has saved me.'" (Judges 7:2)

We see during the time of the judges a cycle: the blessing of God, the prosperity of the people, the rebellion of the people, the wrath of God, the repentance of the people, God's forgiveness and a spirit of revival—His blessing again. Unfortunately, as these cycles continued, there was a progressive deterioration in the character of the people. The cycles became vicious cycles—a downward spiral. The Israelites were in serious trouble.

- Joshua and the Conquest of Canaan
- The Cycle of Judges
- **The Monarchy Begins**

Every year, Great Britain spends hundreds of millions of dollars on "the Royals" (no reference here to the American League baseball team in Kansas City). If you have visited London, you have seen the fabulous palaces surrounded by the daily pomp of horse parades and meticulously outfitted guards. And on special occasions, the daily opulence of the monarchy is thoroughly overshadowed by even *more* lavishness.

If you have dropped in on the Tower of London, you've seen the crown jewels—inestimable gems the size of baseballs, speaking of the Royals.

But who pays for all of this extravagance? Who foots the bill to guard those priceless trinkets? Who picks up the tab for all those tall, fuzzy hats and great red outfits? Who keeps fuel in the fleet of royal jets? Incredibly, the people do—rich people, average people, and commoners.

> With Him, victory is never a numbers game; it is always an adventure into the consequences of obedience. And He expects to get the glory.

So why aren't there rioting and civil disobedience in the streets over this unthinkable squander? Why don't Britishers storm Buckingham Palace, demanding their money back? Good questions.

If you and I were to walk the streets of London with a microphone and a tape recorder, interviewing the British, what do you think we would hear about the royal family? Don't you suspect that most of those we'd ask about this incredible (and strategically unnecessary) national expenditure would tell us that they'd just as soon spend their tax money on schools, medical research, housing initiatives, and the military?

Surprise. Even people who live from paycheck to paycheck, barely eking out a subsistent living, love the monarchy. They *love* it.

But why? How can they stand all that ostentation . . . at *their* expense?

Well, I have the answer. You may think that I'm being a little snippy to be so confident. But I *know* the answer. I know why. And do you want to know where I get my information? It comes directly from the Old Testament—from the Israelites.

For generations, these people, the children of the Patriarchs, had been led by commoners—mostly shepherds and farmers. From Abraham to Moses to Samson, their leaders looked just like them. There were no grand parades. No one gilded to the teeth in gold and dripping in diamonds. And they were tired of it.

Or worse, the Jews were led by a King they couldn't even see. I can only imagine how they had to endure the relentless mocking from their neighbors. "Who are you praying to, your imaginary king?" they must have chided. "Aren't you a little old for make-believe? When are you going to get a *real* king?"

"Other nations have their monarchs," these sniveling Hebrews whined. "Why can't we?"

And so began the most significant shift in the composure of the Israelites to date. Instead of being satisfied with a government ruled by an invisible God, they demanded a king with skin on.

But I'm getting a little ahead of myself . . .

SAMUEL

The book of 1 Samuel introduces us to a godly woman who is in terrible straits. Hannah was dealing with, for that particular culture, the worst kind of curse—barrenness. Every year when she and her husband, Elkanah, journeyed to the Temple in Shiloh to worship, Hannah would pray, pleading with God to give her a son.

Elkanah loved Hannah very much and was truly sorry that she had borne no children. He tried to console her.

> *Then Elkanah her husband said to her,*
> *"Hannah, why do you weep? Why do you not eat?*
> *And why is your heart grieved?*
> *Am I not better to you than ten sons?"* (1 Samuel 1:8)

I cannot help but smile at this conversation. Elkanah was genuinely trying to console his childless wife. He asked her a question to which the Scripture records no answer. "It's okay, honey," Elkanah was saying to Hannah. "I know you don't have any sons, but you have *me*."

Hannah does not say anything. She doesn't tell her husband that, to be perfectly honest, he *isn't* better than ten sons. Poor Elkanah.

On one of her visits to the Temple in Shiloh, Hannah poured out her heart to God. And she made a very important promise.

> *Then [Hannah] made a vow and said,*
> *"O LORD of hosts,*
> *if You will indeed look on the affliction of Your maidservant*
> *and remember me, and not forget Your maidservant,*
> *but will give Your maidservant a male child,*
> *then I will give him to the LORD all the days of his life,*
> *and no razor shall come upon his head."* (1 Samuel 1:11)

Eli the priest saw Hannah praying. In fact, her prayer was so demonstrative that he thought she was intoxicated and tried to shame her for coming into the Temple drunk. She explained that she was not a wicked woman, rather a sorrowful woman, praying for the Lord to grant her a son.

> *Then Eli answered and said,*
> *"Go in peace,*
> *and the God of Israel grant your petition*
> *which you have asked of Him."* (1 Samuel 1:17)

Hannah was so full of faith that when she heard Eli's promise, she "went her way and ate, and her face was no longer sad."

And God was faithful, and Hannah conceived and gave birth to a son. She named the boy Samuel, meaning "heard of God," "because I have asked for him from the LORD." And, according to her promise, after she had weaned him, Hannah took Samuel back to the Temple.

In the same way that Christians today bring their children before their congregations in baptism or dedication, Hannah and Elkanah brought Samuel before the Lord to remind themselves that their child was not their possession, but that he was on loan, a blessing from a Sovereign God.

When we bring our children to the church to receive a public confession of God's blessing, we take them back home to raise them. When Samuel's parents brought him to the Temple, it was a one-way trip. According to Hannah's promise, they left their son behind to be raised by Eli, the priest and judge of Israel.

In many ways, the presence of Samuel in his home must have been a relief to Eli. The Scripture makes it clear that Eli's two sons were a veritable nightmare to their dad. Not only were they rebellious and vile, but they had nothing but disdain for God's call on their father's life. They even had no reverence for the Almighty.

> *Therefore the sin of the young men was very great before the LORD,*
> *for [they] abhorred the offering of the LORD.* (1 Samuel 2:17)

Eli's failure as a father would force God, later in his life, to lift His blessing from Eli and his rebellious offspring. What a joy it must have been to Eli to welcome Samuel as a permanent resident in the Temple. Very soon, Eli realized that this was not only an unusual boy, but Samuel was also a "called" child.

What is especially peculiar about this time in Jewish history is that, after generations of frequent dialogue with God, there had been very little in the way of divine encounters. Perhaps the abject waywardness of the Hebrews had something to do with God's silence.

> *Now the boy Samuel ministered to the LORD before Eli.*
> *And the word of the LORD was rare in those days;*
> *there was no widespread revelation.* (1 Samuel 3:1)

However, as He always eventually does, the Holy One spoke up. The Lord's silence had been extraordinary, but now it was time to speak.

One evening, after everyone had gone to bed, Samuel was awakened by the sound of a voice calling his name: "Samuel." Thinking that Eli must have come to his room in the night, Samuel responded to the sound of his name, "Here I am." But looking around he realized that Eli was not there, so Samuel ran to Eli's room.

"Here I am," Samuel said to Eli. "For you called me."

Rolling over in his cot in the darkness to try to see who was speaking to him, Eli responded to the young boy, "I did not call; lie down again."

> *Then the LORD called yet again,*
> *"Samuel!"*
> *So Samuel arose and went to Eli, and said,*

> *"Here I am, for you called me."*
> *[Eli] answered,*
> *"I did not call, my son; lie down again."* (1 Samuel 3:6)

The very next verse makes a critically important theological statement. Don't miss this.

> *(Now Samuel did not yet know the LORD,*
> *nor was the word of the LORD yet revealed to him.)* (1 Samuel 3:7)

IT TAKES BOTH

An encounter with the Sovereign God is a two-part transaction. In order for there to be a connection, God must first reveal Himself to us and then He must open our eyes to see Him. At the close of the gospel of Luke, there is an event that underscores this idea.

Two men were walking the seven miles from Jerusalem to the town of Emmaus. They were buzzing with the events that had happened the previous weekend—the mock trial, crucifixion, and burial of Jesus Christ, the hoped-for Messiah. As they walked along, the Savior joined them.

"What are you talking about?" Jesus said to the men. "And why are you sad?"

"What's the matter with You?" they responded indignantly. "Are You the only stranger in Jerusalem who doesn't know the things that have happened in the past few days?"

What an irony, you might be saying. Here were these men—apparent followers of the Son of Man—discussing the amazing events leading up to Jesus' execution and, suddenly, there He is. Walking right alongside them. But they didn't recognize Him. How can that be?

> *But their eyes were restrained,*
> *so that they did not know Him.* (Luke 24:16)

There it is. There's the critical biblical truth, repeated again and again throughout Holy Scripture. Before we can have an encounter with God, He first must reveal Himself to us. And *then*, He must open our eyes. Without His initiative, we will never see Him.

Later that same day, as the two men sat at dinner with Jesus, continuing their recollection of the amazing events of the previous few days, they suddenly recognized Him. But it wasn't *their* doing.

> *Now it came to pass, as [Jesus] sat at the table with them,*
> *that He took bread, blessed and broke it, and gave it to them.*
> *Then their eyes were opened and they knew Him;*
> *and He vanished from their sight.*
> *And they said to one another,*
> *"Did not our heart burn within us while He talked with us on the road,*
> *and while He opened the Scriptures to us?"* (Luke 24:30–32)

Please don't miss this truth. Like little Samuel hearing God's voice but not recognizing it, these men had no idea Who they had been talking to until "their eyes were opened." It wasn't their decision to open their eyes; Someone opened their eyes *for* them.

Thankfully, for Samuel, God was ready to open his ears to hear the voice of a Holy God.

> *The Lord called Samuel a third time,*
> *and Samuel got up and went to Eli and said,*
> *"Here I am; you called me."*
> *Then Eli realized that the Lord was calling the boy.*
> *So Eli told Samuel,*
> *"Go and lie down, and if he calls you, say,*
> *'Speak, Lord, for your servant is listening.'"*
> *So Samuel went and lay down in his place.* (1 Samuel 3:8–9 NIV)

Although there are far more visually impressive moments in the Old Testament—the Creation, the Flood, the parting of the Red Sea—this is truly one of the greatest moments of all.

A little boy, skipping back to his room and lying on his pallet, waiting to hear the voice of the God of Abraham, Isaac, and Jacob. Here was a child filled with faith and ears at the ready. Not daring to sleep, he knew that at any moment, the Creator God was going to speak.

If you were to say to me at this moment, "R. C., what do you want more than anything else? What is it that you truly long for?"

I would say to you, "I want a heart like Samuel's after the third call. I want the anticipation of God's call to keep me alert, and I want ears, precision-tuned to the voice of God. I want Him to open my ears as only He can and the courage to be obedient. You can withhold everything else from me, but please give me these things."

Samuel was ready.

> Then the LORD said to Samuel:
> "Behold, I will do something in Israel at which both ears
> of everyone who hears it will tingle.
> In that day I will perform against Eli all that I have spoken concerning his house,
> from beginning to end.
> For I have told him that I will judge his house forever
> for the iniquity which he knows, because his sons made themselves vile,
> and he did not restrain them." (1 Samuel 3:11–13)

The next morning, Eli asked Samuel if God had called again. Samuel told Eli that God had called. Then Eli asked him what God had said. As a young man, Samuel was understandably afraid to tell Eli that God was displeased with his sons . . . and their father. But Eli pleaded and Samuel acquiesced.

Once Samuel had told Eli all that God had told him, Eli's response was profound. "It is the Lord," he confessed. "Let Him do what seems good to Him." Eli knew that God's punishment for his failure and Samuel's eventual leadership among God's people were certain.

And over the next few years, God's blessing on Samuel became more and more evident.

> So Samuel grew, and the LORD was with him
> and let none of his words fall to the ground.

And all Israel from Dan to Beersheba knew that Samuel had been established
as a prophet of the LORD.
Then the LORD appeared again in Shiloh.
For the LORD revealed Himself to Samuel in Shiloh
by the word of the LORD. (1 Samuel 3:19–21)

Soon the time came for God to discipline Eli's house.

In one of the bloodiest battles of the Old Testament, Israel went to war against the Philistines. Not only did the Philistines kill thirty thousand men, including Eli's two sons, but they stole the ark of the covenant as well. It was certainly a case of adding insult to injury.

And not only did they embezzle the Jews' most sacred heirloom, they placed it before the image of their pagan god, Dagon. When Eli received this news, he literally fell backward on his chair and broke his neck. When Eli's pregnant daughter-in-law heard that her husband, her brother-in-law, and father-in-law were dead, and that the ark of the covenant had been captured, she also died. Not, however, before giving birth to a son and naming him Ichabod, meaning "the glory has departed from Israel."

Fortunately, God's glory was not tarnished at all. Just ask the Philistines.

Then the Philistines took the ark of God and brought it
from Ebenezer to Ashdod.
When the Philistines took the ark of God,
they brought it into the house of Dagon and set it by Dagon.
And when the people of Ashdod arose early in the morning,
there was Dagon, fallen on its face to the earth before the ark of the LORD.
So they took Dagon and set it in its place again.
And when they arose early the next morning,
there was Dagon, fallen on its face to the ground before the ark of the LORD.
The head of Dagon and both the palms of its hands
were broken off on the threshold;
only Dagon's torso was left of it.
Therefore neither the priests of Dagon nor any who come into Dagon's house
tread on the threshold of Dagon in Ashdod to this day. (1 Samuel 5:1–5)

For the next seven months, the Philistines moved the ark of the covenant from city to city. And everywhere it went, the people were infected with tumors and many died. Once again, God was unequivocal regarding the demonstration of His holiness. As we have seen time and time again, this is something He *will* do, whether there's obedience or disobedience, righteousness or sin.

Finally, in desperation and fear, the Philistines returned the ark to the Israelites, placing it on a cart pulled by two cows and surrounded by golden trinkets as an offering to God.

When the ark arrived at Kirjath Jearim, the Israelites were understandably thrilled to see it again. However, they foolishly lifted the cover and looked inside, something they knew was against God's Law. This blatant act of disobedience cost many of them their lives.

Eventually the ark was taken to the house of Abinadab where it stayed for twenty years. And during this time, as Samuel continued to reign as judge of Israel, they enjoyed a time of prosperity and peace.

Tragically, as Samuel had seen in the house of his mentor, Eli, Samuel's sons did not walk in God's ways. They "turned aside after dishonest gain, took bribes, and perverted justice." What a heartbreak this must have been for their father.

> *Then all the elders of Israel gathered together*
> *and came to Samuel at Ramah, and said to him,*
> *"Look, you are old, and your sons do not walk in your ways.*
> *Now make us a king to judge us like all the nations." . . .*
> *And the LORD said to Samuel,*
> *"Heed the voice of the people in all that they say to you;*
> *for they have not rejected you, but they have rejected Me,*
> *that I should not reign over them."*

Then God added:

> *However, you shall solemnly forewarn them, and show them the behavior*
> *of the king who will reign over them. (1 Samuel 8:4–5, 7, 9)*

"Go ahead and give them a king," God was saying to Samuel. "But be sure to make it clear to them what they're in for." And so he did in great detail, telling the people that this king would take their sons as charioteers, horsemen, runners, plowmen, and manufacturers of weapons. And he would take their daughters and make of them perfumers, cooks, and bakers.

> It was in God's plan all along, and He would work in, with, or against the wills of the Israelites to accomplish His purposes.

Samuel added that the king would take the best of their fields, their vineyards, and their olive groves and give them to his servants. There would be taxes on grain, grapes, and sheep. The king would co-op the people's maidservants and manservants—their finest young men—and put them to his work.

And as a final warning, Samuel cautioned the Israelites:

> *And you will cry out in that day because of your king*
> *whom you have chosen for yourselves,*
> *and the LORD will not hear you in that day.* (1 Samuel 8:18)

But would Samuel's words change the people's minds? Would they no longer be influenced by all their neighbors who sported a king?

> *Nevertheless the people refused to obey the voice of Samuel;*
> *and they said, "No, but we will have a king over us,*
> *that we also may be like all the nations,*
> *and that our king may judge us and go out before us and fight our battles." . . .*
> *So the LORD said to Samuel,*
> *"Heed their voice, and make them a king."* (1 Samuel 8:19–20, 22)

First, Israel had been tempted by idolatry, to worship like the other countries. Now, Israel wanted a government like their neighbors. Of course, their idol worship was an anathema to a Holy God, but was their demand for an earthly king also against His will?

While their motive in having a king was clearly one of parroting pagan neighbors, the reality of their need for a visible king was one that God had foreordained. Though God was displeased at Israel's motives—giving them a rotten king to start with—He was not surprised at their need for a king. It was in His plan all along, and He would work in, with, or against the wills of the Israelites to accomplish His purposes.

There's that theme again—regardless of what happens, God will *always* be glorified.

And so Samuel goes looking for a monarch.

> *There was a man of Benjamin whose name was Kish . . .*
> *And he had a choice and handsome son whose name was Saul.*
> *There was not a more handsome person than he among the children of Israel.*
> *From his shoulders upward he was taller*
> *than any of the people.* (1 Samuel 9:1–2)

WARNING
Do not select your kings on the basis of their good looks or their stature. If you do, you will be very sorry.

Unfortunately for the Israelites, King Saul did not have this warning embroidered on his tunic. It was not posted above his throne nor was it chiseled into the cornerstone of the palace. If it had been, God's people could have been saved a great deal of grief and loss.

But, fortunately for the Israelites, Samuel was still in place. And the second time around, once God had removed His blessing from Saul because he had blasphemed a sacrifice, Samuel found the *right* man for the job.

SUMMARY
■ JOSHUA AND THE CONQUEST OF CANAAN

The book of Joshua tells the story of the military conquest of the Promised Land—Canaan. It was the same land God promised to Abraham as he obediently left his homeland of Ur centuries before. Canaan was the land God swore to Moses as he led the Hebrews from captivity in Egypt. But there was a problem. Getting back to the land to possess it meant that someone already living there had to be removed. So if the Israelites were to reinhabit the land, someone would have to go. And of course, they wouldn't go easily.

Joshua was a prominent figure in this occupation. His armies went up against well-fortified cities, sometimes several at once, with inexperienced men and low-quality weaponry. It was an obvious miracle every time the relatively tiny forces of Israel won in battle, and it took a man of great faith to lead them into those frightening situations.

"Make no mistake about it," God was saying to Joshua. "I *will* continue the patriarchal blessing upon this covenant people through you. Stay close to the Book of the Law, Joshua. Think about it, speak about it, and obey it. And I will bless you."

With this solemn charge, Joshua began his work. But as always, with the blessings came responsibilities. In the midst of these affirmations, God made it clear that the requirements of the Law had not been diminished.

But why was it necessary to God that those living on His land be completely evicted? Why couldn't Israel live peacefully alongside the pagans? The reason was because *syncretism*—attempts to unify inharmonious philosophies—would destroy this young nation. God's people would have been quickly seduced by the advanced nations surrounding them. And God's redemptive purposes would not have been accomplished through an amalgam of assimilated people. So the nations in the way of Israel's reclamation of Canaan had to be purged.

Holy devotion to God alone was not negotiable.

■ THE CYCLE OF JUDGES

Although Judges covers 350 years in Jewish history, the book itself is relatively brief. The author of the book concentrated on the information he believed was most important. Judges describes a transitional period of Jewish history where Israel existed as a loose confederation of city-states. Between the time of Joshua's death (1405 B.C.) and the coronation of King Saul (1050

B.C.), the nation of Israel had no single leader. During this time, instead of one king ruling the entire nation, there were many autonomous civil groups, united primarily by a common heritage and mutual religious concerns and led by individuals called judges.

Now these were not judges in a Western civilization sense. They did not wear black robes and smack their gavels demanding silence in their courtrooms. No, they were leaders, appointed and empowered by the Holy Spirit to deliver Israel from their enemies and to exercise priestly duties (Samuel), military leadership (Samson), or administrative skills (Deborah).

Unfortunately, even when good judges reigned, the people's character and conduct were contemptible. But mankind's sinfulness always becomes a laboratory for God's relentless grace.

The book of Judges provides us with a great gallery to view how God's mercy is sure, the implications of "He will never leave us or forsake us." Though we are faithless at times, God remains faithful to discipline those whom He loves.

■ THE MONARCHY BEGINS

For generations, the children of the Patriarchs had been led by commoners—mostly shepherds and farmers. From Abraham to Moses to Samson, their leaders looked just like they did. There were no grand parades. No one gilded to the teeth in gold and dripping in diamonds. And they were tired of it.

Or worse, the Jews were led by a King they couldn't even see. I can only imagine how they had to endure the relentless mocking from their neighbors. "Who are you praying to, your imaginary king?" they must have chided. "Aren't you a little old for make-believe? When are you going to get a *real* king?"

"Other nations have their monarchs," these sniveling Hebrews whined. "Why can't we?"

And so began the most significant shift in the composure of the Israelites to date. Instead of being satisfied with a theocracy, they demanded a king with skin on.

Unfortunately for the Israelites, Saul, their first king, was handsome and gifted . . . and arrogant. He was more interested in his own agenda than God's. So God removed His blessing from Saul.

Fortunately for the Israelites, the second time around, the *right* man for the job was found.

CHAPTER FIVE

THE KINGS

- David
- Solomon and the Temple
- The Divided Kingdom

There was a little girl
Who had a little curl right in the middle of her forehead.
When she was good, she was very good,
But when she was bad, she was horrid.

There was a little king . . .

Although we do not know if he was "little" or if King David had any "curls," we do know that the rest of this child's poem matches him quite perfectly. Perhaps this is why David is one of the people I long to meet when I get to heaven. He did nothing halfheartedly. If there ever was a Renaissance man, it was King David. He was multifaceted, extremely complex—a wild bunch of contradictions. He threw himself into life with reckless abandon. His success was beyond limits. His failures were atrocious. But his repentance was unabashed and desperately sincere.

I'll never forget my first visit to the Holy Land. People had told me that it would have a profound effect on my life. They were right. Spending time where the men and women of the Bible lived out their days was a remarkable experience.

We stayed in a hotel near the Mount of Olives, overlooking the Valley of Kidron. Across the hollow lay Jerusalem herself. One night I walked out onto the patio behind the hotel, taking a long look at Jerusalem. Floodlights darted over her walls. I searched until my eyes found a small, thirteen-acre parcel of land in the corner of modern Jerusalem that was, in David's time, the entire city. There in the darkness, I imagined David the king, fleeing from his palace, across the Kidron, from the advance of the armies of his own son, Absalom. I was overcome by a sense of history as I remembered the passage that told of David, wailing as he crossed the valley, his heart desperately broken over the events that had so quickly transpired.

The first time he had fled Jerusalem through this same valley, King Saul was trying to kill him, but this time it was David's own son who wanted to wrest the throne from God's anointed one.

Sören Kierkegaard lamented that the greatest sin of his own Danish people was not that they were overly wicked, but that they were paltry, lacking passion. When he was fed up with the surface-level righteousness of his own culture, the great theologian would turn to the pages of the Old Testament, where people like David would lie, kill, steal, commit adultery, and then repent. No paper saints were these—they had real sin to repent of . . . and they did. This is the model he saw in David's life, and it is what makes this great sinner so commendable.

As we saw with many of those who carried the mantle of God's covenant blessing, David's selection came as a complete surprise. Samuel, who was understandably broken by the failure of Saul as king, was sent by God to visit the home of Jesse, a Bethlehemite from the family of Judah. (Remember Jacob's selection of Judah as the heir to the blessing before he died in Egypt?) "For I have provided Myself a king among his sons," the Sovereign God announced to Samuel.

Knowing that the unpredictable Saul would have him flogged, Samuel quietly visited Jesse's home in order to meet the new king. One by one, Samuel visited with Jesse's sons. First he saw Eliab. Liking what he saw—his appearance and his stature looked kingly—Samuel said, "Surely the LORD's anointed is before Him!"

God's response at this moment to Samuel's first impression of Eliab says more about His final selection of David than we could ever learn elsewhere. It also summarizes the reason why Saul, qualified though he may have been for the monarchical assignment, did not measure up.

> But the LORD said to Samuel,
> "Do not look at his appearance or at his physical stature,
> because I have refused him . . .
> For man looks at the outward appearance,
> but the LORD looks at the heart." (1 Samuel 16:7)

God's anointing did not fall on David because of his good looks. And, as we learn by closely following him throughout the remainder of his life, the blessing didn't become his because he was always good. The covenant blessing of leadership became David's because of his heart.

> The covenant blessing of leadership became David's because of his heart.

Time and time again, we are ushered into the chambers of David's tender heart, even when he would have had the right to be angry or vindictive.

Remember that Saul, the first king of Israel, had risen like a meteor. Unfortunately, his fall was just as swift. Slipping in and out of madness, he even threatened to kill those who tried to help him. Often a target for Saul's vitriol, David should have celebrated this madman's demise—not to mention that his death would have meant an immediate coronation as his successor. But when the news of Saul's death came to him . . .

> David lamented with this lamentation over Saul and over Jonathan his son,
> and he told them to teach the children of Judah . . .
> "The beauty of Israel is slain on your high places!
> How the mighty have fallen!
> Tell it not in Gath,
> Proclaim it not in the streets of Ashkelon—
> Lest the daughters of the Philistines rejoice,
> Lest the daughters of the uncircumcised triumph.
> O mountains of Gilboa,
> Let there be no dew nor rain upon you,
> Nor fields of offerings.
> For the shield of the mighty is cast away there!
> The shield of Saul, not anointed with oil.

From the blood of the slain,
From the fat of the mighty,
The bow of Jonathan did not turn back,
And the sword of Saul did not return empty.
Saul and Jonathan were beloved and pleasant in their lives,
And in their death they were not divided;
They were swifter than eagles,
They were stronger than lions.
O daughters of Israel, weep over Saul,
Who clothed you in scarlet, with luxury;
Who put ornaments of gold on your apparel.
How the mighty have fallen in the midst of the battle!" (2 Samuel 1:17–25a)

Can you imagine? David's heart was broken by the loss of these two men, Jonathan and Saul. And even though he and Jonathan had one of the most remarkable friendships recorded in the Bible, David put Jonathan in the same statement of mourning as Saul, the man who had made repeated attempts to kill him—the man who had literally stolen David's wife from him. How forgiveness must have reigned in David. Therefore, he is able to write this poignant lamentation for King Saul and his son with a clear conscience. He had done all he could do to serve this wicked, insane king while he lived, for Saul was God's anointed.

Is it any wonder that David's epitaph, for time in memoriam, became this?

KING DAVID
A man after God's own heart

David was a prodigious child, far advanced beyond his years as a musician, poet, and warrior. He wrote or participated in the writing of most of the psalms—many of his deepest emotions emerging through their words.

His abilities as an accomplished and brave mercenary started out in private as he risked his life to save his sheep—a fitting precursor to his eminent role of covenant-bearer. From those skills and through his faith in God to deliver him from righteous battles, David dodged the spears of Saul and killed innumerable enemies of God. Before taking the throne, David killed Goliath, in a one-on-one showdown, viewed by the great armies of the Philistines and the Israelites. This story (1 Samuel 17) is not a simple moral tale, and it's not a hero's myth. It is a complicated story showing many things about the nature of two men, but mostly we see David as a man of character and faith . . . and a rather accurate sling. No wonder this boy became an instant hero to the people of Israel.

David was the greatest king of Israel's history. He was the supreme symbol of kingship in the Old Testament and the New. He brought unity to his fractured people, extending the borders of Israel in remarkable ways and nearly accomplishing the command made a thousand years earlier to Moses to drive the pagans from God's chosen land. This tiny nation, which linked three continents, experienced its golden age during David's reign.

David was not only strong and benevolent, but also a good administrator and master diplomat. One of his most brilliant diplomatic decisions was the selection and location of Israel's capital. He took a newly conquered town that had belonged to the Jebusites—and therefore not allied with any political faction in Israel—in the center of the nation and made this his capital. His headquarters became Jerusalem, the city of peace. This city became a symbol for everything that made Israel unique, and it rose to great prominence under David's capable leadership.

ONE SPRING DAY

Unfortunately, David was also an accomplished sinner. Even his transgressions were larger than life. Blinded by lust, he stooped to adultery and murder to secure the affections of a beautiful woman, Bathsheba. It was during the spring when kings traditionally visited their battle sites that David stayed home, taking the few days of rest that eventually cost him dearly: the life of his baby son, unthinkable treachery within his own house, and family chaos for the remainder of his days.

God sent the prophet Nathan to visit with David. His purpose was to confront the king with his heinous sin, but his clever and tender approach tore at the very soul of this man with a great heart. Nathan told David a simple allegory about a lamb—remember David had risked his life repeatedly to protect these little creatures against powerful predators—telling the story as though it were a true account.

> *"There were two men in one city,*
> *one rich and the other poor.*
> *The rich man had exceedingly many flocks and herds.*
> *But the poor man had nothing,*
> *except one little ewe lamb which he had bought and nourished;*
> *and it grew up together with him and with his children.*
> *It ate of his own food and drank from his own cup and lay in his bosom;*
> *and it was like a daughter to him.*
> *And a traveler came to the rich man,*
> *who refused to take from his own flock and from his own herd*
> *to prepare one for the wayfaring man who had come to him;*
> *but he took the poor man's lamb and prepared it for the man*
> *who had come to him."*
> *So David's anger was greatly aroused against the man,*
> *and he said to Nathan,*
> *"As the LORD lives, the man who has done this shall surely die!*
> *And he shall restore fourfold for the lamb,*
> *because he did this thing and because he had no pity."*
> *Then Nathan said to David,*
> *"You are the man!"* (2 Samuel 12:1b–7a)

Can you imagine the passion of this moment? Nathan's story of the innocent little lamb and the helpless poor man is making David's heart pound with fury. And at the pinnacle of his anger, as he called for the execution of the rich man, Nathan turned the tables on the king. "You are the man."

Yes, God's punishment is inconceivably severe. But David's wrath is turned on himself and his own unconscionable deed. Psalm 51 gives us the text of his passionate confessional prayer. If you want to understand the heart of a man in agony over his own sin, you must read this prayer.

I acknowledge my transgressions,
And my sin is always before me.
Against You, You only, have I sinned,
And done this evil in Your sight . . .
Purge me with hyssop, and I shall be clean;
Wash me, and I shall be whiter than snow . . .
Create in me a clean heart, O God,
And renew a steadfast spirit within me . . .
Restore to me the joy of Your salvation . . .
The sacrifices of God are a broken spirit,
A broken and a contrite heart—
These, O God, You will not despise. (Psalm 51:3–4, 7, 10, 12, 17)

If David was more accomplished at something other than military strategy, political prowess, or leadership savvy, it was the art of genuine confession and repentance. Here is an example of what it means to lay ourselves bare before a Holy and Righteous God and to rely on His mercy alone.

- David
- **Solomon and the Temple**
- The Divided Kingdom

Sibling rivalry has been with us since Cain and Abel, the two sons of Adam and Eve. We have seen it time and time again, especially when God's covenant anointing didn't fall on the firstborn son. You'll remember Ishmael, Esau, and Reuben, elder brothers whose fathers bypassed them.

Now we have another firstborn to add to the list, Adonijah, David's oldest son.

Then Adonijah the son of Haggith exalted himself,
saying, "I will be king"; and he prepared for himself
chariots and horsemen, and
fifty men to run before him. (1 Kings 1:5)

Who can blame Adonijah for wanting to succeed his father, David? Unfortunately, the covenant blessing was God's decision, and no amount of coercion or show of strength would sway Him.

Centuries later, the word of the Lord would come to King Zerubbabel:

> *"Not by might nor by power,*
> *but by My Spirit,"*
> *Says the LORD of hosts.* (Zechariah 4:6b)

God's decisions are always His own. So, just as the other firstborn sons had been, Adonijah was unsuccessful in muscling the blessing from his father.

> *Now the days of David drew near that he should die,*
> *and he charged Solomon his son, saying:*
> *"I go the way of all the earth;*
> *be strong, therefore, and prove yourself a man.*
> *And keep the charge of the LORD your God:*
> *to walk in His ways, to keep His statutes,*
> *His commandments, His judgments, and His testimonies,*
> *as it is written in the Law of Moses, that you may*
> *prosper in all that you do and wherever you turn."* (1 Kings 2:1–3)

Years ago, I saw the actor Burt Reynolds being interviewed on television. The discussion that day centered on transitions, particularly the progression from childhood to manhood. The interviewer asked Burt Reynolds, "How do you know when you have become a man?"

Reynolds replied in his predictable country twang, "You know you're a man when your daddy *says* you're a man." Although the audience chuckled at his answer, I knew he had spoken perfectly

> If David was more accomplished at something other than military strategy, political prowess, or leadership savvy, it was the art of genuine confession and repentance.

about the deeply rooted truth in all men. There is nothing quite as powerful as the words of your own father: "You are now an adult, a grownup." Or, in the words of an aged King David to his son Solomon, "Be strong . . . prove yourself a man."

So the covenant mantle was passed to Solomon. And like many of the leaders before him, Solomon was a man of great contrasts.

> *Now Solomon made a treaty with Pharaoh king of Egypt,*
> *and married Pharaoh's daughter;*
> *then he brought her to the City of David*
> *until he had finished building his own house,*
> *and the house of the LORD, and the wall all around Jerusalem . . .*
> *And Solomon loved the LORD,*
> *walking in the statutes of his father David,*
> *except that he sacrificed and burned incense*
> *at the high places.* (1 Kings 3:1, 3)

The spiritual height of the Hebrews' monarchy was at its zenith under David's rule. If David's reign was the golden age of Israel, it would be safe to say that the gold began to tarnish under Solomon. And, because of Solomon's sin, especially near the end of his life, that discoloration turned to pure rust.

> If David's reign was the golden age of Israel, it would be safe to say that the gold began to tarnish under Solomon.

But what made Solomon so successful, and why did God bless him with such monumental prosperity? Sitting on the side of a hill, many generations later, God spoke through His Incarnate Son, Jesus:

> *Ask, and it will be given to you;*
> *seek, and you will find;*
> *knock, and it will be opened to you.*
> *For everyone who asks receives,*
> *and he who seeks finds, and to him*
> *who knocks it will be opened.* (Matthew 7:7–8)

The apostle James, who most certainly heard these words from the Master, years later would add:

If any of you lacks wisdom,
let him ask of God,
who gives to all liberally and without reproach,
and it will be given to him. (James 1:5)

What Jesus and James were challenging their listeners to do, Solomon had done once the throne of his father was his. I have always been fascinated with the fairy tales of people being visited by genies who have promised them the fulfillment of a wish. But what if that visitation were the Sovereign God and no child's tale at all?

At Gibeon the LORD appeared to Solomon in a dream by night;
and God said, "Ask! What shall I give you?"
And Solomon said:
"You have shown great mercy to Your servant David my father,
because he walked before You in truth,
in righteousness, and in uprightness of heart with You;
You have continued this great kindness for him,
and You have given him a son to sit on his throne, as it is this day.
Now, O LORD my God,
You have made Your servant king instead of my father David,
but I am a little child;
I do not know how to go out or come in.
And Your servant is in the midst of Your people whom You have chosen,
a great people, too numerous to be numbered or counted.
Therefore give to Your servant an understanding heart to judge Your people,
that I may discern between good and evil.
For who is able to judge this great people of Yours?"
The speech pleased the LORD, that Solomon had asked this thing.
Then God said to him:
"Because you have asked this thing,
and have not asked long life for yourself,
nor have asked riches for yourself,
nor have asked the life of your enemies,

but have asked for yourself understanding to discern justice,
behold, I have done according to your words;
see, I have given you a wise and understanding heart,
so that there has not been anyone like you before you,
nor shall any like you arise after you.
And I have also given you what you have not asked:
both riches and honor,
so that there shall not be anyone like you among the kings all your days.
So if you walk in My ways, to keep My statutes and My commandments,
as your father David walked,
then I will lengthen your days." (1 Kings 3:5–14)

Given all the things Solomon could have asked God for, he chose wisdom—an understanding heart to judge . . . to discern between good and evil. In this conversation, the new king exudes humility. Understandably overwhelmed by the task of filling his father's sandals, Solomon readily confesses that he could not do this without God's sovereign help. He does not ask for fame, fortune, the deaths of his enemies, or even eternal life—as you and I might be tempted to ask of a genie. No, Solomon asks for wisdom—a wonderfully intelligent request from a young man. And to this day, his name is synonymous with his choice.

> "Therefore give to Your servant an understanding heart to judge Your people, that I may discern between good and evil."

God promises to give Solomon what he asked for, and many of those things he did not request. But, like many of the promises of God, these were contingent upon Solomon's obedience.

THE TEMPLE

Solomon's greatest work was the construction of the Temple. When it was completed, the ark of the covenant was ceremoniously placed in the Most Holy Place—the equivalent of the Holy of Holies in the Tabernacle.

And it came to pass,
when the priests came out of the holy place,
that the cloud filled the house of the LORD,
so that the priests could not continue ministering
because of the cloud; for the glory of the LORD
filled the house of the LORD. (1 Kings 8:10–11)

As we have seen many times before in Scripture, we see the results of a direct encounter with a Holy God. Even the priests—professional speakers who spent their careers in His presence—were filled with awe and stricken with silence.

At the building's dedication (1 Kings 8:14–53) King Solomon revealed a life of devotion and obedience. This prayer and consecration of God's permanent dwelling place is perhaps the most pious, magnificent section of the historical narratives. Read this narrative and savor the sweetness of its words, imitate its cadences, and weep at what happens almost immediately afterward.

Tragically, there was a dark side to the king, a growing shadow cast across his character. Aristotle said, "In the brain of the wisest of men always resides the corner of the fool." Aristotle could well have been thinking of Solomon because this describes him very well.

Solomon's tragic flaw was his love for beautiful—and foreign—women. His wives and concubines were legion. As we have seen, God warned the Israelites against intermarrying with non-Jews because of the unavoidable collision of convictions. And even the powerful and wise King Solomon fell victim to this inappropriate amalgam of beliefs, traditions, and holy allegiances.

This was not the equivalent of someone making secret trips down to the local palm reader. Solomon was making peace with savage and sexually perverted religions. Incredibly, Solomon not only allowed these unthinkable things to occur in Israel but likely participated in them as well.

Finally, in his zeal to make his kingdom great, Solomon instituted the corvée (pronounced cor-vey). This policy forced subscription of men and women, even some Jews, into slave labor camps. These were despised by his people and eventually were the greatest factor in the threatening civil war between the northern and southern sections of the nation, Israel and Judah.

- David
- Solomon and the Temple
- **The Divided Kingdom**

Like a snowball rolling down the face of a mountain, Israel's problems grew in both size and velocity. What had begun with Solomon's disobedience before God continued cascading down from generation to generation.

Jeroboam, a "mighty man of valor" and an "industrious" man, was hired by King Solomon to oversee the slaves taken from Joseph's house.

> *Now it happened at that time,*
> *when Jeroboam went out of Jerusalem,*
> *that the prophet Ahijah the Shilonite met him on the way;*
> *and [Jeroboam] had clothed himself with a new garment,*
> *and the two were alone in the field.*
> *Then Ahijah took hold of the new garment that was on him,*
> *and tore it into twelve pieces.*
> *And he said to Jeroboam,*
> *"Take for yourself ten pieces, for thus says the* LORD,
> *the God of Israel:*
> *'Behold, I will tear the kingdom out of the hand of Solomon*
> *and will give ten tribes to you . . .*
> *I will take the kingdom out of his son's hand*
> *and give it to you—ten tribes.*
> *And to his son I will give one tribe,*
> *that My servant David may always have a lamp before Me in Jerusalem,*
> *the city which I have chosen for Myself,*
> *to put My name there.*
> *So I will take you, and you shall reign over all your heart desires,*
> *and you shall be king over Israel.*
> *Then it shall be, if you heed all that I command you,*
> *walk in My ways, and do what is right in My sight,*
> *to keep My statutes and My commandments,*

> *as My servant David did,*
> *then I will be with you and build for you an enduring house,*
> *as I built for David,*
> *and will give Israel to you.'"* (1 Kings 11:29–31, 35–38)

However, as often happens with kings, the word of this conversation between Jeroboam and Ahijah reached Solomon. He was furious at the prediction of the demise of his kingdom and sought to kill Jeroboam. In fear, Jeroboam fled to Egypt until Solomon was dead. And when he died, Solomon's son Rehoboam assumed his father's throne.

When Jeroboam heard the news, he returned to Jerusalem and, along with the elders of each of the tribes, asked for an audience with King Rehoboam.

> *"Your father made our yoke heavy;*
> *now therefore, lighten the burdensome service of your father,*
> *and his heavy yoke which he put on us, and we will serve you."*
> *So he said to them,*
> *"Depart for three days, then come back to me."*
> *And the people departed.* (1 Kings 12:4–5)

These men wanted the corvée lifted. They were tired of seeing their sons and daughters taken away. They resented having their children's most productive years given over to government projects. But Rehoboam was resistant, putting them off for three days.

Not knowing what to do, the king sought the counsel of his father's former associates—judicious men who had served under the wisest king of all. Their advice was sound:

> *If you will be a servant to these people today, and serve them,*
> *and answer them, and speak good words to them,*
> *then they will be your servants forever.* (1 Kings 12:7)

Sure enough. These veteran advisers to King Solomon gave Rehoboam great advice for kings, parents, or leaders of any kind. "If you will be willing to serve your people as their king, then they will serve you."

BAD ADVICE

Sadly, Rehoboam, the young, full-of-himself king, didn't like the advice. So he looked for a second opinion among his court companions—young ruffians with whom he had grown up. Predictably they tickled the king's ears with the advice that pleased him:

> *Thus you should speak to this people who have spoken to you,*
> *saying, . . . "Whereas my father put a heavy yoke on you,*
> *I will add to your yoke;*
> *my father chastised you with whips,*
> *but I will chastise you with scourges!"* (1 Kings 12:10–11)

Of course, the foolish Rehoboam took his cronies' recommendation and "answered the people roughly, and rejected the counsel which the elders had given him." So the people rebelled.

> *Now it came to pass when all Israel heard that Jeroboam had come back,*
> *they sent for him and called him to the congregation,*
> *and made him king over all Israel.*
> *There was none who followed the house of David,*
> *but the tribe of Judah only.* (1 Kings 12:20)

When Rehoboam heard that ten tribes of Israel had defected from his kingdom, he assembled 180,000 men from the families of Judah and Benjamin to engage in what would have been the bloodiest civil war in the history of the Jews.

But in His mercy, God spoke to one of His obedient servants named Shemaiah:

> *Speak to Rehoboam the son of Solomon, king of Judah,*
> *to all the house of Judah and Benjamin,*
> *and to the rest of the people, saying,*
> *"Thus says the LORD:*

'You shall not go up nor fight against your brethren the children of Israel.
Let every man return to his house, for this thing is from Me.'"
Therefore they obeyed the word of the LORD,
and turned back, according to the word of the LORD. (1 Kings 12:23–24)

Can you imagine the intensity of this moment, and the courage of this godly man, Shemaiah? Through this man's obedience and God's mercy, literally thousands were saved. And isn't it also remarkable that the strident King Rehoboam, sensing that Shemaiah's words were straight from the mouth of a Holy God, agreed to retreat?

THE NORTH AND THE SOUTH

At that moment, Israel was forever divided. In the South, the family of Judah—including the city of Jerusalem—established a nation called "Judah." The ten northern families kept the name "Israel" and were ruled by Jeroboam. The tribe of Levi remained in Jerusalem, managing the affairs of the Temple.

> "If you will be willing to serve your people as their king, then they will serve you."

The subsequent history of the kings of these nations reads like a rogue's gallery. In fact, no sooner had Jeroboam separated from Rehoboam than he consecrated two rival worship sites, ordered the making of golden calves, and announced, "It is too much for you to go up to Jerusalem. Here are your gods, O Israel, which brought you up from the land of Egypt!"

The audacity of Jeroboam is unthinkable. Here was an opportunity—separated from King Rehoboam and his hooligans—to establish a godly nation once more. In fact, didn't the word of the Lord delivered from Ahijah the Shilonite burn in his ears? "If you heed all that I command you, walk in My ways, and do what is right in My sight, to keep My statutes and My commandments, as My servant David did, then I will be with you and build for you an enduring house, as I built for David, and I will give Israel to you."

But these words of covenant blessing were lost on Jeroboam. And, of course, God did not overlook such idolatry. We will find out later how He dealt with this problem.

The history that unfolds in the years that followed is crucial to understanding the remainder of the Old Testament.

Israel: The Northern Kingdom	Judah: The Southern Kingdom
20 kings	20 kings
9 dynasties	1 dynasty
200-year history before destruction	350-year history before destruction
Fell in 722 B.C. to the Assyrians	Fell in 586 B.C. to the Babylonians

Notice that with a much longer history in Judah, the same number of kings reigned. One family, the house of David, ruled in the South. But in the North, nine families—even foreign families—led Israel, with such characters as Ahab and Jezebel ruling Israel. Eventually, both fell, with Israel utterly annihilated and Judah carried off to exile.

The prophet Amos proclaimed that God would restore the fallen house of David by the reign of Christ. In Christ, the promises made to the house of David in ancient Israel would be fulfilled. Faithless kings could not stop a Sovereign God from working in and with the remnant of elect Jews. He continued to keep the hope alive that all the world would be blessed through the promises He had made to Abraham, Isaac, Jacob, and David.

SUMMARY
■ DAVID

David did nothing halfheartedly. If there ever was a Renaissance man, it was King David. He was multifaceted, extremely complex—a wild bunch of contradictions. He threw himself into life with reckless abandon. His success was beyond limits. His failures were atrocious. But his repentance was unabashed and desperately sincere.

As we saw with many of those who carried the mantle of God's covenant blessing, David's selection came as a complete surprise. Samuel, who was understandably broken by the failure of Saul as king, was sent by God to visit the home of Jesse, a Bethlehemite from the family of Judah. "For I have provided Myself a king among his sons," the Sovereign God announced to Samuel.

God's anointing did not fall on David because of his good looks. And, as we learn as we closely follow him throughout the remainder of his life, the blessing didn't become his because he was always good. The covenant blessing of leadership became David's because of his heart.

David was the greatest king in Israel's history. He was the supreme symbol of kingship in the Old Testament and the New. David was not only strong and benevolent, he was also a good administrator and a master diplomat.

But if David was more accomplished at something other than military strategy, political prowess, or leadership savvy, it was the art of genuine confession and repentance.

■ SOLOMON AND THE TEMPLE

The golden age of the Hebrews' monarchy was at its zenith under David's rule. And it would be safe to say that the gold began to tarnish under Solomon. And, because of Solomon's sin, especially near the end of his life, that discoloration turned to pure rust.

But what made Solomon so successful, and why did God bless him with such monumental prosperity? In this conversation recorded in the book of 1 Kings, Solomon exudes humility. Understandably overwhelmed by the task of filling his father's sandals, Solomon readily confesses that he could not do this without God's sovereign help. He does not ask for fame, fortune, the deaths of his enemies, or even eternal life—as you and I might be tempted to ask of a genie. No, Solomon asks for wisdom—a wonderfully intelligent request from a young man. And to this day, his name is synonymous with this wise choice.

God promises to give Solomon what he asked for, and many of those things he did not request. But, like many of the promises of God, these were contingent upon Solomon's obedience. Solomon's greatest work was the construction of the Temple.

Tragically, there was a dark side to the king, a growing shadow cast across his character. Solomon's Achilles heel was his love for beautiful—and foreign—women. His wives and concubines were legion. As we have seen, God warned the Israelites against intermarrying with non-Jews because of the unavoidable syncretism. And even the powerful and wise King Solomon fell victim to this inappropriate amalgam of beliefs, traditions, and holy allegiances.

This was not the equivalent of someone making secret trips down to the palm reader. Solomon was making peace with bloody, savage, and sexually perverted religion. Incredibly, Solomon not only allowed these unthinkable things to occur in Israel, but likely participated in them as well.

■ THE DIVIDED KINGDOM

Like a snowball rolling down the face of a mountain, Israel's problems grew in both size and velocity. What had begun with Solomon's disobedience before God continued cascading down from generation to generation.

Jeroboam, a "mighty man of valor" and an "industrious" man, was hired by King Solomon to oversee the slaves taken from Joseph's house. However, Ahijah the prophet had a conversation in which Jeroboam was identified as Solomon's successor over his son. Solomon was furious at the prediction of the demise of his kingdom and sought to kill Jeroboam. In fear, Jeroboam fled to Egypt until Solomon was dead. And when he died, Solomon's son Rehoboam assumed his father's throne.

When Jeroboam heard the news, he returned to Jerusalem and, along with the elders of each of the tribes, asked for an audience with King Rehoboam. Jeroboam openly challenged the king's policies and arrogant attitude. Drawing a line in the sand, the king forced the elders to take sides, which they soon did. It was not good news for King Rehoboam. Ten tribes of Israel had defected from his kingdom, choosing Jeroboam as their king.

At that moment, Israel was forever divided. In the south, the family of Judah—including the city of Jerusalem—established a nation, called "Judah." The ten northern families kept the name "Israel" and were ruled by Jeroboam. The tribe of Levi remained in Jerusalem, managing the affairs of the Temple.

One family, the house of David, ruled in the South. But in the North, nine families—even foreign families—led Israel, with such characters as Ahab and Jezebel ruling Israel. Eventually, both fell, with Israel utterly annihilated and Judah carried off to exile.

The prophet Amos proclaimed that God would restore the fallen house of David by the reign of Christ. In Christ, the promises made to the house of David in ancient Israel would be fulfilled. Faithless kings could not stop a Sovereign God from working in and with the remnant of elect Jews. He continued to keep the hope alive that all the world would be blessed through the promises He had made to Abraham, Isaac, Jacob, and David.

CHAPTER SIX

THE MAJOR PROPHETS I

- Elijah
- Isaiah
- Jeremiah

"Look at me when I'm talking to you."

There isn't a parent alive who hasn't said these words to their disobedient child. Actually, there are good reasons why youngsters in trouble with their mother or dad don't make a lot of eye contact. Who wants to be looking into the face of the one who is about to lower the boom on you? So it was with the Hebrews.

Most of the Israelites had left their moorings. They had completely forgotten the covenant promise God had spoken to the Patriarchs, and they had thoroughly abandoned the One Who had delivered them from captivity. The Hebrews had taken "disobedience" to a whole new level—the word doesn't even begin to tell the story. And so they had stopped worshiping. They no longer entered God's presence. They determined that the best way to continue in their immoral ways was to no longer look into the face of the Holy One of Israel.

> The Hebrews had taken "disobedience" to a whole new level—the word doesn't even begin to tell the story.

Although I don't have any hard data on this, my guess is that temple attendance during this time was way down. Sunday school was probably even worse. No one wanted to see the symbols of repentance before a Holy God when there was no inkling of remorse to be found in their hearts.

The role of the Old Testament prophets was to go and find the people where they were, stand in front of them, and say, "Thus says the Lord." And when they were ignored because no one wanted to hear what the immortal, invisible God had to say, the prophets would shout, "Look at me when I'm talking to you." Or, better, "Look into the face of God because He's talking to you."

Not only was this a dangerous assignment—prophets were attacked, tortured, thrown into pits, given to wild animals, sawn in half—but it was also an overwhelmingly lonely assignment. These sinful Jews did what every guilty child tries to do when they've been caught. They ran, they avoided the truth, and they desperately tried to look the other way. They did everything they could to discredit and sometimes even attacked these godly men.

But the prophets were relentless in their pursuit. And they were more than mere noisy carnival barkers, attracting attention for a forgotten God. For once they had the people's eyes and ears, the prophets functioned as prosecuting attorneys on behalf of the covenant, building their cases against those who had arrogantly broken the Law. They even pronounced the likely sentence for the perpetrators' crimes.

> God had gone above and beyond the call of duty in keeping His end of the bargain; but the Israelites had not. Now it was time for them to face the truth.

Remember that when Israel was established, it was founded on a treaty between God and His people. God had gone above and beyond the call of duty in keeping His end of the bargain, but the Israelites had not. Now it was time for them to face the truth. And it was the prophets who were assigned the job of exposing it.

The first five prophets listed in the Old Testament—Elijah, Isaiah, Jeremiah, Ezekiel, and Daniel—are often referred to as the "major" prophets. All the others who follow them are frequently called "minor" prophets. This distinction only refers to the amount of text we have that chronicles the lives of these men. It has nothing to do with their impact for God on the people of Israel and Judah. Because each was distinctly called of God to call people to repentance, each one is significant.

Finally, *prophets*, as the word is often used today, were much more than fortunetellers or foretellers of future events. In fact they did very little of this. Their primary role was to be *forthtellers*—bold and courageous purveyors of God's unbending word. And this is exactly what they did. "Stop whatever you're doing. Look into the face of a Holy God, if you dare . . . He's speaking to you."

ELIJAH

No prophet was more significant to the history of the Israelites than Elijah. Here is the final prophecy recorded in the Old Testament and spoken by the prophet Malachi:

> *Remember the Law of Moses, My servant,*
> *Which I commanded him in Horeb for all Israel,*
> *With the statutes and judgments.*
> *Behold, I will send you Elijah the prophet*
> *Before the coming*
> *of the great and dreadful day of the LORD.*
> *And he will turn*
> *The hearts of the fathers to the children,*
> *And the hearts of the children to their fathers,*
> *Lest I come and strike the earth with a curse.* (Malachi 4:4–6)

Elijah was the first and greatest of God's messengers to His people in the Old Testament. Not only was Elijah a prophet who lived at a particular time, he often symbolized the focal point of God's message of judgment for sin and promised pardon.

Some people seem important for a brief period, but as time passes their notability fades. Others seem somewhat significant during their lifetimes, but grow in prominence as time passes. Elijah belongs to the latter class. As we look ahead in the history of redemption, the need to understand the prophet Elijah becomes more, not less, notable.

When contemporary Jews celebrate the Passover in their homes, there is always an empty chair at the table. This place is reserved for Elijah. Because they do not believe that the Messiah has yet come, modern Israelites keep a place for Elijah, hoping he will ultimately return to usher in the Day of the Lord.

At the beginning of his ministry, when religious leaders came to John the Baptist and asked him who he was, they weren't asking him his name. They wanted to know if John was the fulfillment of Malachi's prophecy. Was he

Elijah? And although he answered no to their question—meaning he was not a reincarnated Elijah—he clearly was one, as the angel said to Zechariah his father, who came in the "spirit and power of Elijah."

Even Jesus affirmed this idea concerning John the Baptist.

> *For all the prophets and the law prophesied until John.*
> *And if you are willing to receive it,*
>   *he is Elijah who is to come.*
> *He who has ears to hear, let him hear!* (Matthew 11:13–14)

Jesus Christ confirmed that John the Baptist was continuing the tradition and responsibility of the prophets, beginning with Elijah. Jesus also added what the prophets had been saying all along, "Listen to Me (look at Me) when I'm talking to you."

Another affirmation of the importance of Elijah in redemptive history was his appearance with Moses and Jesus on the Mount of Transfiguration. Jesus had taken three of His disciples—Peter, James, and John—away to share a glimpse of His holiness and glory (Matthew 17:1–8; Mark 9:2–8; Luke 9:28–36). During this surreal moment of intense light, sudden cloud cover, and a voice from heaven, the disciples saw Elijah talking with Moses and Jesus. There in one moment were three common men in the presence of three very uncommon men. Peter, James, and John were seeing Moses, the giver of the Law; Jesus, the Incarnate Son of God; and Elijah, the man who was called to be God's mouthpiece to those who had received and broken the Law—people desperately in need of the Savior.

So there they stood, Moses, Elijah, and Jesus, demonstrating to the disciples that, although He was superior to them, Christ was in perfect relationship to the Law and the prophets.

During his lifetime, Elijah wore the prophetic mantle in many courageous ways. The most notable was his confrontation of the evil King Ahab and his wicked wife, Jezebel. Not only had Ahab brought a foreign woman into the palace, he himself participated in the worship of the pagan god Baal. He had even funded the construction of a wooden idol to the honor of this helpless deity.

Elijah was moved with indignation and paid a visit to Ahab.

And Elijah . . . said to Ahab,
"As the LORD God of Israel lives, before whom I stand,
there shall not be dew nor rain these years, except at my word." (1 Kings 17:1)

Understandably afraid for his own safety, Elijah escaped to the River Cherith, one of the tributaries feeding into the Jordan River. There God sent ravens to bring him food. Once the river had dried up because of the drought, God told Elijah to relocate in Zarephath where "a widow [will] provide for you."

> "This is not about me," Elijah was saying to the evil king. "This is about you. Look into God's face because He's talking to you."

Elijah's encounter with the widow and her dying son represented a defining experience in his prophetic work. First, he performed a miracle, multiplying the widow's flour and oil, underscoring God's faithful provision. Then, Elijah raised the widow's son from the dead, demonstrating God's redemptive power. Imagine how Elijah must have felt when he heard the woman speak these words:

Now by this I know that you are a man of God,
and that the word of the LORD in your mouth is the truth. (1 Kings 17:24)

After three years of drought, Elijah again encountered Ahab, who greeted him with, "Is that you, O troubler of Israel?"

In that moment, Elijah fulfilled his prophetic call with his answer to Ahab:

I have not troubled Israel,
but you and your father's house have,
in that you have forsaken the commandments of the LORD
and have followed the Baals. (1 Kings 18:18)

"This is not about me," Elijah was saying to the evil king. "This is about you. Look into God's face because He's talking to you."

To confirm that God was truly speaking, Elijah challenged Ahab, the 450 prophets of Baal, and the 400 prophets of Asherah to a showdown on Mount Carmel. What happened was, like God's appearance to Moses in the burning bush or the dividing of the Red Sea, one of the snowcapped peaks in the Old Testament. This was a great moment, a visible revelation of the works of a Holy God.

Before the great confrontation, Elijah went to the Israelites.

> *And Elijah came to all the people, and said,*
> *"How long will you falter between two opinions?*
> *If the LORD is God, follow Him;*
> *but if Baal, follow him."*
> *But the people answered him not a word.* (1 Kings 18:21)

An altar was assembled on the mountain. The prophets of Baal and Asherah killed a bull in honor of their god and placed it on the altar. Then they prayed, asking Baal to bring down fire to consume the sacrifice. They prayed all morning, "but there was no voice; no one answered." Then these devout men—850 of them—began to dance around the altar.

Pretending to be sincere, Elijah chided the wizards:

> *Cry aloud, for he is a god;*
> *either he is meditating, or he is busy,*
> *or he is on a journey,*
> *or perhaps he is sleeping and must be awakened.* (1 Kings 18:27)

So they cried aloud, and cut themselves with knives until the blood gushed out on them. By the end of the day, after these men had nearly killed themselves to get their god's attention, there was still silence—"no voice; no one answered, no one paid attention."

> *Then Elijah said to all the people,*
> *"Come near to me."*
> *So all the people came near to him.*

And he repaired the altar of the LORD that was broken down.
And Elijah took twelve stones,
according to the number of the tribes of the sons of Jacob,
to whom the word of the LORD had come, saying,
"Israel shall be your name."
Then with the stones he built an altar in the name of the LORD;
and he made a trench around the altar . . .
and said, "Fill four waterpots with water,
and pour it on the burnt sacrifice and on the wood."
Then he said, "Do it a second time," . . .
and he said, "Do it a third time." . . .
So the water ran all around the altar;
and he also filled the trench with water.
And it came to pass, at the time of the offering of the evening sacrifice,
that Elijah the prophet came near and said,
"LORD God of Abraham, Isaac, and Israel,
let it be known this day that You are God in Israel
and I am Your servant,
and that I have done all these things at Your word.
Hear me, O LORD, hear me,
that this people may know that You are the LORD God,
and that You have turned their hearts back to You again."
Then the fire of the LORD fell and consumed the burnt sacrifice,
and the wood and the stones and the dust,
and it licked up the water that was in the trench.
Now when all the people saw it, they fell on their faces;
and they said, "The LORD, He is God!
The LORD, He is God!" (1 Kings 18:30–39)

Can you imagine the passion and grandeur of this scene? The pagan prophets had spent all day pleading with their god and lacerating themselves. Then Elijah, the prophet of the living God, bowed and spoke to his Father in quiet tones. God saw his heart, heard his prayer, and sent fire from heaven, consuming everything on the altar, even turning the water to a cloud of hissing steam.

And because of what they had seen and because of Elijah's courage and faithfulness, the people shouted their allegiance once again to the God of their fathers. What a moment this must have been for Elijah.

One of the most remarkable notabilities of Elijah was the way he died, or rather, the way he *didn't* die. In a spectacle as wonderful as His blazing visitation on Mount Carmel, God sent "a chariot of fire with horses of fire" to sweep the prophet to heaven in a whirlwind. It might as well have been God's holy signature on the life of Elijah, a sign of His favor, a final stamp of approval on his ministry.

- Elijah
- **Isaiah**
- Jeremiah

Most successful enterprises have a mission statement. This brief proclamation not only summarizes the essence of the endeavor, but it also becomes the banner under which every activity is carried out. Businesses often have their mission statement posted in the reception areas, hallways, and lunchrooms. No one working there can possibly miss it.

> God saw his heart, heard his prayer, and sent fire from heaven, consuming everything on the altar, even turning the water to a cloud of hissing steam.

We know very little about Isaiah's life. But his distinction is that he was the most cultured of the prophets. His family was well educated, in contrast to most of the prophets who came from rural or agricultural backgrounds. His job was like that of a modern-day ambassador, with full access to the powerful leaders of the day—even the courts of royalty.

Given this frame of background and experience surrounding Isaiah's work, is it any wonder that, in the sovereignty of God, this would be the prophet who penned the mission statement for the ministry of Jesus Christ, the Messiah?

The Spirit of the Lord GOD is upon Me,
Because the LORD has anointed Me

> To preach good tidings to the poor;
> He has sent Me to heal the brokenhearted,
> To proclaim liberty to the captives,
> And the opening of the prison to those who are bound;
> To proclaim the acceptable year of the LORD,
> And the day of vengeance of our God. (Isaiah 61:1–2)

How can I so boldly identify this as Jesus' mission statement? Couldn't it have been that Isaiah was saying these things about himself?

Seven centuries later, at the very beginning of His ministry, we get the answer from the Messiah Himself.

> So [Jesus] came to Nazareth, where He had been brought up.
> And as His custom was, He went into the synagogue on the Sabbath day,
> and stood up to read.
> And He was handed the book of the prophet Isaiah.
> And when He had opened the book,
> He found the place where it was written:
> "The Spirit of the LORD is upon Me,
> Because He has anointed Me
> To preach the gospel to the poor;
> He has sent Me to heal the brokenhearted,
> To proclaim liberty to the captives
> And recovery of sight to the blind,
> To set at liberty those who are oppressed;
> To preach the acceptable year of the LORD."
> Then He closed the book,
> and gave it back to the attendant and sat down.
> And the eyes of all who were in the synagogue were fixed on Him.
> And [Jesus] began to say to them,
> "Today this Scripture is fulfilled in your hearing." (Luke 4:16–21)

Can you see these religious people sitting aghast? They had read this prophecy many times. It may have been posted over the water fountains of commerce and in the courtyards of worship. But, until that moment, they had considered it to be Isaiah's mission statement, an important summary of the great prophet's ministry. Now, they were hearing that God had granted Isaiah the privilege of arranging these words for Someone else—a construct for the coming Messiah.

How was it that God chose Isaiah for this assignment? What was it about his life experience that drew his heart toward the coming Savior? To answer that, we must visit the moment when God called Isaiah to be His mouthpiece—and prosecuting attorney—to the wayward and sinful Hebrews.

The first five chapters of the book of Isaiah read like the words of a stenographer, scrawling words for all to see, the voice of God to His people. They are filled with summaries of the people's blatant disregard for the Holy One of Israel and the surety of their punishment.

> But Isaiah was about to have the most significant experience of his life. He was about to come face to face with the One Whom he had been representing.

No doubt Isaiah was a bit full of himself one day as he entered the Temple (chap. 6) to worship. Guilty of what plagues many contemporary ministers, Isaiah was filled with pride, knowing God had selected him to deliver His sovereign message to common folk.

But Isaiah was about to have the most significant experience of his life. He was about to come face to face with the One Whom he had been representing. It was God's "look at Me when I'm talking to you" charge to this gifted communicator. In fact, for a time, the awesomeness of the moment left the articulate Isaiah speechless.

> *In the year that King Uzziah died,*
> *I saw the LORD sitting on a throne, high and lifted up,*
> *and the train of His robe filled the temple.*
> *Above it stood seraphim; each one had six wings:*
> *with two he covered his face,*
> *with two he covered his feet,*
> *and with two he flew.*
> *And one cried to another and said:*

> *"Holy, holy, holy is the LORD of hosts;*
> *The whole earth is full of His glory!"*
> *And the posts of the door were shaken by the voice of him who cried out,*
> *and the house was filled with smoke.*
> *So I said:*
> *"Woe is me, for I am undone!*
> *Because I am a man of unclean lips,*
> *And I dwell in the midst of a people of unclean lips;*
> *For my eyes have seen the King,*
> *The LORD of hosts."*
> *Then one of the seraphim flew to me, having in his hand a live coal*
> *which he had taken with the tongs from the altar.*
> *And he touched my mouth with it, and said:*
> *"Behold, this has touched your lips;*
> *Your iniquity is taken away,*
> *And your sin purged."*
> *Also I heard the voice of the Lord, saying:*
> *"Whom shall I send,*
> *And who will go for Us?"*
> *Then I said, "Here am I! Send me."* (Isaiah 6:1–8)

What a life-changing moment this was for the prophet. He had thought this assignment was going to be one of passing judgment to all *those* incorrigible Jews—*those* unclean sinners. But now Isaiah realized that this was *first* a call to personal contrition, *then* the calling of others to that same repentance.

As with nearly every project you and I have ever undertaken, Isaiah was brutally awakened to the fact that this job was going to be a lot more work than he ever thought it was going to be. But, he was up to the task . . . "Here am I," Isaiah said, after coming face to face with the exalted God. "Send me."

What followed Isaiah's willing words was truly unbelievable.

Instead of an affirming pat on the back, God gave Isaiah a summary of how unsuccessful he was going to be. "The people will not understand nor will they perceive. Their hearts will be dull, their ears heavy, and they will shut their eyes" (see Isaiah 6:9–10).

Isaiah should have been furious with this information. With this forecast of failure, you would have thought that the message of Isaiah would be one flamethrowing sermon after another. I'm not sure that I could lovingly and joyfully preach the Gospel, knowing that not a single person in the audience was ever going to believe one word I was saying.

Yet when we consider the messianic treasure found in the book of Isaiah, a message filled with both judgment *and* hope, is it any wonder that God chose this man for this difficult task?

Thankfully, out of all the terror and destruction, God gave Isaiah a promise:

> *The LORD has removed men far away,*
> *And the forsaken places are many in the midst of the land.*
> *But yet a tenth will be in it,*
> *And will return and be for consuming,*
> *As a terebinth tree or as an oak,*
> *Whose stump remains when it is cut down.*
> *So the holy seed shall be its stump.* (Isaiah 6:12–13)

God promised to save a remnant, a tithe of people who would be purified by their suffering and elected by God for salvation. From those, the Messiah would step forward. This is why Isaiah is remembered as the prophet of the Redeemer. No prophet is quoted more in the New Testament because Isaiah gives us the best picture of the coming Messiah. It is through Isaiah's ministry that the authenticity of Jesus' ministry is seen most clearly.

> *Who has believed our report?*
> *And to whom has the arm of the LORD been revealed?*
> *For He shall grow up before Him as a tender plant,*
> *And as a root out of dry ground.*
> *He has no form or comeliness;*
> *And when we see Him,*
> *There is no beauty that we should desire Him.*
> *He is despised and rejected by men,*
> *A Man of sorrows and acquainted with grief.*

And we hid, as it were, our faces from Him;
He was despised, and we did not esteem Him.
Surely He has borne our griefs
And carried our sorrows;
Yet we esteemed Him stricken,
Smitten by God, and afflicted.
But He was wounded for our transgressions,
He was bruised for our iniquities;
The chastisement for our peace was upon Him,
And by His stripes we are healed.
All we like sheep have gone astray;
We have turned, every one, to his own way;
And the LORD has laid on Him
the iniquity of us all. (Isaiah 53:1–6)

This was the most critical prophecy of Isaiah concerning Christ. It fills out our understanding of Him and His atoning work on the cross. With magnifying glass–like detail, we are given a picture of the Messiah and His sacrifice on our behalf.

The book of Isaiah is filled with glimpses of the coming Messiah, words that would have been hard to understand or believe in the midst of severe judgment. But, from God's perspective, they were as sure as tomorrow's sunrise. There is no doubt, from our post–New Testament perspective, that Isaiah's words foreshadowed the coming of Christ in supernatural detail. And that God chose this remarkable prophet to hand-deliver the message.

- Elijah
- Isaiah
- **Jeremiah**

Don't let anyone look down on you because you are young,
but set an example for the believers in speech,
in life, in love, in faith and in purity. (1 Timothy 4:12 NIV)

Although the prophet Jeremiah had died almost seven hundred years before these words were written by the apostle Paul, he lived his life as though he had written them himself.

In the mid-sixties, I was enrolled in graduate studies at the Free University of Amsterdam. Vesta and I lived in a tiny room with a bed and a sink. Next to the sink was barely enough room for a small student's desk. I sat at this desk soaking up comprehensive documents and books of theology for twelve hours a day. Soon after beginning this program of study, I decided that if I was going to be spending this much time examining works *about* the Scriptures, I would do well to take ample time to examine them myself. So I made a commitment to read and carefully study one book of the Bible each day.

> There is no doubt, from our post–New Testament perspective, that Isaiah's words foreshadowed the coming of Christ in supernatural detail.

It was during these months of intensive work that the prophet Jeremiah became my friend—my associate and my comrade. Like me, Jeremiah felt the call of God as a young man and like the apostle Paul, I wanted to be faithful to His call, accepting the challenge of being a worthy ambassador of the Savior's grace.

One of the things I loved about Jeremiah was his tender heart. With the study of the prophets, it's only natural to think of them as harsh, mean-spirited, and without pity—flamethrowers with an attitude. But during his ministry, Jeremiah picked up a nickname. He was known as "the Weeping Prophet."

Hear and give ear;
Do not be proud,
For the LORD has spoken.
Give glory to the LORD your God
Before He causes darkness,
And before your feet stumble
On the dark mountains,
And while you are looking for light,
He turns it into the shadow of death

> *And makes it dense darkness.*
> *But if you will not hear it,*
> *My soul will weep in secret for your pride;*
> *My eyes will weep bitterly*
> *And run down with tears,*
> *Because the LORD's flock has been taken captive.* (Jeremiah 13:15–17)

Can you hear it in his voice? Jeremiah could be rubbing his hands together with delight. He could be saying to himself, "Israel's finally getting what's coming to her." No, when he returned to his chamber at the end of an exhausting day of preaching, he wept. Instead of being angry and self-righteous, tears ran down his face on behalf of his wayward people.

> One of the things I loved about Jeremiah was his tender heart.

In the early fifties a young preacher named Bob Pierce visited the Orient and saw the postwar devastation, not only on the land but on the children as well. Upon his return home he wrote, "Let my heart be broken by the things that break the heart of God." On these words he founded World Vision, a ministry that has for more than half a century fed and clothed millions of broken souls. God's voice falling on a compassionate heart can produce supernatural results.

Jeremiah's heart was broken because he knew that his people's sinfulness was breaking God's heart as well. So it was to this tender young man that God's call came. In fact, God's voice to Jeremiah was heard before he had drawn his first breath.

> *Then the word of the LORD came to me, saying:*
> *"Before I formed you in the womb I knew you;*
> *Before you were born I sanctified you;*
> *I ordained you a prophet to the nations."* (Jeremiah 1:4–5)

The prophet was called (set apart, sanctified) even before he was born to be God's chosen instrument. As a twenty-year-old, when he first heard this divine summons, Jeremiah responded as any inexperienced young person might have.

> Then said I:
> "Ah, Lord GOD!
> Behold, I cannot speak, for I am a youth."
> But the LORD said to me:
> "Do not say, 'I am a youth,'
> For you shall go to all to whom I send you,
> And whatever I command you, you shall speak.
> Do not be afraid of their faces,
> For I am with you to deliver you," says the LORD.
> Then the LORD put forth His hand and touched my mouth,
> and the LORD said to me:
> "Behold, I have put My words in your mouth.
> See, I have this day set you over the nations and over the kingdoms,
> To root out and to pull down,
> To destroy and to throw down,
> to build and to plant." (Jeremiah 1:6–10)

Don't these words sound like the apostle Paul's words to his young protégé, Timothy? "Don't let anyone look down on you because you're young . . . instead, be an example." And just like God's call to Isaiah when he was standing in the Temple, God admonished Jeremiah to add words of hope to his words of doom: "Root out, pull down, destroy, and throw down," the Holy One told him. "But don't forget to build and plant."

> God's voice falling on a compassionate heart can produce supernatural results.

What's interesting to me about Jeremiah's divine call is that it was "to the nations." This is interesting because as his story unfolded, it became clear that he was speaking to religious leaders. Isaiah stood before kings, but Jeremiah went to Jewish priests and prophets. Then what did God have in mind by calling him to the nations?

Could it be that Jeremiah had a personal ministry to the Gentiles that we don't know about? Or is it possible that his words of blessing and cursing spread through the Israelites to their pagan tormentors? What we do know is that Jeremiah's ministry extended for more than fifty years and that his obedience to God's call lasted well beyond his lifetime—even to a young theological student in the Netherlands crammed into that little space between the sink and the wall.

The young prophet was fearless. His prophetic message went straight to the places of worship, where religious leaders would hear his words.

> *The word that came to Jeremiah from the LORD, saying,*
> *"Stand in the gate of the LORD's house, and proclaim there this word, and say,*
> *'Hear the word of the LORD, all you of Judah who enter in at these gates*
> *to worship the LORD!'"*
> *Thus says the LORD of hosts, the God of Israel:*
> *"Amend your ways and your doings,*
> *and I will cause you to dwell in this place.*
> *Do not trust in these lying words, saying,*
> *'The temple of the LORD, the temple of the LORD,*
> *the temple of the LORD are these.'"* (Jeremiah 7:1–4)

Jeremiah was a reformer to biblical Judaism. He was trying to help his people see that their holy clan had degenerated into meaningless ritualism, and that this would soon lead to their destruction. They still had their religious activity, but it was superficial. Jeremiah was not telling them to get rid of the rituals, the ceremonies, and the external forms of religion. God had prescribed these. Jeremiah was telling them to *apply* these grand truths to their hearts, calling them to genuine repentance, not vain repetition.

As was true with the other prophets, Jeremiah had a very unpopular ministry. Can you imagine someone coming to your local television station or writing a column in your newspaper announcing that the capital of your country was going to be destroyed because of your sin? This person would be lambasted, attacked, and ridiculed—especially if his forecast didn't come true immediately. Well, Jeremiah's message concerning the destruction of Jerusalem was just that.

The religious leaders were furious with him. His detractors used his prophecies against him, pinning him with whatever bigoted label they could find. And how do you think Jeremiah took this ridicule?

O Lord, You induced me, and I was persuaded;
You are stronger than I, and have prevailed.
I am in derision daily;
Everyone mocks me. (Jeremiah 20:7)

Jeremiah was wiped out, exhausted with the burden of his work and the weightiness of his message. He was about to turn in his prophet's badge.

But, in just a few verses, Jeremiah seemed encouraged and renewed.

But the Lord is with me as a mighty, awesome One.
Therefore my persecutors will stumble, and will not prevail.
They will be greatly ashamed, for they will not prosper.
Their everlasting confusion will never be forgotten . . .
Sing to the Lord! Praise the Lord!
For He has delivered the life of the poor
From the hand of evildoers. (Jeremiah 20:11, 13)

I can hear myself shouting encouragement to Jeremiah. "Go for it, friend. Yes, God has delivered the life of the poor, and He will deliver you, too."

But as is so often the case with tender-hearted people, Jeremiah's tone swings wildly back to pain and self-doubt.

Cursed be the day in which I was born!
Let the day not be blessed in which my mother bore me!
Let the man be cursed
Who brought news to my father, saying,
"A male child has been born to you!"
Making him very glad . . .
Why did I come forth from the womb to see labor and sorrow,
That my days should be consumed with shame? (Jeremiah 20:14–15, 18)

Almost every faithful minister of God's Word faces this kind of stress and pain because they serve in the darkness of the world, which does not have fellowship with the light of the Gospel. This can be an incredibly lonely experience.

Thankfully, as with the prophet Isaiah, Jeremiah drew his strength not just from his confidence in the word of the Lord, but from his hope for the coming Messiah as well.

> "Behold, the days are coming," says the LORD,
> "That I will raise to David a Branch of righteousness;
> A King shall reign and prosper,
> And execute judgment and righteousness in the earth.
> In His days Judah will be saved,
> And Israel will dwell safely;
> Now this is His name by which He will be called:
> THE LORD OUR RIGHTEOUSNESS." (Jeremiah 23:5–6)

In spite of the pain of confronting people he knew and loved with the truth of their own peril, and in spite of the loneliness of carrying this message day after day, Jeremiah *knew* that one day his Savior would come—a King who would reign and prosper. And, although there seemed to be little hope of holiness among the people, this King would execute judgment, and righteousness would prevail.

SUMMARY
■ ELIJAH

Most of the Israelites had left their moorings. They had completely forgotten the covenant promise God had spoken to the Patriarchs, and they had thoroughly abandoned the One Who had delivered them from captivity. The Hebrews had taken "disobedience" to a whole new level and so they had stopped worshiping. They no longer entered God's presence. They determined that the best way to continue in their immoral ways was to no longer look into the face of the Holy One of Israel.

The role of the Old Testament prophets was to go and find the people where they were, stand in front of them, and say, "Thus says the Lord." And when they were ignored because no one wanted to hear what the immortal, invisible God had to say, the prophets would shout, "Look at me when I'm talking to you." Or, better, "Look into the face of God because He's talking to you."

The first five prophets listed in the Old Testament—Elijah, Isaiah, Jeremiah, Ezekiel, and Daniel—are often referred to as the "major" prophets. All the others who follow them are frequently called "minor" prophets. This distinction refers only to the amount of text we have that chronicles the lives of these men. It has nothing to do with their impact for God on the people of Israel and Judah. Because each was distinctly called of God to call people to repentance, each one is significant.

No prophet was more significant to the history of the Israelites than Elijah. He was the first and greatest of God's messengers to His people in the Old Testament. Not only was Elijah a prophet who lived at a particular time, he often symbolized the focal point of God's message of judgment for sin and promised pardon.

During his lifetime, Elijah wore the prophetic mantle in many courageous ways. The most notable was his confrontation of the evil King Ahab and his wicked wife, Jezebel.

One of the most remarkable notabilities of Elijah was the way he died, or rather, the way he *didn't* die. In a spectacle as wonderful as God's blazing visitation on Mount Carmel, He sent "a chariot of fire with horses of fire" to sweep the prophet to heaven in a whirlwind. It might as well have been God's holy signature on the life of Elijah, a sign of His favor, a final stamp of approval on Elijah's ministry.

■ ISAIAH

We know very little about Isaiah's life. But his distinction is that he was the most cultured of the prophets. His family was well educated, in contrast to most of the prophets who came from rural or agricultural backgrounds. His job was like that of a modern-day ambassador, with full access to the powerful leaders of the day—even the courts of royalty.

Given this frame of background and experience surrounding Isaiah's work, is it any wonder that, in the sovereignty of God, this would be the prophet who penned the mission statement for the ministry of the Messiah?

How was it that God chose Isaiah for this assignment? What was it about his life experience that drew his heart toward the coming Savior? To answer that, we must visit the moment when God called Isaiah to be His mouth-piece—and prosecuting attorney—to the wayward and sinful Hebrews.

What started out as a routine visit to the Temple became a life-changing experience. Isaiah chapter six records a surprise personal encounter between this prophet and a Holy God.

What a watershed moment this was for Isaiah. He had thought this assign-ment was going to be one of passing judgment to all *those* incorrigible Jews—*those* unclean sinners. But now Isaiah realized that this was first a call to personal contrition, *then* the calling of others to that same repentance.

The book of Isaiah is filled with glimpses of the coming Messiah, words that would have been hard to understand or believe in the midst of severe judg-ment. But, from God's perspective, they were as sure as tomorrow's sunrise. There is no doubt, from our post–New Testament perspective, that Isaiah's work and words foreshadowed the coming of Christ in supernatural detail. And that God chose this remarkable prophet to hand-deliver the message.

■ JEREMIAH

One of the things I loved about Jeremiah was his tender heart. With the study of the prophets, it's only natural to think of them as harsh, mean-spirited, and without pity—flamethrowers with an attitude. But during his ministry, Jeremiah picked up a nickname. He was known as "the Weeping Prophet."

Jeremiah's heart was broken because he knew that his people's sinfulness was breaking God's heart as well. So it was to this tender young man that God's call came.

What's interesting to me about Jeremiah's divine call is that it was "to the nations." This is interesting because as his story unfolded, it became clear that he was speaking to religious leaders. Isaiah stood before kings but Jeremiah went to Jewish priests and prophets. Then what did God have in mind by call-ing him to the nations?

Could it be that Jeremiah had a personal ministry to the Gentiles that we don't know about? Or is it possible that his words of blessing and cursing spread through the Israelites to their pagan tormentors? What we do know is that Jeremiah's ministry extended for more than fifty years and that his obedience to God's call lasted well beyond his lifetime.

In spite of the pain of confronting people he knew and loved with the truth of their own peril, and in spite of the loneliness of carrying this message day after day, Jeremiah *knew* that one day his Savior would come—a King who would reign and prosper. And, although there seemed to be little hope of holiness among the people, this King would execute judgment, and righteousness would prevail.

CHAPTER SEVEN

THE MAJOR PROPHETS II

- **The Exile**
- Ezekiel
- Daniel

If you were to take a handful of seeds and throw them onto a freshly tilled piece of land, eventually something would grow. You would not see any activity for days, or even weeks, but you could be certain that from those seeds, plants would ultimately emerge.

This is one of the most important principles in all of Holy Scripture—every action carries with it an imminent consequence. There is no escaping this. Centuries after the prophets, the apostle Paul summarized it this way:

> *Do not be deceived, God is not mocked; for whatever*
> *a man sows, that he will also reap.* (Galatians 6:7)

Or as the prophet Hosea would say, "They sow the wind, and reap the whirlwind."

This is a picture of the Hebrews. They sowed seeds of disobedience, idolatry, and gross sinfulness. The prophets got in their faces and tried to get their attention. But their efforts essentially proved fruitless. Seeds of wickedness turned to thick underbrush of rebellion and separation from God. So He decided to remove the people from their beloved homeland. Like a mother who warns her sons in church, "You boys better behave or I'll have to separate you," God tore the Israelites from the Promised Land.

The Jews sowed seeds, those seeds grew, and harvesttime came: Foreign powers broke through the borders and killed, scattered, or captured God's chosen people—this is known as the Exile.

But why would anyone want to conquer Israel? It was merely a thin strip of land, only about 150 miles long and 75 miles wide, with craggy deserts and piercing valleys.

Israel's value was not *who* she was but *where* she was.

Israel was, and continues to be, a strategic strip of land, a literal gold mine. It functioned as a land bridge between three continents—Asia, Europe, and Africa—which made it a critical hub for commerce and the mother lode for taxation. There was only one good way to get through Israel, on the "King's Highway" that ran along its western side, adjacent to the Mediterranean Sea. That road had to be patrolled to keep it safe and, as a bonus, those "patrols" made certain that everyone who passed through paid their fair share.

> Seeds of wickedness turned to thick underbrush of rebellion and separation from God.

Today, with the proliferation of air travel, Israel's property value is somewhat diminished. But it is still an important plot of land, consequential enough that plenty of nations continue to lust after it. In spite of what we might hear about this desire, many of the ethnic and religious protests are not entirely genuine. People long to occupy the land because of business—Israel is still a gold mine.

THE EXILE

The Northern Kingdom—Israel—fell to the Assyrians in 722 B.C. The ten families, all the Hebrews except the descendants of Judah and Levi, were scattered to the winds. As they were known to do, the Assyrians killed those not captured, and the cities that held no future military value were leveled. God had judged Israel for its idolatry by completely destroying it, just as He had promised. The Northern Kingdom had sown and now it was time for reaping—the Assyrians were God's harvesters of choice.

The Southern Kingdom—Judah—survived for almost 140 more years, but was destroyed by the Babylonians in 586 B.C.

Ironically, it had been the Assyrians' intention to take the Southern Kingdom following their conquering of the North. But God intervened under the rule of Hezekiah and turned the Assyrians and their commander, Sennacherib (seh-nak-er-rib), away. A combination of illness, broken supply lines, threats in their homeland, and the sovereignty of God—*mostly* the latter—caused the Assyrians to break camp and head home.

> The Northern Kingdom had sown and now it was time for reaping—the Assyrians were God's harvesters of choice.

The time between the fall of Israel and the demise of Judah was one of unmatched turbulence in the Southern Kingdom. It was during this time that Hezekiah reigned as king. He was a good king, a godly king. It was his desire to restore Judah to obedience and proper worship. But Hezekiah's reign and God's blessing on Jerusalem lasted only a few years. His son, Manasseh, a very wicked king, replaced the righteous and God-fearing Hezekiah. Not only did Manasseh establish pagan images in the hilltop sites—high places—around Jerusalem, he also brought a pagan image into the very Temple of God. Incredibly, and by God's grace, Manasseh repented as an old man. His successor, unfortunately, was his nefarious son, who had learned by his father's early example. Until Josiah came to power, Judah found itself in an ongoing and terrible descent.

JOSIAH

Josiah's reign over Judah (starting in 637 B.C.) was marked by the greatest period of reform during this time. Like Jeremiah the prophet, Josiah was unafraid of obedience at a very early age.

> *Josiah was eight years old when he became king,*
> *and he reigned thirty-one years in Jerusalem.*
> *His mother's name was Jedidah the daughter of Adaiah of Bozkath.*
> *And he did what was right in the sight of the LORD,*
> *and walked in all the ways of his father David;*
> *he did not turn aside to the right hand or to the left.* (2 Kings 22:1–2)

It's especially interesting to me that Josiah's mother, Jedidah, is mentioned immediately after we meet the new king. Is it possible, or even likely, that her name is here because, in spite of her husband's incredible failure as the king of Judah, she led her son in the ways of King David, Hezekiah, and their God? I think so. Oh, the power of a godly mother.

Imagine the relief and hope that Josiah represented, especially to the faithful remnant still found in Judah. His obedient leadership could perhaps stabilize this floundering nation. Can't you imagine these people praying for this to be true?

The first thing Josiah did as king was to call for the repairing of the Temple. He knew the importance of what Moses had first established in building the Tabernacle, a "dwelling place" for the Lord. Josiah made certain that this holy place was restored both physically and spiritually. In the process of renovation, the high priest discovered something.

> Like Jeremiah the prophet, Josiah was unafraid of obedience at a very early age.

Then Hilkiah the high priest said to Shaphan the scribe,
"I have found the Book of the Law in the house of the LORD."
And Hilkiah gave the book to Shaphan, and he read it.
So Shaphan the scribe went to the king,
bringing the king word, saying,
"Your servants have gathered the money that was found in the house,
and have delivered it into the hand of those who do the work,
who oversee the house of the LORD."
Then Shaphan the scribe showed the king, saying,
"Hilkiah the priest has given me a book."
And Shaphan read it before the king.
Now it happened, when the king heard the words of the Book of the Law,
that he tore his clothes . . .
[The king said,] "Go, inquire of the LORD for me,
for the people and for all Judah,
concerning the words of this book that has been found;
for great is the wrath of the LORD that is aroused against us,
because our fathers have not obeyed the words of this book,
to do according to all that is written concerning us." (2 Kings 22:8–11, 13)

What was truly remarkable about this discovery was that even Josiah, the righteous king, was unfamiliar with it; or perhaps he was reminded that the people hadn't read it for generations. In either case, his reaction to the reading of the Book of the Law was to tear his kingly garments, a sign of deepest grief.

The truth and power of the word of the Lord delivered to Joshua generations earlier were underscored once again.

> *This Book of the Law shall not depart from your mouth,*
> *but you shall meditate in it day and night,*
> *that you may observe to do according to all that is written in it.*
> *For then you will make your way prosperous,*
> *and then you will have good success.* (Joshua 1:8)

The interesting thing about God's Law is that it is true as written, and it is also inversely true. What Josiah realized at the hearing of the Book of the Law was this: *Allowing* the book to depart from the people's mouths, *not* meditating on it, and *not* observing it would result in certain failure.

So Josiah's first act was to bring about reforms in worship, and God was pleased.

Sadly, Josiah's great reformation was short-lived. At the age of thirty-nine, he was cut down in battle, killed by Egyptian arrows. Ironically, Necho, the king of Egypt, tried to warn Josiah against participating in the skirmish. "I'm not here to fight you," Necho told Josiah. And then Necho said an amazing thing:

> *Refrain from meddling with God, who is with me,*
> *lest He destroy you.* (2 Chronicles 35:21b)

How is this possible? How could a pagan king claim God's sovereignty over one of God's chosen, especially the obedient and prosperous Josiah?

Here is an unmistakable principle, found throughout Scripture. We have seen this before, and we will see it again. God will use whatever or whomever He wants to use in order to accomplish His purposes. We saw this fleshed out in God's leadership of His people through the godless Pharaoh. We saw it again in His unorthodox selection of the Patriarchs. We uncovered this principle in the punishment of the Northern Kingdom by the pagan Assyrians. And now we see it appear again in the life, and death, of a good king who, for one unfortunate battle, overlooked this unchangeable truth. God will use whatever or whomever He wants to use in order to accomplish His purposes.

Judah's crown went to Josiah's son, Jehoahaz, but he reigned for only three months. The king of Egypt deposed him and appointed his own brother, Jehoiakim, instead. Of course, Jehoiakim was heavily influenced by Egypt, which treated Judah as sovereign property. To show his contempt for God's Word, Jehoiakim burned one of Jeremiah's prophetic scrolls. Imagine the contrast in Judah's leadership over just a few short years: Josiah the king who tore his clothes at the hearing of the Book of the Law, and Jehoiakim who burned it.

In 605 B.C., twenty years before Judah fell, the Egyptians went to war against the Babylonians. Because the Babylonians prevailed, part of their booty was paid with Hebrews, turned over as slaves. The great prophet Daniel and his friends were among the Jews who were sent to the Babylonians. This was the first stage of Judah's ultimate demise and exile.

Seven years later, Judah's king and all his nobles were taken away to Babylon, along with the prophet Ezekiel. In 586 B.C., Babylon invaded Judah and completely destroyed it. As a final act of treachery, they killed the children of the king in his presence, they gouged out his eyes, bound him, and led him off into slavery.

Make no mistake about it. Whatever a man—or a nation—sows, that he will also reap.

- The Exile
- **Ezekiel**
- Daniel

As we know, the task of the prophet was to get the people's attention: to admonish them with "Thus says the Lord." It was the equivalent to a parent's "Look at me when I'm talking to you."

The prophet Ezekiel took his prophetic assignment to the next level. More than sixty times he wrote, "That they might know that I am the Lord." David used a similar admonition time and time again in the Psalms: "Be still and know that I am God." Some may think of these statements as a gentle pat on the head or a tender embrace by the Sovereign Lord. Not so. Translated into the vernacular, these statements were the equivalent of: "Sit down. Shut up. And pay attention. I am God."

As we have seen, the Israelites had been mercilessly yanked from their homeland. Surrounded by nothing familiar, they were slaves in Babylon. Because of their wickedness, God had sent a pagan nation to crash through Judah's borders and drag His people into slavery—or should I say, *back* into slavery. The difference, however, between bondage in Egypt and slavery in Babylon was something Martin Luther King Jr. reminded us about during the civil rights era in America. Dr. King said that our country was a melting pot, filled with people from diverse ethnic origins, seeking to be free. But one group of Americans was dragged here not to seek freedom, but to be conscripted as slaves.

> Translated into the vernacular, these statements were the equivalent of: "Sit down. Shut up. And pay attention. I am God."

This is precisely how the Hebrews were in their new homeland of Babylon. In Judah, these people were princes, kings, scholars, priests, artisans, experts, farmers, and parents. Now they were trifling chattel—pure riffraff. It is not too difficult to understand that the abuse and disrespect that defined slaves were almost too much for them to bear.

Down through the centuries, many have wondered how a loving Father could have been so cruel. How could He have granted the Babylonians entrance to the Promised Land? And how could He have given these savages their way with His chosen people? And why doesn't God protect His people today from pain and suffering? These questions are often asked of me. And, actually, the answer is quite straightforward. Over and over again, the Scriptures remind us of this truth: God punishes His children *because* He is their loving Father.

And you have forgotten the exhortation
which speaks to you as to sons:
"My son, do not despise the chastening of the LORD,
Nor be discouraged when you are rebuked by Him;
For whom the LORD loves He chastens,
And scourges every son whom He receives." (Hebrews 12:5–6)

In fact, God's ultimate punishment is not when He disciplines, but when He walks away. His final act of reproof is when He allows His children to live unfettered and undisciplined lives *without* His chastening.

For the wrath of God is revealed from heaven
against all ungodliness and unrighteousness of men,
who suppress the truth in unrighteousness,
because what may be known of God is manifest in them,
for God has shown it to them . . .
Therefore God also gave them up to uncleanness,
in the lusts of their hearts,
to dishonor their bodies among themselves,
who exchanged the truth of God for the lie,
and worshiped and served the creature rather than the Creator,
who is blessed forever. Amen. For this reason
God gave them up to vile passions. (Romans 1:18–19, 24–26a)

Do you see it? God's final verdict on the sinfulness of mankind is not in the invoking of His discipline, it's the *stopping* of His punishment—He walks away; He "gives them up."

So, although I'm confident that being slaves in Babylon didn't *feel* like the activity of a faithful God, it was, in fact, a clear example of God's manifest love to the

> God punishes His children because He is their loving Father.

Israelites. Ezekiel's task was to help the people understand this, and he was uniquely qualified.

Usually, there was a clear separation between the activities of priests and prophets. The former performed activities in the Temple; the latter preached everywhere. Priests were concerned with absolution and ceremony; prophets with repentance. The priest usually faced the altar with his back to the congregation, pleading the case of the people before a Holy God. But, as we have seen, the prophet faced the people, sometimes going nose to nose. The prophet reminded the people, in no uncertain terms, of God's judgment on their sin.

Ezekiel was both a priest and a prophet. He was born into a priestly family, but at the age of thirty, he was called to be a prophet as well. So his writings reflect this dual role—confronting the people with their sinfulness (prophet), then pleading with the Sovereign God on behalf of these same people (priest).

As a prophet, Ezekiel explained to the Israelites that their oppression was not a sign of God's abandonment, but of their sin.

> *And [God] said to me,*
> *"Son of man, stand on your feet, and I will speak to you."*
> *Then the Spirit entered me when He spoke to me, and set me on my feet;*
> *and I heard Him who spoke to me.*
> *And He said to me:*
> *"Son of man, I am sending you to the children of Israel,*
> *to a rebellious nation that has rebelled against Me;*
> *they and their fathers have transgressed against Me to this very day.*
> *For they are impudent and stubborn children.*
> *I am sending you to them, and you shall say to them,*
> *'Thus says the Lord God.'*
> *As for them, whether they hear or whether they refuse—*
> *for they are a rebellious house—*
> *yet they will know that a prophet has been among them.*
> *And you, son of man, do not be afraid of them nor be afraid of their words,*
> *though briers and thorns are with you and you dwell among scorpions;*
> *do not be afraid of their words or dismayed by their looks,*
> *though they are a rebellious house.*
> *You shall speak My words to them,*
> *whether they hear or whether they refuse,*

for they are rebellious.
But you, son of man, hear what I say to you." (Ezekiel 2:1–8a)

God's message to the prophet was clear. "The situation the Israelites find themselves in is *their* doing. Do not be afraid, Ezekiel. You are speaking on My behalf." So it was not because of God's speech being muted or distorted that the people did not obey. Their punishment was not God's fault; their sin—and its predictable consequence—was their doing.

The uniqueness of Ezekiel's approach was his use of outlandish imagery. Certainly a forerunner to the world of special effects in cinema, Ezekiel told the story of God's redemptive purposes and the people's disobedience in fantastic word pictures. Here's an example.

Then I looked, and behold, a whirlwind was coming out of the north,
a great cloud with raging fire engulfing itself;
and brightness was all around it and radiating out of its midst
like the color of amber, out of the midst of the fire.
Also from within it came the likeness of four living creatures.
And this was their appearance:
they had the likeness of a man.
Each one had four faces, and each one had four wings . . .
Now as I looked at the living creatures,
behold, a wheel was on the earth beside each living creature
with its four faces.
The appearance of the wheels and their workings
was like the color of beryl,
and all four had the same likeness.
The appearance of their workings was, as it were,
a wheel in the middle of a wheel.
When they moved,
they went toward any one of four directions;
they did not turn aside when they went.
As for their rims, they were so high they were awesome;
and their rims were full of eyes,

> *all around the four of them.*
> *When the living creatures went,*
> *the wheels went beside them;*
> *and when the living creatures were lifted up from the earth,*
> *the wheels were lifted up.* (Ezekiel 1:4–6, 15–19)

The people must have been scratching their heads. "What in the world is this, Ezekiel?" they must have asked. "How are we supposed to understand what you're saying?"

Ezekiel's prophetic vision was a visible representation of God's judgment seat. The "wheel" was not the first time God had communicated truths about Himself by a physical manifestation. Remember how God had traveled with the Israelites in their journeys, going from place to place in a pillar of cloud by day and a pillar of fire by night?

This time, the use of the imagery was to communicate a message of judgment. We know this because judgment was the topic of most of the prose that surrounded the vision. Another hint was the use of fire, usually used in the Old Testament as God's cleansing judgment. What was truly unique about this judgment throne, however, was its mobility. Since God was willing to be worshiped in a mobile Tabernacle, then He was willing to move His chastisement of sin from place to place as well.

THE SCROLL

Turning to his role as priest, Ezekiel changed the vision to something even more strange than the spinning wheel covered with eyes.

> *Now when I looked,*
> *there was a hand stretched out to me;*
> *and behold, a scroll of a book was in it.*
> *Then He spread it before me; and there was writing on the inside*
> *and on the outside,*
> *and written on it were lamentations and mourning and woe.*
> *Moreover He said to me, . . .*

"Son of man, feed your belly, and fill your stomach
with this scroll that I give you."
So I ate, and it was in my mouth
like honey in sweetness. (Ezekiel 2:9–3:1a, 3)

Imagine the consequences of all the sins of all God's chosen people being recorded on a scroll—Ezekiel called them lamentations, mourning, and woe. What a horrible document that must have been. Then God tells Ezekiel to eat the scroll, to literally ingest it, paper and all—enough to make a man sick. With this vision, you would think that God was telling Ezekiel that the sins of the Israelites are enough to make Him nauseated. But there's a wonderful twist to the vision.

The scroll tasted like honey. Not only did it not sicken the prophet, it was pleasing to his palate. As a priest, it was Ezekiel's job to plead the people's case before the righteous Judge, to bring their sins before Him. And now he was experiencing in a palpable way, the assurance—and the sweetness—of God's ultimate grace extended to the children of Israel.

DRY BONES

Even better known than Ezekiel's wheel or edible scroll was his vision of the valley of dry bones. As with the sweet-tasting scroll, this was another priestly vision.

The hand of the LORD came upon me
and brought me out in the Spirit of the LORD,
and set me down in the midst of the valley;
and it was full of bones.
Then He caused me to pass by them all around,
and behold, there were very many in the open valley;
and indeed they were very dry.
And He said to me,
"Son of man, can these bones live?"
So I answered, "O Lord GOD, You know."

> *Again He said to me,*
> *"Prophesy to these bones, and say to them,*
> *'O dry bones, hear the word of the LORD!*
> *Thus says the Lord GOD to these bones:*
> *"Surely I will cause breath to enter into you,*
> *and you shall live.*
> *I will put sinews on you and bring flesh upon you,*
> *cover you with skin and put breath in you;*
> *and you shall live.*
> *Then you shall know that I am the LORD.""'* (Ezekiel 37:4–6)

This was a vision with a deadly serious message. "The Israelites are dead and their bones have been scattered," God is saying to Ezekiel. "They have no breath left in them. But when they hear My word again, I, the Lord God of your fathers, will bind them together. I will take death and bring it to life. Those who hear the word of the Lord, especially My covenant community, will be made alive."

This was the message of Ezekiel the prophet and the priest—a word of warning and hope.

- The Exile
- Ezekiel
- **Daniel**

If special appearances by the Sovereign God in the Old Testament are like individual snowcapped peaks, visible at any distance, then the account of Daniel is a range of crests all by itself. But, unlike the other appearances—or near appearances—of God Himself, the stories surrounding this young man are a nearly perfect representation of what it looks like when a person is wholly committed to the Holy One of Israel.

Years ago a little song appeared in children's Sunday school classrooms around the country. The chorus went like this:

Dare to be a Daniel,
Dare to stand alone.
Dare to make a purpose firm,
Dare to make it known.

Like Joseph in Egypt centuries earlier, Daniel was a common laborer in a foreign land. One day, King Nebuchadnezzar decided to assemble the best and the brightest young men in the land to serve in the palace. He selected these young men from among the Babylonians and the Hebrews. Because Daniel and his friends were handsome and fit, they were chosen for the king's "A-Team."

Soon after entering the palace, Daniel and his Jewish friends were unimpressed with the rich food and wine the young men were being fed. So they asked the steward, the chief servant of the king, "Please test us for ten days and let them give us vegetables to eat and water to drink." Then he challenged the steward to see if this sound diet would produce visible results.

Sure enough.

At the end of ten days [the Hebrews'] features
appeared better and fatter in flesh than all the young men
who ate the portion of the king's delicacies.
Thus the steward took away their portion
of delicacies and the wine that they were to drink,
and gave them vegetables. (Daniel 1:15–16)

This was the first of many "dare to be a Daniels."

NEBUCHADNEZZAR

Also like Joseph, Daniel gained entrance to the courts of the king because of his ability to interpret dreams. In the second year of Nebuchadnezzar's reign, the king had a dream. Apparently the dream was more like a nightmare because "his spirit was so troubled that his sleep left him." Night sweats will get even a pompous monarch's attention.

What was different about this situation compared to Joseph's interpretation of the pharaoh's dream was that King Nebuchadnezzar wasn't even willing to tell his "magicians, astrologers, sorcerers, or Chaldeans" the content of the dream. Naturally, these wizards wanted to at least have the benefit of knowing what the dream contained before attempting to translate it. Not one to mince words, King Nebuchadnezzar answered:

> *My decision is firm:*
> *if you do not make known the dream to me,*
> *and its interpretation,*
> *you shall be cut in pieces,*
> *and your houses shall be made an ash heap.*
> *However, if you tell the dream and its interpretation,*
> *you shall receive from me gifts, rewards, and great honor.*
> *Therefore tell me the dream and its interpretation.* (Daniel 2:5–6)

The heads of these wizards and wise men must have been spinning. They had just been given two options: win the lottery or get the death penalty. No middle ground here.

> Night sweats will get even a pompous monarch's attention.

As you might imagine, these experts were thoroughly unsuccessful; in fact, they didn't even try. Then the king issued a decree: Kill all the wise men of Babylon, including Daniel and his Jewish friends on the king's "A-Team."

In order to save his life, Daniel prepared for his next courageous "dare."

> *So Daniel went in and asked the king to give him time,*
> *that he might tell the king the interpretation.*
> *Then Daniel went to his house,*
> *and made the decision known to . . . his companions,*
> *that they might seek mercies from the God*
> *of heaven concerning this secret,*
> *so that Daniel and his companions might not perish*
> *with the rest of the wise men of Babylon.*

Then the secret was revealed to Daniel in a night vision.
So Daniel blessed the God of heaven. (Daniel 2:16–19)

Is it any wonder that God chose to bless Daniel? Like young David staring down the mighty Goliath, Daniel placed his dependence entirely on God's mercy. With no presumption, Daniel implored God to give him wisdom, then praised Him when the answer came. In fact, listen to King Nebuchadnezzar's words once the interpretation is complete and the king is prostrate before the Hebrew in gratitude.

> *"Truly your God is the God of gods, the Lord of kings,*
> *and a revealer of secrets,*
> *since you could reveal this secret."*
> *Then the king promoted Daniel*
> *and gave him many great gifts;*
> *and he made him ruler of the whole province of Babylon,*
> *and chief administrator over all the wise men of Babylon.* (Daniel 2:47b–48)

Daniel's interpretation of Nebuchadnezzar's dream involved a summary of the military and political powers that would come to prominence over the next several centuries. This dream featuring things that had not yet happened stunned all who heard it. And even today, skeptical scholars are baffled at the accuracy with which Daniel's prophecy ultimately unfolded.

Daniel's explanation was, however, quite simple.

> *Blessed be the name of God forever and ever,*
> *For wisdom and might are His.* (Daniel 2:20)

THE FIERY FURNACE

Although Daniel held a prominent position of leadership under Nebuchadnezzar, it was clear that the king's fear of God was not the predominant view in Babylon. And even though the king had given verbal homage to the Holy One of Israel, he didn't have the courage to truly believe. Witness the following:

> *Nebuchadnezzar the king made an image of gold,*
> *whose height was [90 feet] and its width [9 feet].*
> *He set it up in the plain of Dura, in the province of Babylon.*
> *And King Nebuchadnezzar sent word to gather together . . .*
> *all the officials of the provinces, to come to the dedication*
> *of the image which King Nebuchadnezzar had set up . . .*
> *Then a herald cried aloud:*
> *"To you it is commanded, O peoples, nations, and languages,*
> *that at the time you hear the sound of the . . . music,*
> *you shall fall down and worship the gold image*
> *that King Nebuchadnezzar has set up;*
> *and whoever does not fall down and worship shall be cast immediately*
> *into the midst of a burning fiery furnace."* (Daniel 3:1–2, 4–6)

"Dare to be a Daniel, dare to stand alone."

Jealousy had arisen over the positions of leadership that Daniel and his three friends had achieved, so certain Chaldeans plotted to trap the Hebrews by Nebuchadnezzar's edict. And it should come as no surprise to us that when these men were brought into the presence of the golden image and the music began, they held their positions. They did not bow down.

In a fury, Nebuchadnezzar brought the men before him, offering to give them one more chance. "With all due respect, Your Excellency," these courageous men responded, "don't bother."

> *Shadrach, Meshach, and Abed-Nego answered and said to the king,*
> *"O Nebuchadnezzar, we have no need to answer you in this matter.*
> *If that is the case, our God whom we serve is able to deliver us from the burning*
> *fiery furnace, and He will deliver us from your hand, O king.*
> *But if not, let it be known to you, O king,*
> *that we do not serve your gods, nor will we*
> *worship the gold image which you have set up."* (Daniel 3:16–18)

Nebuchadnezzar was blind with rage. Public embarrassment was never treated casually by someone as arrogant as Nebuchadnezzar. He ordered the furnace to be heated to seven times its original heat, the first heat severe enough for smelting iron. Incredibly, the fires were so hot that those who were assigned to throw the three Jews into the mouth of the furnace were instantly killed. But the three Hebrew men were unharmed.

> *Then King Nebuchadnezzar was astonished;*
> *and he rose in haste and spoke, saying to his counselors,*
> *"Did we not cast three men bound into the midst of the fire?"*
> *They answered and said to the king, "True, O king."*
> *"Look!" he answered, "I see four men loose,*
> *walking in the midst of the fire;*
> *and they are not hurt, and the form of the fourth*
> *is like the Son of God." (Daniel 3:24–25)*

Nebuchadnezzar covered his face because of the intense heat, straining to see inside the furnace. And, like others who had dared to look into the face of the holiness of God, he was completely overwhelmed by the experience. Like Moses gazing at the bush that would not be consumed, the Israelites peering into the face of Moses at the base of Mount Sinai, or Isaiah standing in the presence of the Almighty, this pagan king was awestruck.

> Public embarrassment was never treated casually by someone as arrogant as Nebuchadnezzar.

> *Blessed be the God of Shadrach, Meshach, and Abed-Nego,*
> *who sent His Angel and delivered His servants*
> *who trusted in Him,*
> *and they have frustrated the king's word,*
> *and yielded their bodies,*
> *that they should not serve nor worship any god*
> *except their own God! (Daniel 3:28)*

Although King Nebuchadnezzar did not go so far as to declare God's sovereignty in the land, he made a decree that no one was to "speak anything amiss against the God of Shadrach, Meshach, and Abed-Nego." Quite a bold statement for a man of Nebuchadnezzar's prominence. But we cannot forget that these words were coming from a man who had been in God's unmistakable presence. How could anyone ever be the same again?

In the mid-eighties, when the Berlin Wall fell and the Soviet Union collapsed, I was fascinated with the immediate spread of the Gospel into these countries. Christian leaders from around the world were welcomed into the halls of power where atheism had been the state religion for more than seventy years. It reminded me of Babylon's King Nebuchadnezzar, seeing for the first time in his life the unmistakable power of an Almighty God and being completely overwhelmed by it.

After the Hebrews survived the furnace, Nebuchadnezzar promoted them to greater positions of leadership in Babylon. Daniel also served with distinction.

ANOTHER INTERPRETATION FOR A VILLAIN

Nebuchadnezzar's son, Belshazzar, succeeded him to the throne of Babylon. And, as you might expect for the king of a prosperous and pagan nation, King Belshazzar enjoyed the good life. One night, during an unusually raucous party—one where the king and his wives and mistresses were drinking wine from the sacred golden vessels taken from the holy Temple in Jerusalem—Belshazzar was rudely interrupted.

> *In the same hour the fingers of a man's hand appeared*
> *and wrote opposite the lampstand on the plaster of the wall*
> *of the king's palace; and the king saw the part of the hand that wrote.*
> *Then the king's countenance changed,*
> *and his thoughts troubled him,*
> *so that the joints of his hips were loosened*
> *and his knees knocked against each other . . .*
> *Now all the king's wise men came,*
> *but they could not read the writing,*
> *or make known to the king its interpretation.*
> *Then King Belshazzar was greatly troubled,*

> *his countenance was changed,*
> *and his lords were astonished.* (Daniel 5:5–9)

Like his father before him who had dreamed a troubling dream, Belshazzar had experienced something supernatural, and its impact was overwhelming. So the king sought out the wise men in Babylon to help him understand the words that had been written on the wall.

Not surprisingly, the Babylonian wizards were again unsuccessful. But Daniel was called into the presence of the king, daring once more to speak truth to this heathen monarch.

> *Then Daniel was brought in before the king.*
> *The king spoke, and said to Daniel,*
> *"Are you that Daniel who is one of the captives from Judah,*
> *whom my father the king brought from Judah?*
> *I have heard of you,*
> *that the Spirit of God is in you,*
> *and that light and understanding and excellent wisdom*
> *are found in you."* (Daniel 5:13–14)

Like Joseph in Egypt, Daniel's reputation had preceded him. But it wasn't simply Daniel's handsome appearance or his strategic leadership skills that had set him apart from the rest. It was the fact that "the Spirit of God" was in him—that "light and understanding and excellent wisdom" were found in Daniel.

THE LIONS' DEN

One final test of Daniel's daring came when Darius, Belshazzar's successor, came to power. The kingdom had been divided into three provinces and Daniel presided over one of these. Darius even considered setting him over the entire realm.

But the king's advisers were scandalized by the thought of having a Hebrew rule over them. Their contemptible jealousy of Daniel drove them to set a trap against him. They approached King Darius with a proposition filled with flattery and deceit.

> *So these governors and satraps thronged before the king,*
> *and said thus to him:*
> *"King Darius, live forever!*
> *All the governors of the kingdom, the administrators and satraps,*
> *the counselors and advisors,*
> *have consulted together to establish a royal statute and to make a firm decree,*
> *that whoever petitions any god or man for thirty days, except you, O king,*
> *shall be cast into the den of lions.*
> *Now, O king, establish the decree and sign the writing,*
> *so that it cannot be changed,*
> *according to the law of the Medes and Persians,*
> *which does not alter."*
> *Therefore King Darius signed the written decree.* (Daniel 6:6–9)

Once the decree was irrevocably signed by his friend the king, Daniel went straight home, opened the window that faced Jerusalem, and knelt and prayed. Daniel gave thanks to his God, "as was his custom since early days."

Believing that they had him right where they wanted him, the advisers returned to King Darius with the report that Daniel had broken the law. When the king received the report, he "was greatly displeased with himself," realizing that his envious subordinates had duped him.

King Darius had no choice but to execute Daniel; the method of the edict was to throw him into a cave inhabited by hungry lions. Just before being cast to his certain death, King Darius gave Daniel his blessing: "Your God, whom you serve continually, He will deliver you."

Early the next morning, after a sleepless night, Darius came to the mouth of the lions' den.

> *And when he came to the den,*
> *he cried out with a lamenting voice to Daniel.*
> *The king spoke, saying to Daniel,*

"Daniel, servant of the living God, has your God,
whom you serve continually, been able to deliver you from the lions?"
Then Daniel said to the king,
"O king, live forever!
My God sent His angel and shut the lions' mouths,
so that they have not hurt me,
because I was found innocent before Him; and also, O king,
I have done no wrong before you." (Daniel 6:20–22)

Holy Scripture tells us that the king was "exceedingly glad" that Daniel had been miraculously spared. The king was also exceedingly angry at those who had framed Daniel. He brought them to the mouth of the cave, along with their entire families, and threw them in. The biblical record affirms that "before they ever came to the bottom of the den," the lions had completely devoured them all.

Just as Achan and his family had learned under Joshua's leadership, these men discovered that defying a Holy God is always dangerous business.

At the height of his dominance as history's most skilled and celebrated basketball player, a popular sports drink sponsored a television advertising campaign promoting Michael Jordan as their spokesperson. The advertisement featured children, young boys primarily, singing a little tune. "I want to be like Mike," they sang over and over, "be like Mike."

> Just as Achan and his family had learned under Joshua's leadership, these men discovered that defying a Holy God is always dangerous business.

Don't get me wrong. I like basketball. And I liked Michael Jordan and believed that when ESPN named him the Male Athlete of the Nineties, that it was recognition well deserved. It's just that I think those kids in Sunday school several decades ago had a better lyric than the one promoting a sports drink. "Dare to be a Daniel." Can you imagine if that would catch on?

After the historical narratives of the first six chapters, the rest of the book of Daniel is taken up by his prophecies. Down through the years, these have been very controversial writings, especially related to questions as to what times they are predicting. They are either addressing the advent of Christ (which I tend to favor) or the events that occurred during the reign of Antiochus Epiphanes (175–164 B.C.).

In either case, Daniel's prophecies hammer home the same truth taught in his narratives: God is in control of history.

SUMMARY
■ THE EXILE

If you were to take a handful of seeds and throw them onto a freshly tilled piece of land, eventually something would grow. You would not see any activity for days, or even weeks, but you could be certain that from those seeds, plants would ultimately emerge.

This is one of the most important principles in all of Holy Scripture—every action carries with it an imminent consequence. There is no escaping this.

The Jews sowed seeds of disobedience, idolatry, and gross sinfulness. Those seeds grew, and harvesttime came: Foreign powers broke through the borders and killed, scattered, or captured God's chosen people—this is known as the Exile.

The Northern Kingdom—Israel—fell to the Assyrians in 722 B.C. The ten families, all the Hebrews except the descendants of Judah and Levi, were scattered to the winds. As they were known to do, the Assyrians killed those not captured, and the cities that held no future military value were leveled. God had judged Israel for her idolatry by completely destroying her, just as He had promised. The Northern Kingdom had sown and now it was time for reaping—the Assyrians were God's harvesters of choice.

The Southern Kingdom—Judah—survived for almost 140 more years, but was destroyed by the Babylonians in 586 B.C.

Make no mistake about it. Whatever a man—or a nation—sows, that he will also reap.

■ EZEKIEL

The prophet Ezekiel took his prophetic assignment to the next level. More than sixty times he wrote, "That they might know that I am the Lord." David used a similar admonition time and time again in the Psalms: "Be still and know that I am God." Some may think of these statements as a gentle pat on the head or a tender embrace by the Sovereign Lord. Not so. Translated into the vernacular, these statements were the equivalent of: "Sit down. Shut up. And pay attention. I am God."

As we have seen, the Israelites had been mercilessly yanked from their homeland. Surrounded by nothing familiar, they were slaves in Babylon. Because of their wickedness, God had sent a pagan nation to crash through Judah's borders and drag His people into slavery—or should I say, *back* into slavery.

This is precisely how the Hebrews were in their new homeland of Babylon. In Judah, these people were princes, kings, scholars, priests, artisans, experts, farmers, and parents. Now they were trifling chattel—pure riffraff. It is not too difficult to understand that the abuse and disrespect that defined slaves were almost too much for them to bear.

Down through the centuries, many have wondered how a loving Father could have been so cruel. How could He have granted the Babylonians entrance to the Promised Land? And how could He have given these savages their way with His chosen people? And why doesn't God protect His people today from pain and suffering? These questions are often asked of me. And, actually, the answer is quite straightforward. Over and over again, the Scriptures remind us of this truth: God punishes His children *because* He is their loving Father.

In fact, God's ultimate punishment is not when He disciplines, but when He walks away. His final act of reproof is when He allows His children to live unfettered and undisciplined lives *without* His chastening.

Ezekiel was both a priest and a prophet. He was born into a priestly family, but at the age of thirty, he was called to be a prophet as well. So his writings reflect this dual role—confronting the people with their sinfulness (prophet), then pleading with the Sovereign God on behalf of these same people (priest).

As a prophet, Ezekiel explained to the Israelites that their oppression was not a sign of God's abandonment, but of their sin. As priest, Ezekiel changed his message to one of hope. Through outlandish visions of spinning wheels covered with eyes, sweet-tasting scrolls, and valleys filled with bones, Ezekiel was delivering the assurance of God's ultimate grace extended to the children of Israel.

■ DANIEL

Like Joseph in Egypt centuries earlier, Daniel was a common laborer in a foreign land. One day, King Nebuchadnezzar decided to assemble the best and the brightest young men in the land to serve in the palace. He selected these young men among the Babylonians and the Hebrews. Because Daniel and his friends were handsome and fit, they were chosen for the king's "A-Team."

Soon after entering the palace, Daniel and his Jewish friends were unimpressed with the rich food and wine the young men were being fed. So they asked the steward, the chief servant of the king, "Please test us for ten days and let them give us vegetables to eat and water to drink." Then he challenged the steward to see if this sound diet would produce visible results.

Sure enough.

Also like Joseph, Daniel gained entrance to the courts of King Nebuchadnezzar because of his ability to interpret dreams.

Although Daniel held a prominent position of leadership, it was clear that his fear of God was not the predominant view in Babylon. And even though Nebuchadnezzar had given verbal homage to the Holy One of Israel, he didn't have the courage to truly believe. His delight over edicts that forced his subjects to bow down to him overshadowed any interest in paying homage to God.

Nebuchadnezzar's son, Belshazzar, succeeded him to the throne of Babylon. Like his father before him who had dreamed a troubling dream, Belshazzar called Daniel into his presence. Not surprisingly, Daniel spoke the truth to this heathen monarch.

Like Joseph in Egypt, Daniel's reputation had preceded him. But it wasn't simply Daniel's handsome appearance, dream-interpretation abilities, or his strategic leadership skills that had set him apart from the rest. It was the fact that "the Spirit of God" was in him—that "light and understanding and wisdom" were found in Daniel.

One final test of Daniel's daring came when Darius, Belshazzar's successor, came to power. The kingdom had been divided into three provinces and Daniel presided over one of these. Darius even considered setting him over the entire realm. But the king's advisers were scandalized by the thought of having a Hebrew to rule over them. Their contemptible jealousy of Daniel drove them to set a trap against him.

King Darius had no choice but to execute Daniel; the method of the edict was to throw him into a cave inhabited by hungry lions. Just before being cast to his certain death, King Darius gave Daniel his blessing: "Your God, whom you serve continually, He will deliver you."

And He did.

CHAPTER EIGHT

THE MINOR PROPHETS

- Amos and Hosea
- Joel, Micah, and Habakkuk
- Jonah

Living in Central Florida means living close to new-home construction. When we moved to Florida from western Pennsylvania in the mid-eighties, there were approximately ten million people living in Florida. By the turn of the twenty-first century, that number had jumped to fifteen million. New buildings are springing up everywhere.

The next time I drive past a house under construction, I may just stop and strike up a conversation with one of the carpenters. Actually, there would be a purpose for this talk, because I have a question for him. The prophet Amos has given me an idea, and I'd like to know if it's a good one.

Here's my question for the carpenter: "What's the most important tool you use when you frame a house?"

Having known builders over the years, I have a strong suspicion that I know what he will tell me. I know he has a literal truckload of things he uses when he sets the walls and frames the roof, but I want to know which is the *most* important tool. What do you think he'll say?

Although a carpenter couldn't survive without hammers, tape measures, and framing squares, when I stop to ask him, he'll probably tell me that the *most* important tool in his truck is his level. If walls and floors aren't perfectly vertical and horizontal—the carpenter will refer to this as "plumb"—he might as well pull his crew off the job and go home. A crooked building is a complete waste of time and materials.

AMOS

The prophet Amos was not a happy man. Here are the opening lines in his book:

> *The LORD roars from Zion,*
> *And utters His voice from Jerusalem;*
> *The pastures of the shepherds mourn,*
> *And the top of Carmel withers.* (Amos 1:2)

In summarizing the situation among the Israelites, Amos made reference to what he knew as a herdsman and a fruit grower. "The pastures mourn" and "the top of Carmel withers." These were things that would have ruined his life as a tradesman, and he was about to tell the Jews that their lives were a wreck as well.

But what about the carpenter's level, and what does this have to do with Amos?

Tucked into the second half of the book, Amos drew an analogy that gives us a clue as to why Amos was so upset and what tool he thought was the most important.

> *Thus [the Lord GOD] showed me:*
> *Behold, the Lord stood on a wall made with a plumb line,*
> *with a plumb line in His hand.*
> *And the LORD said to me, "Amos, what do you see?"*
> *And I said, "A plumb line."*
> *Then the Lord said:*
> *"Behold, I am setting a plumb line*
> *In the midst of My people Israel;*
> *I will not pass by them anymore.*
> *The high places of Isaac shall be desolate,*
> *And the sanctuaries of Israel shall be laid waste.*
> *I will rise with the sword against the house of Jeroboam."* (Amos 7:7–9)

The image was powerful. The Lord God stood on a wall that represented His people, the Israelites. Although He didn't say it here, I surmise that the wall was not straight and true. Either the original builder had been sloppy in his construction, or time and weather had deteriorated the wall, rendering it crooked. Either way it didn't matter. The wall was not straight. In order to make His point, God dropped a plumb line—a long string with a heavy weight at one end—next to the wall. To the naked eye, the wall may have seemed fine. But next to the perfectly vertical plumb line, the wall's imperfection became readily apparent.

This is why Amos wrote:

> *Therefore the* LORD *God of hosts, the Lord, says this:*
> *"There shall be wailing in all streets,*
> *And they shall say in all the highways,*
> *'Alas! Alas!'*
> *They shall call the farmer to mourning,*
> *And skillful lamenters to wailing.*
> *In all the vineyards there shall be wailing,*
> *For I will pass through you,"*
> *Says the* LORD. (Amos 5:16–17)

The focus of Amos's word to God's chosen people was immorality, religious apostasy, and social injustice. All of these things render a nation's walls deformed and useless—good for nothing but tearing down.

> *But let justice run down like water,*
> *And righteousness like a mighty stream.* (Amos 5:24)

During the years of the civil rights movement in America, this was one of Dr. Martin Luther King Jr.'s favorite biblical passages. He knew what Amos knew: A nation that disregards the cries of the poor and the respectful treatment of all her citizenry is a nation in peril—a nation out of plumb.

As with Dr. King's upbraiding of complacent Americans, Amos got in the faces of the Jews. He warned them that their offerings and sacrifices were a stench to God's nostrils because while they were outwardly performing their religious duties, they were treating one another with disregard. The poor were "sold for a pair of shoes" while the women had "become like the fatted cows of Bashan."

Justice did not prevail because, during Amos's time, it was common for judges to accept bribes, so that the rich would always be declared innocent and the poor would be thrown into prison, or worse.

> The "Day of the Lord" was to be a good day for saints, but a bad day for the unrepentant sinner.

Amos preached on a subject that predated the ministry of the prophets: the "Day of the Lord." For thousands of years, Jews had longed for the day that God Himself would come to destroy the wicked and save the righteous. This was to be a good day for saints, but a bad day for the unrepentant sinner.

In the New Testament, the father of John the Baptist sings of this "Day of the Lord" as a good day—a moment in time when God will visit His people with a Redeemer.

> *Blessed is the Lord God of Israel,*
> *For He has visited and redeemed His people . . .*
> *As He spoke by the mouth of His holy prophets,*
> *Who have been since the world began,*
> *That we should be saved from our enemies*
> *And from the hand of all who hate us.* (Luke 1:68, 70–71)

But this "day" was also bad news for impenitent Jews. Like Amos, Jesus Christ, the Redeemer Zecharias was speaking of, *warned* His people of the "Day of the Lord." Jesus lamented that destruction would come upon Jerusalem because they were not ready for God in their "day." His words came true forty years after His resurrection when, in A.D. 70, the Romans utterly destroyed Jerusalem.

Amos prophesied that those who were looking for the Day of the Lord would be surprised, because while they were looking for God to judge other nations, other people, other tribes—He would first judge them. The people may walk into the street, only to be chased by a lion. They would flee down an alley, only to run into a bear. And if they finally reached the safety of their own home, they would close the door behind them, breathe a sigh of relief, put out their hand to steady themselves, and a snake would bite them. For some, the Day of the Lord will be a very, very bad day, indeed.

As we have seen, the life of a prophet was often a lonely one. The task called up all of the emotional and spiritual reserves these men had in their personal arsenals.

As a prophet from the Southern Kingdom, Amos incurred the wrath of those from the North, particularly Amaziah, the priest of Bethel. Amaziah accused Amos of mounting a conspiracy against Israel.

> *Go, you seer!*
> *Flee to the land of Judah.*
> *There eat bread,*
> *And there prophesy.*
> *But never again prophesy at Bethel,*
> *For it is the king's sanctuary,*
> *And it is the royal residence.* (Amos 7:12–13)

But Amos's reply to Amaziah was fascinating.

> *I was no prophet,*
> *Nor was I a son of a prophet,*
> *But I was a sheepbreeder*
> *And a tender of sycamore fruit.*
> *Then the LORD took me as I followed the flock,*
> *And the LORD said to me,*
> *"Go, prophesy to My people Israel."*
> *Now therefore, hear the word of the LORD:*
> *You say, "Do not prophesy against Israel,*
> *And do not spout against the house of Isaac."*
> *Therefore thus says the LORD:*
> *"Your wife shall be a harlot in the city;*
> *Your sons and daughters shall fall by the sword;*

Your land shall be divided by survey line;
You shall die in a defiled land;
And Israel shall surely be led away captive
From his own land." (Amos 7:14–17)

Amos established his credibility with Amaziah by telling him that he was *not* a prophet. It was as though he was telling his accuser, "Hey, I was minding my own business, tending flocks and caring for my fruit trees. I didn't ask for this assignment; God called me to it."

Did you notice that Amaziah referred to Amos as a "seer" ? This referred to a group of professional "prophets"—Elmer Gantrys of sorts—traveling preachers who, with their dog and pony shows, were not official. These professional entertainers were on their own and not called of God.

But Amos corrected his accuser, telling him that he was not a prophet-for-hire, but a real prophet, set apart by God Himself. He made his living from sheep and figs, not from the collection plate.

Although he was a prophet whose message was primarily doom, Amos closed his book with a promise of God's mercy for those who repent.

On that day I will raise up
The tabernacle of David, which has fallen down,
and repair its damages;
I will raise up its ruins,
And rebuild it as in the days of old. (Amos 9:11)

HOSEA

When Jesus was finishing His earthly ministry, He gathered His disciples together. Like Amos, they were uniquely set apart for ministry.

But you shall receive power when the Holy Spirit has come upon you;
and you shall be witnesses to Me in Jerusalem,
and in all Judea and Samaria,
and to the end of the earth. (Acts 1:8)

Notice that Jesus did not give His disciples a glossary of effective words to use or a stack of pamphlets to pass out. He told them to "be" His witnesses. "You may be the only 'Jesus' people see or the only 'Bible' they read," I remember hearing from the pulpit one day many years ago. This is quite an assignment.

It reminds me of Hosea, another called man.

> *When the LORD began to speak by Hosea,*
> *the LORD said to Hosea:*
> *"Go, take yourself a wife of harlotry*
> *And children of harlotry,*
> *For the land has committed great harlotry*
> *By departing from the LORD." (Hosea 1:2)*

Exactly as Jesus had commanded His disciples to "go and be," the Sovereign God told Hosea to *experience* the message before *preaching* it. "Just so you know what it feels like to be Me," the Lord was saying to the prophet, "go marry someone who has no idea what faithfulness, loyalty, and fidelity mean."

Obediently, Hosea sought a prostitute named Gomer to be his bride. By his wife, Hosea had three children: two sons and a daughter. God directed Hosea to name his children, "God plants," "she received no compassion," and "not my people."

Not only did God call Hosea to say to the people, "thus says the LORD," He also filled Hosea's family scrapbook with visible reminders of, "given how You have treated Me, this is how it feels to be God."

In many ways, Hosea became the incarnation—a word in human flesh—of God's message of judgment and redemption.

Once the children had been born, God ordered Hosea to release his wife, divorce her, and turn her loose . . . another reminder of God's ultimate judgment on His people recorded in Romans chapter one: turning them over to their own lusts. But even in returning to the streets, Gomer would not find satisfaction.

> *"Therefore, behold,*
> *I will hedge up your way with thorns,*
> *And wall her in,*

So that she cannot find her paths.
She will chase her lovers,
But will not overtake them;
Yes, she will seek them, but not find them.
Then she will say,
'I will go and return to my first husband,
For then it was better for me than now.' . . .
I will also cause all her mirth to cease,
Her feast days,
Her New Moons,
Her Sabbaths—
All her appointed feasts . . .
I will punish her
For the days of the Baals to which she burned incense.
She decked herself with her earrings and jewelry,
And went after her lovers;
But Me she forgot" says the LORD. (Hosea 2:6–7, 11, 13)

Unfortunately for Hosea, God was not finished with him.

Then the LORD said to me,
"Go again, love a woman who is loved by a lover
and is committing adultery, just like the love
of the LORD for the children of Israel,
who look to other gods and love the raisin cakes of the pagans."
So I bought her for myself for fifteen shekels of silver,
and one and one-half homers of barley.
And I said to her,
"You shall stay with me many days;
you shall not play the harlot, nor shall you have a man—
so, too, will I be toward you." (Hosea 3:1–3)

Like no other prophet, Hosea placed his own life on the altar of fairness. God seemingly took advantage of his availability and obedience, forcing him into fathering a pathetic and broken family. But instead of being filled with anger and resentment, Hosea's prophetic message to his people was filled with tenderness and compassion. No wonder God chose him for this horrific assignment.

In fact, Hosea's word to his people included an amazing forecast of the substitutionary death and reconciling resurrection of the Savior.

> *Come, and let us return to the LORD;*
> *For He has torn, but He will heal us;*
> *He has stricken, but He will bind us up.*
> *After two days He will revive us;*
> *On the third day He will raise us up,*
> *That we may live in His sight.* (Hosea 6:1–2)

Hosea concludes his sacrificial ministry with these words:

> *Who is wise?*
> *Let him understand these things.*
> *Who is prudent?*
> *Let him know them.*
> *For the ways of the LORD are right;*
> *The righteous walk in them,*
> *But transgressors stumble in them.* (Hosea 14:9)

The message to Israel from Hosea was specific, but it has universal applications. A faithful God relentlessly loves His unfaithful people. There is a sweeping call for all of us who read these words to understand their truths.

- Amos and Hosea
- **Joel, Micah, and Habakkuk**
- Jonah

It might be interesting to survey a few people at the local shopping mall, asking them what they think of when someone says the word *prophet*. More than once we would probably get the image of a man, walking back and forth on a city sidewalk and wearing one of those antiquated "sandwich boards." Boldly printed on this board, front and back, would be a single word: REPENT. The idea of this image makes me smile.

But the concept of repentance is no laughing matter.

JOEL

For the prophet Joel, whose very name means "Jehovah is God," repentance was serious business. His message was filled with it. Unfortunately, many people—even Christian believers—consider repentance to be a rather dry event. But the words that Joel associates with repentance are active and painful ones, not easily tossed aside with a "hey I'm sorry" prayer on the run. "Weep, wail, lament, be ashamed, consecrate a fast, call a sacred assembly, cry out to the Lord, turn to God with all your heart, and rend your heart." Joel used these animated words of painful emotion and penitent activity to describe the trauma of genuine remorse.

> Joel used these animated words of painful emotion and penitent activity to describe the trauma of genuine remorse.

Like Amos, Joel visited the theme of the "Day of the Lord." This was a very sad day for those who had rebelled against the Lord, and that included those living in Jerusalem—there was no home-field advantage there.

> Blow the trumpet in Zion,
> And sound an alarm in My holy mountain!
> Let all the inhabitants of the land tremble;
> For the day of the Lord is coming,
> For it is at hand:
> A day of darkness and gloominess,
> A day of clouds and thick darkness,
> Like the morning clouds spread over the mountains.
> A people come, great and strong,
> The like of whom has never been;

> *Nor will there ever be any such after them,*
> *Even for many successive generations.*
> *A fire devours before them,*
> *And behind them a flame burns;*
> *The land is like the Garden of Eden before them,*
> *And behind them a desolate wilderness;*
> *Surely nothing shall escape them.* (Joel 2:1–3)

Joel was saying that the Day of the Lord would be a terrible time of pillage and plunder, worse than anything that had been wrought on the Israelites by their enemies. In fact, later in this same chapter, this vicious army was designated as an army under the command of a Holy and Righteous God.

But God's mercy continues to be poured out on His undeserving nation.

> *"Now, therefore," says the LORD,*
> *"Turn to Me with all your heart,*
> *With fasting, with weeping, and with mourning."*
> *So rend your heart, and not your garments;*
> *Return to the LORD your God,*
> *For He is gracious and merciful,*
> *Slow to anger, and of great kindness;*
> *And He relents from doing harm.* (Joel 2:12–13)

In the same spirit of Hosea, who was called to "be" rather than "say," Joel admonished the tradition-bound Jews to do more than symbolic things that represented contrition. "Break your heart," he admonished, "don't just do something external like tear your clothing. Truly repent."

Perhaps the best-known passage from Joel is the following:

> *And it shall come to pass afterward*
> *That I will pour out My Spirit on all flesh;*
> *Your sons and your daughters shall prophesy,*
> *Your old men shall dream dreams,*
> *Your young men shall see visions.*

And also on My menservants and on My maidservants
I will pour out My Spirit in those days.
And I will show wonders in the heavens and in the earth:
Blood and fire and pillars of smoke.
The sun shall be turned into darkness,
And the moon into blood,
Before the coming of the great and awesome day of the LORD.
And it shall come to pass
That whoever calls on the name of the LORD Shall be saved.
For in Mount Zion and in Jerusalem there shall be deliverance,
As the LORD has said,
Among the remnant whom the LORD calls. (Joel 2:28–32)

The apostle Peter spoke these words on the Day of Pentecost. Forty days had passed since the ascension of Jesus to heaven. Many believers were gathered, and suddenly, there was a mighty rushing wind that blew through the crowd. Just as suddenly, flames appeared over the heads of the believers. The followers of Christ began to praise Him, many in languages they had never spoken before. Some in the crowd mocked them, but Peter pointed to this prophecy, calling that Day of Pentecost the fulfillment of Joel's words.

MICAH

Any quick scan of late-night television programming is sure to produce a plethora of feature-length advertisements—infomercials—selling car wax and weight loss, relationship mending videos and power tools. One of the things you'll notice about these plunderers of the airwaves is that their solutions to people's problems are quick and painless: "Weight loss without work," or "It's as easy as one, two, three."

I have been involved in adult education all my life. As I teach, especially in the areas of theology or doctrine, I often enter some fairly deep waters, uncovering rather complicated ideas. Often, someone will raise an objection.

"R. C.," they'll plead, "we're supposed to have the faith of a child, not of a philosopher. Why can't you just keep it simple?"

My response is usually that while God *does* require a child-*like* faith, He does not approve of a child-*ish* conviction. Coming into fellowship with God is a simple act of responding to God's mercy and love. But comprehending His truth, and experiencing a lifetime of fruitfulness, takes sheer discipline—a lot of hard work. The study of the things of God requires a rigorous use of our minds. Most of the time, our religion is not as easy as A, B, C.

Notice that I say, "most of the time," because sometimes in Holy Scripture, the essence of our faith is consolidated into terse and succinct summaries, profound in their simplicity. Such a statement is found in the prophecy of Micah.

> *[God] has shown you, O man, what is good;*
> *And what does the LORD require of you*
> *But to do justly,*
> *To love mercy,*
> *And to walk humbly with your God?* (Micah 6:8)

Although this may make good infomercial copy because it gets right to the point, no one would ever be able to say that these things are "easy" steps: to act justly, love mercy, or walk humbly with God.

To the contrary, these three dimensions of obedience before a Holy God take a lifetime of discipline and self-denial.

Act Justly

For the believer, doing justly is not optional, it's standard equipment. Whether enacting justice involves a social issue or one of personal conduct—doing the right thing—God requires that we not look the other way when His precepts are blatantly disregarded.

Love Mercy

God requires that we not only do what is right, but also that our relationships be characterized by love and loyalty. The Hebrew word here, translated as "mercy," also means "steadfast or loyal love." This is no easy task; Jesus admonished us to "love our enemies; bless those who curse us; do good to those who hate us; and pray for those who spitefully use and persecute us."

Actually, I misspoke. Loving mercy isn't a *difficult* task at all; it's *impossible* apart from God's grace and indwelling power.

Walk Humbly with God

For many years, *Coram Deo* has been the banner under which our ministry has been operated. This is a Latin phrase, which means "before the face of God." As a business leader, a teacher, and a man, I must live my life in consistent awareness that everything I do, say, and think is before the presence of a Holy God.

As I said, Micah boiled a lifetime of hard work into three succinct phrases. These are simple to understand, but far from simplistic.

Micah's prophecy was unswerving in its announcement of God's judgment on the sins of the people. He courageously went nose to nose with them, especially those in leadership who had abandoned their call.

> *Now hear this,*
> *You heads of the house of Jacob*
> *And rulers of the house of Israel,*
> *Who abhor justice*
> *And pervert all equity,*
> *Who build up Zion with bloodshed*
> *And Jerusalem with iniquity:*
> *Her heads judge for a bribe,*
> *Her priests teach for pay,*
> *And her prophets divine for money.*
> *Yet they lean on the LORD, and say,*
> *"Is not the LORD among us?*
> *No harm can come upon us."*
> *Therefore because of you*
> *Zion shall be plowed like a field,*
> *Jerusalem shall become heaps of ruins,*
> *And the mountain of the temple*
> *Like the bare hills of the forest.* (Micah 3:9–12)

Like several other prophets whom you and I have met, Micah was given the privilege of looking into the future and announcing the coming Incarnate Son of God. Micah told the people exactly where Jesus was to be born.

> *But you, Bethlehem Ephrathah,*
> *Though you are little among the thousands of Judah,*
> *Yet out of you shall come forth to Me*
> *The One to be Ruler in Israel,*
> *Whose goings forth are from of old,*
> *From everlasting.* (Micah 5:2)

Micah not only gave us the one, two, three of obedience to God, he gave us the newborn Messiah's mailing address, too. What a prophet.

HABAKKUK

This was a prophet filled with intense passion. Habakkuk reminds me of a coach, impatiently pacing the sidelines and calling orders to his players on the field. Listen to his words.

> *O LORD, how long shall I cry,*
> *And You will not hear?*
> *Even cry out to You, "Violence!"*
> *And You will not save.*
> *Why do You show me iniquity,*
> *And cause me to see trouble?*
> *For plundering and violence are before me;*
> *There is strife, and contention arises.*
> *Therefore the law is powerless,*
> *And justice never goes forth.*
> *For the wicked surround the righteous;*
> *Therefore perverse judgment proceeds.* (Habakkuk 1:2–4)

Habakkuk's words have a familiar ring to them. Christians down through the ages have cried out to God, "How long, O Lord?" In the face of injustice, pain, and hunger, believers have struggled to see their way toward resolution. We cannot imagine how God can be good and powerful and allow such sin to continue, especially among His own people.

The restless and impatient prophet climbed a symbolic military tower to call again to the Lord. I'm not sure what he hoped to accomplish by doing this, but it was rarely productive to get in the way of an impetuous prophet.

This time, God replied to Habakkuk's pleadings.

> Then the LORD answered me and said:
> "Write the vision
> And make it plain on tablets,
> That he may run who reads it.
> For the vision is yet for an appointed time;
> But at the end it will speak, and it will not lie.
> Though it tarries, wait for it;
> Because it will surely come, It will not tarry.
> Behold the proud,
> His soul is not upright in him;
> But the just shall live by his faith." (Habakkuk 2:2–4)

"Be patient," God told Habakkuk. "My word will come in My time." And then the Sovereign God gave Habakkuk the single most significant doctrinal truth found in all of Holy Scripture. This was a truth carried throughout the New Testament, especially by the apostle Paul and his writings found in the book of Romans. In the sixteenth century, it became the watch-cry of the Protestant Reformers. "The just shall live by faith."

The prophet Habakkuk, here at the close of the Old Testament, gives us another account of a man who had the singular privilege and terrorizing opportunity to enter the presence of a Holy God.

> God came from Teman,
> The Holy One from Mount Paran.
> His glory covered the heavens,

And the earth was full of His praise.

His brightness was like the light;

He had rays flashing from His hand,

And there His power was hidden . . .

When I heard, my body trembled;

My lips quivered at the voice;

Rottenness entered my bones;

And I trembled in myself,

That I might rest in the day of trouble.

When he comes up to the people,

He will invade them with his troops. (Habakkuk 3:3–4, 16)

What a familiar story this has become: Moses, Isaiah, and even Nebuchadnezzar . . . seeing the reflected glory of a Holy God and being completely overwhelmed by the experience.

Finally, the great hymn of conquering faith at the end of the record of Habakkuk's prophecies is one of the most inspiring passages in the Scriptures.

Though the fig tree may not blossom,

Nor fruit be on the vines;

Though the labor of the olive may fail,

And the fields yield no food;

Though the flock may be cut off from the fold,

And there be no herd in the stalls—

Yet I will rejoice in the LORD,

I will joy in the God of my salvation.

The LORD God is my strength;

He will make my feet like deer's feet,

And He will make me walk on my high hills. (Habakkuk 3:17–19)

Habakkuk had learned his lesson. He could wait on the blessings of the Lord as well as the justice of God, and be of good courage because God alone knew the right time to deliver them both.

- Amos and Hosea
- Joel, Micah, and Habakkuk
- **Jonah**

Once upon a time a great fish swallowed a rebellious prophet. After a few days, the fish threw up, sending the same prophet, his skin probably bleached white by the intestinal fluids of this sea monster, onto the beach.

When someone tells you a story that seems outrageous, even though they purport to be telling the truth, you look for other, perhaps more reliable, sources to confirm the story's veracity—a second opinion. What if Jesus Christ Himself confirmed accuracy of the tale?

> *For as Jonah was three days and three nights*
> *in the belly of the great fish,*
> *so will the Son of Man be three days and three nights*
> *in the heart of the earth.* (Matthew 12:40)

In the case of most of the other prophets, we learn of their message by reading their words, their bold declarations to the people. But in the book of Jonah, we discover something of God's judgment and mercy in the narrative of one man's life.

Jonah, a prophet of the Northern Kingdom, was the son of Amittai, also a prophet of God. We are not told what time of day it was when the word of the Lord came to him, but it may have been in the night. Scripture tells us that once he had heard God's voice and had determined to disobey, "Jonah *arose* to flee to Tarshish from the presence of the LORD."

Can you see this man, tired of facing God's wayward and sinful people, soundly sleeping, trying to rest from the rigors of the call? And can you see him being rudely awakened by the sound of a voice—a familiar voice, One Who had welcomed him into the ministry? And can you see him arising—getting out of bed in a flash—packing a few of his things and taking off in the other direction?

It is interesting to me that there is no record of Jonah arguing with God. Life was tough enough exposing the sin of God's people and calling them to repentance. But an assignment to Nineveh was sheer madness. This was a city of 600,000 people, the capital of Assyria. One man against this godless metropolis, warning the pagan leaders of divine judgment, was certain suicide.

> Life was tough enough exposing the sin of God's people and calling them to repentance.

So instead of taking the five-hundred-mile journey to the east, Jonah boarded a Spain-bound ship, going two thousand miles to the west.

Jonah may have been tired. The mantle of the prophet of God may have become unbearably heavy. But Jonah should have known better. He should have known *much* better than this.

> *But Jonah arose to flee to Tarshish*
> *from the presence of the Lord.* (Jonah 1:3a)

Can you imagine a prophet of God, a man completely familiar with the mighty acts of the Holy One of Israel, deciding to run from His presence? But fatigue, even fatigue from doing God's work, can lead a man to do foolish things.

> *And let us not grow weary while doing good,*
> *for in due season we shall reap*
> *if we do not lose heart.* (Galatians 6:9)

Jonah must have lost heart. He must have got tired of "doing good." He must have lost the assurance that when God called a man, He always promised to go first.

Even more miraculous than God sending a fish to swallow the prophet is listening in on Jonah's conversation with God from the belly of the fish, and seeing a profound change of heart.

> *In my distress I called to the Lord,*
> *and he answered me.*
> *From the depths of the grave I called for help,*
> *and you listened to my cry.*

You hurled me into the deep,
into the very heart of the seas,
and the currents swirled about me;
all your waves and breakers swept over me.
I said, "I have been banished from your sight;
yet I will look again toward your holy temple." . . .
When my life was ebbing away,
I remembered you, LORD,
and my prayer rose to you, to your holy temple.
Those who cling to worthless idols
forfeit the grace that could be theirs.
But I, with a song of thanksgiving, will sacrifice to you.
What I have vowed I will make good.
Salvation comes from the LORD. (Jonah 2:1b–4, 7–9 NIV)

One of the most rampant sins that had beset the Hebrews was the sin of idolatry. Time and time again, God's promise of punishment and death came to those who had crafted images to worship. But from the inside of a fish, swimming deep somewhere in the Eastern Mediterranean Sea, the prophet, a man of God, got a glimpse of his own "worthless idols," in contrast to the priceless gifts from his Creator. They were all Jonah's, free for the taking.

The message of the prophet Jonah is a message to those who are involved in "welldoing." As a teacher of good things and author of good words, I can identify with this. I can identify with placing too much stock in my calling, assigning eternal value to these gifts because they have spiritual content— worshiping the "creation" rather than the "Creator."

And as a son of Adam, I can certainly identify with "growing weary."

All of these are worthless idols. Jonah learned of them and faced them the hard way, seaweed wrapped around his head in the dank entrails of the great fish appointed by God.

But Jonah's message to you and me is a simple one: "You cling to these idols, you forfeit God's mighty gift of grace."

This was a message Jonah needed to hear. And one you and I ought to listen to as well.

SUMMARY

■ AMOS

The prophet Amos was not a happy man. The opening lines in his book told the Jews that their lives were a wreck.

He used an easily understandable analogy of a carpenter's level—a plumb line—to point out how far they had tilted from the truth. The image was powerful. The Lord God stood on a wall that represented His people, the Israelites. Although He didn't say it here, I surmise that the wall was not straight and true. Either the original builder had been sloppy in his construction or time and weather had deteriorated the wall, rendering it crooked. Either way it didn't matter. The wall was not straight. In order to make His point, God dropped a plumb line—a long string with a heavy weight at one end—next to the wall. To the naked eye, the wall may have seemed fine. But next to the perfectly vertical plumb line, the wall's imperfection became readily apparent.

The focus of Amos's word to God's chosen people was immorality, religious apostasy, and social injustice. All of these things render a nation's walls deformed and useless—good for nothing but tearing down.

Amos preached on a subject that predated the ministry of the prophets: the "Day of the Lord." For thousands of years, Jews had longed for the day that God Himself would come to destroy the wicked and save the righteous. This was to be a good day for saints, but a bad day for the unrepentant sinner.

Amos prophesied that those who were looking for the Day of the Lord would be surprised, because while they were looking for God to judge other nations, other people, other tribes—He would first judge them. The people may walk into the street, only to be chased by a lion. They would flee down an alley, only to run into a bear. And if they finally reached the safety of their own home, they would close the door behind them, breathe a sigh of relief, put out their hand to steady themselves, and a snake would bite them. For some, the Day of the Lord will be a very, very bad day, indeed.

■ HOSEA

Exactly as Jesus had commanded His disciples to "go and be," the Sovereign God told Hosea to *experience* the message before *preaching* it. "Just so you know what it feels like to be Me," the Lord was saying to the prophet, "go marry someone who has no idea what faithfulness, loyalty, and fidelity mean."

Obediently, Hosea sought a prostitute named Gomer to be his bride. By his wife, Hosea had three children: two sons and a daughter. God directed Hosea to name his children "God plants," "she received no compassion," and "not my people."

Not only did God call Hosea to say to the people, "thus says the LORD," He also filled Hosea's family scrapbook with visible reminders of "given how You have treated Me, this is how it feels to be God."

In many ways, Hosea became the incarnation—a word in human flesh—of God's message of judgment and redemption.

Once the children had been born, God ordered Hosea to release his wife, divorce her, and turn her loose. But even in returning to the streets, Gomer would not find satisfaction.

Unfortunately for Hosea, God was not finished with him. God told Hosea to go find his estranged wife, bring her home, and marry her again.

Like no other prophet, Hosea placed his own life on the altar of fairness. God seemingly took advantage of his availability and obedience, forcing him into fathering a pathetic and broken family. But instead of being filled with anger and resentment, Hosea's prophetic message to his people was filled with tenderness and compassion. No wonder God chose him for this horrific assignment.

■ JOEL

For the prophet Joel, repentance was serious business. His message was filled with it. Unfortunately, many people—even Christian believers—consider repentance to be a rather dry event. But the words that Joel associates with repentance are active and painful ones, not easily tossed aside with a "hey I'm sorry" prayer on the run. "Weep, wail, lament, be ashamed, consecrate a fast, call a sacred assembly, cry out to the Lord, turn to God with all your heart, and rend your heart." Joel used these animated words of painful emotion and penitent activity to describe the trauma of genuine remorse.

Joel reminded the people that God's judgment would be worse than anything that had been wrought on the Israelites by their enemies. But God's mercy continued to be poured out on His undeserving nation.

In the same spirit of Hosea, who was called to "be" rather than "say," Joel admonished the tradition-bound Jews to do more than symbolic things that represented contrition. "Break your heart," he admonished, "not just your clothing. Truly repent."

▪ MICAH

For the prophet Micah, the essence of our faith is consolidated into terse and succinct summaries, profound in their simplicity. Such a statement is found in the prophecy of Micah: Do justly, love mercy, and walk humbly with your God.

These three dimensions of obedience before a Holy God take a lifetime of discipline and self-denial. Micah boiled a lifetime of hard work into three succinct phrases. These are simple to understand, but far from simplistic.

Micah's prophecy was unswerving in its announcement of God's judgment on the sins of the people. He courageously went nose to nose with them, especially those in leadership who had abandoned their call.

Like several other prophets, Micah was given the privilege of looking into the future and announcing the coming Incarnate Son of God. Micah told the people exactly where Jesus was to be born.

▪ HABAKKUK

Habakkuk was a prophet filled with intense passion. Christians down through the ages have cried out to God, "How long, O Lord?" In the face of injustice, pain, and hunger, believers have struggled to see their way toward resolution. We cannot imagine how God can be good and powerful and allow such sin to continue, especially among His own people.

The restless and impatient prophet climbed a symbolic military tower to call again to the Lord. I'm not sure what he hoped to accomplish by doing this, but it was rarely productive to get in the way of an impetuous prophet.

"Be patient," God told Habakkuk. "My word will come in My time." And then the Sovereign God gave Habakkuk the single most significant doctrinal truth found in all of Holy Scripture. This was a truth carried throughout the New Testament, especially by the apostle Paul and his writings found in the book of Romans. In the sixteenth century, it became the watch-cry of the Protestant reformers: "The just shall live by faith."

▓ JONAH

In the case of most of the other prophets, we learn of their message by reading their words, their bold declarations to the people. But in the book of Jonah, we discover something of God's judgment and mercy in the narrative of one man's life.

Jonah, a prophet of the Northern Kingdom, was the son of Amittai, also a prophet of God. We are not told what time of day it was when the word of the Lord came to him, but it may have been in the night. Scripture tells us that once he had heard God's voice and had determined to disobey, "Jonah *arose* to flee to Tarshish from the presence of the LORD."

Can you see this man, tired of facing God's wayward and sinful people, soundly sleeping, trying to rest from the rigors of the call? And can you see him being rudely awakened by the sound of a voice—a familiar voice, One who had welcomed him into the ministry? And can you see him arising—getting out of bed in a flash—packing a few of his things and taking off in the other direction?

Can you imagine a prophet of God, a man completely familiar with the mighty acts of the Holy One of Israel, deciding to run from His presence? But fatigue, even fatigue from doing God's work, can lead a man to do foolish things.

Even more miraculous than God sending a fish to swallow the prophet is listening in on Jonah's conversation with God from the belly of the fish, and seeing a profound change of heart.

CHAPTER NINE

RETURNING HOME

- Ezra and Nehemiah

There's just something about going home.

If you ever went to camp as a kid you know this feeling. And even though most eighteen-year-olds don't like to admit it, during that first semester at college—far from home—there were profound experiences of homesickness, too.

Coming home after camp or that first glimpse of the old homestead after a few months in a dormitory filled your heart with indescribable joy. Remember?

EZRA

The historical book, probably one of the final books to be written in the Old Testament, that describes the resettlement of the Hebrew people in their homeland was written by Ezra the priest. After fifty years of exile, many of the Israelites were desperately homesick.

The Persian Empire had defeated Babylon. However, unlike the Babylonians, Persia allowed the inhabitants of its conquered nations to stay in place, sending in a resident ruling governor to lead them. Traditionally, the Persians were known for their religious tolerance, which explains the proclamation of King Cyrus allowing the Jewish people to return to Jerusalem and rebuild their Temple. He would have also been in favor of spreading his domain several hundred miles to the west.

> *Thus says Cyrus king of Persia:*
> *All the kingdoms of the earth the LORD God of heaven has given me.*
> *And He has commanded me to build Him a house at Jerusalem*
> *which is in Judah.*

> *Who is among you of all His people?*
> *May his God be with him,*
> *and let him go up to Jerusalem which is in Judah,*
> *and build the house of the LORD God of Israel (He is God),*
> *which is in Jerusalem.* (Ezra 1:2–3)

The book of Ezra opens with King Cyrus issuing a decree that "the word of the LORD by the mouth of Jeremiah might be fulfilled." The text adds, "The LORD stirred up the spirit of Cyrus king of Persia." Remember that this man was the monarch of a thoroughly pagan empire that worshiped multiple gods. Cyrus would not have been a viable candidate to teach the adult Sunday school class down at First Presbyterian Church. So how is it that his decree sounds as though it could have been written by a prophet or a priest? Good question.

As we have seen throughout the movements of the Sovereign God of Abraham, Isaac, and Jacob, He will do whatever needs to be done with whomever He needs to move—willing or not—to accomplish His purposes. In fact, throughout the process of the return, the Hebrews praised God, not Cyrus, for the chance to return to Jerusalem. Of course, I'm sure they were grateful to the Persian king, but he was only following orders from the King of kings.

So the people packed their belongings and made the journey to their homeland, all 42,360 of them, not counting 7,337 servants and the 200 members of the Israeli choir.

When they arrived at the ruins of what was once their revered and holy Temple, they presented a sacrifice to God.

> *And when the seventh month had come,*
> *and the children of Israel were in the cities,*
> *the people gathered together as one man to Jerusalem.*
> *Then Jeshua the son of Jozadak and his brethren the priests,*
> *and Zerubbabel the son of Shealtiel and his brethren,*
> *arose and built the altar of the God of Israel,*
> *to offer burnt offerings on it,*

as it is written in the Law of Moses
the man of God.
Though fear had come upon them
because of the people of those countries,
they set the altar on its bases;
and they offered burnt offerings on it to the LORD,
both the morning and evening burnt offerings.
They also kept the Feast of Tabernacles,
as it is written, and offered the daily burnt offerings
in the number required by ordinance for each day. (Ezra 3:1–4)

What an amazing scene this was. The people had finished their journey back to their homeland. And they knew, even though they had been guilty of idolatry and disobedience for generations, that the first order of business was to worship. And so they gathered together "as one man"—a perfect word picture for the apostle Paul's reference to God's worshiping people as "the body of Christ"—to praise the Holy One of Israel.

> As these Jews stood among the ruins, broken shards of marble and stone crunching beneath their feet, their repentant souls were ready to be in God's presence, and He was pleased. His sanctuary—their hearts—was not in disrepair.

Where once they had stood among the beauty and grandeur of Solomon's Temple, crumbled walls and debris now surrounded them. But it did not matter. God had warned Samuel when he was selecting a new king from among Jesse's sons, "Man looks on the outward appearance, but God looks on the heart." As these Jews stood among the ruins, broken shards of marble and stone crunching beneath their feet, their repentant souls were ready to be in God's presence, and He was pleased. His sanctuary—their hearts—was not in disrepair.

And so began the process of the rebuilding of the great Temple. Once the rubble had been cleared the work was under way. One of the great moments of this return came when the workers had completed the reconstructed foundation.

> *When the builders laid the foundation of the temple of the LORD,*
> *the priests stood in their apparel with trumpets,*
> *and the Levites, the sons of Asaph, with cymbals, to praise the LORD,*
> *according to the ordinance of David king of Israel.*
> *And they sang responsively,*
> *praising and giving thanks to the LORD:*
> *"For He is good,*
> *For His mercy endures forever toward Israel."*
> *Then all the people shouted with a great shout,*
> *when they praised the LORD,*
> *because the foundation of the house of the LORD*
> *was laid.* (Ezra 3:10–11)

Can you imagine this sight? All of this music and celebration . . . and for what . . . the laying of the foundation?

Absolutely. These people were ecstatic because they were home, and now the place where they gathered as one people, God's house, was under way. This was no ordinary foundation.

> *For we are God's fellow workers;*
> *you are God's field, you are God's building . . .*
> *For no other foundation can anyone lay than that which is laid,*
> *which is Jesus Christ . . .*
> *Do you not know that you are the temple of God and that*
> *the Spirit of God dwells in you?* (1 Corinthians 3:9, 11, 16)

The author of these words was the apostle Paul, a devout and educated Jew. He knew full well what had happened that day at the celebration of the laying of the Temple foundation. This was far more than a building project. It represented God's mercy, it represented God's plan for redemption through the promised Messiah, and it represented the presence of the Holy Spirit within the hearts of His chosen people.

Without any hesitation, I can assure you that the elderly men who witnessed the completion of the foundation also understood.

But many of the priests and Levites
and heads of the fathers' houses,
old men who had seen the first temple,
wept with a loud voice when the foundation of the temple
was laid before their eyes.
Yet many shouted aloud for joy,
so that the people could not discern the noise of the shout of joy
from the noise of the weeping of the people,
for the people shouted with a loud shout,
and the sound was heard afar off. (Ezra 3:12–13)

Any man who has witnessed the birth of his child, the successful completion of a business plan, or his favorite team winning the Super Bowl or the World Series can fully appreciate this moment—an indescribable blend of weeping and euphoria. These old men had seen it all. Although Ezra does not mention this, I wonder if they were a part of the 10 percent remnant promised to Isaiah (Isa. 6). They had endured the troubling reigns of idolatrous kings and vile practices within the walls of this holy Temple. They had faithfully prayed for this moment, no doubt on their knees with one another—sometimes in the midst of seeming hopelessness. And now, "before their eyes" was the fulfillment of their greatest dream. No wonder there were tears of joy.

The work on the Temple was steady while Cyrus was in power, but when his successor, Artaxerxes, ascended to the throne of Persia, the work on the Temple was halted for a time. Ezra returned to Babylon to settle a dispute that arose among Artaxerxes' administration regarding the Israelites' rebuilding of their "rebellious and evil" city. In fact, troops were dispatched to Jerusalem to stop the reconstruction.

Eventually, the dispute was settled and the Temple was completed.

Then the children of Israel,
the priests and the Levites and the rest of the descendants of the captivity,
celebrated the dedication of this house of God with joy.
And they offered sacrifices at the dedication of this house of God,
one hundred bulls, two hundred rams, four hundred lambs,

and as a sin offering for all Israel twelve male goats,
according to the number of the tribes of Israel.
They assigned the priests to their divisions
and the Levites to their divisions,
over the service of God in Jerusalem,
as it is written in the Book of Moses. (Ezra 6:16–18)

Not only was the physical structure of the Temple now completed, but the Israelites also reestablished the purposes of the House of God—contrition by way of a costly sacrifice and entrance to the presence of a Holy God through worship.

As is always the case when God's people repent and reverence Him, they were bound together in love and fellowship.

> Not only was the physical structure of the Temple now completed, but the Israelites also reestablished the purposes of the House of God.

Then the children of Israel who had returned from the captivity
ate together with all who had separated themselves from the filth
of the nations of the land
in order to seek the LORD God of Israel. (Ezra 6:21)

There will be a covered-dish supper
On the Eastern Porch
Immediately following the sin sacrifice and worship
Praising God for the
Newly Rebuilt Temple
Reuben, Simeon, Levi: vegetables
Judah, Issachar, Zebulun: wheat loaves
Dan, Naphtali, Gad: fruits and nuts
Asher, Joseph, Benjamin: milk and honey
Bring your own wineskin.
Grilled beef and mutton will be provided.

It isn't very hard to imagine that over the past fifty years in Babylon, the Israelites had picked up some bad habits, in spite of the faithful ministries of Ezekiel, Jeremiah, and Daniel. And pagan behavior wasn't all they had picked up—they had also married forbidden foreigners.

Ezra spoke to the people regarding this breach of the covenant with God, concerned that the extent of this sin might lead to His ultimate judgment on them. He was afraid that even a remnant might not survive if God were to judge them for the magnitude of this sin. He remembered that God had spoken so clearly that if Israel disregarded the Law, she would forfeit the blessings and have to endure the punishment for it.

As we have seen so many times before, Ezra didn't try to make a defense. He quoted from the Book of the Law, which was perfectly capable of speaking for itself.

> When the LORD your God brings you into the land
> which you go to possess,
> and has cast out many nations before you . . .
> And when the LORD your God delivers them over to you,
> you shall conquer them and utterly destroy them.
> You shall make no covenant with them nor show mercy to them.
> Nor shall you make marriages with them.
> You shall not give your daughter to their son,
> nor take their daughter for your son.
> For they will turn your sons away from following Me,
> to serve other gods;
> so the anger of the LORD will be aroused against you
> and destroy you suddenly. (Deuteronomy 7:1–4)

Ezra was understandably frightened at the specter of the final phrase from this command coming true, so he urged the release of these illegitimate brides (nothing is said of the grooms). Imagine the pain the people must have experienced in obeying Ezra. They knew that they had disobeyed the Law and must repent. Is there any doubt that there was an outpouring of grief across the land as these husbands said good-bye to their wives, with wailing children clinging to their mothers' skirts? Disobedience to the commands of a Holy God had devastating consequences.

The words of the prophet Joel had to be ringing in their ears.

> *Rend your heart . . .*
> *Return to the LORD your God,*
> *For He is gracious and merciful,*
> *Slow to anger, and of great kindness.* (Joel 2:13)

Repentance—separation from sinful deeds—was painful, but not as severe as facing the anger of the Sovereign God. And so the people obeyed.

With the Temple reconstructed, the people of God once again had a place to sacrifice, to worship, and to gather. However, because the city and its surrounding wall had been destroyed by the Babylonians, the Temple was vulnerable to the aggression of foreign powers.

> Repentance—separation from sinful deeds—was painful, but not as severe as facing the anger of the Sovereign God. And so the people obeyed.

Someone had to do something about the wall.

NEHEMIAH

On January 17, 1994, at 3:35 in the morning, an earthquake rocked Southern California. Hitting 7.1 on the Richter scale, the Northridge earthquake collapsed buildings and highway overpasses as though they were children's toys.

Joni Eareckson Tada and her husband, Ken, were sound asleep when the quake hit. Since they're veteran residents of this part of the world, they knew exactly what was happening. Ken immediately threw himself on top of his wife's body, since Joni is a quadriplegic and could do nothing to protect herself from falling objects. In thirty-five seconds, the earthquake was over, but its devastating effects were everywhere.

Even though Joni and Ken were not hurt and their house was not structurally damaged, the kitchen cabinets had been summarily emptied of their contents. Wedding china and pantry staples had fallen from their shelves, and framed pictures had come crashing down from the walls.

Before beginning the process of cleaning up, Ken wheeled Joni to their back porch, overlooking the valley where the earthquake had just struck. As she gazed into the darkness, with flashing lights from emergency units just beginning to arrive all across the basin below, Joni looked up at the early morning sky, still dark but filled with a panoply of stars.

As she frequently does, Joni began to sing. She chose one of her favorite songs.

> *Our God is an awesome God,*
> *He reigns from heaven above,*
> *With wisdom, power, and love,*
> *Our God is an awesome God.*

Early that chilly winter morning, God had spoken.

Throughout history, God has spoken in earthquakes, windstorms, and still, small voices. But how do you know when God is calling you? And how did the people in the Old Testament know when He was calling them?

For Nehemiah, God's call came in the form of a broken heart.

> *It came to pass . . . that Hanani one of my brethren*
> *came with men from Judah;*
> *and I asked them concerning the Jews who had escaped,*
> *who had survived the captivity,*
> *and concerning Jerusalem.*
> *And they said to me,*
> *"The survivors who are left from the captivity in the province*
> *are there in great distress and reproach.*
> *The wall of Jerusalem is also broken down,*
> *and its gates are burned with fire."*
> *So it was, when I heard these words,*
> *that I sat down and wept, and mourned for many days; I was fasting*
> *and praying before the God of heaven.* (Nehemiah 1:1b–4)

Nehemiah was the cupbearer to King Artaxerxes. This was not the "food taster" of medieval courts, but a high-ranking position that involved offering counsel to the king. Nehemiah was a member of the royal court, a highly trusted individual. In his position, he would have lived in the palace of the king, surrounded by opulence he would never have known in Judah. But the riches surrounding him could not stop the tears over the broken walls and gates of Jerusalem.

> You can take a man out of the Promised Land, but you cannot take the Promised Land out of a man—at least not Nehemiah.

You can take a man out of the Promised Land, but you cannot take the Promised Land out of a man—at least not Nehemiah. His broken spirit and longing for his homeland drove him to his knees.

> *I pray, LORD God of heaven, O great and awesome God,*
> *You who keep Your covenant and mercy with those who love You*
> *and observe Your commandments, please let Your ear be attentive*
> *and Your eyes open, that You may hear the prayer of Your servant*
> *which I pray before You now, day and night,*
> *for the children of Israel Your servants,*
> *and confess the sins of the children of Israel*
> *which we have sinned against You.*
> *Both my father's house and I have sinned.* (Nehemiah 1:5–6)

This certainly doesn't sound like the prayer of a man who is struck with the reality of evil in the world. There's no hint of, "Oh, God, how could You let this happen to Your people?" This is a prayer of adoration, reverence, and clear acknowledgment of the sovereignty of a Holy God.

Nehemiah knew full well why the destruction of Jerusalem and the exile had fallen on the Southern Kingdom; his nation, his "father's house," and Nehemiah himself had sinned.

And Nehemiah knew that God was calling him to return to Jerusalem to direct the rebuilding of the wall. As his prayer continued, Nehemiah asked that the heart of Artaxerxes be softened to his request for a leave of absence.

And it came to pass . . . that I took the wine and gave it to the king.
Now I had never been sad in his presence before.
Therefore the king said to me,
"Why is your face sad, since you are not sick?
This is nothing but sorrow of heart."
So I became dreadfully afraid, and said to the king,
"May the king live forever!
Why should my face not be sad,
when the city, the place of my fathers' tombs,
lies waste, and its gates are burned with fire?"
Then the king said to me, "What do you request?"
So I prayed to the God of heaven. And I said to the king,
"If it pleases the king, and if your servant has found favor in your sight,
I ask that you send me to Judah,
to the city of my fathers' tombs, that I may rebuild it."
Then the king said to me (the queen also sitting beside him),
"How long will your journey be? And when will you return?"
So it pleased the king to send me; and I set him a time. (Nehemiah 2:1–6)

God graciously answered Nehemiah's prayer. The king's heart was pre-pared to hear Nehemiah's request; in fact, he was *so* ready that he initiated the conversation. "What's wrong?" Artaxerxes asked Nehemiah. "You look sad."

This comment from the king seemed tender and sensitive. So why did it strike fear in Nehemiah's heart? Nehemiah was terrified because in the court of the Medo-Persian kings, it was forbidden to show any negative emotions upon punishment of death. But Nehemiah was filled with courage as he over-came his fear and concisely told the king what was troubling him.

The king heard his plight and asked what he could do to help. As any of us would do under the same circumstances, Nehemiah shot up one of those prayers: "O God, please help me quick!" Miraculously, the king granted his request.

Can you imagine? Just as God had done with King Cyrus by opening his heart to allow the people to return to Jerusalem, *another* Persian king was divinely led to listen to God's voice and respond in obedience.

Our God *is* an awesome God.

What follows is one of the most dramatic chapters in Jewish history. Nehemiah and his entourage were given safe passage from Babylon to Jerusalem with papers that identified them as on a mission from the king. They were even given permission to gather the building materials they needed along their way to Jerusalem.

But once they arrived, the sheer physical challenge of rebuilding the wall wouldn't be the only challenge Nehemiah and his associates would face.

> *But it so happened, when Sanballat heard that we were rebuilding the wall,*
> *that he was furious and very indignant,*
> *and mocked the Jews.*
> *And he spoke before his brethren and the army of Samaria, and said,*
> *"What are these feeble Jews doing? Will they fortify themselves?*
> *Will they offer sacrifices? Will they complete it in a day?*
> *Will they revive the stones from the heaps of rubbish—*
> *stones that are burned?"*
> *Now Tobiah the Ammonite was beside him, and he said,*
> *"Whatever they build, if even a fox goes up on it,*
> *he will break down their stone wall."* (Nehemiah 4:1–3)

When you and I were kids, we were accomplices to one of the world's most vicious lies. We chanted it in our neighborhoods and it made us feel tough . . . but it wasn't the truth.

> *Sticks and stones may break my bones,*
> *But words will never hurt me.*

The words *did* hurt. The spirits of Nehemiah and his men were wounded by the mocking, but they were resolute to finish the task.

> *Hear, O our God,*
> *for we are despised;*
> *turn their reproach on their own heads,*

> *and give them as plunder to a land of captivity!* . . .
> *So we built the wall,*
> *and the entire wall was joined together up to half its height,*
> *for the people had a mind to work.* (Nehemiah 4:4, 6)

Sanballat and Tobiah saw that their derision had not done its work, so they conspired to attack the workers on the wall and, if necessary, to kill them. When Nehemiah heard of this plan, he set guards at the openings, ready to defend themselves. He also made a short speech to his leaders.

> *And I looked, and arose and said to the nobles, to the leaders,*
> *and to the rest of the people,*
> *"Do not be afraid of them.*
> *Remember the Lord, great and awesome,*
> *and fight for your brethren, your sons,*
> *your daughters, your wives, and your houses."*
> *And it happened, when our enemies heard that it was known to us,*
> *and that God had brought their plot to nothing,*
> *that all of us returned to the wall,*
> *everyone to his work.* (Nehemiah 4:14–15)

Once again, the Sovereign God intervened. He not only gave Nehemiah and his people the strength to defend their work, He went behind enemy lines and let Sanballat, Tobiah, and their fellow scoundrels know that they were up against far more than just a band of Hebrews. Even when the wall was completed, Nehemiah's adversaries truly knew why the Israelites had been successful.

> *So the wall was finished . . . in fifty-two days.*
> *And it happened, when all our enemies heard of it,* . . .
> *that they were very disheartened in their own eyes, for they perceived*
> *that this work was done by our God.* (Nehemiah 6:15–16)

Nehemiah's God . . . an awesome God indeed.

When the wall was completed, the task was not over. The Jews needed thorough reformation, a complete break with pagan comingling. Again, they had taken non-Israelites for wives and entrenched themselves in pagan customs—just what Ezra had warned against. Corruption even invaded the priesthood, but Nehemiah persevered in cleansing the Temple of disobedient clergy.

Nehemiah's story is a stark reminder that even under the most capable leadership, the people still needed a Savior. One who could bring more than reformation, but forgiveness of sin and binding reconciliation with a Holy God.

What they couldn't have known is that they would have to wait four hundred years for that dream to become a reality.

SUMMARY
■ EZRA

The book of Ezra opens with King Cyrus issuing a decree that "the word of the LORD spoken by the mouth of Jeremiah might be fulfilled." The text adds, "The LORD stirred up the spirit of Cyrus king of Persia."

He issued a decree, allowing the Jews to return to their homeland. As we have seen throughout the movements of the Sovereign God of Abraham, Isaac, and Jacob, He will do whatever needs to be done with whomever He needs to move—willing or not—to accomplish His purposes. In fact, throughout the process of the return, the Hebrews praised God, not Cyrus, for the chance to return to Jerusalem.

So the people packed their belongings and made the journey to their homeland, all 42,360 of them, not counting 7,337 servants and the 200 members of the Israeli choir.

When they arrived at the ruins of what was once their revered and holy Temple, they presented a sacrifice to God.

What an amazing scene this was. The people had finished their journey back to their homeland. And they knew, even though they had been guilty of idolatry and disobedience for generations, that the first order of business was to worship. And so they gathered together "as one man"—a perfect word picture for the apostle Paul's reference to God's worshiping people as "the body of Christ"—to praise the Holy One of Israel.

Where once they had stood among the beauty and grandeur of Solomon's Temple, crumbled walls and debris now surrounded them. But it did not matter. God had warned Samuel when he was selecting a new king from among Jesse's sons, "Man looks on the outward appearance, but God looks on the heart." As these Jews stood among the ruins, broken shards of marble and stone crunching beneath their feet, their repentant souls were ready to be in God's presence and He was pleased. His sanctuary—their hearts—was not in disrepair.

And so began the process of the rebuilding of the great Temple. Once the rubble had been cleared the work was under way. One of the great moments of this return came when the workers had completed the reconstructed foundation.

Can you imagine this sight? All of this music and celebration . . . and for what . . . the laying of the *foundation*?

Absolutely. These people were ecstatic because they were home and now the place where they gathered as one people, God's house, was under way. This was no ordinary foundation. This was far more than a building project. It represented God's mercy, it represented God's plan for redemption through the promised Messiah, and it represented the presence of the Holy Spirit within the hearts of His chosen people.

With the Temple reconstructed, the people of God once again had a place to sacrifice, to worship, and to gather. However, because the city and its surrounding wall had been destroyed by the Babylonians, the Temple was vulnerable to the aggression of foreign powers.

Someone had to do something about the wall.

■ NEHEMIAH

Throughout history, God has spoken in earthquakes, windstorms, and still, small voices. But how do you know when God is calling you? And how did the people in the Old Testament know when He was calling them?

For Nehemiah, God's call came in the form of a broken heart. He was a member of the royal court, a highly trusted individual. In his position, he would have lived in the palace of the king, surrounded by opulence he would never have known in Judah. But the riches surrounding him could not stop the tears over the broken walls and gates of Jerusalem. His longing for his homeland drove him to his knees.

Nehemiah knew full well why the destruction of Jerusalem and the Exile had fallen on the Southern Kingdom; his nation, his "father's house," and Nehemiah himself had sinned.

And Nehemiah knew that God was calling him to return to Jerusalem to direct the rebuilding of the wall. As his prayer continued, Nehemiah asked that the heart of Artaxerxes be softened to his request for a leave of absence.

God graciously answered Nehemiah's prayer. The king's heart was prepared to hear Nehemiah's request.

What follows is one of the most dramatic chapters in Jewish history. Nehemiah and his entourage were given safe passage from Babylon to Jerusalem with papers that identified them as on a mission from the king. They were even given permission to gather the building materials they needed along their way to Jerusalem.

But once they arrived, the sheer physical exertion of rebuilding the wall wouldn't be the only challenge Nehemiah and his associates would face. They were forced to deal with the discouragement that came from the verbal assaults of neighbors.

When the wall was completed, the task was not over. The Jews needed thorough reformation, a complete break with pagan comingling. Again, they had taken non-Israelites for wives and entrenched themselves in pagan customs—just what Ezra had warned against. Corruption even invaded the priesthood, but Nehemiah persevered in cleansing the Temple of disobedient clergy.

Nehemiah's story is a stark reminder that even under the most capable leadership, the people still needed a Savior. One who could bring more than reformation, but forgiveness of sin and binding reconciliation with a Holy God.

CHAPTER TEN

THE WISDOM BOOKS

- **Characteristics of Wisdom Literature**
- Psalms
- Ecclesiastes
- Job

Car racing: It's the number one spectator sport in the world. Right down the road from where we live is the Daytona International Speedway. Not long ago, on a quiet Sunday afternoon, I watched an hour of the greatest of all Winston Cup events, the Daytona 500.

All stereotypes aside, auto racing is an amazing sport. Around and around the two-and-a-half-mile track, the 3,500-pound machines traveled at 170 to 195 miles per hour. When all forty cars were packed together, no more than inches apart, they looked like a giant flock of birds, in perfect sequence and formation.

The noise from these unmuffled engines was deafening.

On this particular day, Dale Jarrett took the checkered flag. It was the third time he had won this race over the past decade. The CBS Sports announcer hurried his microphone to the pit area to get an interview with the crew chief. "Well, Todd," the announcer started, preparing to deliver another one of those brilliant postgame questions, "you did it." As it turned out, it wasn't a question at all.

The crew chief didn't say anything. I thought he must have been distracted or perhaps was not paying attention. And then I saw something I never would have expected in such a setting. I saw tears. "He could lose his credentials for this," I whispered to myself.

With the emotion of the moment and the tears that ensued, it took Todd Parrott, crew chief and card-carrying tough guy, a full minute to recover enough to speak a single word.

That Sunday afternoon, I saw an interesting snapshot of life. The race—the apostle Paul refers to life as a race—can be brutal. It's a dog-eat-dog, winner-take-all, and don't-make-a-mistake-or-you'll-get-passed-by-or-run-over world.

But what motivates us to run? Why do we do what we do? Where do we hide our anxieties and our fears? Who are we . . . really? When we look into our hearts, what do we see?

The tears of Dale Jarrett's crew chief that Sunday afternoon brought these questions to the forefront of my mind. They reminded me of the books of the Bible we call the Wisdom Books. And just as auto racing and tears are not incompatible, life and poetry can be harmonious friends.

Life in biblical times got pretty raucous: wars, slavery, avarice, adultery, murder, sibling rivalry, deception—sounds like a stock car race to me. But what was really happening in these people's hearts? Why did they act the way they did? What were their fears and motives? And how did all of these things affect them—on the inside? What was in their hearts?

As [a man] thinks in his heart, so is he. (Proverbs 23:7)

Solomon, the wisest of them all, knew that although some men may try to hide this fact, it's their *hearts* that make their decisions for them. A man's heart—the seat of all his emotions—motivates his drives and desires. Most of the time, it's a man's heart that affects his thinking, not the other way around.

The Bible's Wisdom Literature speaks to our hearts.

HEBREW POETRY

There were three books in the Old Testament canon that the Jews recognized as poetry. Those books were Psalms, Proverbs, and Job. They were plainly written in Hebrew verse. In contemporary biblical scholarship, we have a group of Bible books known as Wisdom Literature: Job, Psalms, Proverbs, Song of Solomon, Ecclesiastes, and in the New Testament, James. These books focus on philosophy, not the abstract speculation of the ancient Greeks, but a very practical love of wisdom.

The goal of the Wisdom Literature was a full understanding of how to live

a godly life, not simply the rigors of answering abstract questions—as important as that can be. This understanding could be known only when human
hearts and souls were in a posture of submission and humility before the
Lord: when men—and women—had stopped running the race and begun to
contemplate, to consider, and to feel.

To understand these books, we need to know something of poetry.
You and I have read poetry, perhaps even tried our hand at writing it. We
know about meter, rhythm, rhyme, and other elements in Western poetry.
But ancient Hebrew poetry was simpler. Rather than the rhyming of
sounds, Hebrew poetry rhymed ideas. The Jewish poets made plays on
words, puns, and used special meter. And, try as we might, all of it cannot
be translated.

During my time of study in Amsterdam several decades ago, I personally
experienced this challenge of translation. One day I walked downstairs and
happened to meet the landlady. She looked at me quizzically, as if to ask what
I was doing. "I'm taking a break from my studies," I tried to say in Dutch.
Unfortunately, "taking a break" does not translate well, so I changed the
word for "break" to *paus*. And, apparently, I didn't pronounce it well. What I
actually said to my Dutch friend was, "The pope has a hernia." A big fan of
the pontiff, she was very concerned.

In any case, even though translation of Hebrew poetry can be a challenge,
there are some clues to understanding it.

The primary rhetorical device in Hebrew poetry is parallelism. This is
used in every language to keep the reader interested, to communicate deeper
ideas than plain prose can, and to simply beautify the sentence. There are
three kinds of parallelism; the first is *synonymous parallelism*. This form is
found mainly, but not exclusively, in the poetic books. Look at the elegance
of this familiar benediction:

> *The Lord bless you and keep you;*
> *The Lord make His face shine upon you,*
> *And be gracious to you;*
> *The Lord lift up His countenance upon you,*
> *And give you peace.* (Numbers 6:24–26)

Each of these three sentences says the same thing. They are synonymous, and, all together, they magnify and expand one another. What does it mean for the Lord to bless you and me? It means that His face will shine on us. When God's face is shining on us, what does it mean? It means that His face is turned benevolently toward us in love and mercy.

This kind of parallelism makes Hebrew poetry beautiful in any language and shows God's wisdom in giving us the Old Testament, which often communicates mystical truth in this understandable form.

A second form of parallelism used in the Scripture is *antithetical parallelism*. This is often used in the Proverbs.

> *A soft answer turns away wrath,*
> *But a harsh word stirs up anger.* (Proverbs 15:1)

Can you see how the second sentence repeats the first but is in contrast to it? Solomon tells us that if you want to lower the chances for an argument, return caustic remarks with a "soft answer." Then he tells us the opposite truth: If you use harsh words, you'll escalate the fight. Again, parallelism helps to create a deeper understanding of the truth.

The third form of parallelism in the Bible is *synthetic parallelism*. The opening phrase makes a statement, the second magnifies it.

> *Keep your heart with all diligence,*
> *For out of it spring the issues of life.* (Proverbs 4:23)

The writer is reminding us of the principle of planting and harvesting—something we have seen in Scripture before. "Plant" diligence in your heart, because the things that sprout will result from what you plant. This is like another version of the first proverb we read, "As he thinks in his heart, so is he." You sow a diligent mind, you'll reap a faithful life.

As important as it is to study and obey the precepts of Holy Scripture, it is critical to understand and feel God's movement in the hearts of those who followed after Him.

- Characteristics of Wisdom Literature
- **Psalms**
- Ecclesiastes
- Job

Church historians have discovered that at the heart of most of the great revivals was a renewed love for the book of Psalms. Martin Luther, certainly one of history's most consequential Reformers, called the Psalms his "little Bible." Luther saw in it a microcosm of the themes from all of Scripture standing on the essential practice of prayer.

The last thing I would ever do is to question the words or wisdom of Jesus. But when His disciples asked Him, "Lord, teach us to pray," Jesus did not answer them the way I thought He would. I'm sure He had His reasons for walking them through the "Lord's Prayer," but He could have pointed them to 150 God-inspired prayers. No doubt He did this off-camera.

If you and I want to learn how to pray, there is no better place to start than reading and praying through the Psalms. Even though there are times when it seems as if I'm eavesdropping on the precious prayers of the saints, I can think of no better way to pray than to be mentored by King David, the author of most of these corporate prayers.

There are seven basic types of psalms:

Psalm Type	Key Example	Other Examples
1. Praise	"O LORD, our Lord, how excellent is Your name in all the earth." (Ps. 8:1)	Psalms 113–18, 145–50
2. Wisdom	"Blessed is the man who walks not in the counsel of the ungodly, nor stands in the path of sinners, nor sits in the seat of the scornful." (Ps. 1:1)	Psalms 19, 37, 49, 127, 138, 133
3. Lament	"Hear my prayer, O LORD, and let my cry come to You." (Ps. 102:1)	Psalms 12, 25, 39, 86, 120, 129

4. Messianic	*"The LORD said to my Lord, 'Sit at My right hand, till I make Your enemies Your footstool.'" (Ps. 110:1)*	Psalms 2, 16, 21, 22, 40
5. Penitence	*"Have mercy upon me, O God, according to Your lovingkindness; according to the multitude of Your tender mercies, blot out my transgressions." (Ps. 51:1)*	Psalms 6, 38, 102, 130, 143
6. Imprecation	*"Let their table become a snare before them, and their well-being a trap." (Ps. 69:22)*	Psalms 35, 88, 109, 137, 140
7. Thanks-giving	*"I will give thanks to You, O LORD, among the Gentiles, and sing praises to Your name." (Ps. 18:49)*	Psalms 66, 108, 118, 119, 135

Psalms of Praise

The center of worship in the Old Testament was the sacrifice. The most important thing to bring to the altar, however, was not the most perfect sheep or the biggest ram, it was a heart filled with praise. A sacrifice of praise and adoration was what the Holy God wanted from His people.

Psalms of Wisdom

To those who desire to be wise—and who *doesn't* want this?—these psalms make it clear: Meditate on Scripture. To those who want to perish, it is also very clear: Ignore the truth of God's Word and you will not be able to stand before God in judgment.

Psalms of Lament

There are some who think there is something unspiritual about lamenting (we must think positive—happy, happy, happy), but the Jewish people understood that godly sorrow was a good thing. These people were hurting, so they brought their pain before God's throne. Expressing deep sorrow before God was truly an acquired spiritual strength.

Messianic Psalms

These psalms promised royal authority to One who was both David's off-spring and David's Lord, seen by many New Testament authors as fulfilled in Jesus Christ. They are also called Royal Psalms or Coronation Psalms.

Psalms of Penitence

If Christians want to see what it looks like to be truly repentant, these psalms provide a perfect template. Daily reading from these helps us to understand godly contrition.

Psalms of Imprecation

Some Christian professionals squirm over the content of these psalms that call down God's holy wrath on our enemies. The qualification to be able to pray these psalms is that we need to understand the person—or the activity of a person—whom God truly hates. The Scripture calls this a "perfect" hatred and a perfect love, which means that it is possible to "hate" our enemies' behaviors without eluding the command to love our enemies as well.

Psalms of Thanksgiving

Extolling the goodness of the law of God is an important part of our prayer life. It is the primary concern of the book of Psalms. Psalms of thanksgiving sometimes follow psalms of lament; the psalmist pours out his grief-filled heart then fills it again with gratitude.

I encourage you to take time to pray, using these forms as a guide. It may feel mechanical at first, but I promise that as you do this, you will deeply enhance the experience of entering the presence of a Holy God.

- Characteristics of Wisdom Literature
- Psalms
- **Ecclesiastes**
- Job

Perhaps taking his cue from King Solomon, one of the best-selling authors of the twentieth century began his biggest book this way: "Life is hard and then you die." So began M. Scott Peck's hugely successful book, *The Road Less Traveled.*

The cue Peck may have taken from Solomon is found in the first quoted words of the book of Ecclesiastes: "Vanity of vanities, all is vanity." Or if the words had been written today, "Futility of futilities, all is futile."

This may come as a surprise to you, but Ecclesiastes is one of my favorite books in the Old Testament. Although it isn't a long book, it expresses, as no other, the wisdom of God when directly compared to a prevailing cultural atmosphere of skepticism—as true in the twenty-first century as it was almost one thousand years before the birth of Christ.

The other reason why I love this book is that God used it to get my attention, which,

> The most important thing to bring to the altar, however, was not the most perfect sheep or the biggest ram, it was a heart filled with praise.

as a result, led to my conversion. The person who was telling me of God's grace quoted an obscure passage from this Wisdom Book.

> *If a tree falls to the south or the north,*
> *In the place where the tree falls,*
> *there it shall lie.* (Ecclesiastes 11:3b)

Of course, I've discovered, since that moment I received God's amazing grace, that God can use anything He chooses to draw people into His mercy—including the New York City Yellow Pages, if necessary—but this passage from Ecclesiastes hit me like a straight left to the jaw. I may be the only one in the history of the church who has ever been converted by this verse, but hearing it was a profound experience of illumination. I saw myself lying on the ground like a fallen tree, going nowhere, rotting and disintegrating. At that moment I knew that I needed to respond to God's offer of salvation. And by His grace, I did.

The book of Ecclesiastes is puzzling to the novice reader because its skepticism can be overwhelming. Those who are not prepared for such a philosophical book wonder if, as a joke, an atheist sneaked into the printer and stuck his own ramblings into the middle of Holy Scripture.

Ernest Hemingway, one of literature's most consistent revolutionaries, admired Ecclesiastes. He integrated its truths into several of his books, including *The Sun Also Rises*. The text of the song "Turn, Turn, Turn," made popular in the late sixties by the group "The Byrds," is taken from this book. Herman Melville, the author of *Moby-Dick*, picked up the teaching of Ecclesiastes in his book *Redburn*. It is interesting that this support from such an eclectic assembly of secular minds has only fueled the concerns of many more conservative scholars regarding the veracity of Ecclesiastes.

But for me this book was—and continues to be—a watershed.

Ecclesiastes clearly presents two competing world-views: "under heaven" and "under the sun." The perspective of a Sovereign God is the former, and the perspective of mortal men is the latter. The conflict between these two realms is sharply and candidly presented here.

> Those who are not prepared for such a philosophical book wonder if, as a joke, an atheist sneaked into the printer and stuck his own ramblings into the middle of Holy Scripture.

Too often in Christian writings, perspectives on opposing world-views are not presented fairly. But the writer of this book—probably Solomon—gives a cogent and persuasive view of naturalism for the reader to judge as he sees fit. Ecclesiastes opens with an introduction of a cyclical view of life.

> *One generation passes away,*
> *and another generation comes;*
> *But the earth abides forever.*
> *The sun also rises, and the sun goes down,*
> *And hastens to the place where it arose.*
> *The wind goes toward the south,*
> *And turns around to the north;*
> *The wind whirls about continually,*
> *And comes again on its circuit.*
> *All the rivers run into the sea,*
> *Yet the sea is not full;*
> *To the place from which the rivers come,*
> *There they return again.* (Ecclesiastes 1:4–7)

Can you see it? Life is presented as an endless cycle with no beginning and no end. In the first chapter of this book I talked about God raising His hand like the starter in a race, and squeezing the trigger. "In the beginning," the book of Genesis opens.

But in fairness to those who believe that all of life is cyclical, vanity is the order of the day. The sun comes up and the sun goes down. The wind comes from the south, then turns from the north. What difference does today make if tomorrow brings it back again? Everything in the world is going around in circles. If this is true, vanity, hopelessness, and cynicism make perfect sense.

In the early seventies, we were introduced to a young Jane Fonda in the movie *They Shoot Horses, Don't They?* This film introduced this hopeless, cyclical world-view.

The movie is set during the Great Depression. A large prize was offered to a couple who had the stamina to win a dance marathon. Poor couples came from all over town to participate. They danced for hours and hours. When the marathon reached twenty-four hours of dancing, the emcee sped up the music, calling out, "Round and round and round they go, and where they stop, nobody knows!"

"Life is a meaningless rat race," the movie told us. "We spin in a 'rat race' until we drop exhausted to the floor. Then we die."

This idea is taken straight from the opening pages of Ecclesiastes. And the reader is challenged to examine this world-view's accuracy.

Throughout Ecclesiastes, the writer, who calls himself the "Preacher," analyzes the value of living in light of the sacred or the secular. In our youth, we have similar tests we perform as we weigh the perceived loss of freedom to follow Christ versus the unbridled freedom in following our passions. As adults, we see a perceived loss of pleasure, power, or purpose if the Bible is to be believed and obeyed. Most people, the Preacher concludes, decide

> God has created us to be restless until we find our rest in Him.

at some point in their lives whether or not to believe, "You only go 'round once in life; you might as well grab for all the gusto."

It is not clear whether the author actually participated in the activities he discusses in this book or whether he is simply making an illustration, but if his stories are real, he lived a debauched life in his early years. This is consistent with what we know about Solomon as he lived a life of fluctuating obedience to God. It also demonstrates that the hedonism of the twenty-first century matches the sensualism of ancient times. Living for ourselves, for the moment, and without eternal consequences is a universal desire. Round and round we go . . .

> *What has man for all his labor,*
> *and for the striving of his heart*
> *with which he has toiled under the sun?* (Ecclesiastes 2:22)

Futility is a cancer. Its effects are perilous and terminal. If there is no purpose to life, then why *not* be led by our infatuations? Away with the eternal; live for the moment.

> *So I commended enjoyment,*
> *because a man has nothing better under the sun than to*
> *eat, drink, and be merry;*
> *for this will remain with him in his labor*
> *all the days of his life*
> *which God gives him under the sun.* (Ecclesiastes 8:15)

If a man pursues pleasure and he finds it, he will eventually be bored with even the greatest indulgences. If a man pursues pleasure and never finds it, then he will forever live in anger, resentment, and cynicism. So, it appears impossible for humanity to be satisfied with hedonism.

God has created us to be restless until we find our rest in Him.

Ecclesiastes teaches that death comes to us all, but God gives hope for His cherished who die.

> *Remember now your Creator in the days of your youth,*
> *Before the difficult days come,*
> *And the years draw near when you say,*
> *"I have no pleasure in them."* (Ecclesiastes 12:1)

The book closes with a fitting overview of what Solomon has taught us.

> *And moreover, because the Preacher was wise,*
> *he still taught the people knowledge;*
> *yes, he pondered and sought out and set in order many proverbs.*
> *The Preacher sought to find acceptable words;*
> *and what was written was upright—words of truth.*
> *The words of the wise are like goads,*
> *and the words of scholars are like well-driven nails,*
> *given by one Shepherd . . .*
> *Let us hear the conclusion of the whole matter:*
> *Fear God and keep His commandments,*
> *For this is man's all.*
> *For God will bring every work into judgment,*
> *Including every secret thing,*
> *Whether good or evil.* (Ecclesiastes 12:9–11, 13–14)

If we fear God, life will not be meaningless. The wisdom that comes from fearing God will give us the ability to discern what is valuable in life and what is not.

- Characteristics of Wisdom Literature
- Psalms
- Ecclesiastes
- Job

"Do I have to eat this broccoli?" is the cry of most red-blooded children, hoping for a "bye" on the vicious stuff in exchange for the sugary delights of dessert. But no diligent parent would grant their request.

For many Old Testament readers, the accounts in the life of Job are the biblical cooked vegetables they'd like to leave on their plates. But, like every good parent, God had a plan for putting Job's story here. A full understanding of its message is spiritual nutrition at its best.

The book of Job deals head-on with the problem of evil and suffering. It touches us all as we read it because all of us struggle with unexplained affliction. As I have, I'm sure you've looked up to heaven and said, "Why me? Why now? Is this how You treat Your friends?"

These are the most profound questions we have to face as mortals, and they require nothing less than an encounter with a Holy God to answer them. The facts that clarify an understanding of pain and suffering are found throughout Scripture, but concerning this problem in the extreme, there is no other book quite like Job.

The setting for Job takes place during the patriarchal period, long before the chronology of its placement in the Old Testament. We don't know exactly when the story of Job was recorded, but its form and vocabulary suggest that it may be the oldest book in the Old Testament, written five hundred or more years prior to Moses' reception of the Law.

Some scholars believe that the book of Job was never intended to be taken as a literal book of history, that it was only a story used to teach theological truths. As a highly artistic literary work, it is more poetic than any history you will ever read in Scripture. It contains scenes, dialogues, and soliloquies. However, the majority of conservative scholars throughout history believe that this is a story about a real man named Job, dramatized and stylized into an incredible work of art as well as an ancient historical narrative.

> As I have, I'm sure you've looked up to heaven and said, "Why me? Why now? Is this how You treat Your friends?"

The beginning of the book of Job gives us a fascinating look into the life of this man:

> There was a man in the land of Uz, whose name was Job;
> and that man was blameless and upright,
> and one who feared God and shunned evil.
> And seven sons and three daughters were born to him.
> Also, his possessions were seven thousand sheep,
> three thousand camels, five hundred yoke of oxen,
> five hundred female donkeys, and a very large household,

so that this man was the greatest
of all the people of the East. (Job 1:1–3)

This was a man of immense wealth, dwarfing even that of Abraham. He was not only the wealthiest man of that time, but the most spiritual man as well—what an incredible combination. He was a man truly blessed by God in every dimension of life, physical and spiritual.

The scene then changes to the throne room of God. The stage is being set for a showdown between God and Satan.

Now there was a day when the sons of God
came to present themselves before the LORD,
and Satan also came among them.
And the LORD said to Satan,
"From where do you come?"
So Satan answered the LORD and said,
"From going to and fro on the earth,
and from walking back and forth on it."
Then the LORD said to Satan,
"Have you considered My servant Job,
that there is none like him on the earth,
a blameless and upright man,
one who fears God and shuns evil?"
So Satan answered the LORD and said,
"Does Job fear God for nothing?
Have You not made a hedge around him, around his household,
and around all that he has on every side?
You have blessed the work of his hands,
and his possessions have increased in the land.
But now, stretch out Your hand and touch all that he has,
and he will surely curse You to Your face!"
And the LORD said to Satan,
"Behold, all that he has is in your power;
only do not lay a hand on his person." (Job 1:6–12)

In this remarkable scene, Satan was bragging to God about his domain—walking to and fro—no doubt pleased with his accomplishments. With the profound exception of the man named Job. God told Satan that not all the world is his realm—there is God's servant who is righteous.

"No wonder Job is righteous," Satan snaps. "You've given him all he could ever want."

Knowing that Job's faithfulness is not connected to his blessings, God turns Satan loose to remove these tangible things from Job's personal net worth. Job's servants, his livestock, even his children were decimated. But Job remained faithful.

This scene demonstrates God's relationship to suffering. Even in the evil actions and decisions of Satan, even in the sin and madness of humankind, there is a kind of concurrence. Running side by side, there are two wills being worked out. But the motives are different.

When Joseph's brothers threw him into a pit to die, then sold him to slave traders, they meant it for evil. But God, who saw their every move and allowed each event to occur, meant it for good (Genesis 50:20). Similarly, both God and Satan were involved in the attacks on Job's personal property. But who was responsible? Was it the Chaldeans? The devil? God?

The answer is "yes." All these are players in the drama of history.

> "No wonder Job is righteous," Satan snaps. "You've given him all he could ever want."

But when the Chaldeans stand before God on Judgment Day, and God accuses them of destroying Job's property, what will they say—"The Devil made us do it"? And when Satan is brought before the tribunal of God and charged with his activities, what will he say—"I was only carrying out the will of God. How can you punish me for this?"

Those cattle-rustling Chaldeans had had their eyes on Job's bounty for years, and when God took that hedge of protection down, it didn't take much prodding from Satan to motivate them to attack Job's livestock. The Chaldeans were quite agreeable to assist Satan, and they freely chose to attack Job. Neither Satan nor the Chaldeans were coerced in choosing this evil. They willingly chose violence over peace, and, since there was no coercion from

God, they and every other unrepentant sinner can be judged for their evil. Concurrence does not equal coercion.

God's sovereignty does not remove us from the responsibility for our actions. And we can be absolutely certain that His judgments will be sure.

So, the book of Job is an argument for God's righteous punishment of sinners, and an argument against blaming Him for directly causing all the evil in the world—also known as a *theodiocy*. This question was specifically raised in the New Testament when, faced with a man sightless from birth, the disciples asked Jesus, "Why was this man born blind? Was it from his sin, or the sin of his parents?" (see John 9).

Jesus answered tersely: "It was for neither reason . . . but for the glory of God."

Notice that the disciples' question assumed that there must have been a local sin to cause this man to be born blind. Suffering and pain in this world were, according to first-century Jewish thought, always caused by a sin done by someone directly associated with the situation. But the disciples had committed the informal fallacy of the false dilemma—the "either-or" fallacy.

Does this mean that there is no relationship between sin and suffering? No, for if there were no sin, there would be no suffering either. Pain and death are direct consequences of living in a fallen world. But the error the disciples made was in thinking that there was always a one-to-one correspondence between personal sin and personal pain. We cannot ever make that assumption.

Throughout Scripture, people suffered *because* of their fidelity with God:

> [Jesus said,] "Blessed are you when they revile and persecute you,
>   and say all kinds of evil against you falsely for My sake.
> Rejoice and be exceedingly glad, for great is your reward in heaven,
> for so they persecuted the prophets who were before you." (Matthew 5:11–12)

The apostle Paul suffered because of God's desire to purify him:

> And lest I should be exalted above measure
>   by the abundance of the revelations,
>   a thorn in the flesh was given to me,

> *a messenger of Satan to buffet me,*
> *lest I be exalted above measure.* (2 Corinthians 12:7)

To strengthen the depth of our fellowship with Him:

> *That I may know Him and the power of His resurrection,*
> *and the fellowship of His sufferings,*
> *being conformed to His death,*
> *if, by any means, I may attain to the resurrection*
> *from the dead.* (Philippians 3:10–11)

And sometimes God brings suffering to divinely discipline us:

> *For whom the LORD loves He chastens,*
> *And scourges every son whom He receives.* (Hebrews 12:6)

We cannot assume that our sin has nothing to do with our suffering, and we cannot assume that our suffering has everything to do with our sin. On this point, Jesus' teaching is quite clear, and the book of Job confirms that teaching as well. Indeed, "the secret things belong to the LORD" (Deuteronomy 29:29), and we cannot know exactly why God is disposed to allow certain tragedies and blessings to occur. However, we wait in faith for Him to resolve these difficult questions, which He, in His time, will do.

> The heart of their argument was that Job must be the biggest sinner the world had ever known, since he was suffering more than anyone they had ever known.

In Job's case, his suffering increased. He was tormented, finally covered by sores and afflicted by disease. His so-called friends came to him and presented their concerns. The heart of their argument was that Job must be the biggest sinner the world had ever known, since he was suffering more than anyone they had ever known. Some kind of comfort this must have been.

Their solution was to tell Job to repent of his sins and confess them to God. Job's response was to honestly tell them that he didn't know what else he could confess. He had done everything he knew to do to serve God. Their response was brutal. "Look how proud you are. Look how unteachable. You are compounding your trials by lying about your sin. Repent!"

Finally, Job's wife jumped in. "Curse God," she wailed to her husband, "and die."

I suppose that in desperation over seeing the agony of Job, she had decided to submit to whatever deity was the opposite of God. Nothing, she thought, could possibly be worse than this, and perhaps his plight would improve if he separated himself from God.

Toward the end of the book, God responded to Job's questions. Truthfully, it wasn't much of a two-way conversation—more of a monologue with Job on the receiving end.

> *Who is this who darkens counsel*
> *By words without knowledge?*
> *Now prepare yourself like a man;*
> *I will question you,*
> *and you shall answer Me.*
> *Where were you when I laid the foundations of the earth?*
> *Tell Me, if you have understanding.*
> *Who determined its measurements?*
> *Surely you know! . . .*
> *Or who laid its cornerstone,*
> *When the morning stars sang together,*
> *And all the sons of God shouted for joy?* (Job 38:2–7)

It was the ultimate Dutch-uncle talk—you know it's going to be a tough one when the Sovereign God of the universe tells you to "take it like a man." God challenges Job's right to question Him. Again we see the theme of so many passages of Scripture when God answers our questions with: "Because I said so. Any questions?"

Job finally answered, timidly waving the white flag at God's verbal assault. Once again, we have one of the Old Testament's snowcapped peaks where God made His holy presence known.

> *Then Job answered the LORD and said:*
> *"Behold, I am vile;*
> *What shall I answer you?*
> *I lay my hand over my mouth.*
> *Once I have spoken, but I will not answer;*
> *Yes, twice, but I will proceed no further."* (Job 40:3–5)

God's holiness was released in all its fury. "Would you condemn Me," He said to Job, "that you might be justified?"

This is the key question that all who suffer must answer.

Finally, Job answered God again, this time in a barely audible whisper. "No Sir," he replied. "No, Sir."

Job repented, not of any past sins that might have caused his travail, but of his mistrust of God in the midst of it.

Ultimately, God never answered Job's questions. Job never actually found out why all of this loss and horror had occurred. It was as if the answer to Job's queries was simply God's presence. The Holy One of Israel was saying, "If you know Who I am, then you will trust Me. That will be enough."

In the final scene, Job was restored. God triumphed over the mockeries of Satan. Job's possessions were multiplied and the story was complete.

> Job repented, not of any past sins that might have caused his travail, but of his mistrust of God in the midst of it.

Although coming from the oldest book in the Old Testament, this is clearly the message of the New Testament. Those who join in the redemptive sufferings of Christ will be delivered; ultimately they will be transported to a place more glorious than anything they could ever have imagined.

SUMMARY
■ CHARACTERISTICS OF WISDOM LITERATURE

Life in biblical times got pretty raucous: wars, slavery, avarice, adultery, murder, sibling rivalry, and deception. But what was really happening in these people's hearts? Why did they act the way they did? What were their fears and motives? And how did all of these things affect them—on the inside? What was in their hearts?

Solomon, the wisest of them all, knew that although some men may try to hide this fact, it's their *hearts* that make their decisions for them. Man's heart—the seat of all his emotions—motivates his drives and desires. Most of the time, it's a man's heart that affects his thinking, not the other way around.

The Bible's Wisdom Literature speaks to our hearts.

■ PSALMS

Church historians have discovered that at the heart of most of the great revivals was a renewed love for the book of Psalms. Martin Luther, certainly one of history's most consequential Reformers, called the Psalms his "little Bible."

There are seven basic types of Psalms: (1) Praise; (2) Wisdom; (3) Lament; (4) Messianic; (5) Penitence; (6) Imprecation; and (7) Thanksgiving.

King David wrote most of the psalms, which have been used for centuries as models for prayer and lyrics for song.

■ ECCLESIASTES

The book of Ecclesiastes is puzzling to the novice reader because its skepticism can be overwhelming. Those who are not prepared for such a philosophical book wonder if, as a joke, an atheist sneaked into the printer and stuck his own ramblings into the middle of Holy Scripture.

Ecclesiastes clearly presents two competing world-views: "under heaven" and "under the sun." The perspective of a Sovereign God is the former, and the perspective of mortal men is the latter. The conflict between these two realms is sharply and candidly presented here.

Too often in Christian writings, perspectives on opposing world-views are not presented fairly. But the writer of this book—probably Solomon—gives a cogent and persuasive view of naturalism for the reader to judge as he sees fit.

For the unbeliever, life is an endless cycle with no beginning and no end. The sun comes up and the sun goes down. The wind comes from the south, then turns from the north. What difference does today make if tomorrow brings it back again? Everything in the world is going around in circles. If this is true, vanity, hopelessness, and cynicism make perfect sense.

Life is a meaningless rat race. We spin until we drop exhausted to the floor. Then we die.

Throughout Ecclesiastes, the writer analyzes the value of living in light of the sacred or the secular. It is not clear whether the author actually participated in the activities he discusses in this book or whether he is simply making an illustration, but if his stories are real, he lived a debauched life in his early years. This is consistent with what we know about Solomon as he lived a life of fluctuating obedience to' God. It also demonstrates that the hedonism of the twenty-first century matches the sensualism of ancient times. Living for ourselves, for the moment, and without eternal consequences is a universal desire.

Futility is a cancer. Its effects are perilous and terminal. If there is no purpose to life, then why *not* be led by our infatuations? Away with the eternal; live for the moment.

If a man pursues pleasure and he finds it, he will eventually be bored with even the greatest indulgences. If a man pursues pleasure and never finds it, then he will forever live in anger, resentment, and cynicism. So, it appears impossible for humanity to be satisfied with hedonism.

God has created us to be restless until we find our rest in Him. If we fear God, life will not be meaningless. The wisdom that comes from fearing God will give us the ability to discern what is valuable in life and what is not.

▪ JOB

The book of Job deals head-on with the problem of evil and suffering. It touches us all as we read it because all of us struggle with unexplained affliction. As I have, I'm sure you've looked up to heaven and said, "Why me? Why now? Is this how You treat Your friends?"

These are the most profound questions we have to face as mortals, and they require nothing less than an encounter with a Holy God to answer them. The facts that clarify an understanding of pain and suffering are found throughout Scripture, but concerning this problem in the extreme, there is no other book quite like Job.

This was a man of immense wealth, dwarfing even that of Abraham. Job was a man who sacrificed for himself and his children. He was not only the wealthiest man of that time, but the most spiritual man as well—what an incredible combination. He was a man truly blessed by God in every dimension of life, physical and spiritual.

The scene then changes to the throne room of God. The stage is being set for a showdown. Satan was bragging to God about his domain—walking to and fro—no doubt pleased with his accomplishments. With the profound exception of the man named Job. God told Satan that not all the world is his realm—there is God's servant who is righteous.

"No wonder Job is righteous," Satan snaps. "You've given him all he could ever want."

Knowing that Job's faithfulness is not connected to his blessings, God turns Satan loose to remove these tangible things from Job's personal net worth. Job's servants, his livestock, even his children were decimated. But Job remained faithful.

Although coming from the oldest book in the Old Testament, this is clearly the message of the New Testament. Those who join in the redemptive sufferings of Christ will be delivered; ultimately they will be transported to a place more glorious than anything they could ever have imagined.

CHAPTER ELEVEN

PREPARATION FOR THE COMING MESSIAH

- **The Intertestamental Period**
- John the Baptist
- The Birth of Jesus
- The Early Years of Jesus' Life

When you attend a stage play, something happens between scenes that gives the production director and stagehands enough time to rearrange the set for the next act; the curtain closes. You sit quietly for a few minutes, knowing that the movements and rearrangement of the sets and props and actors will be important for the next portion of the play.

The Old Testament period had finished. The sound of Malachi's voice delivering his final prophecy had faded into silence. And then, because this act was completed, the curtain dropped. The stage needed to be prepared for the next of God's visible activities.

But unlike the plays you and I have seen where the curtain is closed for a couple of minutes, this time the patrons sat in the audience for a long time, waiting for the next scene to unfold. In fact, this was even longer than a thirty-minute intermission. For the story of the Israelites, God's chosen people, the curtain remained closed for four hundred years—four centuries of rearrangement and preparation for the greatest drama in human history.

> *But when the fullness of the time had come,*
> *God sent forth His Son, born of a woman, born under the law,*
> *to redeem those who were under the law,*
> *that we might receive the adoption as sons.* (Galatians 4:4–5)

The *pleroma*—the fullness of time—tells us that the stage was being set for the coming of Jesus. This was going to be the focal point of history. He came at the right time, the perfect instant, fulfilling all the prophecies in one moment in time. God's plan of redemption was about to come to pass.

ALEXANDER THE GREAT

Just because the curtain was closed does not mean that this period of time was insignificant. Following Nehemiah's reconstruction of the walls in 445 B.C., the Medo-Persians controlled Jerusalem for one hundred more years. But in 331 B.C., the Medo-Persians were conquered by Alexander the Great's Greek Empire.

The story of Alexander is fascinating. With memories of men like the youthful King David and King Josiah, Alexander was putting the finishing touches on his conquest of the Persian Empire when he was only twenty-four years old. Prior to Alexander's reign, the three titans of Greek civilization had profoundly shaped the thinking of this soon-to-be dominant force in the world: Socrates, Plato, and Aristotle. And, the most famous pupil of Aristotle was a young man named Alexander.

He was not known as a thinker or a philosopher, but as a strategic military genius. How did those studies fit into Alexander's gifts? As a teacher, Aristotle searched for a unifying system of knowledge. He searched for scientific and philosophical unity. He and his students wrestled with the coalescence of multiple ideas and complex theories into one cogent way of thinking.

> He came at the right time, the perfect instant, fulfilling all the prophecies in one moment in time.

As Alexander studied, he dreamed of creating that same kind of unity . . . militarily and politically. If diverse schools of thought can be organized into a singular, dominant system, then peoples and lands can be similarly unified. So Alexander did both. He conquered with his forces, and he conquered with the philosophies of his master.

So thoroughly did Alexander saturate surrounding kingdoms with Greek culture that, to this day, we have a special word for what he did: *Hellenize.* Alexander unified the known world in a way that Aristotle was unable to do with ideas alone, but his impact on the world was not simply that of a master soldier. He was also a great evangelist for the Greek world-view. Alexander commanded that the people speak Greek, think Greek, write Greek, and live Greek. So pervasive and so successful were Alexander's efforts that, more than three centuries later when the text of the New Testament was penned— mostly by Hebrews—it was written in Greek.

Although, as I said, the curtain was closed on our understanding of what was happening among God's people, we can certainly imagine how the remnant of devout Jews must have fought against the pervasiveness of Greek thinking. In their conquests, the Greeks had co-opted the pagan gods of Egypt, Asia Minor, and Persia and given them new names. Because these gods promised immortality, they were far more appealing to the Greeks, so right along with taking possession of the lands and peoples, they assumed the ownership of the gods as well. In order to avoid confusion, they gave these new gods the names of their old ones. Their religion was a come-one-come-all, the-more-the-merrier religion. "If you've got the time, we've got a god."

> Their religion was a come-one-come-all, the-more-the-merrier religion. "If you've got the time, we've got a god."

During the ministry of the apostle Paul in Athens—the Greek's capital city—we discover that the Greeks had even erected a massive altar, with the inscription, "To the Unknown God." With their multideity philosophy, they just couldn't be too careful . . . a special altar to a spare god, just in case of an unforeseen emergency when they might need another.

In addition to having many gods, renewed interest in astrology during this time led to widespread belief that the planets governed the lives and destinies of human beings.

Can you imagine how the faithful Israelites—the truly devout ones—must have been utterly scandalized by this? It was horrific enough to have been batted around like chattel for generations among pagan kingdoms that claimed raw hedonism as their god. But now their conquerors were challenging the purity—the essence—of who they were and what they believed by filling the skies with false deities.

No wonder the Israelites were ready for a Savior.

THE PTOLEMIES AND THE SELEUCIDS

In 327 B.C., Alexander the Great was stricken with an illness and died as he was conquering Babylon. Upon his death, his kingdom was divided among his eight surviving generals. As you might imagine, without the singular leadership of Alexander, chaos ensued. When the dust had settled, Alexander's conquered lands were divided into two groups: the Ptolemies and the Seleucids. Initially, Palestine (the name given to Israel around this time) was controlled by the Ptolemaic dynasty, which also controlled Egypt. The Seleucids ruled over Syria and the territories to the north and east.

> Unfortunately, by the time we meet the Pharisees in the New Testament, they have been reduced to a sniveling gaggle of hypocrites, concerned only with the externals of the Law.

After more than one hundred years under the Ptolemies, Antiochus III fought for and won control of Palestine for the Seleucids. Antiochus had an ardent passion for spreading Greek culture among the chosen people. Knowing that the Jews had so adamantly opposed syncretism over the generations, it's understandable that they resisted this. Groups of Jews began forming in resistance to this cultural and spiritual attempt at assimilation.

The Hassidians—the "Pious Ones"—were earnest in their desire to maintain the Jewish culture and belief in the One True God. Other groups tried to maintain the purity of their traditions, such as the Pharisees. These were the original "Puritans." They were pious in their obedience to the Law, genuinely godly men. Unfortunately, by the time we meet them in the New Testament, they have been reduced to a sniveling gaggle of hypocrites, concerned only with the externals of the Law.

Following the short reign of Antiochus III, Antiochus Epiphanes came to power. He assumed the title "epiphanes" because the word means "manifest god." Antiochus's reign was related to the Old Testament because his vicious and radical steps against Israel were specifically foretold by the prophets. Pious Jews didn't call him by his given name. Instead, they called him Antiochus Epimanes, which meant "Antiochus the Insane."

The monarch lived up to this second name. He was demented, with a messianic complex unrivaled by any leader of that time. Antiochus implemented a radical anti-Jewish initiative, one so harsh that even the most non-devout Jews hated him. He was the "Hitler" of the second century B.C., outlawing the Sabbath, circumcision, and even the possession of the Hebrew Scriptures. These were capital crimes against the state. Breaking the laws was punishable by immediate execution. In the year 167 B.C., Antiochus ordered the sacrifice of a pig on the most sacred altar of the Temple in Jerusalem. This was more than the Jews could bear, and an uprising against Antiochus broke out. Three years later, the Maccabean Revolts began.

JUDAS MACCABAEUS

A man named Mattathias rose in protest against Antiochus. He began to fight a guerrilla war against the Seleucids with his five sons. When Mattathias died, the leadership of the revolt fell to Judas Maccabaeus—Judas the Hammer. Because of his bold raids against the invaders, he became a national hero among the Israelites and remains so today. So successful was Judas Maccabaeus that he actually won concessions from the Greeks, which included the restoration of religious freedom and the reopening of the Temple for sacred worship.

The Feast of Hanukkah is celebrated to this day in memory of this event and the unabashed heroics of Judas the Hammer.

In 142 B.C., the Jews were able to gain their full freedom from domination, which lasted for eighty years. In 63 B.C., however, Palestine was conquered again, this time by General Pompey from the ever-spreading Roman Empire. Twenty-three years later, Herod the Great was appointed by Rome as the local king over the Jews.

Herod founded a dynasty, primarily on the backs of the Hebrews. He was exceptionally cruel to his subjects, which ultimately led to his demise. But it is significant that when our curtain finally rises and the New Testament begins, the people of God are crying out for deliverance under the harrowing rule of Herod the Great.

No wonder the Israelites were ready for a Savior.

- The Intertestamental Period
- **John the Baptist**
- The Birth of Jesus
- The Early Years of Jesus' Life

"Who was the greatest prophet in the Old Testament?"

This is a trick question I have asked my seminary students for years—tormenting them has always been a favorite pastime of mine. The question always starts a debate. Students argue the impact of Isaiah on the life of the people. Some vote for Jeremiah because of his passion for repentance. But Elijah usually wins as the most important Old Testament prophet. The frequent New Testament references to him are the *coup de grâce.*

> The Feast of Hanukkah is celebrated to this day in memory of this event and the unabashed heroics of Judas the Hammer.

Once they've finished with their intramural squabble, I announce that John the Baptist is clearly the most important prophet in the Old Testament. They look at me with consternation, telling me that John the Baptist's record is found in the *New* Testament. After thanking them for that reminder, I tell them that, while his story is recorded in the New Testament, he was, in fact, under the Old Covenant. Jesus said that the Law and the prophets ruled until John the Baptist (Luke 16:16), and the word *until* means "up to and including."

Now that I've put this trick question and the answer in a book, I'm going to have to come up with another one to annoy my students. This won't be too difficult.

Of all the people we meet in the New Testament, the most underrated person is John the Baptist. It has always perplexed me why Christian scholars and lay teachers have given so little credit to him. They certainly didn't get this depreciation of John from the Scriptures. In the four Gospels, only two even mention the birth of Jesus, but all four discuss the significance of John the Baptist and his ministry. Even secular historians treat John as a national celebrity.

So why does John get so much attention?

For four hundred years—more than 150 years longer than the United States of America has been in existence—the prophets of God had been silent. Generation after generation passed without anyone hearing the words, "Thus says the Lord." Can you imagine how difficult it must have been for the priests to preach with any passion or for their words to gain entrance into the hearts of the people?

Then came John. He was the first prophet in four centuries to speak God's Word with divine authority. He brought the prophet Malachi's words to life.

> *Behold, I will send you Elijah the prophet*
> *Before the coming of the great and dreadful day of the LORD.*
> *And he will turn*
> *The hearts of the fathers to the children,*
> *And the hearts of the children to their fathers,*
> *Lest I come and strike the earth with a curse.* (Malachi 4:5–6)

The return of a Holy God was—and will always be—good news for the faithful but a very, very unhappy thing for His enemies.

The words of the last prophet, Malachi, in the Old Testament and the opening words of Mark's gospel in the New Testament bear an uncanny resemblance.

> *Behold, I send My messenger before Your face,*
> *Who will prepare Your way before You.*
> *The voice of one crying in the wilderness:*
> *"Prepare the way of the LORD;*
> *Make His paths straight."* (Mark 1:2–3)

Malachi called this new prophet "Elijah." And given John's wardrobe, diet, and lifestyle, he was certainly a worthy successor to Elijah, the second greatest prophet in the Old Testament.

BEHOLD THE LAMB OF GOD

Like many prophets before him, John talked about the Day of the Lord. What was significant about John's message was that, unlike the prophets of old, he did not talk about the "coming" of that great and awesome day. John the Baptist said that the day is *here*. He used two images to describe this concept: the ax at the root of a tree and the fan in the farmer's hand. Remember that the Day of the Lord was bad news to God's enemies, including "good, upstanding citizens" who had for generations ignored their need for sacrifice, contrition, and worship.

John told them that this One would be like an ax, felling those who had forgotten God or who were unwilling to repent. The Messiah would be like the tool that farmers used to separate the wheat from the chaff. From the wheat people were fed, but the chaff was only good for burning.

I can picture the religious leaders of the day beginning to squirm in their seats. The coming of a prophet, ushering in the Messiah, sounded like good news at first. After all,

> The return of a Holy God was—and will always be—good news for the faithful but a very, very unhappy thing for His enemies.

Herod the Great was having his way with the Israelites and these Jewish leaders were looking for some help. But John's words sounded more like a visit to the woodshed, and they were at the top of his list.

> *When [John] saw many of the Pharisees and Sadducees*
> *coming to his baptism, he said to them,*
> *"Brood of vipers! Who warned you to flee*
> *from the wrath to come?"* (Matthew 3:7)

In addition to being brutally courageous with his words, John also pushed the edges on something called baptism. Many other rabbis baptized their students in the ceremonial baths under the stairs leading to the Temple. Gentile converts to Judaism had to undergo a baptism as well. But John called all, not just his intimate disciples or Gentile converts, to be baptized. And was John accusing the Jews of being unclean, like the Gentiles, and in need of a ceremonial bath?

Well, actually, yes. That's exactly what he was doing.

This created quite a shouting match between John and the other rabbis. It's what precipitated his outburst when he called them a bunch of snakes. These pious men were furious. But John was resolute and was not to be intimidated by a heap of bleached-bone boxes—as he later called them. As far as John was concerned, the Messiah was coming down the road; the King was at the door;

> John's words sounded more like a visit to the woodshed, and they were at the top of his list.

and they, of all people who should have been ready for Him, were not. These fine, upstanding, religion-leading, card-carrying-sacramental-Jews-only club members were unclean.

Before the Messiah comes, you are going to need to take a bath . . . inside and out.

After John had upset nearly everyone in Judea, the teachers from Jerusalem came out to question him.

> Now this is the testimony of John,
> when the Jews sent priests and Levites from Jerusalem to ask him,
> "Who are you?"
> He confessed, and did not deny, but confessed,
> "I am not the Christ."
> And they asked him,
> "What then? Are you Elijah?"
> He said, "I am not."
> "Are you the prophet?"
> And he answered, "No."
> Then they said to him,
> "Who are you, that we may give an answer to those who sent us?
> What do you say about yourself?"
> He said: "I am
> The voice of one crying in the wilderness:
> 'Make straight the way of the LORD,'
> as the prophet Isaiah said."
> Now those who were sent were from the Pharisees.
> And they asked him, saying,
> "Why then do you baptize if you are not the Christ,
> nor Elijah, nor the Prophet?"
> John answered them, saying,
> "I baptize with water, but there stands One among you

whom you do not know.
It is He who, coming after me,
is preferred before me,
whose sandal strap I am not worthy to loose. " (John 1:19–27)

Can you picture this? These religious leaders, quite full of themselves, are getting a closer look at this wild man from the desert. And not only did John the Baptist level them with his words, calling them serpents and candy-coated crypts, but he told them that there was Someone in their midst who was about to make them look really, really bad. In fact, the way John tells them this—right after they ask him if he is the Messiah—is to announce that he's not worthy even to untie the shoes of this One.

> The Savior of the world, the perfect Sacrifice, the Hope of all mankind—Jews, Gentiles, and Romans—had finally come.

This was the most important dimension of John's calling, bearing witness to the coming Messiah, Jesus Christ. Even before he was born, John did a cartwheel inside his mother's womb at the sound of Jesus' mother's precious voice.

One day when John was preaching and baptizing in the Jordan River, he looked up and saw Jesus walking toward him, directly into the water. John's life and divine calling must have flashed before his eyes.

"Behold!" John exclaimed. "The Lamb of God who takes away the sin of the world!"

The Savior of the world, the perfect Sacrifice, the Hope of all mankind—Jews, Gentiles, and Romans—had finally come.

- The Intertestamental Period
- John the Baptist
- **The Birth of Jesus**
- The Early Years of Jesus' Life

The miracles recorded in the Bible do not have a rating system. I guess that a miracle—any divine intervention breaking through the codes of natural law—was . . . a miracle. But if there *were* a rating system: The fish swallowing Jonah would have been a "3" on a scale of 1 to 10, the Red Sea parting a "5,"

> That starry night in the City of David, God sent God to earth.

and the sun standing still a "7"; the creation of the earth and the birth of Jesus Christ would both be "10s." That is, *if* there *were* a scoring grid.

In the first chapter of this book, we looked at the incredible wonder of creation: God putting everything in place *ex nihilo*—out of nothing. And we learned that Scripture tells us that He did all of these things simply by using His voice. There was nothing at all. Then He spoke. There it was; everything was in its place. In Chapter Two, I referred to this as the first snowcapped peak on the landscape of the Bible.

The birth of Jesus was just as indescribably wonderful as Creation—perhaps even more so. Why would I say such a thing? Because the birth of the Savior involved a Holy God doing something that involved Himself. That starry night in the City of David, God sent God to earth.

Jesus Christ, God the Son, did not first come into being in Bethlehem. He was eternally existent, before the foundations of the earth. He, too, was the Creator of the universe.

> *[Jesus Christ] is the image of the invisible God,*
> *the firstborn over all creation.*
> *For by Him all things were created*
> *that are in heaven and that are on earth,*
> *visible and invisible, whether thrones or dominions*
> *or principalities or powers.*
> *All things were created through Him and for Him.*
> *And He is before all things,*
> *and in Him all things consist.* (Colossians 1:15–17)

The miracle of Christmas wasn't simply that the Messiah was born, but that God the Son willingly condescended from His own holy throne. Having eternally existed and never having been limited by time or space, He quietly took upon Himself the nature of a helpless baby boy. Jesus became a child whose ethnic lineage was, and continues to be, the most persecuted in all of human history.

His mother conceived Him before she was married. And although she and Joseph, her fiancé, were visited by angels confirming the Holy Spirit's participation in this conception, no one else had the same vision. The pregnant single girl raised eyebrows even among the most liberated Jews, not to mention pompous outrage from those who were staunch keepers of the Law.

As heaven's resident for all eternity, God's Son had never known physical pain, hunger, thirst, winter's chill, summer's heat, exhaustion, or poverty. Now He would experience all of these in His human nature, starting with His birth in a cattle trough.

As a boy, Jesus Christ grew up as a poor "illegitimate" boy—an outsider—among a people who were under the domination of a foreign power. Politically, He didn't stand a chance.

> In His mercy, God delivered His message of the coming Messiah to someone else . . . someone Mary loved and trusted.

His ministry was ushered in by John the Baptist, whose personal style and diplomatic skills made a wild boar look like a puppy. This was the way the Son of God was introduced.

Finally, He came on a mission: to die a humiliating and unthinkable death, bearing the sins of the world.

To think that God willingly did this to *Himself* makes the miracle of the birth of Jesus Christ truly indescribable. This is exactly what happened.

THE ANNUNCIATION

> *The whole thing narrows and narrows,*
> *until at last it comes down to a little point,*
> *small as the point of a spear—*
> *a Jewish girl at her prayers.* (C. S. Lewis)

An angel approached a young woman who was betrothed to a man but not yet married. The angel told Mary to rejoice because she had found favor with God and would receive a profound blessing. Her initial response was to be rather troubled. This may sound strange to you and me. If an angel came to us and told us to be happy, we would probably comply—unless, of course, the assignment was as overwhelming as the one delivered to Mary.

I'm sure that Mary doubted her senses, or perhaps wondered if she was ill. And if she really became pregnant because of a visitation of the Holy Spirit, how would she tell her beloved Joseph? The angel went on to clarify exactly who her son would be, giving her a powerful summary of Christ's deity and authority.

> *He will be great, and will be called the Son of the Highest;*
> *and the Lord God will give Him the throne of His father David.*
> *And He will reign over the house of Jacob forever,*
> *and of His kingdom there will be no end.* (Luke 1:32–33)

Mary was confused. She was beginning to understand that she was going to have a baby and that this baby was going to be a very important person. But she knew for sure that she was a virgin, and virgins didn't have babies.

The angel replied with something of an explanation.

> *The Holy Spirit will come upon you,*
> *and the power of the Highest will overshadow you;*
> *therefore, also, that Holy One who is to be born*
> *will be called the Son of God.* (Luke 1:35)

These words remind me of the beginning of Creation, when "the Spirit of God was hovering over the face of the waters." With Mary, the same Spirit was hovering over her, creating a fertilized embryo—Jesus—inside of her. And then as a confirmation, the angel told Mary that her cousin, a woman well past her childbearing years, was also pregnant.

In one of the most succinct statements in all of Scripture, the angel, almost as an afterthought, summarized for Mary the efforts of man compared to the works of a Sovereign God.

> *For with God nothing will be impossible.* (Luke 1:37)

Mary hurried off to see Elizabeth. The moment that Mary entered the house and greeted her pregnant cousin, the baby inside Elizabeth's womb jumped for joy. With no prompting, Elizabeth spoke words to Mary that were exactly what she needed to hear.

> *Then [Elizabeth] spoke out with a loud voice and said,*
> *"Blessed are you among women,*
> *and blessed is the fruit of your womb!"* (Luke 1:42)

Before she even had time to tell Elizabeth her story, Mary heard the identical words that had been spoken to her by the angel when he first came to her. Can you imagine how reassuring and comforting this must have been to her? In His mercy, God delivered His message of the coming Messiah to someone else . . . someone Mary loved and trusted. These words from her friend must have confirmed in her heart that what she had heard and experienced from the angel was authentic.

THE MAGNIFICAT

Then Mary responded with a song that has come to be known as the Magnificat. Either it is an example of God selectively and supernaturally revealing truth to her, or Mary was extremely well grounded in the Old Testament Scriptures. In either case, her song is theologically profound.

> *And Mary said:*
> *"My soul magnifies the Lord,*
> *And my spirit has rejoiced in God my Savior.*
> *For He has regarded the lowly state of His maidservant;*
> *For behold, henceforth all generations will call me blessed.*
> *For He who is mighty has done great things for me,*
> *And holy is His name.*
> *And His mercy is on those who fear Him*
> *From generation to generation.*
> *He has shown strength with His arm;*

> *He has scattered the proud in the imagination of their hearts.*
> *He has put down the mighty from their thrones,*
> *And exalted the lowly.*
> *He has filled the hungry with good things,*
> *And the rich He has sent away empty.*
> *He has helped His servant Israel,*
> *In remembrance of His mercy,*
> *As He spoke to our fathers,*
> *To Abraham and to his seed forever."* (Luke 1:46–55)

From these words it is clear Mary understood that the angel had announced to her that she would be giving birth to a king—the King, the Son of David. There is a confounding similarity between her song and the Old Testament prophecies concerning the Messiah.

JOSEPH

But what about Joseph? Would he have to deal with the bitter news of his fiancée's unexpected pregnancy without the benefit of an angelic visitation or the confirmation of a close friend?

> *Then Joseph her husband, being a just man,*
> *and not wanting to make her a public example,*
> *was minded to put her away secretly.*
> *But while he thought about these things,*
> *behold, an angel of the Lord appeared to him in a dream, saying,*
> *"Joseph, son of David, do not be afraid*
> *to take to you Mary your wife,*
> *for that which is conceived in her is of the Holy Spirit.*
> *And she will bring forth a Son, and you shall call His name JESUS,*
> *for He will save His people from their sins."* (Matthew 1:19–21)

At the outset, Joseph did not believe Mary's story. Who can blame him . . . angelic visitations . . . conceived by the Holy Spirit . . . the Son of God? This was outrageous. Rather than publicly humiliate Mary, Joseph's loving plan was to "put her away secretly." Mary would have been consigned either to an asylum or, at the least, to a home for unwed mothers if he had exposed her.

But, once again, in His mercy, God sent an angel to Joseph. The heavenly messenger confirmed for him exactly what Mary had reported, adding that her son would "save His people from their sins."

Joseph did exactly as he had been told, taking Mary as his wife. However, he did not have sexual relations with her until after Jesus was born.

The Scriptures give us the record of Joseph in a very brief, straightforward way, with few details past those found in the birth narratives. We know that he deeply loved Mary, was devout and disciplined, a law-abiding citizen, and he was a construction worker—no doubt, big and strong. The most significant was that Joseph was of the royal lineage of David and had been chosen to participate in fulfilling the promise King David had made.

> [The Lord said,] "I will make the horn of David grow;
> I will prepare a lamp for My Anointed.
> His enemies I will clothe with shame,
> But upon Himself His crown shall flourish." (Psalm 132:17–18)

EVIDENCE OF THE VIRGIN BIRTH

These accounts clearly point to the fact of the virgin birth of Jesus Christ. For some reason, some biblical scholars over the years have taken great delight in doubting this point of doctrine. Some will even believe in the bodily resurrection of the Savior but not the virgin birth.

As we will see, Jesus' earthly life was ablaze in miracles. It began with a miracle, it was filled with miracles, and it ended with the wonder of His resurrection and ascension. But Jesus will not be stripped of the miraculous simply because some may be uncomfortable with the supernatural. It should bring us comfort that both Mary and Joseph doubted. But God intervened, visiting them both and by His Spirit assuring them that He could be believed and trusted. This assurance can also be ours.

From a human standpoint, the accounts of miracles seem impossible.

Fortunately, our Sovereign God specializes in the impossible. It was impossible for God to lie. It was impossible for God's Messiah not to be born just as He predicted. It was impossible for the Holy One to fail in His mission. It was impossible for this risen Heir of David not to reign as King of the universe. It was impossible that He would allow sin to have dominion over His people. And it will be impossible for Christ not to return some day, taking His people home with Him.

> The all-powerful, self-existing God created the vast universe and chose to visit the earth.

The all-powerful, self-existing God created the vast universe and chose to visit the earth. If we take this as our starting point, then we can embrace what the angel said to Mary: "Nothing is impossible with God."

- The Intertestamental Period
- John the Baptist
- The Birth of Jesus
- The Early Years of Jesus' Life

Picture yourself standing on the sidewalk at a busy downtown New York City intersection. A businessman is desperate to get a cab. He hails one, but it's on the other side of the street. So the man, dressed in an expensive navy suit, dashes across the street, deftly dodging traffic in order to keep anyone else from heisting his taxi. He successfully dodges one sedan and a delivery van, but he's not as fortunate with a sporty black import. The driver of the car tries to swerve to miss the man, but he's not successful.

The sports car strikes the man, sending him and his briefcase sprawling. The man lies still on the street. He is injured, but not critically.

In a few moments, you hear sirens from police cars and paramedics. Amazingly, a newspaper reporter arrives on the scene in a flash. She begins to talk to people who were close by and might have seen what happened. Later these onlookers would all be referred to on the police blotter as "eyewitnesses."

If you were to collect each of these firsthand accounts, you would find something fascinating about them. Even though only one specific incident occurred—a businessman was hit by a sports car—each onlooker would underscore different dimensions of the events. One would notice, in great detail, the light green Mercury sedan and the small white Acme delivery van that barely missed him. Another would be able to identify the driver of the sports car. He would report that he looked to be about sixty, salt-and-pepper hair, and wearing a yellow golf shirt. One eyewitness even noticed that the businessman was wearing alligator shoes.

From the very same incident that occurred . . . very different stories would result—all true to the account. The interesting thing about eyewitnesses is that the uniqueness of their views of the story reveals as much about them as it does about the story itself. This is also the case in the eyewitness accounts of the life of Jesus Christ found in the New Testament.

THE GOSPELS

Matthew, Mark, Luke, and John—the Gospels—are four different eye-witness accounts of the life of Jesus. Although they each tell about the same person, in the same location, during the same time in history, they each told their stories from their own unique perspective.

As a tax collector, Matthew was concerned with the credibility of the Messiah from a historical perspective. His gospel is filled with references to Old Testament prophecy. In fact, Matthew begins his story by describing Jesus' family tree—straight from the tribe of Judah and house of King David.

Mark was a young man when Jesus walked in Palestine. His gospel is filled with the emotion and passion of the events he saw—the kind of excitement you'd expect from a young person. Interestingly enough, Mark does not even mention Jesus' nativity. Most young men aren't interested in the details of a woman's pregnancy.

Luke is a physician. Predictably, the conceptions and births of both John the Baptist and Jesus are delivered to us in some detail, even including the move-ments of the preborn baby inside Elizabeth's womb. Luke is the only book that even mentions Jesus as a young man.

John is a disciple. His writing is theological and topical, with most of his gospel arranged around subjects rather than chronology. John's work is chiefly devoted to the final week in Jesus' life. Because he was "the disciple whom Jesus loved," John gives us an intimate portrait of the Savior.

The Gospels are not the complete picture of Jesus Christ. When we consider the volume of material that could have been written about *any* man who lived for thirty-three years, they are very abbreviated. This record of the promised Messiah has been necessarily and divinely edited.

JESUS IN THE TEMPLE

As I said, Luke is the only gospel writer who says anything about Jesus' infancy and youth, and even his account of Jesus' childhood is limited to one story about when Jesus went to the Temple to prepare for His bar mitzvah.

[Jesus'] parents went to Jerusalem every year at the Feast of the Passover.
And when He was twelve years old, they went up to Jerusalem
according to the custom of the feast.
When they had finished the days, as they returned,
the Boy Jesus lingered behind in Jerusalem.
And Joseph and His mother did not know it;
but supposing Him to have been in the company, they went a day's journey,
and sought Him among their relatives and acquaintances.
So when they did not find Him, they returned to Jerusalem, seeking Him.
Now so it was that after three days they found Him in the temple,
sitting in the midst of the teachers,
both listening to them and asking them questions.
And all who heard Him were astonished at His understanding and answers.
So when they saw Him, they were amazed;
and His mother said to Him,
"Son, why have You done this to us?
Look, Your father and I have sought You anxiously."
And He said to them, "Why did you seek Me?
Did you not know that I must be about My Father's business?"
But they did not understand the statement which He spoke to them.
Then He went down with them and came to Nazareth, and was subject to them,

but His mother kept all these things in her heart.

And Jesus increased in wisdom and stature,

and in favor with God and men. (Luke 2:41–52)

This is an amazing story, giving us some very interesting information about the Holy Family. Naturally, it paints Mary and Joseph in quite a bad light. How could Jesus' parents leave town without their young son? How could they travel a full day before they realized that He was not with them? Wasn't this grossly irresponsible of them?

When Jesus was found—four days later—by His frantic parents, He was teaching in the Temple—*teaching* instead of looking for His parents. In fact, Jesus did not seem to realize that His parents must have been agitated. He

> These people were not untouchable legends, but real people with real foibles and real faith.

wasn't visibly sympathetic about what must have been pure terror for them. I used to be a twelve-year-old boy, and I once had a son who was twelve. This kind of thing would *not* have happened in my father's house or in mine . . . at least not without a stiff, don't-ever-do-this-again thrashing.

From my perspective, this story *must* be true. Why? Because, in the early church, the Holy Family was held in reverence and awe. They were idolized and literally worshiped. If this story isn't true, then why would an account of Mary and Joseph looking completely inept as parents and Jesus appearing to be an arrogant little prodigy have survived? Good question.

These people were not untouchable legends, but real people with real foibles and real faith. Joseph and Mary had a *real* preteen. This story has not been airbrushed or revised. We find it in Luke's gospel with all its warts in full view. It makes no intellectual or common sense to do anything but treat this account as genuine.

Now, back to the story for an answer to the question of apparent parental irresponsibility.

Actually, it *is* quite understandable that Joseph and Mary could have got away from Jerusalem without realizing that Jesus was not with them. The journey back to Nazareth after the Passover Feast involved lots of family members—most likely hundreds of people. And, because of the dangers of marauding thugs along the road, people always traveled in groups. And like family caravans today, the kids always begged to travel with their cousins.

There is no question that Jesus' parents *should* have been more responsible in making sure that their son was in one of the family groupings, but again, it's understandable. (Don't forget, Mary couldn't pick up her cell phone to call Uncle Jacob's van to be sure Jesus was on board. These people were walking in a caravan that spread out for miles.)

> The Holy Family was normal, except for one thing. The adolescent boy in their little family was the preexistent, Eternal Sovereign and Holy God, Creator of the universe— "normal" except for that.

It wasn't until the end of the first day of traveling, when immediate families probably collected themselves, that Joseph and Mary realized their son was missing.

The bigger problem with the story had to do with the twelve-year-old.

As I said, the Holy Family was normal, except for one thing. The adolescent boy in their little family was the preexistent, Eternal Sovereign and Holy God, Creator of the universe—"normal" except for that.

When Mary and Jesus saw their boy in the Temple, not just entertaining or even keeping up with the intellectuals of the day, but *teaching* them, Jesus' parents were "amazed." The word used here is exactly the same word that is used later in a story from Jesus' ministry about when He literally cast a demon out of a young boy. Those standing around saw Him do this unspeakable thing and "they were all amazed at the majesty of God." Joseph and Mary's astonishment at their son's intellectual prowess was more than the typical, "My son is an honor student at Nazareth Elementary." These people were awestruck by the same wonder that captivated Moses, Isaiah, Elijah, and Nebuchadnezzar.

What young Jesus experienced in being drawn away from His earthly parents, Joseph and Mary, was the unmistakable tug of His *heavenly* Father. Certainly, this must have been something that He felt many times as a young man. However, it appears that the event was a watershed for the youthful Jesus. The Scripture tells us that, after the temple incident, Jesus went home with His parents and "was subject to them." Perhaps Jesus and His Father had a conversation and decided that it was too soon for Him to teach in the Temple and that it would be best for Him to obediently remain at home with Joseph and Mary.

So the Boy Messiah went back home to be His mother and father's son. And as Jesus grew, the Scripture identifies four distinct areas in which He developed—an ideal model for all children.

Jesus increased in wisdom and stature,
and in favor with God and men. (Luke 2:52)

In Wisdom

The pursuit of knowledge is a powerful thing. Children who diligently seek to learn are, indeed, wealthy beyond measure. Jesus had the very mind of God and passionately understood this. We don't know exactly how Joseph and Mary encouraged Jesus' love of learning, but it is a challenge for parents to model a diligent search for knowledge and truth. Even though I have lived a life immersed in the rigors of study, I fully understand how dangerous it would be to stop learning and growing. So I won't.

In Stature

The story of Daniel and his Hebrew friends will always be one of my favorites. These young men knew that healthy minds would have a greater chance to influence their culture if they resided in healthy bodies—so they ate their vegetables. Jesus understood this.

In Favor with God

When a young person makes a profession of faith and then diligently seeks to obey his heavenly Father, great things are in store for him. Even though Jesus was the Incarnate God, He practiced this. As we follow His life throughout the gospel stories, we see His undying commitment to be in tune with God. In prayer He listened to His Father's voice.

In Favor with Man

Perhaps the greatest measure of a man is in his ability to make friends. I don't know if He was voted "most popular" in His school, but I *do* know that Jesus' closest friends loved Him so much, they would have been willing to die for Him . . . which most of them eventually did. Jesus understood the importance of friendship—favor with men.

The young Jesus grew intellectually, physically, spiritually, and relationally. What a perfect balance for the One who would bring a suffering and sinful world the hope of forgiveness and eternal life, in perfect communion and fellowship with a Holy God.

SUMMARY
■ THE INTERTESTAMENTAL PERIOD

The Old Testament period had finished. The sound of Malachi's voice delivering his final prophecy had faded into four hundred years of silence. And then, because this act was completed, the curtain dropped. The stage needed to be prepared for the next of God's visible activities.

The *pleroma*—the fullness of time—tells us that the stage was being set for the coming of Jesus. This was going to be the focal point of history. He came at the right time, the perfect instant, fulfilling all the prophecies in one moment in time. God's plan of redemption was about to come to pass.

During this time one of Aristotle's most famous students, Alexander the Great, came to power. He conquered with his forces and he conquered with the philosophies of his master. So pervasive and so successful were Alexander's efforts that, more than three centuries later when the text of the New Testament was penned—mostly by Hebrews—it was written in Greek.

In 327 B.C., Alexander the Great was stricken with an illness and died as he was conquering Babylon. Upon his death, his kingdom was divided into two groups: the Ptolemies and the Seleucids.

After more than one hundred years under the Ptolemies, Antiochus III fought for and gained control of Palestine for the Seleucids. Groups of Jews began forming in resistance to his cultural and spiritual attempt at assimilation. The Hassidians—the "Pious Ones"—were earnest in their desire to maintain the Jewish culture and belief in the One True God. Other groups tried to maintain the purity of their traditions, such as the Pharisees. Unfortunately, by the time we meet them in the New Testament, they are concerned only with the externals of the Law.

Following the short reign of Antiochus III, Antiochus Epiphanes came to power. He was demented, with a messianic complex unrivaled by any leader of that time. Three years later, the Maccabean Revolts began.

A man named Mattathias rose in protest against Antiochus. He began to fight a guerrilla war against the Seleucids with his five sons. When Mattathias died, the leadership of the revolt fell to Judas Maccabaeus—Judas the Hammer. Because of his bold raids against the invaders, he became a national hero among the Israelites and remains so today. The Feast of Hanukkah is celebrated to this day in memory of this event and the unabashed heroics of Judas the Hammer.

In 63 B.C. Palestine was conquered again, this time by General Pompey from the ever-spreading Roman Empire. Twenty-three years later, Herod the Great was appointed by Rome as the local king over the Jews.

No wonder the Israelites were ready for a Savior.

■ JOHN THE BAPTIST

Like many prophets before him, John the Baptist talked about the Day of the Lord. What was significant about John's message was that, unlike the prophets of old, he did not talk about the "coming" of that great and awesome day. John the Baptist said that the day is *here*.

John told them that this One would be like an ax, felling those who had forgotten God or who were unwilling to repent. The Messiah would be like the tool that farmers used to separate the wheat from the chaff. From the wheat people were fed, but the chaff was only good for burning.

I can picture the religious leaders of the day beginning to squirm in their seats. The coming of a prophet, ushering in the Messiah, sounded like good news at first. But John's words sounded more like a visit to the woodshed, and they were at the top of his list.

After John had upset nearly everyone in Judea, the teachers from Jerusalem came out to question him. Can you picture this? These religious leaders, quite full of themselves, are getting a closer look at this wild man from the desert. And not only did John the Baptist level them with his words, calling them serpents and candy-coated crypts, but he also told them that there was Someone in their midst who was about to make them look really, really bad.

This was the most important dimension of John's calling, bearing witness to the coming Messiah, Jesus Christ. One day when John was preaching and baptizing in the Jordan River, he looked up and saw Jesus walking toward him, directly into the water. "Behold!" John exclaimed. "The Lamb of God who takes away the sin of the world!"

The Savior of the world, the perfect Sacrifice, the Hope of all mankind—Jews, Gentiles, and Romans—had finally come.

■ THE BIRTH OF JESUS

Jesus Christ, God the Son, did not first come into being in Bethlehem. He was eternally existent, before the foundations of the earth. He, too, was the Creator of the universe.

The miracle of Christmas wasn't simply that the Messiah was born, but that God the Son willingly condescended from His holy throne. Having eternally existed and never having been limited by time or space, He quietly took upon Himself the form of a helpless baby boy. Jesus became a child whose ethnic lineage was, and continues to be, the most persecuted in all of human history.

As heaven's resident for all eternity, God's Son had never known physical pain, hunger, thirst, winter's chill, summer's heat, exhaustion, or poverty. Now He would experience all of these, starting with His birth in a cattle trough. He came on a mission: to die a humiliating and unthinkable death, bearing the sins of the world. As a man, He had nothing to look forward to. To think that God willingly did this to *Himself* makes the miracle of the birth of Jesus Christ truly indescribable. This is exactly what happened.

■ THE EARLY YEARS OF JESUS' LIFE

Matthew, Mark, Luke, and John—the Gospels—are four different eye-witness accounts of the life of Jesus. Although they each tell about the same person, in the same location, during the same time in history, they each told their stories from their own unique perspective.

The Gospels are not the complete picture of Jesus Christ. When we consider the volume of material that could have been written about *any* man who lived for thirty-three years, they are very abbreviated. This record of the promised Messiah has been necessarily and divinely edited.

The young Jesus grew intellectually, physically, spiritually, and relationally. What a perfect balance for the One who would bring a suffering and sinful world the hope of forgiveness and eternal life, in perfect communion and fellowship with a Holy God.

CHAPTER TWELVE

THE EARLY MINISTRY OF JESUS

- **The Baptism and Temptation of Jesus**
- Jesus' Inaugural Address and Public Ministry
- The Teaching of Jesus: Parables
- Interpreting Parables
- The Miracles of Jesus

Not long ago, my wife and I were enjoying dinner with two friends at our favorite restaurant. As often happens when we're with people we enjoy, the conversation included lots of information about our respective families. We talked about how our adult children and their spouses were doing and we talked about grandchildren—we have seven and they have three. What followed, of course, was the unloading of wallets and purses, and oohing and ahing at photos of the representatives of our second and third generations. There's nothing quite like the special kind of pride parents and grandparents feel for their kids. And for the children and grandchildren, knowing their parents and grandparents carry photos of them creates a wonderful sense of security.

If you visit a high school football game and sit in the hometown stands, you'll be sure to see proud moms and dads wearing huge buttons that read, "My Son Is #54." And, even though the teenage toughs running up and down the field would be hard-pressed to admit it, they relish the fact that someone in the stands is wearing a button that bears their number. There's nothing quite like the assurance that your parents are proud of you.

Throughout this book we have seen the snowcapped peaks of God's special visits to planet earth. In every case, these sovereign appointments left the men and women who experienced them changed forever.

One of these mountaintops—perhaps the most wonderful one in all of Scripture—is when God said to His only Son, "I'm proud of You." And can you imagine how powerful these words were to the ears of the Messiah?

You and I have already seen that only Luke included anything about Jesus' childhood and, even then, there's only one story—the one about Jesus in the Temple.

But none of the Gospels contain a single word about Jesus from the age of twelve until the age of thirty—eighteen years of silence. I have often wondered about this. My suspicion is that God was preparing His Son for the incredible assignment that was coming.

I'm reminded of this when I read a story of a well-known celebrity who makes a profession of faith in Christ. During the time when he ought to be quietly soaking in sound teaching and experiencing solid spiritual growth, he's making appearances on Christian television and standing on the platform speaking to thousands at huge Christian conferences. *Where's the preparation? I* often wonder to myself. *It's too soon for ministry.*

> No limousines, no spotlights, no packed auditoriums of "beautiful" people, simply the focal point of a loving God's redemption and grace in human form, Jesus Christ the Messiah.

Even Jesus Christ spent almost twenty years in training, from the time He was called to ministry in the Temple until He made His first public appearance as the Messiah. Perhaps the confirmation that He had prepared well were the words from His Daddy, "I'm proud of You."

THE JORDAN RIVER

Although I spend very little time watching televised awards shows, I'm still fascinated by them: the Emmys, the ESPYs, the Tonys, the Grammys, and the Academy Awards. Huge auditoriums are packed with celebrities who desperately await the sound of their own names at the close of the sentence, "And the winner is . . ."

Once the favorite is announced and the cameras have focused closely on the faces of the losers, squeezing out painful smiles and trying not to look infuriated at the choice, the winner makes his way through the crowd to the podium. Spotlights follow the victor, who often stops to hug a friend on his way to receive his trophy. For these actors, musicians, and athletes, *this* is the moment they have awaited—the split second they have given their lives for.

The eyewitness accounts of three of the four Gospels record the baptism of Jesus and the beginning of His earthly ministry. The last account we had of Him was when He was only twelve. Now, after almost two unrecorded decades, the thirty-year-old Jesus made His way through the crowd and stepped to the banks of the River Jordan.

John the Baptist, standing waist-deep in the placid river, did not ask for an envelope to see whose name he would announce. After having given his entire ministry to prepare for this instant, John knew exactly Who it was standing at the water's threshold.

> *Behold! The Lamb of God who takes away*
> *the sin of the world! This is He . . .* (John 1:29–30)

Do you remember the curtain God closed for four hundred years between the Old and New Testaments—four centuries of rearrangement and preparation for the greatest event in human history? Do you remember the *pleroma*—the fullness of time—when God's answer to the chaos and despair of mankind would step forward?

This was it.

And from His birth in a humble feeding trough and His obscure boyhood in a Galilean carpenter's home, the greatest Man to ever draw a breath quietly and unobtrusively stood ready to change the course of antiquity forever. No limousines, no spotlights, no packed auditoriums of "beautiful" people, simply the focal point of a loving God's redemption and grace in human form, Jesus Christ the Messiah.

"Baptize me," Jesus asked John.

Not one to be easily intimidated, John was understandably overwhelmed by the request.

> *And John tried to prevent Him, saying,*
> *"I need to be baptized by You,*

and are You coming to me?"
But Jesus answered and said to him,
"Permit it to be so now,
for thus it is fitting for us to fulfill all righteousness."
Then he allowed Him.
When He had been baptized,
Jesus came up immediately from the water . . . (Matthew 3:14–16a)

Jesus reminded John that in order to fulfill all righteousness He must be baptized. Every dimension of the Law of God must be fulfilled by Christ. And so it was.

But something unexpected happened when Jesus came out of the water. It was something that those standing on the riverbank must have talked about the rest of their lives. God spoke.

And behold, the heavens were opened to Him,
and He saw the Spirit of God descending like a dove
and alighting upon Him.
And suddenly a voice came from heaven, saying,
"This is My beloved Son,
in whom I am well pleased." (Matthew 3:16b–17)

It would have been wonderfully affirming for Jesus to hear John the Baptist declare to those standing along the river that day, "Behold the Lamb of God." But to literally *hear* the audible voice of His Father must have been indescribable: "Well done, My Son. I'm so proud of You." No boy, after hearing these words from his daddy, is ever the same again.

THE WILDERNESS

The euphoria of the voice from heaven to Jesus was, however, short-lived.

Then Jesus, being filled with the Holy Spirit,
returned from the Jordan and was led by the Spirit into the wilderness,

> *being tempted for forty days by the devil.*
> *And in those days He ate nothing,*
> *and afterward, when they had ended,*
> *He was hungry.* (Luke 4:1–2)

When we began this journey through the Bible, we read how Satan tempted Adam and Eve. We learned how the serpent's wiles had prevailed over them and how they were thrown out of the Garden of Eden. One of the most important motifs in the New Testament is Jesus' fulfilling the role of the new Adam, the new representative of God's people . . . the Son of Man. Since Jesus was to achieve victory where the first Adam had experienced defeat, coming face to face with the persuasive power of evil was the first post-baptism test.

But, unlike Adam, who faced the devil while sauntering around a five-star garden, Jesus was dealing with Satan in a desolate wilderness after forty days with nothing to eat. And the evil one came to Jesus with not just a single proposition, but three seductive offers.

> *And the devil said to Him,*
> *"If You are the Son of God, command this stone to become bread."*
> *But Jesus answered him saying,*
> *"It is written, 'Man shall not live by bread alone,*
> *but by every word of God.'"* (Luke 4:3–4)

The force of this temptation was grand. Satan was appealing to a desperate physical desire for food that, after a forty-day starvation fast, must have been incredible. There is, of course, nothing wrong with eating, but to do so in this case would have meant obedience to God's greatest adversary, and Jesus wasn't going to do it. And, not surprisingly, He used the Holy Scripture to support His decision.

The next temptation is a disturbing one.

> *Then the devil, taking Him up on a high mountain,*
> *showed Him all the kingdoms of the world in a moment of time.*

And the devil said to Him,
"All this authority I will give You, and their glory;
for this has been delivered to me,
and I give it to whomever I wish.
Therefore, if You will worship before me,
all will be Yours."
And Jesus answered and said to him,
"Get behind Me, Satan! For it is written,
'You shall worship the LORD your God,
and Him only you shall serve.'" (Luke 4:5–8)

Satan is offering Jesus a clear shortcut to the fulfillment of His task: "If You are the Son of God, why should You go through all the pain and suffering? No cross, no grief—You can have Your kingdom right now." This would be an attractive offer to anyone, like the advertisements that seem to promise great things with no effort whatsoever. In fact, Satan seemed to be treating Jesus mercifully, like a man offering his friend a gift.

On this very subject, an unforgettable conversation between Jesus and Simon Peter is tucked into the gospel record. Matthew, Mark, and Luke each record it.

From that time Jesus began to show to His disciples that
He must go to Jerusalem,
and suffer many things from the elders and chief priests and scribes,
and be killed, and be raised the third day.
Then Peter took Him aside and began to rebuke Him, saying,
"Far be it from You, Lord;
this shall not happen to You!"
But [Jesus] turned and said to Peter,
"Get behind Me, Satan! You are an offense to Me,
for you are not mindful of the things of God,
but the things of men." (Matthew 16:21–23)

Over the years, students have asked me why Jesus was so tough on Peter. Why was His rejoinder so harsh? Wasn't Peter just trying to protect Jesus? Weren't his words the expressions of an advocate? Perhaps.

But Jesus knew that the assignment of His incarnation was to fulfill His Father's complete will by becoming, as John the Baptist had declared, the *Lamb* of God, taking upon Himself the sins of mankind, and dying as the Law required. Even though it would have been wonderfully convenient to agree to the lure of this temptation, to sidestep the suffering would have been to destine men to die in their own trespasses and sins without a redeeming Savior. So Jesus' words to Peter were direct. He knew that if He didn't suffer, He would be acting in disobedience to His Father.

> Like a child who had just been pummeled by the neighborhood bully, Jesus was tenderly comforted by His Father's special agents.

Jesus was resolved to complete His task until, as He proclaimed from the cross, "it is finished."

In the first two encounters with Satan, Jesus quoted the Scripture in His defense. But in the final temptation, the evil one tries his own hand at referencing the biblical record.

> *Then [the devil] brought [Jesus] to Jerusalem,*
> *set Him on the pinnacle of the temple, and said to Him,*
> *"If You are the Son of God,*
> *throw Yourself down from here.*
> *For it is written:*
> *'He shall give His angels charge over you,*
> *To keep you,' and*
> *'In their hands they shall bear you up,*
> *Lest you dash your foot against a stone.'"*
> *And Jesus answered and said to him,*
> *"It has been said,*
> *'You shall not tempt the LORD your God.'"* (Luke 4:9–12)

One of the most basic rules of biblical interpretation is to let Scripture interpret Scripture and to never set one passage against another. "You have not spoken the whole truth," He was saying to Satan. "Yes, the Scripture *does* say that the angels will take care of Me, but it also says not to put God to the test. I do not have to jump from this tower to prove My Father's trustworthiness."

I love the word picture that Matthew gives us at the close of the temptation ordeal.

> *Then the devil left Him,*
> *and behold, angels came and ministered to Him.* (Matthew 4:11)

Like a child who had just been pummeled by the neighborhood bully, Jesus was tenderly comforted by His Father's special agents. We're not told how long this respite lasted, but can there be any doubt that it was exactly what the Savior needed?

- The Baptism and Temptation of Jesus
- **Jesus' Inaugural Address and Public Ministry**
- The Teaching of Jesus: Parables
- Interpreting Parables
- The Miracles of Jesus

Just like a young soldier having successfully completed the treachery of boot camp, Jesus returned from the desert and went straight to Nazareth, His hometown. He did what any of us would have done; He surrounded Himself with familiar faces and places.

The following Sabbath, Jesus went to the synagogue. This was His "home church," the place where He had sat at the feet of the rabbi, memorizing the Scriptures and learning Hebrew. More parishioners would have known Him as "Joseph and Mary's boy" than by His given name.

On this day, Jesus was handed a scroll containing the writings of the prophet Isaiah. Most likely the word had circulated of John's baptism of Jesus in the Jordan six weeks prior, and the elders wanted to give the new Rabbi a chance to read publicly.

> *And [Jesus] was handed the book of the prophet Isaiah.*
> *And when He had opened the book,*

> *He found the place where it was written:*
> *"The Spirit of the LORD is upon Me,*
> *Because He has anointed Me*
> *To preach the gospel to the poor;*
> *He has sent Me to heal the brokenhearted,*
> *To proclaim liberty to the captives*
> *And recovery of sight to the blind,*
> *To set at liberty those who are oppressed;*
> *To proclaim the acceptable year of the LORD."* (Luke 4:17–19)

Put yourself in the synagogue at that moment. Look around the room into the faces of the men sitting there. How proud they first must have been at Jesus' ability to read the Scripture—the daily lectionary lesson: hometown boy makes good. Can you see them smile? *The tone of His voice is so warm, so gracious,* they must have been thinking.

Once the reading was completed, Jesus handed the scroll back to the temple attendant. He quietly sat down. The Scripture tells us that the eyes of those who were sitting there were "fixed on Him." In the prolonged silence, can you see their smiling faces turn quizzical? *What is He going to say now,* they surely thought.

Jesus' first words must have stunned them. "I'm the very One Whom Isaiah was talking about," He said.

> *Then He closed the book, and gave it back to the attendant and sat down.*
> *And the eyes of all who were in the synagogue were fixed on Him.*
> *And He began to say to them,*
> *"Today this Scripture is fulfilled in your hearing."* (Luke 4:20–21)

Their questioning faces probably first produced thin smiles again, thinking that Jesus was going to add something to what He had just said—something to soften the preposterous claim He had made. But when they realized that He was not speaking euphemistically, someone spoke up.

"Is this not Joseph's son?" he rhetorically asked. No answer was required. Of course, everyone knew exactly Who this was making this unconscionable claim. Their faces must have become filled with a sense of outrage. "Who does this *boy* think He is?"

Perceiving that these religious leaders were not happy with His pretension, Jesus said:

> *No prophet is accepted in his own country.* (Luke 4:24)

And then, in direct and measured tones, Jesus told these men—experts in Jewish history—something they already knew full well: God's revelation is selective. When Elijah had declared drought on the kingdom because of Ahab and Jezebel's sin, he singled out one widow and paid her a visit. Although the nation had many widows, God sent Elijah to just one.

And even though Israel had many lepers, God chose one man, Naaman the Syrian—not even a Jew—to be miraculously healed by the prophet Elisha.

> Their faces must have become filled with a sense of outrage. "Who does this *boy* think He is?"

"God does not *owe* you an appearance," Jesus was saying to them. "If you refuse to recognize Me as the One, then the Sovereign God will send Me to others who will know Who I am. I will reveal Myself to those whom He chooses."

As these Bible scholars listened to Jesus' words, I wonder if any of them were reminded of God's words to Moses centuries earlier:

> *I will be gracious to whom I will be gracious,*
> *and I will have compassion on*
> *whom I will have compassion.* (Exodus 33:19b)

Regardless of what came to their minds, we do know that these pious men were furious at what they perceived was an insult. In fact, they were so blind with rage, they did something that seems unbelievable, given the fact that Jesus and His family were faithful members at this temple.

> *All those in the synagogue, when they heard these things,*
> *were filled with wrath, and rose up and thrust Him out of the city;*

and they led Him to the brow of the hill on which their city was built,
that they might throw Him down over the cliff.
Then passing through the midst of them, He went His way. (Luke 4:28–30)

On the surface, I would say that Jesus' first message did not turn out very well. But, without question, it accomplished its purpose: Jesus identified Himself publicly as the predicted Messiah from Isaiah's prophecy. Jesus' comments also began the process that, three years later, would result in the successful accomplishment of the Jewish leaders' ultimate goal: the death of this messianic impostor.

THE DISCIPLES

Each of the gospel writers included the accounts of Jesus selecting the disciples. This gathering of potential students was not an unusual practice by traveling rabbis. However, His selections *were* highly peculiar. Jesus did not draft the brightest pupils from surrounding religious schools; He picked fishermen, political troublemakers, and a tax collector. He announced His choices by offering them a simple invitation: "Follow Me." And this is exactly what they did. These twelve men packed a few things and took to the road with Joseph and Mary's son.

For the next three years the essence of Jesus' ministry was to travel around the area with a group of friends and students, teaching in the synagogues, preaching the gospel of the kingdom, and healing all kinds of sicknesses and diseases among the people.

> Jesus did not draft the brightest pupils from surrounding religious schools; He picked fishermen, political troublemakers, and a tax collector.

Word of His work spread throughout the region. People brought those with every type of illness and torment—including the demon-possessed. Epileptics and paralytics came, and He healed them. Even the dead were revived. Predictably, multitudes followed Him, some who truly believed and others from sheer curiosity.

The most comprehensive of Jesus' messages is found in Matthew.

THE SERMON ON THE MOUNT

C. S. Lewis wrote that anyone who reads the Sermon on the Mount and is not filled with fear does not understand what Jesus was saying. The reason for this wise commentary is that Lewis understood the sermon's context. Like Old Testament speeches given by Elijah, Isaiah, or Jeremiah, the blessings and warnings of this oracle were prophetic.

Jesus had just said that His mission was to heal the broken, bring freedom to the prisoners, and sight to the blind. He had resolutely identified Himself as the One promised through Isaiah. The location of this presentation was the Mount of Olives. A crowd had

> This was no ordinary sermon; this was a transcendent event that penetrated the hearers' souls with the eternal pleasure of God.

gathered around Jesus, Who was, as Matthew reported, becoming quite famous in the region and beyond. The people were expectant: Miracles, a flash of power, or authoritative preaching provided plenty of entertainment.

First, Jesus used the literary device of the prophetic oracle, a series of divine pronouncements of God's blessing upon those who demonstrate a certain attitude. The rewards to those who obey Jesus' words are deeper than "happiness" and more significant than "joy." Those faithful to the Messiah's admonitions could consider themselves "blessed," being given a heavenly benediction from God Himself. This was no ordinary sermon; this was a transcendent event that penetrated the hearers' souls with the eternal pleasure of God.

The message Jesus gave was filled with irony, the topsy-turvy announcement of His kingdom's values. Under normal circumstances, those who rejoice are blessed and those who are rich throw the parties, but not in this kingdom. Usually those who are oppressed and beaten down remain so, but not where Jesus is King.

In this special place the blind see, the deaf hear, and the poor receive good news. And their suffering and pain bring them blessing. "When you are maligned, despised, or even persecuted for righteousness' sake," Jesus said, "you are blessed."

"So," He tells the crowd gathered on the hillside, "rejoice and be very glad, for great *is* your reward in heaven." God's blessing gave the people a future heavenly hope, but it was also in the present: the here and now. Imagine the impact of Jesus' words on those who listened.

For centuries, liberal scholars have desperately attempted to turn Jesus into a happy humanist who, while saying an occasional odd thing, basically wanted everyone to just get along and love one another unconditionally. According to these folks, the impact of Jesus was not His atonement for our sins or His resurrection; that was mythology. Jesus' great contribution was His ethical insights, the acme of which was the Beatitudes found at the beginning of the Sermon on the Mount.

> His kingdom required both obedience and a personal relationship with the Father. To reject this would result in eternal lostness: So much for being nice.

However, this discourse contains the unique revelation of the person of Jesus Christ that frontally contradicts these flaccid claims. These are not the words of a first-century "Mr. Rogers," but of an individual Who is declaring the eternal fate of every man, woman, and child on the planet. He is pronouncing that those who are persecuted for His sake will be blessed by the Father, and those who reject His message will be forever cursed—not exactly a benign children's story from the mouth of some well-meaning Sunday school volunteer.

Look at the climax of the sermon.

> *Not everyone who says to Me, "Lord, Lord,"*
> *shall enter the kingdom of heaven,*
> *but he who does the will of My Father in heaven.*
> *Many will say to Me in that day,*
> *"Lord, Lord, have we not prophesied in Your name,*
> *cast out demons in Your name,*
> *and done many wonders in Your name?"*
> *And then I will declare to them,*
> *"I never knew you; depart from Me,*
> *you who practice lawlessness!"* (Matthew 7:21–23)

This is not a pleasant sermon on morality. Jesus' words were alarming and strong. He was telling His listeners that there was no wall separating works and faith. His kingdom required both obedience and a personal relationship with the Father. To reject this would result in eternal lostness: So much for being nice.

- The Baptism and Temptation of Jesus
- Jesus' Inaugural Address and Public Ministry
- **The Teaching of Jesus: Parables**
- Interpreting Parables
- The Miracles of Jesus

Everyone loves a good story. Public speakers know that using stories helps to keep the audience eagerly listening. Writers know that stories effectively illustrate their points. Grandfathers, like me, know that stories are often the great connector between generations. "Papa, read me a story," is so compelling that I drop everything to obey. When one of my grandkids is nestled on my lap and I'm reciting something from the printed page, all is well with the world, and I am at peace.

Jesus knew that telling stories would be a profound way of connecting with an audience, illuminating truth, and building relationships. And so He told stories . . . parables.

This unorthodox approach to teaching completely bewildered the Sanhedrin. "Why haven't you captured Him?" the Pharisees queried the officers who had been dispatched to collar the Savior.

> *The officers answered,*
> *"No man ever spoke like this Man!"*
> *Then the Pharisees answered them,*
> *"Are you also deceived?"* (John 7:46–47)

Even these religious spies were spellbound by the simple power of Jesus' approach. In fact, their superiors must have detected that the Messiah's stories had even reached the hearts of the officers, thus the question: "Are you also deceived?" In other words, "He hasn't gotten to you, *too*, has He?"

Others reported that Jesus "taught them as one having authority" (Mark 1:22). For some, the paradox of "simple" stories and "authoritative" command was irreconcilable. But Jesus did exactly that.

The word used here for "authority" (in Greek: *exousia*) can be translated as "being" or "essence." Jesus did not speak lightly, frivolously, or without substance. He spoke with *exousia*, telling it like it was in a format that made truth understandable and application of that truth unforgettable—literally life-changing for many.

Jesus said that His teachings were not created by His own imagination (John 7:16), but were taken directly from God. He said that He did not speak on His own *exousia*, but with the authority of the Father. Jesus was not simply a person with a commanding presence, a charismatic style, or a deep and silvery voice. He spoke with the authority of the Sovereign One and that, coupled with an ability to tell inspired stories, was enough.

> He spoke with the authority of the Sovereign One and that, coupled with an ability to tell inspired stories, was enough.

Over the centuries, even those who do not embrace Christ as the Messiah have written and spoken in admiring terms of Jesus' skill of teaching through parables.

Parables were not similes—stories using "as" or "like" that took a truth and made an exact replica as in "To what shall I liken this generation?" Parables were not metaphors or implied comparisons like "I am the Vine, and you are the branches." Parables were not hyperbole, or intentional exaggeration, such as "faith like a mustard seed."

A parable—meaning "to throw alongside"—was a story that delivered a parallel truth. It was a pithy, fictional story that had one purpose: to underscore the point of the message. Saint Augustine, when he was teaching his students how to interpret Scripture, said that there were three keys to doing so: context, context, and context. The three most important elements of dynamic communication are illustration, illustration, and illustration. And the form of illustration that Jesus used most often was the parable.

Jesus demonstrated that parables could be quite long, as with the story of the prodigal son (Luke 15) or very short:

> And if the blind leads the blind,
> both will fall into a ditch. (Matthew 15:14b)

THE GOOD SAMARITAN AND THE QUIETED LAWYER

Parables were also used like riddles, setting a trap for the listeners. One of the most profound of these was the parable of the good Samaritan. Apparently Jesus was teaching and, at a certain point—perhaps it was an official question-and-answer session—a lawyer stood. Luke gives us a clue as to the motives of the attorney. The text tells us that he "tested" Jesus with the question. This looks like it might be a good time for a riddle.

> And behold, a certain lawyer stood up
> and tested Him, saying,
> "Teacher, what shall I do to inherit eternal life?"
> [Jesus] said to him, "What is written in the law?
> What is your reading of it?"
> So [the lawyer] answered and said,
> "'You shall love the LORD your God with all your heart,
> with all your soul, with all your strength,
> and with all your mind,'
> and, 'your neighbor as yourself.'"
> And [Jesus] said to him,
> "You have answered rightly; do this and you will live." (Luke 10:25–28)

Can you see the wheels turning in the lawyer's mind? How was he going to save face among his friends when he—and, no doubt, they—knew that there was no mortal man who could claim to actually *do* all this. "All" your heart, soul, strength, mind, and neighbor? I don't think so. But the lawyer is still standing there and, of course, he knows the business of cross-examination, so he continues, not with an answer but with another question.

> *But he, wanting to justify himself, said to Jesus,*
> *"And who is my neighbor?" (Luke 10:29)*

Again, Luke's use of the words "justify himself" gives us some important insight into the heart and motives of this man.

"Who's your neighbor?" Jesus could have said to the man. "I thought you wanted to inherit eternal life. Have you loved God with 'all' your heart, soul, strength, and mind? You've got plenty to work on before you start worrying about the definition of *neighbor.*" Jesus could have reduced this arrogant cynic to nothing, like a snowman on a warm spring day—as I would have been tempted to do. He could have looked away from the man, around to the rest of the crowd and said, "Next question, please." But He didn't.

Instead, Jesus told a story.

> *Then Jesus answered and said:*
> *"A certain man went down from Jerusalem to Jericho,*
> *and fell among thieves, who stripped him of his clothing,*
> *wounded him, and departed, leaving him half dead.*
> *Now by chance a certain priest came down that road.*
> *And when he saw him, he passed by on the other side.*
> *Likewise a Levite, when he arrived at the place,*
> *came and looked, and passed by on the other side.*
> *But a certain Samaritan, as he journeyed, came where he was.*
> *And when he saw him, he had compassion.*
> *So he went to him and bandaged his wounds,*
> *pouring on oil and wine;*
> *And he set him on his own animal,*
> *brought him to an inn, and took care of him.*
> *On the next day, when he departed, he took out two denarii,*
> *gave them to the innkeeper, and said to him,*
> *'Take care of him; and whatever more you spend,*
> *when I come again, I will repay you.'*
> *So which of these three do you think was neighbor to him*
> *who fell among the thieves?"*

And [the lawyer] said, "He who showed mercy on him."
Then Jesus said to him, "Go and do likewise." (Luke 10:30–37)

The impact of this simple yet profound story was unmistakable.

Instead of grilling the lawyer on how impossible it was to love God with his heart, soul, strength, and mind, Jesus picked an easy one. "Go love your neighbor." And, as would have been the case with you and me, the lawyer realized how far short he fell in obeying this one . . . much less the entire Law. As a professional in the art of oral argumentation, this legal whip wasn't accustomed to being soundly defeated in public. Of course, he had never been cross-examined by the Creator of the universe.

No doubt the lawyer quietly sat down, determining that the next time he would pick on someone his own size.

THE FOUR SOILS: AN OPPORTUNITY
TO TEACH THE DISCIPLES ABOUT PARABLES

When I'm preparing to speak to a group in Boston, I try to pick up a morning copy of the *Boston Globe* to see what's happening around town. A Red Sox winning streak or a successful downtown Pops concert gives me good material to connect with the local audience. Of course, I didn't come up with this good idea all by myself. It was exactly what Jesus did.

Most of the people Jesus spoke to were farmers, raising livestock and crops. So, as you would expect, the majority of His parables centered on this vocation. There was immediate connection.

"Listen! Behold, a sower went out to sow.
And it happened, as he sowed, that some seed fell by the wayside;
and the birds of the air came and devoured it.
Some fell on stony ground, where it did not have much earth;
and immediately it sprang up because it had no depth of earth.
But when the sun was up it was scorched,
and because it had no root it withered away.
And some seed fell among thorns;

and the thorns grew up and choked it, and it yielded no crop.
But other seed fell on good ground and yielded a crop that sprang up,
increased and produced: some thirtyfold, some sixty, and some a hundred."
And He said to them, "He who has ears to hear, let him hear!" (Mark 4:3–9)

According to the text, Jesus said no more than this to the crowd. He did not tell them Who the Sower was or what the seed and soils represented. Some must have walked away wondering why Jesus was giving them a lesson on planting crops. But other people's conscious minds must have been penetrated with the fact that Jesus was the Sower, the Word was the seed, and *they* were the soils. Many scratched their heads, while others were stunned by the convicting power of the Master's story.

As the crowds were dispersing, the disciples took Jesus aside and asked Him about His approach.

[Jesus said,] "To you it has been given to know
the mystery of the kingdom of God;
but to those who are outside, all things come in parables . . ." (Mark 4:11)

Jesus reminded His disciples that He used stories to draw unbelievers to Himself. With a heart of love and compassion, parables were His way of alerting outsiders to the truths of the kingdom. As an art form, these narratives spoke different things to different listeners, much like the communicating power of music, drama, and art. The prerequisite, regardless of the condition of those in His presence, was that the listeners had "ears to listen." His truth was not primarily intended to open the cynic's resistant ears but to fill the hearts of the hungry.

Before we take a close look at a parable, here are some important principles to use as a guide when you are reading the stories Jesus told.

1. Don't treat parables like allegory. An allegory is most often completely filled with symbolic meaning. Every detail means something that can be traced to the overriding principle that is being illuminated. Parables usually have one basic, central meaning. Trying to oversymbolize them can have the effect of tearing them apart. A person doesn't understand the beauty of a flower by disassembling it. Like a blossom, a parable is best understood by seeing it in its simple and profound entirety.

2. *The Rule of Three.* Like all good storytelling, parables usually follow the Rule of Three. Do you remember the stories you heard as a child—such as "The Three Little Pigs" and "The Three Bears"? Both of these stories are filled with more "threes": three wolves, three beds, three bowls of porridge. Jesus did this often in the telling of the parables. And is it any wonder that many parables deliver three important truths or that most sermons rest on three important points?

3. *The Rule of Two.* Parable characters often follow the Rule of Two. There were usually two people who experienced tension between righteousness and sin, good and evil. When you look for these two elements you will find an important part of the development of the parable.

4. *Code words and phrases.* Jesus' parables used certain phrases and code words that communicated in subtly powerful ways to His audiences. For instance, "How much more" is used to build a bridge from temporal things to spiritual realities. "He who has ears to hear" calls people to critically important issues of spiritual life and death. "Verily, verily, I say to you," means that Jesus is speaking with earnest intensity; don't miss it. Look for these phrases and understand where they're leading you.

One of the advantages to having four Gospels—four separate accounts of Jesus' life and ministry from a quartet of eyewitnesses—is that we can learn something about these writers by seeing where and how they place certain episodes. As they give the scenes different textures and context, we can see the unique concerns of each one. Absolutely no damage is done to divine inspiration to affirm that each human author had different motivations and goals for writing what he wrote.

Many stories and accounts are told by only one, two, or three of the gospel writers. Occasionally, all four give accounts of the same events. We can be certain that when this occurs God truly intended for the church to pay great attention to this oft-repeated lesson. The baptism of Jesus by John the Baptist, the feeding of the five thousand people from one boy's sack lunch, and most of the events of the week leading up to the crucifixion and resurrection of Jesus are told by all four authors.

Some opponents of biblical accuracy point out that some of Jesus' sermons are recorded as having been given in different geographical locations, proving that the gospel writers made mistakes. Their observations are correct, but their logic is not. As a traveling speaker, I can assure you that I've given the same message in multiple locations. I have also given the same message in the *same* location because I thought the audience needed to hear it again. Teachers often repeat their best material and their most important words so that their audiences will be certain to understand it.

Jesus, the greatest Teacher, would have certainly used repetition to help His followers remember His key messages. And His parables accompanied most of His teaching.

In addition to pointing to the number of times a story is repeated to understand how important it is, we can also look at the amount of space—newspaper folks call this "column inches"—certain parables and messages take. One such lengthy account is the parable of the lost things (Luke 15), which follows. See if you can spot some of the above elements.

- The Baptism and Temptation of Jesus
- Jesus' Inaugural Address and Public Ministry
- The Teaching of Jesus: Parables
- **Interpreting Parables**
- The Miracles of Jesus

The Jewish leadership was persecuting Jesus because He commiserated with sinners—human debris as far as these religious fanatics (Pharisees) were concerned. Luke tells of a moment in time when Jesus was enjoying supper with sinners and the Pharisees showed up to gather evidence against Him. Imagine having all three in the same place at the same time: the religious elite, the blatantly irreverent, and the Incarnate Savior of the world. Can't you see the room's floor, filled with disheveled, underdressed men and women, smelling of sweat and spirits? And these pious onlookers, standing around the room's perimeter, beautifully outfitted in their finest apparel and pompously stroking their pointed chins.

What a moment this was for an unforgettable parable . . . or *three* unforgettable parables, giving us a crystal-clear understanding of every person's need for repentance and the reality of God's perfect grace.

> *What man of you, having a hundred sheep,*
> *if he loses one of them, does not leave the ninety-nine in the wilderness,*
> *and go after the one which is lost until he finds it?*
> *And when he has found it, he lays it on his shoulders, rejoicing.*
> *And when he comes home, he calls together his friends and neighbors,*
> *saying to them, "Rejoice with me, for I have found my sheep*
> *which was lost!" (Luke 15:4–6)*

In the minds of the Pharisees, Jesus *must* have been addressing the sinners. "Go for it, Jesus; stick it to these poor, lost souls," they probably whispered among themselves. But then Jesus added a comment, a single sentence that furrowed their arrogant brows.

> *I say to you that likewise there will be more joy in heaven*
> *over one sinner who repents than over ninety-nine just persons*
> *who need no repentance. (Luke 15:7)*

"What do You mean, '*more joy in heaven*'?" they could have said. "Look at us and all the good things we're doing for God. Certainly our hard work is celebrated in heaven . . . isn't it?"

Jesus continued.

> *Or what woman, having ten silver coins,*
> *if she loses one coin, does not light a lamp, sweep the house,*
> *and search carefully until she finds it?*
> *And when she has found it,*
> *she calls her friends and neighbors together, saying,*
> *"Rejoice with me, for I have found the piece which I lost!"*

Likewise, I say to you, there is joy in the presence of the angels of God
over one sinner who repents. (Luke 15:8–10)

The tension lifted from the faces of the Pharisees. Certainly Jesus was talking to the riffraff sitting in front of them. No mention here of those "who need no repentance."

But Jesus wasn't quite finished.

A certain man had two sons.
And the younger of them said to his father,
"Father, give me the portion of goods that falls to me."
So he divided to them his livelihood.
And not many days after, the younger son gathered all together,
journeyed to a far country,
and there wasted his possessions with prodigal living.
But when he had spent all, there arose a severe famine in that land,
and he began to be in want.
Then he went and joined himself to a citizen of that country,
and he sent him into his fields to feed swine.
And he would gladly have filled his stomach with the pods that the swine ate,
and no one gave him anything.
But when he came to himself, he said,
"How many of my father's hired servants have bread enough and to spare,
and I perish with hunger!
I will arise and go to my father, and will say to him,
'Father, I have sinned against heaven and before you,
and I am no longer worthy to be called your son.
Make me like one of your hired servants.'" (Luke 15:11–19)

The Pharisees were home free. *Now* there was no doubt in their minds that Jesus was talking to the sinners. And they were pleased with the progress of the story: brash little brother, accommodating father (only for the purpose of teaching this whippersnapper a thing or two), and hopeless failure in the boy's attempt to survive away from the father . . . and obedience to the Law.

And he arose and came to his father.
But when he was still a great way off, his father saw him and had compassion,
and ran and fell on his neck and kissed him.
And the son said to him,
"Father, I have sinned against heaven and in your sight,
and am no longer worthy to be called your son." (Luke 15:20–21)

The common folk listening to Jesus must have been thrilled with this story. Of course, they would have been pleased with the accounts of the lost sheep and misplaced coin, but this one they really liked. As those who never passed up an opportunity to push the edges of propriety, to scorn the Law and shake their fists in the face of authority, the forgiving father was an image that warmed their hearts.

Even the Pharisees had to be somewhat pleased. Okay, so the father went a little overboard with running down the lane and giving the compassionate embrace to his undeserving son, but as long as the boy was prepared to engage in some serious groveling, they'd be satisfied.

Unfortunately, for the Pharisees, there was more.

But the father said to his servants,
"Bring out the best robe and put it on him,
and put a ring on his hand and sandals on his feet.
And bring the fatted calf here and kill it, and let us eat and be merry;
for this my son was dead and is alive again;
he was lost and is found."
And they began to be merry. (Luke 15:22–24)

Jesus had crossed the line with the religious elite. They were willing to give Jesus the father's dash to hug the kid. They would have been willing, once the boy's prepared speech was finished, for some sort of qualified parental absolution. But to bring out the finest robe and throw a party—*before* the prodigal had even finished his recitation of utter penance. That was unacceptable.

I can see Jesus lifting His eyes from His audience of "prodigals" scattered on the floor to those who stood at the room's perimeter. He wasn't finished.

Now his older son was in the field.
And as he came and drew near to the house, he heard music and dancing.
So he called one of the servants and asked what these things meant.
And he said to him,
"Your brother has come, and because he has received him safe and sound,
your father has killed the fatted calf."
But he was angry and would not go in.
Therefore his father came out and pleaded with him.
So he answered and said to his father,
"Lo, these many years I have been serving you;
I never transgressed your commandment at any time;
and yet you never gave me a young goat, that I might make merry with my friends.
But as soon as this son of yours came,
who has devoured your livelihood with harlots,
you killed the fatted calf for him."
And [the father] said to [the older brother],
"Son, you are always with me, and all that I have is yours.
It was right that we should make merry and be glad,
for your brother was dead and is alive again,
and was lost and is found." (Luke 15:25–32)

The Pharisees were thoroughly scandalized by the conclusion to this story—and it *is* the conclusion. What the young son had done, in their Semitic culture, was heinous . . . unspeakable. And, in telling the story, Jesus didn't even *address* these: disrespect to a father, fleeing the responsibilities of the family farm, harlots (and who knows what else), and wishing for the food being fed to swine. All of this was unconscionable.

> Jesus had blown their cover. They were neither actively recruiting lost people to their religion, nor were they even pleased when depraved people got restored.

Waves of pompous rage must have swept over the religious leaders. Jesus hadn't added that the father apologized to the older brother (a perfect typecast of them) for having overlooked him, promising a you're-such-a-good-boy celebration for him and his friends. No, there was no such promise to the older brother, no pat on the head, and no apology from the father. In fact, there was nothing more to the story.

Jesus had blown their cover. They were neither actively recruiting lost people to their religion, nor were they even pleased when depraved people got restored.

"He's got to go," one of the Pharisees must have said to his cronies as they all walked away. "He's destroying our credibility," another could have replied. "He's treating those lowlifes with more dignity than us," someone else might have added.

But the sinners were still there in the presence of their Savior—the forgiving Father. The look on their faces must have said it all. God was eager to welcome them home from their rebellion and sin—their lostness. Not only that, He was willing to throw the biggest party they had ever seen and pick up the tab. This was too good to be true.

All of this came from the telling of three simple yet profound stories. The power in them is timeless. These unforgettable stories speak to you and me whether we're "older brothers" or young prodigals . . . living in open rebellion or foolishly counting on our "righteousness" to save us. No wonder Jesus used parables.

- • The Baptism and Temptation of Jesus
- • Jesus' Inaugural Address and Public Ministry
- • The Teaching of Jesus: Parables
- • Interpreting Parables
- • **The Miracles of Jesus**

"Step right up," carnival hawkers shout. "See the *amazing* fire-eating, sword-swallowing, bearded midget lady." And like a tray of metal shavings drawn to a powerful magnet, gullible people stream in to see the incredulity.

Over the centuries, Jesus' miracles have been portrayed similarly. Jesus Christ, the Incarnate Holy God, the Savior of the world, attracting humanity's disenfranchised with a derby, a cane, and a little magic. But nothing could be farther from the truth.

If you were to study Greek, the original language of the New Testament, you'd discover that the word *thaumazi*—translated "amazement"—is used more than forty times. Most often, the word describes the reaction of the people to something indescribable that Jesus had just done. There were no words to speak, there was only awe . . . and silent wonder. And those who were "amazed" weren't only the naive, the simpleminded, or the easily impressed.

> *There was a man of the Pharisees named Nicodemus,*
> *a ruler of the Jews.*
> *This man came to Jesus by night and said to Him,*
> *"Rabbi, we know that You are a teacher come from God;*
> *for no one can do these signs that You do unless God is with Him." (John 3:1–2)*

Nicodemus was no vulnerable, uneducated hayseed. He was a well-educated religious leader. The Jews looked to him as an example of law-abiding living. As an expert, with a thorough understanding of the Torah, he was an often-used resource for spiritual discernment and guidance.

No doubt, during his lifetime, Nicodemus had seen his share of messianic impostors. Pharisees were not easily impressed. None of them had "Expect a Miracle!" bumper stickers stuck to the back of their horse carts.

And not only was Nicodemus alone persuaded that Jesus' works could be described only as "miracles," but some of his colleagues in the Sanhedrin were also convinced. "We know that You are . . . sent from God," he confessed in his nocturnal visit to the Son of God. "My friends and I have been talking about You," Nicodemus could have said to Jesus. "And we're amazed—in spite of ourselves."

> Nicodemus was no vulnerable, uneducated hayseed. He was a well-educated religious leader.

A miracle is not something to be readily expected; otherwise, the extraordinary nature of it would be lost. I hear people, often those with a fine understanding of the Bible, saying that the vibrancy of a flower or the birth of a child is a miracle. They are not.

Please don't misunderstand me. I am not saying that these things happen without God's sustaining power. Unlike the deists of the eighteenth century, I believe that God has wondrously created the worlds and all that are in them, and *without* His sustaining power, they would vanish. But there is a difference between God's ordinary interventions into our reality and His extraordinary ones. Miracles, by definition, are the intentional and unusual intervention of a Holy God, disrupting the predictable and drawing attention to Himself.

> Miracles immediately drew unsuspecting mortals into the presence of an awesome God.

Today, when someone makes it from Tampa to Orlando by car in ninety minutes or finds a first-edition copy of *Little Women* at a garage sale down the street, they might describe these things as "miracles." These are marvelous things, but they are not miracles.

Speedy car trips from the Gulf or discovering a treasure at someone's private flea market doesn't qualify as extraordinary, supernatural, and miraculous sovereign intervention.

John Locke, a nineteenth-century British philosopher, said that the primary function of a miracle in the Bible was to bring credit to the Proposer. The act was to prove the truthfulness of the actor and to certify that this individual was endorsed by God, speaking His truth. And if the miracle was of the same caliber as the ones executed by Jesus and His disciples, then the person performing the miracle was an agent of divine revelation. Miracles immediately drew unsuspecting mortals into the presence of an awesome God. If someone was publicly proven to be an unrepentant liar, cheat, or heretic, then God would not ordinarily give them the gift of miracles, for He would be placing His stamp of approval on an unbelieving impostor.

And what was true regarding the character of miracle workers during Jesus' earthly ministry is also true today.

EYEWITNESS ACCOUNTS

There could have been more than enough evidence to find Jesus guilty of fakery. But to the contrary, history does not record any evidence that those who were eyewitnesses to His miracles doubted their authenticity. The reality of Jesus' miracles was not challenged. What people had seen from His hand was extraordinary and they knew it.

The issue in question had to do with the Author of the miracle.

Then one was brought to [Jesus] who was demon-possessed, blind and mute;
and He healed him, so that the blind and mute man both spoke and saw.
And all the multitudes were amazed and said,
"Could this be the Son of David?"
Now when the Pharisees heard it they said,
"This fellow does not cast out demons except by Beelzebub, the ruler of the demons."
But Jesus knew their thoughts, and said to them:
"Every kingdom divided against itself is brought to desolation,
and every city or house divided against itself will not stand.
If Satan casts out Satan, he is divided against himself.
How then will his kingdom stand?
And if I cast out demons by Beelzebub,
by whom do your sons cast them out?
Therefore they shall be your judges.
But if I cast out demons by the Spirit of God,
surely the kingdom of God has come upon you." (Matthew 12:22–28)

A wretched man came to Jesus: unable to see or speak and possessed by an evil spirit. Jesus healed him and all the people were *amazed*—there's our word again. The religious elite, standing on the fringes of the crowd, did not question the reality of what they had just seen. The man had most certainly been healed.

Actually, this story is the account of *two* miracles. The first is the immediate, visible healing of a severely disabled man. This pathetic individual was made whole in a single moment of time, and the people who saw it were filled with awe.

The second miracle was that, without the Pharisees uttering a single word, Jesus "knew their thoughts." Imagine how vulnerable they must have felt as this Galilean gave voice to what was only in their minds: definitely another extraordinary event.

Rudolf Bultmann, the twentieth-century German New Testament scholar, raised serious questions about the reality of miracles. He attributed the miracle stories in the Bible to mythology, pious fiction that developed as men attempted to explain their religious experiences. What Bultmann overlooked was that even the most skeptical men in the crowd that day knew that what they had seen was a supernatural occurrence. There was no explanation other than this.

The Pharisees did not examine the healed man to see if their eyes were playing tricks on them. This was no optical illusion. Even these cynics did not dispute the reality of the miracles surrounding Jesus' ministry. The man *had* been healed. What the Pharisees did do, however, was raise a question as to who had caused the miracle to take place. Which deity was responsible?

Jesus made it clear to the Pharisees that only the Spirit of God could do something as marvelous as what they had witnessed. This could only have been the work of the Holy One of Israel. Remember, *real* miracles immediately drew unsuspecting mortals into the presence of an awesome God.

> *Therefore we must give the more earnest heed to the things we have heard,*
> *lest we drift away.*
> *For if the word spoken through angels proved steadfast,*
> *and every transgression and disobedience received a just reward,*
> *how shall we escape if we neglect so great a salvation,*
> *which at the first began to be spoken by the Lord,*
> *and was confirmed to us by those who heard Him,*
> *God also bearing witness both with signs and wonders,*
> *with various miracles, and gifts of the Holy Spirit,*
> *according to His own will?* (Hebrews 2:1–4)

We often think that bearing witness is something you and I do, as ambassadors of Christ. But God bore witness to Jesus, and the way He did this was by miracles.

So when we see a miraculous account in Holy Scripture, we must ask, "What is the significance of this miracle?" "What is God saying to us about the one who performed the miracle?" "And what was God telling us about Jesus, the One Whose ministry was literally filled with miracles?"

I think the answer is clear.

SUMMARY

■ THE BAPTISM AND TEMPTATION OF JESUS

Very little was written in the Gospels about Jesus' childhood. Luke gives only one account of Him as a preteen. And none of the Gospels contain a single word about Jesus from the age of twelve until the age of thirty—eighteen years of silence. I have often wondered about this. My suspicion is that God was preparing His Son for the incredible assignment that was coming.

The eyewitness accounts of three of the four Gospels record the baptism of Jesus and the beginning of His earthly ministry. The last account we had of Him was when He was only twelve. Now, after almost two unrecorded decades, the thirty-year-old Jesus made His way through the crowd and stepped to the banks of the River Jordan.

John the Baptist knew exactly Who it was standing at the water's threshold. Do you remember the curtain God closed for four hundred years between the Old and New Testaments—four centuries of rearrangement and preparation for the greatest event in human history? Do you remember the *pleroma*—the fullness of time—when God's answer to the chaos and despair of mankind would step forward?

This was it.

As soon as Jesus came out of the water from His baptism, God spoke. "This is My beloved Son, in Whom I am well pleased."

The euphoria of the voice from heaven to Jesus was short-lived. Jesus retreated to the wilderness and, after a forty-day fast, dealt one-on-one with Satan himself, who came to Jesus with three seductive offers.

Following the temptations, like a child who had just been pummeled by the neighborhood bully, Jesus was tenderly comforted by His Father's special agents. We're not told how long this respite lasted, but can there be any doubt that it was exactly what the Savior needed?

■ JESUS' INAUGURAL ADDRESS AND PUBLIC MINISTRY

Just like a soldier having successfully completed the treachery of boot camp, Jesus returned from the desert and went straight to Nazareth, His hometown. He did what any of us would have done; He surrounded Himself with familiar faces and places.

The following Sabbath, Jesus went to the synagogue. Jesus was handed a scroll containing the writings of the prophet Isaiah. Once the reading was completed, Jesus handed the scroll back to the temple attendant. He quietly sat down. Jesus' first words must have stunned them: "I'm the very One Whom Isaiah was talking about," He said.

Regardless of what came to their minds, we do know that these pious men were furious at what they perceived as an insult. In fact, they were so blind with rage, they did something that seems unbelievable, given the fact that Jesus and His family were faithful members at this temple. They took Him to the outskirts of town with the intention of murdering Him. However, He escaped.

Each of the gospel writers included the accounts of Jesus selecting the disciples. Jesus did not draft the brightest pupils from surrounding religious schools; He picked fishermen, political troublemakers, and a tax collector. He announced His choices by offering them a simple invitation: "Follow Me." And this is exactly what they did.

For the next three years the essence of Jesus' ministry was to travel around the area with a group of friends and students, teaching in the synagogues, preaching the gospel of the kingdom, and healing all kinds of sicknesses and diseases among the people. The most comprehensive of Jesus' messages is the Sermon on the Mount, found in Matthew.

The message Jesus gave was filled with irony, the topsy-turvy announcement of His kingdom's values. Under normal circumstances, those who rejoice are blessed and those who are rich throw the parties, but not in this kingdom. Usually those who are oppressed and beaten down remain so, but not where Jesus is King.

In this special place the blind see, the deaf hear, and the poor receive good news. And their suffering and pain bring them blessing. "When you are maligned, despised, or even persecuted for righteousness' sake," Jesus said, "you are blessed."

"So," He tells the crowd gathered on the hillside, "rejoice and be very glad, for great is your reward in heaven." God's blessing gave the people a future heavenly hope, but it was also in the present: the here and now. Imagine the impact of Jesus' words on those who listened.

■ THE TEACHING OF JESUS: PARABLES

Jesus knew that telling stories would be a profound way of connecting with an audience, illuminating truth, and building relationships. And so He told stories . . . parables.

Even the religious leaders were spellbound by the simple power of Jesus' approach. Others reported that Jesus "taught them as one having authority" (Mark 1:22). For some, the paradox of "simple" stories and "authoritative" command was irreconcilable. But Jesus did exactly that.

■ THE MIRACLES OF JESUS

"Step right up," carnival hawkers shout. "See the *amazing* fire-eating, sword-swallowing, bearded midget lady." And like a tray of metal shavings drawn to a powerful magnet, gullible people stream in to see the incredulity.

Over the centuries, Jesus' miracles have been portrayed similarly. Jesus Christ, the Incarnate Holy God, the Savior of the world, attracting humanity's disenfranchised with a derby, a cane, and a little magic. But nothing could be farther from the truth.

If you were to study Greek, the original language of the New Testament, you'd discover that the word *thaumazi*—translated "amazement"—is used more than forty times. Most often, the word describes the reaction of the people to something indescribable that Jesus had just done. There were no words to speak, there was only awe . . . and silent wonder. And those who were "amazed" weren't only the naive, the simpleminded, or the easily impressed.

A miracle is not something to be readily expected; otherwise, the extraordinary nature of it would be lost. I hear people, often those with a fine understanding of the Bible, saying that the vibrancy of a flower or the birth of a child are miracles. They are not. Miracles immediately drew unsuspecting mortals into the presence of an awesome God. What people had seen from His hand was extraordinary and they knew it.

A wretched man came to Jesus: unable to see or speak and possessed by an evil spirit. Jesus healed him and all the people were *amazed*—there's our word again. The religious elite, standing on the fringes of the crowd, did not question the reality of what they had just seen. The man had most certainly been healed.

Actually, this story is the account of *two* miracles. The first is the immediate, visible healing of a severely disabled man. The second miracle was that, without the Pharisees uttering a single word, Jesus "knew their thoughts."

When we see a miraculous account in Holy Scripture, we must ask, "What is the significance of this miracle?" "What is God saying to us about the one who performed the miracle?" "And what was God telling us about Jesus, the One Whose ministry was literally filled with miracles?"

I think the answer is clear.

CHAPTER THIRTEEN

THE LATER MINISTRY OF JESUS

- **The Caesarea-Philippi Confession**
- The Transfiguration
- The Triumphal Entry
- The Cross
- The Resurrection
- The Ascension

It's clear, even from a brief overview of the New Testament, that Jesus Christ is the central character. And, as we study the Old Testament, we clearly see that this record is Christocentric—focusing on Jesus as the pivotal figure—as well. The prophets called Him the Suffering Servant (Isaiah 53), Moses referred to Him as the great prophet to come (Deuteronomy 18), and the office of the Davidic line of kings pointed to Him as the ultimate King of the universe (Psalm 2).

When we think of the Messiah's name, we think of "Jesus Christ." Actually, His name was "Jesus," but His title was "Christ." This word corresponded to the Old Testament word *Messiah*. Predictably, of all the names or titles ascribed to Jesus in the New Testament, the most frequently used—more than 550 times—was the name "Christ." This was in contrast to "Lord," which was used fewer than 150 times.

When Jesus was called Christ, what was really being said was "Jesus the Messiah." This was the earliest confession of the Christian faith, as the early church acknowledged that Jesus was the long-awaited Messiah. Interestingly, when we look at the teachings of Jesus, something strange happens in connection to His name. We discover that He shows great reluctance in identifying Himself as the Messiah. This is called the "messianic secret."

Over the past few decades, I have written quite a number of books and have had the privilege of teaching and preaching at hundreds of churches and conferences around the world. Because of this visibility, every once in a while someone walks up to me and says, "Aren't you R. C. Sproul?"

I suppose that I consider myself well known, but I am *not* famous—and have no aspiration to be. Famous is Tiger Woods. Famous is Luciano Pavarotti. Famous is Harrison Ford. This is a whole different thing.

Because I'm only well known and not famous, I have no hesitance about walking around in public. But if I *were* famous, much of my life would need to be lived in secret. Before Woods won the Masters, before Pavarotti walked onto the stage at Carnegie Hall, and before Ford stepped in front of a movie camera, they had no qualms about being in the marketplace. However, once their names and faces were known the world over, they were forced to hide.

But as famous as these men are, who could compare to the eminence of the Messiah, the long-awaited-prophesied-for-centuries Savior of the world? No one.

Jesus' reticence for fame was not primarily to avoid being crushed by autograph seekers among the masses. He avoided open and repeated references to Himself as the Messiah because the people of Israel were looking for the Redeemer to be a political leader, a religious revolutionary, who would single-handedly cast off the Romans and restore Israel to her place among the nations. And since this was not why Jesus came, He was careful not to identify Himself with a title that was so widely misunderstood. This is sometimes called the "messianic secret."

When it came time to teach His disciples this potentially explosive truth about Himself—that He *was* the Messiah—Jesus pulled them aside, away from the normal places He taught.

THE SECRET IS REVEALED

At the extreme northern section of Palestine lies the beautiful Caesarea-Philippi. It was a gift to Herod from Augustus Caesar, and Herod built a temple in Caesar's honor there. Jesus and His disciples traveled around the foot of Mount Hermon, through the Hulah Valley, into the lush area at its base, and stopped at an ancient cultic worship site, dedicated to the god Pan, but also used for emperor worship. Along the walls of the cliff, notches were cut out that held altars to Pan and other gods. Out from a cave at the base of the cliff, a large stream flowed—and continues to flow to this day. This cave bore the name "the Gates of Hell." It was used as a part of pagan worship that had taken place at this site for as long as anyone could remember. This provided the backdrop for Jesus' private meeting with His disciples.

> *When Jesus came into the region of Caesarea Philippi,*
> *He asked His disciples, saying,*
> *"Who do men say that I, the Son of Man, am?"* (Matthew 16:13)

Remember that Jesus was addressing neither the multitudes nor the Pharisees. He was asking His closest followers and friends for a report. Based on this, they responded.

> *So they said, "Some say John the Baptist,*
> *some Elijah, and others Jeremiah or one of the prophets."* (Matthew 16:14)

When John the Baptist disappeared, not everyone knew he had been taken prisoner and killed. Others living in remote villages didn't know that Jesus and John had been active at the same time, believing that Jesus was John the Baptist raised from the dead. Others were still holding out for the reappearance of Elijah as foretold by Malachi. But notice the theme: All these were prophets.

Public opinion was that Jesus of Nazareth was a great prophet. But Jesus wanted to teach them that He was so much more than a prophet.

Public opinion was that Jesus of Nazareth was a great prophet. But Jesus wanted to teach them that He was so much more than a prophet. So He confronted His disciples with the ultimate challenge, a question they could not hide from.

> *He said to them, "But who do you say that I am?"*
> *Simon Peter answered and said,*
> *"You are the Christ, the Son of the living God."* (Matthew 16:15–16)

So far in this brief exchange, we have three titles for Jesus. "Christ," as we have seen, has a messianic implication. "Son of God" and "Son of Man" have aspects of humanity and deity in them. When the angel Gabriel announced to Mary that she was to give birth to a child, conceived by the power of the Holy Spirit, he declared "that [the] Holy One who is to be born will be called the Son of God" (Luke 1:35b). Can you see the blending of the human with the divine?

But what about the "Son of Man"? When Jesus used this term He was pointing back to the Old Testament book of Daniel (chap. 7). His disciples would have picked up on the setting of this title as quickly as someone in the Western world would know the context of "Mary Had a Little Lamb."

> I was watching in the night visions,
> And behold, One like the Son of Man,
> Coming with the clouds of heaven!
> He came to the Ancient of Days,
> And they brought Him near before Him.
> Then to Him was given dominion and glory and a kingdom,
> That all peoples, nations, and languages should serve Him.
> His dominion is an everlasting dominion,
> Which shall not pass away,
> And His kingdom the one
> Which shall not be destroyed. (Daniel 7:13–14)

When Jesus called Himself the Son of Man, the crowds were astonished. "He's claiming to be the One Who stands with the Father in heaven and receives all the authority foretold in Daniel," they must have whispered to one another.

Is it any wonder that the Pharisees were threatened? They knew He was claiming to be God. This was not a title of humility, but a claim of absolute authority. When He healed on the Sabbath and was rebuked, what did He say? "I have done this that you might know the Son of Man is Lord of the Sabbath."

When He created an uproar by forgiving sins, His enemies shouted that only God could forgive sins. Can't you hear the loudmouths from the back of the crowd? In calm reply, He said that He did this so that they might know that the Son of Man has authority on earth to forgive sins.

So when Jesus heard Simon Peter's answer to the question of "Who do you say that I am?" Jesus did not contradict the charge. He taught them that the One Who stood before them was the Ancient of Days, the Son of Man. He was God, just as much as the Father was God. It was in this setting that Peter gave his great confession: "You are the Christ, the Son of the living God."

Immediately Jesus blessed Simon Peter.

> *Jesus answered and said to him,*
> *"Blessed are you, Simon Bar-Jonah,*
> *for flesh and blood has not revealed this to you,*
> *but My Father who is in heaven."* (Matthew 16:17)

Why was Peter singled out to receive this blessing? Because he had not thought this up on his own. He had supernaturally been given this information by the Father, because until that moment, Jesus had been concealing His full identity. How else could Peter have known except by divine revelation?

> Announcing that "the gates of hell" would not prevail against the church was the same as saying that the pagan religions and political powers, forever enemies of God's people, would not prevail against the church.

With all that the disciples had witnessed already, we may wonder why they hadn't realized this before. But we shouldn't judge these men too harshly. For Jesus' contemporaries, it was difficult to discern the messianic impostors from the true Son of God. Even John the Baptist, at the end of his life, was uncertain about Jesus' true identity. So it was necessary for a blessing from God to free Peter's mind from its blinders concerning Who Jesus was.

Then Jesus added:

> *And I also say to you that you are Peter,*
> *and on this rock I will build My church, and the gates*
> *of Hades [hell] shall not prevail against it.* (Matthew 16:18)

Notice the phrase "the gates of [hell]." Remember that the setting for this intimate conversation between Jesus and His disciples was the mouth of a cave bearing that name. Standing in a place that was known around the region as a seedbed of pagan worship, Jesus was making a powerful religious and political statement. It's no wonder that He had to tell the disciples this in private. Announcing that "the gates of hell" would not prevail against the church was the same as saying that the pagan religions and political powers, forever ene-

> Premature exposure of His deity would short-circuit His assignment, most certainly bringing immediate trial and execution.

mies of God's people, would not prevail against the church. In fact, the church would prevail against them, storming their gates and setting those imprisoned by unbelief wholly free.

The extent of Jesus' blessing following Peter's confession is especially important for the Roman Catholic Church. For centuries, Catholics have used it as the basis for their church government. Was the "this" in Jesus statement—"On *this* rock I will build My church"—the man, Peter, or the confession, "You are the Christ, the Son of the living God"?

If we had been there, we would have been able to tell by the inflection in Jesus' voice whether He was referring to the man or the message. If we had been there, we would have seen Him pointing to Peter when He spoke these words. Or we would know if He spread His arms wide or even pointed to Himself, letting the disciples know that it was His deity that would form the foundation of the church.

Jesus continued.

> *And I will give you the keys of the kingdom of heaven,*
> *and whatever you bind on earth will be bound in heaven,*
> *and whatever you loose on earth*
> *will be loosed in heaven.* (Matthew 16:19)

In his commentary on this passage, Dr. Sinclair Ferguson wrote, "It is difficult to exegete gesticulations." (Don't you just love the way scholars can turn a phrase?) In other words, without seeing Jesus' motions, it's a challenge for us to know for sure what He was referring to. Actually, it's impossible to know for certain.

The Roman Catholic Church has always held that Jesus was referring to the man Peter—"The church will be built on you"—creating a case for the papacy. Protestants differ on whether Jesus was speaking of Peter or of Peter's confession.

But if Peter was the first vice-regent of the church, his first official act was to scold Jesus.

> *From that time Jesus began to show to*
> *His disciples that He must go to Jerusalem,*
> *and suffer many things from the elders and chief priests and scribes,*
> *and be killed, and be raised the third day.*
> *Then Peter took [Jesus] aside and began to rebuke Him, saying,*
> *"Far be it from You, Lord; this shall not happen to You!"* (Matthew 16:21–22)

And if these *were* the words of a pontiff, Jesus' response was hardly befitting a comment to a pope.

> *But [Jesus] turned and said to Peter,*
> *"Get behind Me, Satan!*
> *You are an offense to Me,*
> *for you are not mindful of the things of God,*
> *but the things of men."* (Matthew 16:23)

Remember that Jesus did all this in a secluded place, treating His disciples as trusted confidants. It was not the right time for Him to reveal this "messianic secret."

> *Then He commanded His disciples that they should tell no one*
> *that He was Jesus the Christ.* (Matthew 16:20)

How odd this seems to you and me, living in a publicity-seeking, media-driven culture. Isn't the mission of the church to proclaim Jesus as Lord to as many people as possible? Most of us think so. Then why would Jesus tell His closest friends to keep quiet?

Yes, the purpose of the church *is* to go into the entire world and preach the Gospel. But for Jesus, the timing of His messianic announcement had to be just right. Premature exposure of His deity would short-circuit His assignment, most certainly bringing immediate trial and execution.

So, with the full revelation of Who Jesus was, burning in their hearts, the disciples waited for His word to release it.

- The Caesarea-Philippi Confession
- **The Transfiguration**
- The Triumphal Entry
- The Cross
- The Resurrection
- The Ascension

Centuries before Jesus was born, Moses made a special request to the Lord God. Like a boy trying to sneak into a baseball game without a ticket, Moses begged God to let him do the unthinkable—to see His glory.

> And [Moses] said, "Please, show me Your glory." . . .
> But [God] said, "You cannot see My face;
>   for no man shall see Me, and live."
> And the Lord said, "Here is a place by Me,
>   and you shall stand on the rock.
> So it shall be, while My glory passes by,
>   that I will put you in the cleft of the rock,
>   and will cover you with My hand while I pass by.
> Then I will take away My hand, and you shall see My back;
>   but My face shall not be seen." (Exodus 33:18, 20–23)

Can you picture the boy, unable to gain legitimate entrance to the ballpark, peeking through a crack in the fence to catch a glimpse of a game?

God rejected Moses' request to see His glory straight on, but gave him permission to peer through a breach in a rock, enough to see His back. It wasn't that God was being stingy with His glory; it was for Moses' own protection. "If I would give you what you're asking for and you would actually see Me," the Sovereign God was saying to Moses, "you wouldn't be able to handle it. You would literally drop dead."

> *So Moses made haste*
> *and bowed his head toward the earth,*
> *and worshiped.* (Exodus 34:8)

Is it any wonder that, having seen a little of God's glory even through a thin slice in a rock, Moses was completely overwhelmed?

Centuries later, the articulate and upbeat Isaiah, when faced with the glorified presence of the Almighty in the Temple, was breathless and stunned, filled with the truth of his own depravity and unworthiness.

> *"Woe to me!" I cried. "I am ruined!*
> *For I am a man of unclean lips, and I live among a people of unclean lips,*
> *and my eyes have seen the King, the LORD Almighty."* (Isaiah 6:5 NIV)

Glory. It's one of the most important concepts in all of Holy Scripture. The Hebrew word—*kabod*—that is translated "glory" literally means the "weight" and therefore the "worth" of something. Sometimes when we speak of the worth of a person, we say that his word carries "a lot of weight." The glory of God is His worthiness, His holiness . . . His "God-ness." And this carries a tremendous amount of weight. Nothing in all of human knowledge, history, or experience carries more.

For most of His earthly ministry, God's Son set aside His glory. He did not, as we would say, "throw His weight around."

The apostle Paul said it this way:

> *[Jesus], being in very nature God,*
> *did not consider equality with God something to be grasped,*

but made himself nothing, taking the very nature of a servant,
being made in human likeness.
And being found in appearance as a man,
he humbled himself and became obedient to death—
even death on a cross!
Therefore God exalted him to the highest place
and gave him the name that is above every name,
that at the name of Jesus every knee should bow,
in heaven and on earth and under the earth,
and every tongue confess that Jesus Christ is Lord,
to the glory of God the Father. (Philippians 2:6–11 NIV)

Can you see it? The life of Jesus Christ was a remarkable demonstration of humility—fully possessing the nature of a Holy God but setting aside the glory. And this passage also assures us that once Jesus' task was, as He said on the cross, "finished," then the glory would once again be His.

The life of the Savior moved from degradation (starting with His birth in a cattle barn) to more debasement (scorn, misunderstanding, hatred) to His greatest humiliation during the final week of His life. But in the Gospels, glimpses of glory come peeking through.

> It wasn't that God was being stingy with His glory; it was for Moses' own protection.

This is an account—one of those glimpses of glory—of the most important intrusion of the full weight of a Holy God during Jesus' ministry. It is commonly known as the Transfiguration.

Now after six days Jesus took Peter, James, and John his brother,
led them up on a high mountain by themselves;
and He was transfigured before them.
His face shone like the sun, and His clothes became as white as the light.
And behold, Moses and Elijah appeared to them, talking with Him.
Then Peter answered and said to Jesus,
"Lord, it is good for us to be here;
if You wish, let us make here three tabernacles:

one for You, one for Moses, and one for Elijah."
While he was still speaking, behold,
a bright cloud overshadowed them;
and suddenly a voice came out of the cloud, saying,
"This is My beloved Son, in whom I am well pleased.
Hear Him!"
And when the disciples heard it,
they fell on their faces and were greatly afraid.
But Jesus came and touched them and said,
"Arise, and do not be afraid."
When they had lifted up their eyes,
they saw no one but Jesus only.
Now as they came down from the mountain, Jesus commanded them, saying,
"Tell the vision to no one until the
Son of Man is risen from the dead." (Matthew 17:1–9)

They had seen God's glory and lived. They fell to the ground in worship and awe in the presence of *kabod* and at the sound of the *vox dei*, the voice of God. But, in His tender love and compassion, Jesus reached down, took them by the hands, and helped them to their feet.

If these three disciples hadn't fully understood the spoken message of the "messianic secret" at Caesarea-Philippi, they should have now. Like Moses catching a glimpse of God's amazing glory and Isaiah being filled in the Temple, Jesus had shown Peter, James, and John a flash of His "God-ness," and it scared them to death. Then Jesus ordered them to keep all of this to themselves.

Their mortal minds surely were dazed. What these men saw that day was beyond anything a human could ever hope to see. God must have supernaturally sustained them to be able to bear the sight and live. We know that this moment made a lasting impression on them. In fact, Peter mentioned "the glory" many times in his writings. And in the opening of his gospel, John wraps Jesus' nature in a heavy blanket of *kabod*:

And the Word became flesh and dwelt among us,
and we beheld His glory,

the glory as of the only begotten of the Father,
full of grace and truth. (John 1:14)

In Jesus Christ, glory was cloaked in human form. However that shroud, when peeled back, left men stunned and speechless . . . an overwhelming awe that should fill you and me with wonder every time we think of Him.

- The Caesarea-Philippi Confession
- The Transfiguration
- **The Triumphal Entry**
- The Cross
- The Resurrection
- The Ascension

Around the world, the church celebrates Palm Sunday and the account of Jesus' victorious entry into the City of David just a few days before His crucifixion and resurrection.

Now when they drew near Jerusalem,
and came to Bethphage, at the Mount of Olives,
then Jesus sent two disciples, saying to them,
"Go into the village opposite you,
and immediately you will find a donkey tied, and a colt with her.
Loose them and bring them to Me.
And if anyone says anything to you, you shall say,
'The Lord has need of them,' and immediately he will send them."
All this was done that it might be fulfilled which
was spoken by the prophet, saying:
"Tell the daughter of Zion,
'Behold, your King is coming to you,
Lowly, and sitting on a donkey,
A colt, the foal of a donkey.'"
So the disciples went and did as Jesus commanded them.

> *They brought the donkey and the colt,*
> *laid their clothes on them, and set Him on them.*
> *And a very great multitude spread their clothes on the road;*
> *others cut down branches from the trees and spread them on the road.*
> *Then the multitudes who went before and those who followed cried out, saying:*
> *"Hosanna to the Son of David!*
> *'Blessed is He who comes in the name of the LORD!'*
> *Hosanna in the highest!"* (Matthew 21:1–9)

Jesus' time had come. No longer was He pressing His disciples to keep the secret. He approached Jerusalem willing to make a public display of His iden-tification with the Old Testament prophecy of the Messiah. But for us, the image of Jesus riding on a lowly animal, His feet no doubt dragging on either side of the colt, hardly seems royal enough for the Son of the Most High.

Actually, in the culture of that day, the residents of the Holy City were truly "rolling out the red carpet" for the Savior.

The Messiah riding on a donkey's colt was the fulfillment of Zechariah's prophecy. Many of the people in the crowd that day would have known this. So, as Sir Walter Raleigh did before Queen Mary, they threw their garments on the roadway. This was a gesture of honor and respect for Jesus. Finally, they shouted "Hosanna." This may have been because the people thought that Jesus was about to declare His messiahship and overthrow the Romans—the waving of palm branches was often done to celebrate military victories.

Then something very interesting happened. Some of the religious elite standing on the fringes of the celebrating crowd hollered out to Jesus.

> *And some of the Pharisees called to [Jesus] from the crowd,*
> *"Teacher, rebuke Your disciples."*
> *But He answered and said to them,*
> *"I can tell you that if these should keep silent,*
> *the stones would immediately cry out."* (Luke 19:39–40)

These Pharisees had become accustomed to Jesus keeping His "messianic secret." Certainly they must have heard Him downplay His claim to the "throne of David." But even though He must have known that many of those in the crowd were misunderstanding the moment, Jesus allowed the festivity to continue. In fact He told them that if He even tried to stop the party, the cobblestones would stand and praise Him. So much for the secret.

The Pharisees were likely seething with rage. "Who does He think He is?" they must have muttered to one another. And so they aggressively pursued their plan to execute the Savior.

- The Caesarea-Philippi Confession
- The Transfiguration
- The Triumphal Entry
- **The Cross**
- The Resurrection
- The Ascension

For the past hundred years, executions in the Western world have taken place under the cover of night. We may read an account in the newspaper of what happened—the lethal injection or the electric chair—but there are no photographs in the morning paper, no video replays.

Given what we know about the circumstances surrounding capital punishment throughout history, the secrecy that we have come to expect is actually quite unusual. For most of recorded history, the taking of someone's life as chastisement for a heinous offense was as much a public spectacle as a sporting event or a royal wedding. Civil authorities have for centuries believed that executions accomplished two very important things: (1) the perpetrator had been eliminated, and (2) the onlookers had been soundly warned.

> The Almighty not only allowed the crucifixion of Jesus to take place; He literally commanded it for the atonement of the sin of all mankind.

Men, women, and even children witnessed hangings, firing squads, and even beheadings. Can you imagine the impact these violent killings had on common people?

The public crucifixion of Jesus was meant to accomplish two objectives for the Romans and the Jewish leaders: first, to exterminate the troublemaker; and second, to send a message to His followers that such lawlessness—opposition to them—would not be tolerated.

During the time of the Roman Empire, tens of thousands of criminals were crucified. But this One was different. What the perpetrators didn't know was that a Holy God also had a purpose in allowing His precious Son to be sacrificed, far different from their foolish objectives. And the Almighty not only allowed the crucifixion of Jesus to take place; He literally commanded it for the atonement of the sin of all mankind. Although they must have been proud of themselves for successfully executing Jesus, if God hadn't foreordained His Son's sacrifice, their plot would have failed pathetically.

In spite of his belief in the Savior's innocence, the Roman governor, Pilate, had a purpose in allowing Jesus to be treated as an ordinary criminal. It was his way of restoring the allegiance of the Jewish leaders to his rule.

> From then on Pilate sought to release [Jesus],
> but the Jews cried out, saying,
> "If you let this Man go, you are not Caesar's friend.
> Whoever makes himself a king speaks against Caesar."
> When Pilate therefore heard that saying,
> he brought Jesus out and sat down in the judgment seat
> in a place that is called the Pavement, but in Hebrew, Gabbatha.
> Now it was the Preparation Day of the Passover,
> and about the sixth hour.
> And [Pilate] said to the Jews, "Behold your King!"
> But they cried out, "Away with Him, away with Him! Crucify Him!"
> Pilate said to them, "Shall I crucify your King?"
> The chief priests answered, "We have no king but Caesar!" (John 19:12–15)

Against his own conscience but in order to ensure his subjects' loyalty, Pilate acquiesced.

The motives of the corrupt Jewish leaders—Pharisees and Sadducees—were clear. Jesus' death was pure expediency. That one man be sacrificed for the preservation of their religious system was a relatively small matter.

Likewise the chief priests also, mocking with the scribes and elders, said,
"He saved others; Himself He cannot save.
If He is the King of Israel, let Him now come down from the cross,
and we will believe Him. He trusted in God;
let Him deliver Him now if He will have Him;
for He said, 'I am the Son of God.'" (Matthew 27:41–43)

For skeptics, the Crucifixion was the unequivocal confirmation of their doubt. Perhaps these people had truly wanted to believe, but didn't have the courage. Perhaps their cynicism had cost them friends and family who had chosen to follow the Master. Now the venom of their unbelief and alienation came pouring out.

And those who passed by blasphemed Him, wagging their heads and saying,
"You who destroy the temple and build it in three days,
save Yourself! If You are the Son of God,
come down from the cross." (Matthew 27:39–40)

Can't you hear these degenerates, making complete fools of themselves?
For most of Jesus' followers, including His disciples and family, the Crucifixion represented the abrupt end of a dream. The One Whom they had followed, believed, and loved had been violently taken from them. For them, life no longer had purpose. Their grief and loneliness knew no bounds.

Now from [noon to three o'clock] there was darkness over all the land.
And about [three o'clock] Jesus cried out with a loud voice, saying,
"Eli, Eli, lama sabachthani?" that is, "My God, My God,
why have You forsaken Me?" (Matthew 27:45–46)

It may seem odd that Jesus, at the moment of greatest agony, shouts poetry from the cross. He is quoting from a psalm of David (Psalm 22), which mourns the pain and affliction of the righteous at the hands of the wicked. These words alert us that Jesus knew, moments before His death, that this was a moment of prophetic fulfillment.

> *My God, My God, why have You forsaken Me?*
> *Why are You so far from helping Me,*
> *And from the words of My groaning? . . .*
> *All those who see Me ridicule Me;*
> *They shoot out the lip, they shake the head, saying,*
> *"He trusted in the LORD, let Him rescue Him;*
> *Let Him deliver Him, since He delights in Him!" . . .*
> *I am poured out like water,*
> *And all My bones are out of joint;*
> *My heart is like wax;*
> *It has melted within Me . . .*
> *They divide My garments among them,*
> *And for My clothing they cast lots.*
> *But You, O LORD, do not be far from Me;*
> *O My Strength, hasten to help Me! (Psalm 22:1, 7–8, 14, 18–19)*

When Jesus cried out, He was not simply *feeling* forsaken. Jesus *was* forsaken because He *had* to be forsaken. And that abandonment was dramatized in every tiny dimension of the moment. In order for Him to satisfy the demands of the justice of God, He had to bear the full measure of divine wrath.

We know that Jesus was innocent. Like Pilate, we "find no fault in Him." However, the corporate wickedness of God's elect was concentrated on Him. After voluntarily becoming the spotless Lamb of God and taking upon Himself the sins of the world, Jesus Christ became the most obscene creature in the universe.

> When Jesus cried out, He was not simply *feeling* forsaken. Jesus was forsaken because He *had* to be forsaken.

The apostle Paul described the impact of this moment in his letter to the Galatians.

> *For as many as are of the works of the law are under the curse;*
> *for it is written, "Cursed is everyone who does not continue in all things*

which are written in the book of the law, to do them."
But that no one is justified by the law
in the sight of God is evident,
for "the just shall live by faith." . . .
Christ has redeemed us from the curse of the law,
having become a curse for us
(for it is written, "Cursed is everyone who hangs on a tree"),
that the blessing of Abraham might come upon
the Gentiles in Christ Jesus,
that we might receive the promise
of the Spirit through faith. (Galatians 3:10–11, 13–14)

The language Paul used described Jesus' death in Old Testament terminology. In the book of Deuteronomy, God described the rules of the covenant He made with Israel. There were blessings for the repentant Jew, and there were cursings for the unrepentant breakers of the Law of God.

But it shall come to pass, if you do not obey
the voice of the LORD your God,
to observe carefully all His commandments and
His statutes which I command you today,
that all these curses will come upon you and overtake you:
Cursed shall you be in the city,
and cursed shall you be in the country.
Cursed shall be your basket and your kneading bowl.
Cursed shall be the fruit of your body and the produce of your land,
the increase of your cattle and the offspring of your flocks.
Cursed shall you be when you come in,
and cursed shall you be when you go out.
The LORD will send on you cursing, confusion,
and rebuke in all that you set your hand to do,
until you are destroyed and until you perish quickly,
because of the wickedness of your doings
in which you have forsaken Me. (Deuteronomy 28:15–20)

This is why Paul spoke of Jesus being cursed—He suffered the covenant sanctions so that we would not have to. We live in God's blessing, as His adopted children, welcomed before our Father's throne. All these blessings belong to God's people because Jesus was cursed in His death.

THE LOCATION OF THE CROSS

Another important dimension of Jesus' death is that He was executed outside the city of Jerusalem. For centuries leading up to the Crucifixion, in the ceremony marking the Day of Atonement, there were two animals used to illustrate God's forgiveness of sin (Leviticus 16:1–34). One was a goat that was sacrificed as a burnt offering, but the other was called the "scapegoat." The priest would lay his hands on the goat's head and symbolically place the sins of Israel on him. Then he would turn the scapegoat loose to face the perils of the barren wilderness.

As Jesus was crucified outside of Jerusalem, this fulfills both the role of the sin offering and the scapegoat. He was "sent outside the camp," away from the protection and blessings of God, to be forsaken so that we could be free from the curse and predictable consequences of sin.

The apostle John ends his description of the Crucifixion with the following:

> *After this, Jesus, knowing that all things were now accomplished,*
> *that the Scripture might be fulfilled, said, "I thirst!"*
> *Now a vessel full of sour wine was sitting there;*
> *and they filled a sponge with sour wine,*
> *put it on hyssop, and put it to His mouth.*
> *So when Jesus had received the sour wine, He said,*
> *"It is finished!"*
> *And bowing His head, He gave up His spirit.* (John 19:28–30)

Jesus had obediently done His assignment. His suffering was complete. For the moment, He was finished. But His mission was not yet fully accomplished.

- The Caesarea-Philippi Confession
- The Transfiguration
- The Triumphal Entry
- The Cross
- **The Resurrection**
- The Ascension

When criminals were executed during this time, their bodies were literally thrown on the city's smoldering garbage dump known as Gehenna. But the body of the Savior was not subjected to this humiliation. In fact, when His life-less form was taken down from the cross, a complete stranger, Joseph of Arimathea, offered his own burial tomb. In this we begin to see the transition from a life of abasement to the *kabod* that awaited Jesus.

In fact, the care of Jesus' body through the events that immediately followed the Cross represented the ongoing fulfillment of Old Testament prophecy concerning Him. His body was not "to see corruption" (Psalm 16:10), and He was to be laid in a borrowed tomb (Isaiah 53).

One of the most poignant—and important—scenes in all of Holy Scripture is the scene of the first Easter. It's the story of a small contingent of women who return to the burial place of Jesus on Sunday morning.

> *Now on the first day of the week, very early in the morning,*
> *they, and certain other women with them,*
> *came to the tomb bringing the spices which they had prepared.*
> *But they found the stone rolled away from the tomb.*
> *Then they went in and did not find the body of the Lord Jesus. (Luke 24:1–3)*

Mark, in his gospel, names three of the women who visited the tomb that terrible morning: Mary, the mother of Jesus; Mary Magdalene; and a woman named Salome.

Imagine how horrible these bereaved women must have felt. Their son and their Savior had died an unthinkable death and then, without the proper cere-monial anointing, had hurriedly been laid in the tomb of a Gentile stranger.

What an irony. The Jewish elite scorned no living things more than women and Gentiles, except perhaps swine. But here they were, willing to step forward and honor the lifeless body of Jesus.

Is it any wonder that down through the centuries, the church the Messiah had promised would prevail against the "gates of hell" would include the faithfulness, courage, and personal sacrifice of women and Gentiles? Considering the components to the scene on Easter Sunday morning, this is no mystery to me at all.

What these women could never have known was that the truth to be revealed to them over the next few hours would change the course of human history. Certainly another one of the Bible's snowcapped peaks, visible at any distance, is this moment. The Eternal and Holy God concealed in a lifeless corpse not only left His graveclothes behind, but the limitations of His humanity were also abandoned in that borrowed sepulcher. Jesus' *kabod*, briefly visible to Peter, James, and John on the Mount of Transfiguration, was about to be revealed to many others.

When the women entered the crypt, the empty shroud was lying there.

> *Then they went in and did not find the body of the Lord Jesus.*
> *And it happened, as they were greatly perplexed about this,*
> *that behold, two men stood by them in shining garments.*
> *Then, as they were afraid and bowed their faces to the earth, they said to them,*
> *"Why do you seek the living among the dead?*
> *He is not here, but is risen!*
> *Remember how He spoke to you when He was still in Galilee, saying,*
> *'The Son of Man must be delivered into the hands of sinful men,*
> *and be crucified, and the third day rise again.'"*
> *And they remembered His words.*
> *Then they returned from the tomb and told all these things to the eleven*
> *and to all the rest.* (Luke 24:3–9)

The minds of the disciples must have been whirling. Their hearts were filled with unbelief. Most believed that the women had gone crazy. Completely delusional. "This *can't* be true," they must have exclaimed to one another. So Peter and John were dispatched to see for themselves. Sure enough, the tomb was empty. But where was Jesus?

It's very important for you and me to understand that our belief in the bodily resurrection of Jesus is not based only on the fact of the missing body of Jesus. This would be terribly skimpy evidence. If it would be only that the tomb was empty, resurrection would be the last possible scenario; grave robbers would have been far more likely.

> What these women could never have known was that the truth to be revealed to them over the next few hours would change the course of human history.

The reason I believe that the Resurrection is a reliable historic fact is that Jesus made many visits to His people. He appeared to the women, to the disciples, to a couple of traveling men, to a group of five hundred, and to the apostle Paul. It is the extraordinary evidence of people having talked to, eaten with, and touched Jesus that causes us to believe that the Old Testament prophecies have come true.

One of the most fascinating stories surrounding the Resurrection is the account of two men walking to the town of Emmaus. Wouldn't you have loved to have been a witness to this event?

Now behold, two of them were traveling that same day to a village called Emmaus,
which was seven miles from Jerusalem.
And they talked together of all these things which had happened.
So it was, while they conversed and reasoned,
that Jesus Himself drew near and went with them.
But their eyes were restrained, so that they did not know Him.
And He said to them,
"What kind of conversation is this that you have with
one another as you walk and are sad?"
Then the one whose name was Cleopas answered and said to Him,
"Are You the only stranger in Jerusalem,
and have You not known the things which happened there in these days?"
And He said to them, "What things?"
So they said to Him, "The things concerning Jesus of Nazareth,

> *who was a Prophet mighty in deed and word before God and all the people,*
> *and how the chief priests and our rulers delivered Him*
> *to be condemned to death, and crucified Him.*
> *But we were hoping that it was He who was going to redeem Israel.*
> *Indeed, besides all this, today is the third day since these things happened.*
> *Yes, and certain women of our company, who*
> *arrived at the tomb early, astonished us.*
> *When they did not find His body, they came saying*
> *that they had also seen a vision of angels who said He was alive.*
> *And certain of those who were with us went to the tomb*
> *and found it just as the women had said;*
> *but Him they did not see."* (Luke 24:13–24)

These two men had heard accounts of angelic conversations and empty tombs, but because they hadn't seen Jesus, they were unconvinced.

> *Then [Jesus] said to them, "O foolish ones,*
> *and slow of heart to believe in all that the prophets have spoken!*
> *Ought not the Christ to have suffered*
> *these things and to enter into His glory?"*
> *And beginning at Moses and all the Prophets,*
> *He expounded to them in all the Scriptures*
> *the things concerning Himself.* (Luke 24:25–27)

What a tremendous sermon this must have been. In one seamless account, Jesus, the Master Storyteller, wove together the teaching of these men's ancestors with the truth of His own nature and mission. *Who is this man?* they must have silently wondered.

> *Then they drew near to the village where they were going,*
> *and He indicated that He would have gone farther.*
> *But they constrained Him, saying,*
> *"Abide with us, for it is toward evening, and the day is far spent."*
> *And He went in to stay with them.* (Luke 24:28–29)

Imagine this scene: Two unsuspecting men have just invited the Creator of heaven and earth to join them for the evening. If they had known, their breathing would have surely ceased from sheer terror.

Now it came to pass, as He sat at the table with them,
that He took bread, blessed and broke it, and gave it to them. (Luke 24:30)

When my wife and I invite friends to dinner at our home, I usually offer the blessing. Occasionally, I will call on someone else to say grace, but because this is my house I have the prerogative to make this call—either to offer the blessing myself or to invite another person at the table to do so. What Jesus did at this table would have been like one of my dinner guests presumptuously barging in with an uninvited prayer. This would have been bad manners unless, of

> This would have been bad manners unless, of course, you were the Incarnate and now-resurrected Son of a Holy God, in which case you would have been free to do whatever you pleased.

course, you were the Incarnate and now-resurrected Son of a Holy God, in which case you would have been free to do whatever you pleased.

Then their eyes were opened and they knew Him;
and He vanished from their sight. (Luke 24:31)

Before the Crucifixion and the Resurrection, Jesus would have restricted His earthly form from this kind of thing—vanishing from someone's presence. Nowhere in all the Gospels is such an account recorded. But even though Jesus was clearly visible to mortal men after the empty tomb, He now had a glorified body, fully capable of appearing and disappearing. However, as was the case before the Resurrection, He still had the capacity to transform men.

And they said to one another,
"Did not our heart burn within us while He talked with us on the road,
and while He opened the Scriptures to us?"
So they rose up that very hour and returned to Jerusalem,

> *and found the eleven and those who were*
> *with them gathered together, saying,*
> *"The Lord is risen indeed,*
> *and has appeared to Simon!"*
> *And they told about the things that had happened on the road,*
> *and how He was known to them in the breaking of bread.* (Luke 24:32–35)

In many churches, the minister and the congregation have a common public conversation. "He is risen," the cleric declares. "He is risen, indeed," respond the people. Although the first time this antiphonal dialogue had a delay of several hours, it went something like this: "He is not here," announced the angels on Sunday morning, "He is risen."

"He is risen, indeed," the men returning from Emmaus on Sunday night rejoined.

> *Now as they said these things,*
> *Jesus Himself stood in the midst of them,*
> *and said to them,*
> *"Peace to you."*
> *But they were terrified and frightened,*
> *and supposed they had seen a spirit.*
> *And He said to them, "Why are you troubled?*
> *And why do doubts arise in your hearts?*
> *Behold My hands and My feet, that it is I Myself.*
> *Handle Me and see, for a spirit does not*
> *have flesh and bones as you see I have."*
> *When He had said this, He showed them His hands and His feet.*
> *But while they still did not believe for joy, and marveled,*
> *He said to them, "Have you any food here?"*
> *So they gave Him a piece of a broiled fish and some honeycomb.*
> *And He took it and ate in their presence.* (Luke 24:36–43)

He is risen.
He is risen, indeed.

- The Caesarea-Philippi Confession
- The Transfiguration
- The Triumphal Entry
- The Cross
- The Resurrection
- **The Ascension**

> *Good night, good night! parting is such sweet sorrow,*
> *That I shall say good night till it be morrow.*

Who could ever forget the words of history's most famous romantic interlude? Romeo and Juliet's was a forbidden love. But the incompatible class distinction between their families, the Montagues and the Capulets, could not deny them what their hearts knew. Familial prohibitions notwithstanding, Romeo's words said it well. They were desperately in love.

> *With love's light wings did I o'erperch these walls;*
> *For stony limits cannot hold love out,*
> *And what love can do that dares love attempt;*
> *Therefore thy kinsmen are no stop to me.*
> (William Shakespeare, *Romeo and Juliet*, Act II, Scene II)

The hour was late. So, as they prepared to say good night, Juliet asked Romeo what time they would see each other in the morning. "At the hour of nine," he responded.

"I will not fail thee," Juliet pined. "'Tis twenty years till then."

And then she added the familiar words, "Good night, good night! parting is such sweet sorrow."

This love scene makes for tender prose. But these words are more than just a little naive. With apologies to William Shakespeare, my life has had its share of the bitterness of saying good-bye.

Like you, I have stood at the gravesides of some of my dearest friends. The emptiness inside at this good-bye did not taste sweet. Of course, the minister had given us the assurances of a reunion in heaven, but for now the sense of loss was palpable. And it was not pleasant.

As a small boy, I remember sitting on my mother's lap as she daily typed out letters to my father at war. At the close of these letters, she would let me hit the "X" and "O" keys, sending hugs and kisses to the soldier we loved.

When I was three years old, my dad came home on a short leave. My memories of these few days are vivid. But even more graphic is the vision of walking to the bus stop just a few hundred yards from our home, holding his hand. When the gray military bus arrived, he stooped over, kissed me good-bye, and boarded the bus. I stood on the curb watching the bus disappear. Sobs came from deep inside this little boy's soul, as I slowly made my way back home. There was nothing sweet about this good-bye.

A week later, a kind policeman found me walking along the road almost four miles from my home. "I'm going to Italy to see my dad," was my answer to his understandable question as to what I was doing. Because I had no assurance that he would ever return, I remember the stinging bitterness of saying good-bye. There was nothing sweet about it.

Just before His trial and crucifixion, Jesus gathered His disciples together to say farewell. His work was almost complete.

> *Little children, I shall be with you a little while longer.*
> *You will seek Me; and as I said to the Jews,*
> *"Where I am going, you cannot come." (John 13:33)*

Jesus' words were bitter news, and the disciples were understandably overwhelmed. Their grief was ominous and foreboding. Regardless of where Jesus was going, they were determined to join Him. After all, this is exactly what they had done for three years. It was Jesus Himself who had invited them to follow Him. They were certain that there would be nothing sweet about this good-bye.

> *Simon Peter said to [Jesus], "Lord, where are You going?"*
> *Jesus answered him,*
> *"Where I am going you cannot follow Me now,*

> *but you shall follow Me afterward."*
> *Peter said to Him,*
> *"Lord, why can I not follow You now?*
> *I will lay down my life for Your sake." (John 13:36–37)*

I can almost see the rest of the disciples nodding with Simon Peter's words. "Yes, Jesus," they were saying. "We agree with Peter; we want to go with You."

The words that Jesus spoke at this tender moment are, by most surveys, the favorite of all biblical texts among professing Christians.

> *Let not your heart be troubled; you believe in God, believe also in Me.*
> *In My Father's house are many mansions;*
> *if it were not so, I would have told you. I go to prepare a place for you.*
> *And if I go and prepare a place for you,*
> *I will come again and receive you to Myself;*
> *that where I am, there you may be also.*
> *And where I go you know, and the way you know. (John 14:1–4)*

Now the disciples were *really* confused. Jesus was going somewhere, and He told them they couldn't come along. And now He was telling them that some day they *would* be able to join Him. Thomas's question was thoroughly understandable.

> *Thomas said to Him, "Lord, we do not know were You are going,*
> *and how can we know the way?" (John 14:5)*

FAMOUS LAST WORDS

In his book *The Man in the Mirror*, Patrick Morley reminds us that the words of a man on his deathbed are sometimes the most poignant of his life.

"All my life I have been seeking to climb out of the pit of my besetting sins and I cannot do it and I never will unless a hand is let down to draw me up" (Seneca).

"All of the wisdom of this world is but a tiny raft upon which we must set sail when we leave this earth. If only there was a firmer foundation upon which to stand, perhaps some divine word" (Socrates).

"I am about to take my last voyage, a great leap in the dark" (Thomas Hobbes).

"The meager satisfaction that man can extract from reality leaves him starving" (Sigmund Freud).

A lifelong agnostic, W. C. Fields was found reading a Bible moments before his death. "I'm looking for a loophole," he explained.

∽∾∾

Just a few hours before His crucifixion, Jesus' answer to Thomas's question was one of the most important statements in all of Holy Scripture. In these words, Jesus placed a priceless frame around His deity, He articulated His expectation of obedience for His followers, and He promised them the Holy Spirit to empower and inspire them . . . the sweetness of this sorrow.

> Jesus said to [Thomas],
> "I am the way, the truth, and the life.
> No one comes to the Father except through Me.
> If you had known Me, you would have known My Father also;
> and from now on you know Him and have seen Him . . .
> Do you not believe that I am in the Father, and the Father in Me?
> The words that I speak to you I do not speak on My own authority;
> but the Father who dwells in Me does the works . . .
> If you ask anything in My name, I will do it.
> If you love Me, keep My commandments.
> And I will pray the Father, and He will give you another Helper,
> that He may abide with you forever—
> the Spirit of truth, whom the world cannot receive,

because it neither sees Him nor knows Him;
but you know Him, for He dwells with you and will be in you.
I will not leave you orphans; I will come to you.
A little while longer and the world will see Me no more,
but you will see Me.
Because I live, you will live also." (John 14:6–7, 10, 14–19)

The event of Jesus' physical body being lifted into the clouds—the Ascension—was the time when God the Father restored to His Son the glory that had been His from the foundation of the world. In these words John recorded, Jesus was anticipating the end of His humiliation. He was comforting His disciples by telling them that He would, as He was glorified, prepare a place of rest for them.

> Jesus did something that my father could not do—make a covenant to return some day.

Jesus did something that my father could not do—make a covenant to return some day.

And being assembled together with [the disciples],
[Jesus] commanded them not to depart from Jerusalem,
but to wait for the Promise of the Father,
"which," He said, "you have heard from Me;
for John truly baptized with water,
but you shall be baptized with the Holy Spirit not many days from now."
Therefore, when they had come together, they asked Him, saying,
"Lord, will You at this time restore the kingdom to Israel?"
And He said to them, "It is not for you to know times or seasons
which the Father has put in His own authority.
But you shall receive power when the Holy Spirit has come upon you;
and you shall be witnesses to Me in Jerusalem,
and in all Judea and Samaria, and to the end of the earth."
Now when He had spoken these things, while they watched,
He was taken up, and a cloud received Him out of their sight.
And while they looked steadfastly toward heaven as He went up,

> *behold, two men stood by them in white apparel, who also said,*
> *"Men of Galilee, why do you stand gazing up into heaven?*
> *This same Jesus, who was taken up from you into heaven,*
> *will so come in like manner as you saw Him go into heaven."* (Acts 1:4–11)

Heaven is one of the greatest assurances for believers. And we are certain of heaven because we know Jesus walked the earth; from eyewitness accounts He ascended through the clouds, and now He sits at the right hand of the Father in glory. I believe that there is a direct relationship between our confidence in this reality and our obedience to His Word. What a man believes about the future always shapes how he lives in the present. This certainly marked those disciples who were there as He disappeared into the sky.

> *And they worshiped Him,*
> *and returned to Jerusalem with great joy,*
> *and were continually in the temple*
> *praising and blessing God.* (Luke 24:52–53)

Jesus had left the disciples physically, but He had encouraged them with joy and hope for the future. And He had left the Helper . . . the Comforter . . . the Holy Spirit, to be with them and to empower them.

Jesus Christ, the Son of Man, currently reigns as King, primarily revealing Himself to His church . . . for now. But one day, every eye will see Who He really is, and every tongue will confess that Jesus is Lord and King. What a sweet day that will be.

SUMMARY

■ THE CAESAREA-PHILIPPI CONFESSION

Jesus' reticence for fame was not primarily to avoid being crushed by autograph seekers among the masses. He avoided open and repeated references to Himself as the Messiah because the people of Israel were looking for the Redeemer to be a political leader, a religious revolutionary, who would single-handedly cast off the Romans and restore Israel to her place among the nations. And since this was not why Jesus came, He was careful not to identify Himself with a title that was so widely misunderstood. This is called the "messianic secret."

When it came time to teach His disciples this potentially explosive truth about Himself—that He *was* the Messiah—Jesus pulled them aside to a secret location, away from the normal places He taught. In the conversation that ensued, Jesus asked Simon Peter, "Who do you say that I am?" It was in this setting that Peter gives his great confession: "You are the Christ, the Son of the living God."

Immediately Jesus blessed Simon Peter.

Remember that Jesus did all of this in a secluded place, treating His disciples as trusted confidants. It was not the right time for Him to reveal this messianic secret. So with the full revelation of Who Jesus was burning in their hearts, the disciples waited for His word to release it.

■ THE TRANSFIGURATION

Centuries before Jesus was born, Moses made a special request to the Lord God. Moses begged God to let him do the unthinkable—to see His glory.

God rejected Moses' request to see His glory straight on, but gave him permission to peer through a breach in a rock, enough to see His back. It wasn't that God was being stingy with His glory; it was for Moses' own protection. "If I would give you what you're asking for and you would actually see Me," the Sovereign God was saying to Moses, "you wouldn't be able to handle it. You would literally drop dead."

Centuries later, the articulate and upbeat Isaiah, when faced with the glorified presence of the Almighty in the Temple, was breathless, filled with the truth of his own depravity and unworthiness.

The Transfiguration is an account—one of those glimpses of glory—of the most important intrusion of the full weight of a Holy God during Jesus' ministry.

Peter, James, and John had seen God's glory and lived. They fell to the ground in worship and awe in the presence of *kabod* and at the sound of the *vox dei*, the voice of God. But, in His tender love and compassion, Jesus reached down, took them by the hands, and helped them to their feet.

Their mortal minds were dazed. What these men saw that day was beyond anything a human could ever hope to see. God must have supernaturally sustained them to be able to bear the sight and live.

In Jesus Christ, glory was cloaked in human form. However that shroud, when peeled back, left men stunned and speechless . . . an overwhelming awe that should fill you and me with wonder every time we think of Him.

■ THE TRIUMPHAL ENTRY

Around the world, the church celebrates Palm Sunday and the account of Jesus' victorious entry into the City of David just a few days before His crucifixion and resurrection.

Jesus' time had come. No longer was He pressing His disciples to keep the secret. He approached Jerusalem willing to make a public display of His identification with the Old Testament prophecy of the Messiah. But for us, the image of Jesus riding on a lowly animal, His feet no doubt dragging on both sides of the colt, hardly seems royal enough for the Son of the Most High. Actually, in the culture of that day, the residents of the Holy City were truly "rolling out the red carpet" for the Savior.

■ THE CROSS

The public crucifixion of Jesus was meant to accomplish two objectives for the Romans and the Jewish leaders: (1) exterminate the troublemaker; and (2) send a message to His followers that such lawlessness—opposition to them— would not be tolerated.

In spite of his belief in the Savior's innocence, the Roman governor, Pilate, had a purpose in allowing Jesus to be treated as an ordinary criminal. It was his way of restoring the allegiance of the Jewish leaders to his rule.

The motives of the corrupt Jewish leaders—the Pharisees and the Sadducees—were clear. Jesus' death was pure expediency. That one man be sacrificed for the preservation of their religious system was a relatively small matter.

For most of Jesus' followers, including His disciples and family, the

Crucifixion represented the abrupt end of a dream. The One Whom they had followed, believed, and loved had been violently taken from them. For them, life no longer had purpose. Their grief and loneliness knew no bounds.

After voluntarily becoming the spotless Lamb of God and taking upon Himself the sins of the world, Jesus Christ became the most obscene creature in the universe.

■ THE RESURRECTION

When criminals were executed during this time, their bodies were literally thrown on the city's smoldering garbage dump known as Gehenna. But the body of the Savior was not subjected to this humiliation. In fact, when His lifeless form was taken down from the cross, a complete stranger, Joseph of Arimathea, offered his own burial tomb. One of the most poignant—and important—scenes in all of Holy Scripture is the scene of the first Easter. It's the story of a small contingent of women who return to the burial place of Jesus on Sunday morning.

Imagine how horrible these bereaved women must have felt. Their son and their Savior had died an unthinkable death and then, without the proper ceremonial anointing, had hurriedly been laid in the tomb of a Gentile stranger. What an irony. No living thing was scorned by the Jewish elite more than women and Gentiles, except perhaps swine. But here they were, willing to step forward and honor the lifeless body of Jesus.

What these women could never have known was that the truth to be revealed to them over the next few hours would change the course of human history.

When the women entered the crypt, the empty shroud was lying there. Upon hearing the news, the disciples' heads must have been spinning. Their hearts were filled with unbelief. Sure enough, the tomb was empty. But where was Jesus?

It's very important for you and me to understand that our belief in the bodily resurrection of Jesus is based not only on the fact of the missing body of Jesus. It is a reliable historic fact that Jesus made many visits to His people. He appeared to the women, to the disciples, to a couple of traveling men, to a group of five hundred, and to the apostle Paul. It is the extraordinary evidence of people having talked to, eaten with, and touched Jesus that causes us to believe that the Old Testament prophecies have come true.

■ THE ASCENSION

Just before His trial and crucifixion, Jesus gathered His disciples together to say farewell. His work was almost complete. The event of Jesus' physical body being lifted into the clouds—the Ascension—was the time when God the Father restored to His Son the glory that had been His from the foundation of the world.

CHAPTER FOURTEEN

FROM PENTECOST TO PAUL

- Pentecost
- The Expansion of the Church
- The Conversion of Paul

Because my wife and I live in Central Florida, an area of the country where new buildings spring up like weeds, we often see photos in the morning newspaper of "groundbreaking ceremonies." There are banners, marching bands, huge crowds, and prominent men and women wearing suits and dresses, pushing silver-plated shovels into the earth. Brief speeches are delivered, then everyone retires to a huge white tent to munch on fancy hors d'oeuvre and sip on something cold. Strobe lights pop as photographers capture each exciting moment.

The building process has begun and it's time to celebrate.

It makes me smile to think of the *real* workers who show up the next day to begin the *real* work on the building. Can't you see these tough guys, saying to one another in the early morning hours as they sip black coffee from Styrofoam cups, "Hey, where are the marching bands? Where are the dignitaries? Where are the silver shovels? Where are the cameras? Where's the food?"

Actually, they don't say these things. They finish their coffee and get to work. The workers understand that yesterday's hoopla was a necessary celebration of the starting point and they are on site to finish the job.

Shortly after Jesus ascended into heaven, an extremely important thing took place. It was a moment, a celebration, a groundbreaking event that had never happened before and has not happened since: the baptism of the Holy Spirit on the Day of Pentecost.

When the Day of Pentecost had fully come,
they were all with one accord in one place.
And suddenly there came a sound from heaven, as of a rushing mighty wind,
and it filled the whole house where they were sitting.
Then there appeared to them divided tongues, as of fire,
and one sat upon each of them.
And they were all filled with the Holy Spirit
and began to speak with other tongues,
as the Spirit gave them utterance.
And there were dwelling in Jerusalem Jews, devout men,
from every nation under heaven.
And when this sound occurred, the multitude came together, and were confused,
because everyone heard them speak in his own language.
Then they were all amazed and marveled, saying to one another,
"Look, are not all these who speak Galileans?
And how is it that we hear, each in our own language in which we were born?
Parthians and Medes and Elamites, those dwelling in Mesopotamia,
Judea and Cappadocia, Pontus and Asia, Phrygia and Pamphylia,
Egypt and the parts of Libya adjoining Cyrene, visitors from Rome,
both Jews and proselytes, Cretans and Arabs—we hear them speaking
in our own tongues the wonderful works of God."
So they were all amazed and perplexed, saying to one another,
"Whatever could this mean?" (Acts 2:1–12)

These strangers had heard the rushing wind, seen the fire, experienced the strange "speaking in tongues" phenomenon, and their predictable response was, "What in the world is going on here?"

If these signs of the Spirit's presence sound odd to us, imagine how it must have been for those who were there. So Peter stood up and informed the crowd as to what was happening, reminding them that this was exactly what the prophet Joel had predicted when he said that the Holy Spirit would be distributed throughout the nations. No longer would God primarily save a Jewish remnant, but He would call people from all over the world to bend their knee before Him.

This was a groundbreaking moment, so the celebration was completely in order.

What was the Day of Pentecost? Historically, it meant the "Fiftieth Day" after the offering of the barley sheaf at the Feast of Unleavened Bread. It included a holy convocation with the usual restriction on manual labor. Pentecost—also known as the Feast of Harvest—was one of the three greatest annual feasts of Israel, preceded by the Passover and followed by the Feast of Tabernacles.

> These strangers had heard the rushing wind, seen the fire, experienced the strange "speaking in tongues" phenomenon, and their predictable response was, "What in the world is going on here?"

In order for us to truly understand this particularly puzzling Pentecost, we need to journey back to the children of Israel's trek from Egypt to the Promised Land. In the book of Numbers (chap. 11) we read that the people had grown tired of the taste of manna. They groused to Moses, saying that they missed the leeks and onions they had left behind in Egypt, forgetting that they also had been brutalized slaves under the ruthless pharaoh. Nonetheless, they were complaining about camp food and wanted home cooking again.

The Jews rioted and God responded by sending fire among them, burning some of those on the outskirts of the camp. Moses was so furious that he begged God to kill him. He told God that he could no longer bear the pressure and responsibility of leading these rebellious people.

So what's the connection to Pentecost?

So the LORD said to Moses:
"Gather to Me seventy men of the elders of Israel,
whom you know to be the elders of the people and officers over them;
bring them to the tabernacle of meeting, that they may stand there with you.
Then I will come down and talk with you there.
I will take of the Spirit that is upon you and will put the same upon them;
and they shall bear the burden of the people with you,
that you may not bear it yourself alone." (Numbers 11:16–17)

Moses was the covenant mediator for the people of Israel. As the one who stood between the sinful people and a Holy God, Moses was the *charismatic* leader. He did not lead the Jews on the basis of his own natural strength, but he led them by means of a supernatural gift. Does this mean that the people of the Old Testament also had the Holy Spirit? Of course they did. For they couldn't have known God without Him.

But there were more functions and activities of the Holy Spirit than regeneration. The Holy Spirit empowered men and women for specific tasks as well. Kings, judges, prophets, craftsmen, warriors—all are mentioned as bearing the "anointing" of God for specific tasks. In the above text, God dispersed Moses' leadership responsibilities to seventy men, so His work could be done more effectively by being shared.

This is exactly what happened at Pentecost. God's Holy Spirit was scattered among His people, empowering them to carry out His will in the world.

There were three signs of the Holy Spirit's presence on this remarkable day. They provide us with explicit symbols of the reality of God's occupation among His people—then and now.

WIND

The first was a sound like rushing wind. This was no ordinary wind whipped up by some spontaneous cloudburst. This was the unconstrained movement of a Holy God. The Greek word for "spirit" is *pneuma*. In Hebrew, the word is *ruach*. Both of these words mean "wind."

Living in Florida, where hurricane season signals sobriety among us all, the wind is a common visitor. Its impact is profound on the landscape. Although the wind itself cannot be seen, the gale-forces that literally level buildings make headlines around the world. No wonder the Holy Spirit visited these unsuspecting believers in the form of a rushing wind—an invisible force with undeniable results. God's Spirit leaves no one untouched.

The wind blows wherever it pleases.
You hear its sound, but you cannot tell
where it comes from

or where it is going.
So it is with everyone born of the Spirit. (John 3:8 NIV)

FIRE

The second manifestation of this dramatic descent of the Holy Spirit was a visible phenomenon. Those assembled saw tongues of fire resting over each person's head. Like wind, the imagery of fire was a common revelation of God's presence.

As the Israelites journeyed from Egypt in search of Canaan, God led them through the darkness by a pillar of fire. God's Spirit leads. On Mount Carmel, Elijah's blasphemous foes were utterly consumed by divine fire spilling down from the sky. God's Spirit punishes.

> *But who can endure the day of His coming?*
> *And who can stand when He appears?*
> *For He is like a refiner's fire*
> *And like launderers' soap.*
> *He will sit as a refiner and a purifier of silver;*
> *He will purify the sons of Levi,*
> *And purge them as gold and silver,*
> *That they may offer to the LORD*
> *An offering in righteousness.* (Malachi 3:2–3)

Through the process of melting off the dross from raw ore, fire refines precious metals. God's Spirit purifies.

TONGUES

The third experience of Pentecost was the seeming confusion of multiple languages being spoken. Whether this outbreak was a miracle of speech or a miracle of hearing is unclear. Were the people given an ability to speak foreign languages without training, or was there a supernatural work of translation going on here? No doubt this moment involved both.

To those believers present in the house that day, the message of the tongues was unmistakable: When He's ready to speak, God's voice *will* be heard. He *will* do whatever He needs to ensure that His pronouncements *will* be clearly understood. Like scenes you have seen within the chambers of the United Nations where delegates wear headphones connected to translators, Pentecost was not chaos. It was crystalline communication from a Holy God to the hearts of individual men and women—coming through to each one. God's Spirit is strong and clear.

> What makes Pentecost so distinct is that it only happened *once.*

Every believer is a "charismatic" believer. We are empowered and indwelt by the Holy Spirit. And the doctrine once largely confined to Pentecostal and Assemblies of God churches is becoming of central importance to a vast number of Christians around the globe. A sense of excitement and spiritual renewal usually accompanies this fresh discovery of the presence and the power of the Holy Spirit in the church. But in spite of the enthusiasm, care must be taken in understanding the doctrine of the filling of the Holy Spirit.

There are those who hold to the belief that conversion and Holy Spirit baptism are two separate events. The time lapse between the regeneration of the believers in this account of the Day of Pentecost and its veritable explosion of the Holy Spirit's presence give them the notion that two works of grace are necessary. This is an error.

Many who use Pentecost as evidence of the necessity of "something else" in the experience of a believer are taking a historical scenario and giving it the same dogmatic value as a teaching of Jesus or an epistle of John or Paul. While historical narratives have the same accuracy as the propositions and doctrines taught by Jesus, John, or Paul, it can be a terrible mistake to attempt to apply them in the same way in a contemporary setting. They are different kinds of writing, and God was accomplishing very different purposes with each of them.

Clear propositional teaching should always clarify the application of historical biblical events. Narratives should never stand alone without the buttresses of dogma to support them.

What makes Pentecost so distinct is that it only happened *once.* The subsequent episodes of Holy Spirit baptism beyond its inaugural moment should be understood as an extension of Pentecost by which the whole church—the body of Christ—is gifted for ministry. The signs were given to affirm the sovereignty and activity of a Holy God and to affirm that even Gentiles received a full measure of the Holy Spirit. No longer in God's economy was there a distinction between Jews and Greeks.

This particular Day of Pentecost was an unforgettable moment in time. The Holy Spirit had descended on the people in an undeniable, visible way, and a new day in the life of God's people had begun.

But the ceremonies had concluded. The silver-plated shovels were being fitted for the display cases, musicians were returning instruments to their cases, and the white tents were being folded up.

Now it was time to get to work.

- Pentecost
- **The Expansion of the Church**
- The Conversion of Paul

A prophetic overview of the first thirty years following Jesus' ascension was summarized perfectly among His final words to the disciples.

> *For John truly baptized with water,*
> *but you shall be baptized with the Holy Spirit not many days from now . . .*
> *You shall receive power when the Holy Spirit has come upon you;*
> *and you shall be witnesses to Me in Jerusalem,*
> *and in all Judea and Samaria, and to the end of the earth.* (Acts 1:5, 8)

The dramatic events at the Day of Pentecost must have been an epiphany for the disciples who had heard Jesus' words. "We remember Jesus telling us that Holy Spirit baptism was coming," they must have said to one another, "but we had no idea it would be like *this*."

In the same way that Jesus had predicted the events of Pentecost, He had also laid out the strategy for their missionary work in spreading the Gospel and building the church. Like the effect of a pebble dropped in a pond, His followers were to take His message from the center (Jerusalem) out in concentric circles to the world. The rest of the book of Acts demonstrates their remarkable level of obedience.

In some Bibles, the book of Acts is referred to as "The Acts of the Apostles." I think the book could be more appropriately named, "The Acts of the Holy Spirit." From the Day of Pentecost forward, the central character of Acts was not the apostles (those who had been with Jesus and had been specifically commissioned for ministry were called "apostles"), but the Spirit of God. The Holy Spirit went from Pentecost manifesting His power and person in ways no one had ever seen before.

With the elimination of the "King of the Jews," the conniving Jewish leaders had figured that they could safely get on with their old covenant traditions. They were in for an unpleasant surprise.

In crucifying the Savior, their problems were exponentially multiplied. Empowered by the Holy Spirit, the disciples who were incognito during Jesus' trial were now standing front and center, calling people to repentance. So, like state troopers on a holiday weekend, these "holy men" posted speed traps everywhere. They were going to put an end to this.

> When [the high priest and council]
> had called for the apostles and beaten them,
> they commanded that they should not speak in the name of Jesus,
> and let them go.
> So [the apostles] departed from the presence of the council,
> rejoicing that they were counted worthy
> to suffer shame for His name.
> And daily in the temple, and in every house,
> they did not cease teaching and preaching Jesus as the Christ. (Acts 5:40–42)

STEPHEN

But the Jewish council was getting nowhere. Their plan to severely punish these men who were spreading the Gospel was turning on them. Their efforts to *stop* the growth of the church were literally *making* it grow. Capital punishment for the perpetrators would be their only hope. Beatings were proving unsuccessful. They needed a more permanent deterrent.

The story of Stephen is one of the most remarkable accounts of raw courage recorded in the entire Bible. We are introduced to Stephen when a group of converted Gentiles complained to the twelve apostles that their widows were not receiving enough care.

> Then the twelve summoned the multitude of the disciples and said,
> "It is not desirable that we should leave the word of God and serve tables.
> Therefore, brethren, seek out from among you seven men of good reputation,
> full of the Holy Spirit and wisdom,
> whom we may appoint over this business;
> but we will give ourselves continually to prayer
> and to the ministry of the word."
> And the saying pleased the whole multitude.
> And they chose Stephen, a man full of faith and the Holy Spirit,
> and [six other men]. (Acts 6:2–5)

Like a lightning rod perched atop a rural barn, Stephen became the focus of a particular group of devout Jews called the Synagogue of the Freedmen. These men were displeased with Stephen's work and ministry, so they laid a trap, inducing some to say that Stephen had blasphemed Moses, God, the Temple, and the sacred Law.

So they sent a band of mercenaries to seize Stephen, summoning him into their pompous presence.

> And all who sat in the council, looking steadfastly at [Stephen],
> saw his face as the face of an angel. (Acts 6:15)

Can't you see these religious men nervously shifting in their seats as they look into the face of this brave man?

> Then the high priest said,
> "Are these things so?" (Acts 7:1)

There's an old saying that goes, "If you don't want the answer, don't ask the question." The high priest shouldn't have asked the question because Stephen's answer ultimately humiliated and infuriated him. This layman delivered one of the greatest sermons recorded in the Scriptures. Beginning on the common ground of the Patriarchs, Stephen deftly wove a narrative tapestry, pointing to the rebellion of the Israelites and ultimately their rejection of the Messiah. On his way to the conclusion of his address, he verbally leveled the high priest and the council.

> These calculating and deliberate men became like wild animals.

> You stiff-necked and uncircumcised in heart and ears!
> You always resist the Holy Spirit;
> as your fathers did, so do you. (Acts 7:51)

Not taking lightly his oral assault, these arrogant zealots covered their ears like spoiled children, then physically charged Stephen, dragging him to the outskirts of the city. These calculating and deliberate men became like wild animals. Tearing their cloaks from their bodies, they picked up rocks, throwing them full-force into Stephen's angelic face. In the midst of the indescribable violence, this courageous man, filled with the Holy Spirit, spoke.

> Lord Jesus, receive my spirit . . .
> Lord, do not charge them with this sin. (Acts 7:59b–60b)

What a stunning moment this must have been for everyone there, including one of the accomplices, standing guard over the perpetrators' cloaks—a young scholar named Saul.

FUELING THE FIRES

What the Jewish leaders had established as an aggressive plan to extinguish the church was actually accomplishing the opposite. The blood of the martyrs was fueling the fires of evangelism's spread.

At that time a great persecution arose against the church which was at Jerusalem;
and they were all scattered throughout the regions of Judea and Samaria,
except the apostles. (Acts 8:1)

One of the great recurring themes in the Bible is that God will use whomever and whatever He chooses to complete His work. He used the godless Pharaoh and the barbaric Assyrians to purify the Israelites; now through persecution and dispersion, He was using misguided religious fanatics to fulfill the design for His church.

It was also interesting that the apostles stayed home in Jerusalem, sending "common" folks to the surrounding regions. This was a properly practiced doctrine of the "priesthood of the believer" (1 Peter 2). The spread of the Gospel was the result of committed and obedient laymen, filled with the Holy Spirit and properly equipped for ministry by the apostles.

Once the laity had begun to move out from Jerusalem, some of the apostles followed. And what happened was quite remarkable. Philip, for example, traveled to Samaria to preach. As a result, a man named Simon, a popular

> The blood of the martyrs was fueling the fires of evangelism's spread.

practitioner in sorcery and witchcraft, was wonderfully converted. In fact, Simon joined Philip, seeing for himself the indescribable power of the Holy Spirit at work in the hearts of unregenerate men and women.

But, as wonderful as the Spirit's power was through the obedience of ordinary people and through the faithful ministry of the apostles, God's amazing work included His own direct intervention.

There was a certain man in Caesarea called Cornelius,
a centurion of what was called the Italian Regiment,
a devout man and one who feared God with all his household,
who gave alms generously to the people, and prayed to God always.
About the ninth hour of the day he saw clearly in a vision an angel of God
coming in and saying to him, "Cornelius!"
And when he observed him, he was afraid, and said,
"What is it, lord?" So [the angel] said to him,

"Your prayers and your alms have come up for a memorial before God.
Now send men to Joppa, and send for Simon whose surname is Peter.
He is lodging with Simon, a tanner, whose house is by the sea.
He will tell you what you must do."
And when the angel who spoke to him had departed,
Cornelius called two of his household servants and a devout soldier
from among those who waited on him continually.
So when he had explained all these things to them,
he sent them to Joppa. (Acts 10:1–8)

But before Cornelius's emissaries had reached him, Simon Peter had a vision that prepared him for the encounter. In this vision he saw a great object that looked like a sheet filled with all sorts of animals, those traditionally acceptable for Jews to consume and those not permissible to eat.

And a voice came to him, "Rise, Peter; kill and eat."
But Peter said, "Not so, Lord!
For I have never eaten anything common or unclean."
And a voice spoke to him again the second time,
"What God has cleansed you must not call common."
This was done three times.
And the object was taken up into heaven again. (Acts 10:13–16)

Cornelius, a foreigner and a non-Jew, was visited by an ambassador of the living God who told him to call on Simon Peter, a convert to Christ but a proud and exclusive-minded Jew. And this same God visited Peter and prepared him for the meeting with a lesson on inclusiveness—the wideness of His mercy.

Once Cornelius had called on Simon Peter and explained the visitation of the angel of God, Peter was astonished.

Peter opened his mouth and said:
"In truth I perceive that God shows no partiality." (Acts 10:34)

As He had done to encourage the heart of Gideon and his pathetic army and spread fear among the mighty Midianites preparing them for defeat, this could only be the work of the Sovereign Holy Spirit. He prepared the heart of an Italian centurion *and* the apostle for an encounter that led to the conversion of an outsider named Cornelius. Surrounded by his family and close friends, this sincere but lost man heard the message of the atonement and redemption of Jesus Christ from the lips of Simon Peter.

> *While Peter was still speaking these words,*
> *the Holy Spirit fell upon all those who heard the word.*
> *And those [Jews] who believed were astonished, as many as came with Peter,*
> *because the gift of the Holy Spirit had been poured out on the Gentiles also.*
> *For they heard them speak with tongues and magnify God.*
> *Then Peter answered,*
> *"Can anyone forbid water, that these should not be baptized*
> *who have received the Holy Spirit just as we have?"*
> *And he commanded them to be baptized in the name of the Lord.*
> *Then they asked him to stay a few days.* (Acts 10:44–48)

This and other experiences of the Holy Spirit falling on people in extraordinary ways are exactly that: extraordinary. They were special displays of God's glory symbolic of the blessing afforded all believers, then and now—those who speak in tongues and those who do not. With each display in Scripture and since, God has been proclaiming to the church that the same Day of Pentecost grace is theirs. The visible manifestations of filling were only symbols that underscored the Holy Spirit's presence and power going forth to all nations.

When a Holy God acts, His ways are always thorough, and His will is always accomplished.

- Pentecost
- The Expansion of the Church
- **The Conversion of Paul**

As you and I have seen, the Bible is full of the unpredictable activity of God. There's no *logical* explanation for His choice of a stammering Moses to lead

His people out of Egypt as their eloquent leader or His selection of the young-ster David to be Israel's greatest king. There's no *logical* reason why God would have used a great fish to provide transportation for a rebellious prophet or a cattle trough to become a birthing crib for His Holy Son. But this is what He did.

The story of the apostle Paul—the author of almost one-third of the entire New Testament—fits perfectly into this sovereign randomness. You'll remember, at the scene of the brutal execution of Stephen, there was an accomplice watching over the cloaks of the council—the young scholar named Saul.

What would his response have been if you had been able to stand there next to him and quietly whisper to him dur-ing the violence of the moment, "Some day, young man, you'll also be privileged to die as a martyr for Jesus."

> The Bible is full of the unpredictable activity of God.

I'm not quite sure how you'd say "You must be joking" in Greek, but Saul's response would have been the colloquial equivalent to it.

God doesn't seek our permission to affirm His logic; He simply acts as He pleases. And it pleased Him to choose this gifted young man to become Christianity's first apologist—a trained and called defender of the faith.

You'll notice that I have introduced this person as "Saul," but have referred to him as the "apostle (one who had been personally called by Jesus) Paul." It sounds like two different men, doesn't it? Well, it *is* . . . which is exactly the point of the story.

Then Saul, still breathing threats and murder against the disciples of the Lord,
went to the high priest and asked letters from him to the synagogues of Damascus,
so that if he found any who were of the Way, whether men or women,
he might bring them bound to Jerusalem. (Acts 9:1–2)

Saul was zealously attacking Christians. He wanted to rid the world of this heretical sect that appeared to be undermining Judaism. Saul was no ignorant curmudgeon. Having earned the equivalent of two Ph.D.'s by the time he was twenty-one years old, he rationally believed that the followers of Jesus could systematically and eventually undo rabbinical Judaism. And he was not going to stand idly by. Given his training, his passion, and his unregenerate heart, who can blame him?

But that was then. Saul was about to take a journey that would fully change everything.

> As [Saul] journeyed he came near Damascus,
> and suddenly a light shone around him from heaven.
> Then he fell to the ground, and heard a voice saying to him,
> "Saul, Saul, why are you persecuting Me?" (Acts 9:3–4)

Lying there in the dust of the road to Damascus, Saul must have been wholly overwhelmed. His first conscious thought, once he had recovered enough of his wits, must have been to try to intellectually sort out what had just happened. Scholars tend to do this under duress—just ask their spouses.

> God doesn't seek our permission to affirm His logic; He simply acts as He pleases.

Saul had seen a great light. In fact, like the power of a thousand flashbulbs, it had rendered him incapable of seeing. Like someone hurriedly thumbing through a stack of index cards, Saul mentally scanned the Scriptures.

Moses begged God to let him catch a glimpse of His glory but God warned him,

> You cannot see My face; for no man shall see Me, and live. (Exodus 33:20)

Isaiah, who had had his own encounter with a Holy God, said,

> The people who walked in darkness
> Have seen a great light;
> Those who dwelt in the land of the shadow of death,
> Upon them a light has shined. (Isaiah 9:2)

Even the claims of the shepherds on the Judean hillside one starry night,

> *And the glory of the Lord shown around them,*
> *and they were greatly afraid.* (Luke 2:9b)

"Could this be God?" Saul must have wondered. "Or *Jesus?*" he may have feared.

Then the voice calls his name twice, "Saul, Saul."

The scholar facedown in the dirt knew that in the Scriptures this was a rare but significant thing—when a voice repeated a name twice: Moses at the burning bush, Abraham about to take the life of his son, and Elisha calling to his mentor, Elijah. The repetition meant emphasis and intimacy. This, too, got Saul's attention.

> To assail Jesus' church
> is to abuse Him.

Gaining enough strength and courage to open his mouth, Saul spoke:

> *Who are You, Lord?* (Acts 9:5a)

Saul's query makes me smile because he asks a question that contains the answer. Saul knew full well that this was a divine encounter.

> *Then the Lord said,*
> *"I am Jesus, whom you are persecuting.*
> *It is hard for you to kick against the goads."* (Acts 9:5b)

Do you find it curious that Jesus didn't say, "I am Jesus and you are persecuting My people"? He didn't say this because to attack Jesus' followers, to rip into His body of believers, is to assault the person of Christ. To assail His church is to abuse Him.

The "goads" were hard spikes mounted to the front of an ox-drawn wagon, meant to keep the ox from kicking against the wagon it was pulling. An unusually stubborn ox would become infuriated with the pain inflicted by these goads and kick again and again, doing further damage to himself. Jesus was charging Saul with being just such an ox.

God had Saul's full attention.

So [Saul], trembling and astonished, said,
"Lord, what do You want me to do?"
Then the Lord said to him, "Arise and go into the city,
and you will be told what you must do."
And the men who journeyed with him stood speechless,
hearing a voice but seeing no one.
Then Saul arose from the ground,
and when his eyes were opened he saw no one.
But they led him by the hand and brought him into Damascus.
And he was three days without sight,
and neither ate nor drank. (Acts 9:6–9)

Crawling to his feet, like a cowboy having been pounded by a traveling gunslinger in the town square, Saul discovered that he could not see. His companions, unable to speak, helped Saul along and continued their journey to Damascus. What an interesting, almost pathetic, picture this is: mute men leading a blind man—their intellectual mentor—by the hand. But exactly where were they to go?

Now there was a certain disciple at Damascus named Ananias;
and to him the Lord said in a vision, "Ananias."
And he said, "Here I am, Lord."
So the Lord said to him,
"Arise and go to the street called Straight,
and inquire at the house of Judas for one called Saul of Tarsus,
for behold, he is praying.
And in a vision he has seen a man named Ananias
coming in and putting his hand on him, so that he might receive his sight."
Then Ananias answered,
"Lord, I have heard from many about this man,
how much harm he has done to Your saints in Jerusalem.
And here he has authority from the chief priests
to bind all who call on Your name." (Acts 9:10–14)

Once again, God was preparing *both* sides of His sovereign equation.

But I can understand Ananias's apprehension. Perhaps this isn't a vision from God. Maybe it's a bad dream . . . surely God would not want him to present himself to this man who has ravaged the church.

But the Lord said to [Ananias],
"Go, for he is a chosen vessel of Mine
to bear My name before Gentiles, kings, and the children of Israel.
For I will show him how many things he must suffer for My name's sake."
And Ananias went his way and entered the house;
and laying his hands on him he said,
"Brother Saul, the Lord Jesus,
who appeared to you on the road as you came,
has sent me that you may receive your sight
and be filled with the Holy Spirit."
Immediately there fell from his eyes something like scales,
and he received his sight at once;
and he arose and was baptized.
So when he had received food, he was strengthened.
Then Saul spent some days with the disciples at Damascus. (Acts 9:15–19)

This was the defining experience in Saul's life. Never having been one to hide his passions, Saul, who became "Paul," went straight to the temple.

Immediately [Paul] preached the Christ in the synagogues,
that He is the Son of God.
Then all who heard were amazed, and said,
"Is this not he who destroyed those
who called on this name in Jerusalem,
and has come here for that purpose,
so that he might bring them bound to the chief priests?"
But Saul increased all the more in strength,
and confounded the Jews who dwelt in Damascus,
proving that this Jesus is the Christ. (Acts 9:20–22)

Can you imagine the shock of both the Jews and the Christians at the change in Paul? Years later, in his letter to his understudy Timothy, this man would write these words:

> *I thank Christ Jesus our Lord who has enabled me,*
> *because He counted me faithful,*
> *putting me into the ministry,*
> *although I was formerly a blasphemer,*
> *a persecutor, and an insolent man;*
> *but I obtained mercy because I did it ignorantly in unbelief.*
> *And the grace of our Lord was exceedingly abundant,*
> *with faith and love which are in Christ Jesus.*
> *This is a faithful saying and worthy of all acceptance,*
> *that Christ Jesus came into the world to save sinners,*
> *of whom I am chief.* (1 Timothy 1:12–15)

Paul understood God's mercy and his own repentance. The word *metanoyah* meant "change of mind, reversal, or reformation," a concept the author of 1 Timothy certainly knew something about from his "Damascus road experience."

THE APOSTLE?

Remembering back to the Old Testament, there were constant struggles between those who had been called by God and those who were false prophets, not called or empowered by God. First, to distinguish between the true and false prophet was to understand that one could clearly articulate the exact circumstances of their divine call. This explains why most prophets, early in their writings, went to such pains to explain the exact circumstances of their call to speak God's word.

Second, a called prophet was able to say to the people, "Thus says the Lord," with unconditional precision. So, there has always been a general criterion to establish the veracity of God's specially appointed messengers.

Before looking closely at some of Paul's writings, the issue of Paul referring to himself as an "apostle" should be addressed.

As I have mentioned, following Jesus' ascension, the disciples became known as apostles. The apparent criteria for being an apostle were fourfold:

1. Apostles had heard a direct call from Jesus, "Follow Me."
2. Apostles were eyewitnesses of Jesus during His earthly ministry;
3. Apostles were eyewitnesses of the post-resurrected Christ; and
4. The authenticity of these things was verified by the other apostles.

So it was imperative that apostles, just like prophets, had a clear calling. It was also necessary to have had a personal *and* physical encounter with the Savior. However, because these standards are not clearly stated in the Scripture, there is still some uncertainty regarding the right to use the title "apostle" today. While many Christian leaders may be doing apostle-like ministry, such as planting churches and providing oversight to parish ministers, this is not enough. They would need to provide the kind of proof the apostle Paul was forced to furnish to those who doubted his apostleship.

> Can you picture the original apostles welcoming the man who had so recently been the archenemy of their intimate fellowship?

Certainly, Paul received a call. But Luke, the author of the Acts, made it abundantly clear that Paul's call was a direct and audible one. In fact, Paul's traveling companions were credible eyewitnesses to this.

After Paul had seen Jesus and heard His voice, he was sent back to Jerusalem to visit with the other apostles. At first they were understandably apprehensive. But he eventually convinced them of the events that had occurred and received confirmation of the authenticity of his apostleship from those who would know for sure.

> *And when Saul had come to Jerusalem,*
> *he tried to join the disciples; but they were all afraid of him,*
> *and did not believe that he was a disciple.*
> *But Barnabas took him and brought him to the apostles.*
> *And he declared to them how he had seen the Lord on the road,*
> *and that He had spoken to him,*

and how he had preached boldly at Damascus in the name of Jesus.
So he was with them at Jerusalem, coming in and going out. (Acts 9:26–28)

Can you picture the original apostles welcoming the man who had so recently been the archenemy of their intimate fellowship? Although they all knew that there was certain persecution ahead for each one of them, this celebration of friendship must have been awesome.

As you would expect, the word of Paul's admission to the inner circle spread throughout the region.

When the brethren found out,
they brought him down to Caesarea and sent him out to Tarsus.
Then the churches throughout all Judea, Galilee, and Samaria
had peace and were edified.
And walking in the fear of the Lord
and in the comfort of the Holy Spirit, they were multiplied. (Acts 9:30–31)

SUMMARY
■ PENTECOST

Shortly after Jesus ascended into heaven, an extremely important thing took place. It was a moment, a celebration, a groundbreaking event that had never happened before and has not happened since: the baptism of the Holy Spirit on the Day of Pentecost.

These strangers had heard the rushing wind, seen the fire, experienced the strange "speaking in tongues" phenomenon, and their predictable response was, "What in the world is going on here?"

If these signs of the Spirit's presence sound odd to us, imagine how it must have been for those who were there. So Peter stood up and informed the crowd as to what was happening, reminding them that this was exactly what the prophet Joel had predicted when he said that the Holy Spirit would be distributed throughout the nations. No longer would God primarily save a Jewish remnant, but He would call people from all over the world to bend their knee before Him.

This was a groundbreaking moment, so the celebration was completely in order. At Pentecost, God's Holy Spirit was scattered among His people, empowering them to carry out His will in the world. But Pentecost was not chaos. The Holy Spirit had descended on the people in an undeniable, visible way, and a new day in the life of God's people had begun.

■ THE EXPANSION OF THE CHURCH

In the same way that Jesus had predicted the events of Pentecost, He had also laid out the strategy for their missionary work in spreading the Gospel and building the church. Like the effect of a pebble dropped in a pond, His followers were to take His message from the center (Jerusalem) out in concentric circles to the world.

In some Bibles, the book of Acts is referred to as "The Acts of the Apostles." I think the book could be more appropriately named, "The Acts of the Holy Spirit." From the Day of Pentecost forward, the central character of Acts was not the apostles, but the Spirit of God. The Holy Spirit went from Pentecost manifesting His power and person in ways no one had ever seen before.

With the elimination of the "King of the Jews," the conniving Jewish leaders had figured that they could safely get on with their old covenant traditions. They were in for an unpleasant surprise.

In crucifying the Savior, their problems were exponentially multiplied. Empowered by the Holy Spirit, the disciples who were incognito during Jesus' trial were now standing front and center, calling people to repentance. So, like state troopers on a holiday weekend, these "holy men" posted speed traps everywhere. They were going to put an end to this.

The story of Stephen is one of the most remarkable accounts of raw courage recorded in the entire Bible. Like a lightning rod perched atop a rural barn, Stephen became the focus of a particular group of devout Jews called the Synagogue of the Freedmen. These men were displeased with Stephen's work and ministry, so they laid a trap, inducing some to say that Stephen had blasphemed Moses, God, the Temple, and the sacred Law.

So they sent a band of mercenaries to seize Stephen, summoning him into their pompous presence. This layman delivered one of the greatest sermons recorded in the Scriptures. Beginning on the common ground of the Patriarchs, Stephen deftly wove a narrative tapestry, pointing to the rebellion of the Israelites and ultimately their rejection of the Messiah.

Not taking lightly his oral assault, these arrogant zealots covered their ears like spoiled children, then physically charged Stephen, dragging him to the outskirts of the city. What a stunning moment this must have been for everyone there, including one of the accomplices, standing guard over the perpetrators' cloaks—a young scholar named Saul.

■ THE CONVERSION OF PAUL

What would Saul's (later "Paul") response have been if you had been able to stand there next to him and quietly whisper to him during the violence of the execution of Stephen, "Some day, young man, you'll also be privileged to die as a martyr for Jesus."

I'm not quite sure how you'd say "You must be joking" in Greek, but Saul's response would have been the colloquial equivalent to it.

God doesn't seek our permission to affirm His logic; He simply acts as He pleases. And it pleased Him to choose this gifted young man to become Christianity's first apologist—a trained and called defender of the faith.

After a vision that knocked him to the dust of the road to Damascus, Saul must have been wholly overwhelmed. His first conscious thought, once he had recovered enough of his wits, must have been to try to intellectually sort out what had just happened.

Saul had seen a great light. In fact, like the power of a thousand flashbulbs, it had rendered him incapable of seeing. Like someone hurriedly thumbing through a stack of index cards, Saul mentally scanned the Scriptures.

"Could this be God?" Saul must have wondered. "Or *Jesus?*" he may have feared. Then the voice calls his name twice, "Saul, Saul."

The scholar facedown in the dirt knew that in the Scriptures this was a rare but significant thing—that a voice repeated a name twice: Moses at the burning bush, Abraham about to take the life of his son, and Elisha calling to his mentor, Elijah. The repetition meant emphasis and intimacy. God had Saul's full attention.

After Paul had seen Jesus and had heard His voice, he was sent back to Jerusalem to visit with the other apostles. At first they were understandably apprehensive. But he eventually convinced them of the events that had occurred and received confirmation of the authenticity of his apostleship from those who would know for sure.

CHAPTER FIFTEEN

PAUL'S LETTERS TO THE CHURCHES

- Romans
- 1 and 2 Corinthians
- The Prison Epistles
- 1 and 2 Timothy

When was the last time you read through the operations manual for your car? Has it been *that* long ago? Here, in one place, is everything you need to know about your automobile. And the fact that you've not read this booklet recently has nothing to do with its being misplaced. You know where it is, right there in the glove box.

This may seem like a silly question for me to ask you, but it's not. Why? Because the book of Romans is the closest we come in all of Scripture to an operations manual for our faith. And as the first book following the Acts of the Apostles, we know exactly where to find it.

One of the greatest favors God has given the church is the blessing of brilliant thinkers—down through history theologians who have been exceptionally gifted at taking the complexity of religious thought and distilling it into understandable language. There has been no greater theologian in history than the apostle Paul. Certainly Augustine, Luther, Calvin, and Edwards were giants of the Christian faith, but their brilliance pales in the face of Paul.

When you add to this the fact that Romans, and the books that follow it, were written by Paul under the unrestricted inspiration of the Holy Spirit, it becomes clear why this operations manual has no business living in our dark glove boxes. The light of day is where it belongs.

Unlike many thinkers, past and present, Paul was not an "ivory tower" intellectual. He was a missionary, a pastor, and an evangelist. His writings and thoughts came from living in the trenches of first-century ministry . . . and persecution. Because of this, Paul was forced to search for the truths that could inform, encourage, and sustain his converts in a world that was entirely opposed to the truths of Christ.

As the operations manual for our beliefs, Romans is the closest Paul comes to setting down a systematic theology of salvation. And, amazingly, it is relatively brief. George Bernard Shaw once wrote a twelve-page letter to a friend, apologizing at the end for having written such a tome. "Forgive me for going on so long," Shaw groveled. "I didn't have time to write a shorter letter."

Again, under the inspiration of the Spirit of God, Paul took enough time to distill the great themes of our belief system and put them into the sixteen concise chapters of Romans. Over the centuries, God has used Romans to bring revival to more churches than we could count. Saint Augustine, Charles Wesley, and Martin Luther are only a few of those who have been dramatically converted by the truths it contains.

Like any accomplished writer would do, Paul begins the book by telling us what he is going to tell us. He summarizes Romans in what is surely the thesis for this great book.

> For I am not ashamed of the gospel of Christ,
> for it is the power of God to salvation for everyone who believes,
> for the Jew first and also for the Greek.
> For in it the righteousness of God is revealed from faith to faith;
> as it is written,
> "The just shall live by faith." (Romans 1:16–17)

FIRST THE BAD NEWS

Right from the top, Paul tells us what we need to know about living the Christian life. He tells us that we can't . . . without faith. Because we do not possess—and cannot achieve—the righteousness to be acceptable to a Holy God, we can only find righteousness as recipients of the gift of God's righteousness in Christ. Once we do receive this, then we *can* find the ability to live obediently . . . but again, only by the grace of God.

Before we can understand the good news of the Gospel, Paul knew that we first had to understand the bad news. So the first three chapters establish that all are guilty before God, exposed as sinners by the Law of God. And regardless of the ethnic origin of the original recipients of the book of Romans—Jews or Gentiles—everyone is hopelessly culpable.

Paul underscores this truth with a sobering reminder.

> *The law entered that the offense might abound.* (Romans 5:20a)

Over the past few years, I have found it interesting to read editorials, passionately supporting or decrying the posting of the Ten Commandments in schools, government buildings, and other public places. What is fascinating to me is that *if* laws were passed, allowing the decalogue to be seen in common places, the *reason* for its placement would be completely missed. The Law was not given as a summary of what to do and what to avoid.

God conferred the Law to Moses and then to the Israelites as a stark reminder of how impossible it was to obey Him. As a reminder of their need for grace, the Law was offered to the Israelites—and us—to prompt them as to how sinful they were.

> Because we do not possess—and cannot achieve—the righteousness to be acceptable to a Holy God, we can only find righteousness as recipients of the gift of God's righteousness in Christ.

There's even more bad news. Whether or not the Law is posted, Paul reminds us that God has also revealed Himself in nature.

> *For since the creation of the world*
> *His invisible attributes are clearly seen,*
> *being understood by the things that are made,*
> *even His eternal power and Godhead,*
> *so that they are without excuse.* (Romans 1:20)

Remember when Jesus was entering the city of Jerusalem to the sounds of "Hosanna"? And do you remember what He said to the religious elite who told Him to quiet the crowd?

> *I can tell you that if these should keep silent,*
> *the stones would immediately cry out.* (Luke 19:40–41)

This is exactly what Paul is saying. Whether mankind chooses to praise and obey the Sovereign God, all of creation will do it anyway. In other words, for those skeptics who are looking for a sign, there's no excuse. Signs *are* posted everywhere.

For those who ignore Him, God's judgment is often thought of as a consuming fire falling from heaven. But Paul introduces us to another, more devastating punishment.

> *God also gave them up to uncleanness,*
> *in the lusts of their hearts,*
> *to dishonor their bodies among themselves.* (Romans 1:24)

If God's grace is our greatest hope, then the removal of that same grace would represent our most explicit hopelessness. A Holy God's greatest punishment to sinful men is to turn them loose, separating Himself from their thinking and acting. What a perfect description of first-century—and twenty-first-century mankind.

> God conferred the Law to Moses and then to the Israelites as a stark reminder of how impossible it was to obey Him.

The universal response to God's revelation is to disobey. So it is essential that if we are to be holy as God is Holiness, if we are to be righteous as He is Righteousness, we must receive our holiness and our righteousness from Jesus Christ.

One of the ways that Paul teaches in his writing is through "dialecture." In this he presumes a question from the reader, then answers it.

For example, in chapter 4, Paul assumes questions about Patriarchs who lived centuries before the Law was given to Moses . . . long before the incarnation of the Son of God in Bethlehem.

> *What then shall we say that Abraham our father*
> *has found according to the flesh?* (Romans 4:1)

Good question.

The answer is clear and strong. God's grace has been available from the beginning of time. And these men received the blessing of that grace by first receiving the gift of faith.

> *"Abraham believed God,*
> *and it was accounted to him for righteousness."* . . .
> *For the promise that he would be the heir of the world*
> *was not to Abraham or to his seed through the law,*
> *but through the righteousness of faith.* (Romans 4:3b, 13)

The Patriarchs first believed God, then they obeyed. Their works did not save them, but their faith in a Holy God provoked them to righteousness. Obedience was a by-product of belief.

GOD'S PEACE TREATY WITH MANKIND

In the fifth chapter, Paul presumes the questions, "How does Christ take our place?" "From whom have we been saved?" "How should we respond to receiving Christ's righteousness?"

Again, good questions.

> *For when we were still without strength, in due time Christ died for the ungodly.*
> *For scarcely for a righteous man will one die;*
> *yet perhaps for a good man someone would even dare to die.*
> *But God demonstrates His own love toward us,*
> *in that while we were still sinners, Christ died for us.*
> *Much more then, having now been justified by His blood,*
> *we shall be saved from wrath through Him.*
> *For if when we were enemies we were reconciled*
> *to God through the death of His Son,*
> *much more, having been reconciled, we shall be saved by His life.*
> *And not only that, but we also rejoice in God through our Lord Jesus Christ,*
> *through whom we have now received the reconciliation.* (Romans 5:6–11)

Christ willingly took our place because He loved us. We are saved from the wrath of God. (Remember, God used Himself to rescue us from His own wrath.) Our response, once we understand what we've been liberated from, must be spontaneous celebration, an overflow of gratitude to God for the peace treaty He signed with us in Christ's blood.

Chapters 6 and 7 remind us that even though the "war" is over, the battle continues. Surrender is not a simple matter.

> *For I know that in me (that is, in my flesh) nothing good dwells;*
> *for to will is present with me,*
> *but how to perform what is good I do not find.*
> *For the good that I will to do, I do not do;*
> *but the evil I will not to do, that I practice.*
> *Now if I do what I will not to do, it is no longer I who do it,*
> *but sin that dwells in me . . .*
> *O wretched man that I am! Who will deliver me from this body of death?*
> *I thank God—through Jesus Christ our Lord!* (Romans 7:18–20, 24–25a)

Sometimes new believers are disillusioned by the difference between what was promised to them and what their new faith delivers. They were told that their faith would bring them instant peace, happiness, and prosperity. And not only did they not discover these things on the other side of sin, their problems seemed to *increase*.

Given what we have just seen, this escalation of trouble makes perfect sense. The preconversion, easy-street promises made to them were utterly counterfeit. Look at it again.

> If God's grace is our greatest hope, then the removal of that same grace would represent our most explicit hopelessness.

God's punishment for many unbelievers is to turn them loose, running unfettered through the indulgences of sin. The results of those excesses are devastating. Then, through the gifts of faith and grace, a Holy God steps in. Life is no longer lived as an open swamp of lawlessness but within the river boundaries of Jesus Christ's atoning sacrifice. What was experienced without apparent consequences is now understood as the reason for the Cross. What seemed independent and autonomous is now being examined through the eyes of a loving Father. What felt like freedom came at the Savior's personal expense.

Living life with strict boundaries sounds like a jarring life-change to some new believers. But even *this* is good news. The presence of conflict means the close proximity of the Holy Spirit. Our propensity to sin and its perils keep us close to the One who saved us.

> Life is no longer lived as an open swamp of lawlessness but within the river boundaries of Jesus Christ's atoning sacrifice.

"In our lives, how does God work through this difficulty—sanctification—and take us to triumph—glorification?"

This question is answered in Romans chapter 8, one of the most encouraging chapters in the Bible. Here we have the assurance of God's providential care over us.

> *For whom He foreknew, He also predestined*
> *to be conformed to the image of His Son,*
> *that He might be the firstborn among many brethren.*
> *Moreover whom He predestined, these He also called;*
> *whom He called, these He also justified;*
> *and whom He justified, these He also glorified.* (Romans 8:29–30)

And Paul answers forever the question as to whether someone can thwart God's will to save him. "Can our defiance keep Him away?"

> *Yet in all these things we are more than conquerors through Him who loved us.*
> *For I am persuaded that neither death nor life,*
> *nor angels nor principalities nor powers,*
> *nor things present, nor things to come,*
> *nor height nor depth, nor any other created thing,*
> *shall be able to separate us from the love of God*
> *which is in Christ Jesus our Lord.* (Romans 8:37–39)

His love is completely irresistible and unshakable.

PREDESTINATION

"So, this sovereignty of God . . . exactly how does it work in our salvation?" Brace yourself, this is a tough one.

Over the years, the theological questions people have asked me generally fall into three categories: election, election, and election. In spite of Paul's clear articulation of this theological reality, many still find fault with his answers—and mine.

Paul recalls the account of God's choice to use Pharaoh, despite his unapologetic godlessness. He remembers the Sovereign's selection of Jacob over his brother, regardless of Jacob's lack of meritorious works. In these accounts, Paul justified God's competence to make His own choices. And these choices were not based on anything except His will to choose. He elected to do it, and it was done.

In their attempt to wink at the truth of election some say that God looks down the corridor of history seeing those who would choose Him and persevere. Then He predestines these for salvation. Unfortunately, this is the absolute opposite of what is taught here.

> The point is not in God's overlooking of some but in His mercy toward *anyone at all.*

Others will argue that election falls on certain classes or groups of people, that God elects assemblies rather than individuals. But this only moves the argument backward. If this is true, how does God choose whom within the group to include?

Paul does not shrink from the truth of God's election. In fact, he revels in it. Why? The answer is as simple as the view of the partially filled glass. Is it half full or is it half empty?

The fact that God will have mercy on whomever He chooses is an incredible thing. In the early chapters of Romans we see our sinfulness and rebellion. In fact, throughout Scripture, we witness mankind's willful disobedience, even fist-shaking hatred of a Holy God. No one, even the elect, deserves His grace.

The point is not in God's overlooking of some but in His mercy toward *anyone at all.*

COMPLACENCY

It's only natural to wonder, "Since God is sovereign, why not just passively sit here and wait for God to sanctify me?" "Doesn't election promote spiritual complacency?"

The final chapters of Romans are dedicated to the practical application of the fundamental truths of salvation and obedience. The working out of our "calling"demands that our minds be completely renewed.

Because we are a community of redeemed sinners, no two of us are at the same point in our sanctification. So the Holy Spirit grants us particular gifts, then calls us to use those gifts to inspire, support, or challenge other believers.

"Now that we're under God's supremacy, what credence should be given to local and federal magistrates?"

Legitimate civil government is in place at God's command and is granted authority by His will. When I am pulled over by Officer Friendly and given a ticket (even though *everyone* else was driving faster), it is no accident. It was not an arbitrary choice by that policeman but the fulfillment of God's sovereignty. God gives government selected authority. Where it legitimately exercises that authority—where civil laws do not contradict biblical laws—we are to submit with respect and gratitude.

As Paul closes Romans with greetings to those at his various destinations, I wonder if these people knew what they were reading. Did they know that this would become the greatest theological document in human history?

Isn't it amazing what can be learned about our faith after spending a little time in the operations manual?

- Romans
- **1 and 2 Corinthians**
- The Prison Epistles
- 1 and 2 Timothy

Paul was a "task theologian." He was not so much a theorist as he was a problem-solver. His theological skills were intended for application to particular situations and problematic individuals. The letters he wrote to the church at Corinth were meant to help them through a terrific case of spiritual immaturity.

Very disturbing news had come to Paul about the Corinthian church. Unlike other churches that had received his letters, Paul had spent eighteen months with the believers there. Because of a year and a half of his teaching, these people could not claim ignorance. They had no excuse for their childish behavior.

> Within the context of church discipline, "live and let live" has never been God's idea.

Corinth was a difficult place to start a church. It had begun as a Greek city, then it transitioned to a Roman municipality. This created cultural confusion among its citizenry.

With a population of more than a half million people, Corinth was an international hub of commerce and entertainment. And it became known as a center for licentiousness and idol worship throughout the world. For the members of the Corinth church, this pagan influence was apparently unavoidable.

As a geographical crossroad, traveling ministers would visit the church. Naturally, these preachers would have a variety of teaching skills, some eloquent and others not so eloquent. Like children, the members of the Corinth church picked personal favorites, neglecting the leadership that Paul, under the supervision of the Holy Spirit, had appointed inside the church. This had caused strife among members and leaders.

Within the context of church discipline, "live and let live" has never been God's idea. However, one of the members of the Corinth church was sleeping with his stepmother. Not wanting to cause a stir, the church's leadership looked the other way. Paul scolded them for their lack of courage.

In civil matters, church members were suing fellow Christians, submitting themselves to pagan judges and bringing ridicule upon the name of Christ. So much for, "By this will all men know that you are My disciples, because of your love for each other."

At Corinth, people were using their spiritual gifts to impress one another rather than edify one another. Their immaturity was most graphic in this area. Right in the middle of this discussion Paul delivered the great "Love Chapter." The primary motive for using spiritual gifts was to be one of love for each other, bearing with one another's weaknesses and strengths.

Paul closed the first letter to Corinth giving these believers some holy perspective on their conflicts and problems. He counseled them on the proper use of spiritual gifts. He admonished them on their view of death. And he underscored the critical importance of the Resurrection to sound Christian theology.

If Christ is not risen, then our preaching is empty
and your faith is also empty. (1 Corinthians 15:14)

The second letter to the Corinthians is probably an anthology of several letters collected into one. Much of what we know about Paul during this period of time was written in this letter. Chapter 11 presents Paul's argument for his apostleship and requests that the believers listen to him based on his calling and his suffering for the sake of the Gospel.

- Romans
- 1 and 2 Corinthians
- **The Prison Epistles**
- 1 and 2 Timothy

The apostle Paul was in serious trouble. He had lived a life of passion—all the way from persecuting Christians with the infatuation of a zealot to defending the risen Savior with every fiber of his being. So, no one was neutral when it came to their opinions about him. This would have been especially true among Jewish leaders who believed that Paul was a traitor, pure and simple.

From the accounts recorded in the Acts and the summary in 2 Corinthians 11, we see that among Paul's persecutions for the cause of Christ, imprisonment was the most frequent. Some of his incarcerations were brief, such as the overnight stay in the Philippian cell with his colleague, Silas. Some were longer, up to two years in Rome under house arrest.

> Remember where this is coming from: a dank, vermin-infested, putrid-smelling prison cell. This is either the transforming attendance of the Holy Spirit or sheer madness.

It was during these involuntary confinements that Paul wrote four letters: Philippians, Colossians, Ephesians, and a brief note to Philemon.

PHILIPPIANS

As an author, I can tell you that I'm quite particular about my physical surroundings while I'm writing. It's important that I'm comfortable. It's good to have plenty of light, a pleasant view, and an atmosphere that's conducive to crisp and creative thinking. I enjoy having everything "just so."

Writing from a prison cell would not be high on my list of ideal locations in which to compose: poor light, no view, and an ominous, even life-threatening ambiance. Frankly, regardless of what I would have to write from a dirt-floored jail crypt, I know it would have an effect on how I wrote and *what* I wrote.

Throughout church history, the letter to the Philippians has been referred to as the "Epistle of Joy." Sixteen times Paul encourages the believers in Philippi to participate in the joy he is experiencing over his salvation. Remember where this is coming from: a dank, vermin-infested, putrid-smelling prison cell. This is either the transforming attendance of the Holy Spirit or sheer madness.

Having spent a lifetime studying Paul's life, I stand firmly on the side of the presence of the Spirit of a Holy God. In fact, he used the condition of his imprisonment to confirm this truth. According to Paul, when believers manifest true joy in the midst of difficult circumstances, it's a sure sign of the Holy Spirit's power.

Of course, we are to weep with those who weep, and it is natural to be sorrowful over our sin and the graphic effects of sinfulness all around us. But the inhabiting emotional posture in the life of a believer should always be joy.

> *Rejoice in the Lord always. Again I will say, rejoice!*
> *Let your gentleness be known to all men. The Lord is at hand.*
> *Be anxious for nothing, but in everything by prayer and supplication,*
> *with thanksgiving, let your requests be made known to God;*
> *and the peace of God, which surpasses all understanding,*
> *will guard your hearts and minds through Christ Jesus.* (Philippians 4:4–7)

Since Paul was unable to be present in the lives of the Christians living in Philippi, he reminded them that this was all right. Their salvation and their growth as believers were not up to him.

> *Therefore, my beloved, as you have always obeyed,*
> *not as in my presence only, but now much more in my absence,*
> *work out your own salvation with fear and trembling;*
> *for it is God who works in you both to will*
> *and to do for His good pleasure.* (Philippians 2:12–13)

"God is at work in your lives," Paul is saying to his friends at Philippi. "Go for it. Join Him."

In the same way that faith is a gift as well as God's grace, God's work in our lives starts with His transformation of our desires. Then He grants us His power to implement those re-created longings. The gift of faith, then the gift of grace; the fulfillment of His will by the reformation of our desires, then the empowerment to do it. These represent God's perfect synergies.

Sitting in the jail cell, there were times when Paul wished for his release . . . one way or the other. This is perfectly understandable.

> *For I know that this will turn out for my deliverance through your prayer*
> *and the supply of the Spirit of Jesus Christ,*
> *according to my earnest expectation and hope*
> *that in nothing I shall be ashamed, but with all boldness, as always,*
> *so now also Christ will be magnified in my body,*
> *whether by life or by death.*
> *For to me, to live is Christ, and to die is gain.*
> *But if I live on in the flesh, this will mean fruit from my labor;*
> *yet what I shall choose I cannot tell.*
> *For I am hard-pressed between the two,*
> *having a desire to depart and be with Christ, which is far better.*
> *Nevertheless to remain in the flesh is more needful for you.*
> *And being confident of this,*

> *I know that I shall remain and continue with you all*
> *for your progress and joy of faith,*
> *that your rejoicing for me may be more abundant*
> *in Jesus Christ by my coming to you again.* (Philippians 1:19–26)

Paul was in a quandary. He wasn't sure what he wanted more: to die and be with Christ, putting an end to the suffering, or to stay on earth and continue to live out the faith, supporting, encouraging, and ministering to those around him. It's important to understand that Paul was not saying that life was evil. "To live is Christ," certainly sounds like the proclamation of someone who has something to live for. But, he saw the next life as so much better. Paul could hardly wait.

> Jesus didn't lose anything in the Incarnation; He *gained* His humanity.

In what has become one of the most important summaries of the deity and humanity of Jesus Christ, and our need to follow Him, Paul wrote:

> *Let this mind be in you which was also in Christ Jesus,*
> *who, being in the form of God, did not consider it robbery to be equal with God,*
> *but made Himself of no reputation, taking the form of a bondservant,*
> *and coming in the likeness of men.*
> *And being found in appearance as a man, He humbled Himself*
> *and became obedient to the point of death, even the death of the cross.*
> *Therefore God also has highly exalted Him*
> *and given Him the name which is above every name,*
> *that at the name of Jesus every knee should bow,*
> *of those in heaven, and of those on earth, and of those under the earth,*
> *and that every tongue should confess that Jesus Christ is Lord,*
> *to the glory of God the Father.* (Philippians 2:5–11)

These verses address the ancient question: "What did Jesus lose when He became human?"

Some heretics in the early church wanted to teach that Jesus lost His deity. But, in fact, Jesus didn't lose anything in the Incarnation; He *gained* His humanity. He emptied Himself, not of His God-ness, but of His rights, His prerogatives, and His dignity. These verses are a call to you and me to take a position of humility as we serve the risen Christ. They are also a reminder that Jesus set aside His glory—*kabod*—temporarily when He walked the earth. God the Father has completely restored Him to His rightful place in heaven . . . "He is not here; He is risen."

One of the things that suffering often brings is a new kind of perspective. And even though Paul was sitting on the filthy floor of a dark prison cell, his words were from the heart of a man looking over the expanse of life as though he were perched atop a lofty tower.

> *But what things were gain to me, these I have counted loss for Christ.*
> *Yet indeed I also count all things loss for the excellence*
> *of the knowledge of Christ Jesus my Lord,*
> *for whom I have suffered the loss of all things, and count them as rubbish,*
> *that I may gain Christ and be found in Him,*
> *not having my own righteousness, which is from the law,*
> *but that which is through faith in Christ,*
> *the righteousness which is from God by faith;*
> *that I may know Him and the power of His resurrection,*
> *and the fellowship of His sufferings, being conformed to His death,*
> *if, by any means, I may attain to the resurrection from the dead.*
> *Not that I have already attained, or am already perfected;*
> *but I press on, that I may lay hold of that for which*
> *Christ Jesus has also laid hold of me.*
> *Brethren, I do not count myself to have apprehended;*
> *but one thing I do, forgetting those things which are behind*
> *and reaching forward to those things which are ahead,*
> *I press toward the goal for the prize*
> *of the upward call of God in Christ Jesus.* (Philippians 3:7–14)

Forget about yesterday. Forget about past victories and defeats. Focus on pressing forward, regardless of the circumstances. As I said, Paul gives us a veritable clinic in the fine art of perspective. And it wasn't enough to run the race that began with a flash and a voice on the road to Damascus; the race had to be finished.

COLOSSIANS

For centuries, mankind has tried to force the person of Jesus into a mystical ideal—a spiritual Being but not an actual man who was born, lived, died, and was risen. Paul ran into this kind of thinking in a city called Colossae in the first century. In his role as a problem-solving "task theologian," he addressed a creeping heresy among believers called "Gnosticism."

> The Cosmic Christ will not be belittled, only to be given a tacit nod on Sunday morning.

The Gnostics held to a blending of many world-views, which held that only through the mind could we understand God. The world was evil and only spiritual realities were good. According to the Gnostics, Jesus could not be the Incarnate God; they claimed that He was only Spirit, a type of archangel. They imagined a host of deities that functioned as intercessors between mortals and God, and Jesus was simply One among these.

In dealing with this heresy, Paul had to show that Jesus was superior to all angels. Colossians illumines Jesus as the Cosmic Christ. Not only was He the Redeemer, He *was* the eternal Word (John 1:1) and the very brightness of the glory of God (Hebrews 1:3). Jesus is the Lord of the universe, the King over all creation.

> *[Jesus] is the image of the invisible God, the firstborn over all creation.*
> *For by Him all things were created that are in heaven and that are on earth,*
> *visible and invisible, whether thrones or dominions or principalities or powers.*
> *All things were created through Him and for Him. And He is before all things,*
> *and in Him all things consist.* (Colossians 1:15–17)

Jesus did not make His first appearance in the cattle trough in Bethlehem. He was a full participant in Creation. The universe was made by Him, through Him, and for Him. The Cosmic Christ will not be belittled, only to be given a tacit nod on Sunday morning. No, the Christ of the Bible is more grand than we could ever imagine. The church—the body of Christ—is the continuing work of Jesus Christ in the world, and if we are doing His work, worshiping the Cosmic Christ instead of the Consumer Christ, we will participate in His victory by means of His suffering. This is a promise.

EPHESIANS

Another brilliant letter written from prison was the one addressed to the church that was at Ephesus, a city Paul had visited twice in his travels. It's interesting that, unlike other letters, Paul did not mention specific individuals, even though he must have had friends there. Of the theories surrounding this omission, the most plausible is that this letter was to be passed on to other churches.

The book of Ephesians is like a recipe for godly living, set between two bookends. The first bookend is theology, as powerful as Paul's writing in Romans. God's plan, clearly demonstrated in the life of His Son, is concisely summarized.

> *In [Jesus Christ] we have redemption through His blood, the forgiveness of sins,*
> *according to the riches of His grace which He made to abound toward us*
> *in all wisdom and prudence, having made known to us the mystery of His will,*
> *according to His good pleasure which He purposed in Himself,*
> *that in the dispensation of the fullness of the times*
> *He might gather together in one all things in Christ,*
> *both which are in heaven and which are on earth—in Him.*
> *In Him also we have obtained an inheritance,*
> *being predestined according to the purpose of Him*
> *who works all things according to the counsel of His will,*
> *that we who first trusted in Christ*
> *should be to the praise of His glory.* (Ephesians 1:7–12)

The companion bookend is focused on the practical. What does this faith actually look like when it's lived out in a person's life, family, and among fellow

believers? Paul closes the letter with one of the most powerful descriptions of
Satan's strategy and our best defense against it. Here is strong theology made
visual, relevant, and extremely practical.

> *Finally, my brethren, be strong in the Lord and in the power of His might.*
> *Put on the whole armor of God,*
> *that you may be able to stand against the wiles of the devil.*
> *For we do not wrestle against flesh and blood,*
> *but against principalities, against powers,*
> *against the rulers of the darkness of this age,*
> *against spiritual hosts of wickedness in the heavenly places.*
> *Therefore take up the whole armor of God,*
> *that you may be able to withstand in the evil day, and having done all, to stand.*
> *Stand therefore, having girded your waist with truth,*
> *having put on the breastplate of righteousness,*
> *and having shod your feet with the preparation of the gospel of peace;*
> *above all, taking the shield of faith with which you will be able to quench*
> *all the fiery darts of the wicked one.*
> *And take the helmet of salvation, and the sword of the Spirit,*
> *which is the word of God;*
> *praying always with all prayer and supplication in the Spirit,*
> *being watchful to this end with all perseverance*
> *and supplication for all the saints—*
> *and for me, that utterance may be given to me,*
> *that I may open my mouth boldly to make known the mystery of the gospel,*
> *for which I am an ambassador in chains; that in it*
> *I may speak boldly, as I ought to speak.* (Ephesians 6:10–20)

Imagine a group of children playing. Suddenly one of them gets an idea to
do something risky. Once he has described his plan to the others, one of them
surely will say in a voice filled with apprehension, "You go first."

What Paul was telling the churches from his prison cell was that he understood the treachery of dealing with the devil. And, as Christ's ambassador, he
was willing to go first.

PHILEMON

In this tiny letter written to a believer named Philemon, Paul makes a defense for a young man named Onesimus. Onesimus, a slave, had run away from his master, Philemon. During his time of exile from Philemon, the fugitive had encountered Paul and was converted. Paul gave this letter to Onesimus to carry back to his former master.

Some wonder if Onesimus had been arrested, either because of his escape from Philemon or for another reason, encountering Paul as a fellow prisoner. In the letter, Paul implores his "brother" Philemon to receive Onesimus back, not as an escaped captive, but as a "beloved brother." Paul even offers personally to make amends for Onesimus's debts.

Though very brief, this letter from prison is packed with strong, practical reminders of how Christian love works itself out. It is also a fitting glimpse into Paul's tender heart.

- Romans
- 1 and 2 Corinthians
- The Prison Epistles
- **1 and 2 Timothy**

One of the greatest joys I have experienced over the past several decades has been the chance to teach. This has especially been true when my students have been preparing for ministry. Being a teacher to future teachers and a clergyman to prospective clergymen has been a distinct privilege. And becoming a friend to my students has also been my delight.

As Timothy's tutor for ministry, Paul knew this joy as well.

Other than Jesus with His disciples, this is the best example we see in the New Testament of mentoring. The relationship between Paul and Timothy stands out because of its depth of passion. At the close of his second letter to his understudy, Paul delivers some of the most poignant expressions of love and encouragement we read from the apostle's pen.

You therefore, my son, be strong
in the grace that is in Christ Jesus.
And the things that you have heard from me among many witnesses,
commit these to faithful men who will be able to teach others also.
You therefore must endure hardship as a good soldier
of Jesus Christ. (2 Timothy 2:1–3)

Ever the task theologian, Paul focuses on the problem of false doctrine, especially within the confines of the church. In the contemporary church, much emphasis is placed on relationships at the expense of orthodoxy. "Doctrine divides, but Christ unites," proponents of this form of ecclesiology defend. This idea would be utterly foreign to Paul.

> The first line of protection against the proliferation of false doctrine was a right-thinking church.

He saw a symbiotic connection between orthodoxy and practice; right doctrine led to healthy relationships. The first line of protection against the proliferation of false doctrine was a right-thinking church. And the secret of an effective church fell on the shoulders of its leaders. Systematically, Paul addresses the qualifications, requirements, and duties of church leaders.

First, the bishop/elder:

This is a faithful saying:
If a man desires the position of a bishop, he desires a good work.
A bishop then must be blameless, the husband of one wife,
temperate, sober-minded, of good behavior, hospitable, able to teach;
not given to wine, not violent, not greedy for money,
but gentle, not quarrelsome, not covetous;
one who rules his own house well,
having his children in submission with all reverence
(for if a man does not know how to rule his own house,
how will he take care of the church of God?);
not a novice, lest being puffed up with pride
he fall into the same condemnation as the devil.

Moreover he must have a good testimony among those who are outside,
lest he fall into reproach and the snare of the devil. (1 Timothy 3:1–7)

Many who have read this list of qualifications have determined that anyone holding the office of bishop must be completely deceived or living the life of a manifest hypocrite. Blameless? Who could ever qualify? But I believe this is a "panegyric" list—an idealized detailing of character traits not for the sake of seeking an exact match, but to demonstrate the sobriety of the office and the kind of person this office deserves. Given this list, a man appointed as a bishop would be a person who fully understood his need for God's grace to adequately fulfill this assignment.

Qualifications for deacon were also spelled out.

Likewise deacons must be reverent, not double-tongued,
not given to much wine, not greedy for money,
holding the mystery of the faith with a pure conscience.
But let these also first be tested;
then let them serve as deacons, being found blameless.
Likewise, their wives must be reverent,
not slanderers, temperate, faithful in all things.
Let deacons be the husbands of one wife,
ruling their children and their own houses well.
For those who have served well as deacons
obtain for themselves a good standing and great boldness
in the faith which is in Christ Jesus. (1 Timothy 3:8–13)

This list has the same panegyric quality as the one for the bishop/elder. Again, the word *blameless* is our tip-off.

But as with the bishop/elder, does this idealized inventory for the role of deacon mean that the church should turn the other way, setting these qualifications aside as some first-century panacea? Never.

The church is in need of capable, trained, and mature people who have their own houses in order and are willing to take positions of leadership in God's house. The responsibility of governing the church cannot be relegated to one person. To have an impact on its members and the community that surrounds it, leadership must be portioned out to qualified, committed people.

2 TIMOTHY

The apostle Paul must have had a notion that this letter would be among his last. There is a sense in which this document reads like a last will and testament, so, as he says "good-bye," his words to his protégé are filled with tenderness, affection, encouragement, and kindhearted admonition.

> *I thank God, whom I serve with a pure conscience, as my forefathers did,*
> *as without ceasing I remember you in my prayers night and day,*
> *greatly desiring to see you, being mindful of your tears,*
> *that I may be filled with joy,*
> *when I call to remembrance the genuine faith that is in you . . .*
> *Therefore I remind you to stir up the gift of God*
> *which is in you through the laying on of my hands.*
> *For God has not given us a spirit of fear, but of power*
> *and of love and of a sound mind.* (2 Timothy 1:3–5a, 6–7)

Once this affirmation was complete, Paul went right to work. He admonished Timothy—and others in leadership—to crack down on the corruption that was seeping into the church.

> *But know this, that in the last days perilous times will come:*
> *For men will be lovers of themselves, lovers of money,*
> *boasters, proud, blasphemers, disobedient to parents, unthankful, unholy,*
> *unloving, unforgiving, slanderers, without self-control, brutal, despisers of good,*
> *traitors, headstrong, haughty, lovers of pleasure rather than lovers of God,*
> *having a form of godliness but denying its power.*
> *And from such people turn away!* (2 Timothy 3:1–5)

Remember, with this roster of terrible, horrible, very bad folks, Paul was not describing godless savages who knew no better than to act like this, he was talking about church people. And he was exhorting Timothy to go after such people, commanding them to change their ways or get out because their influence was affecting those around them. Yes, relationships are important. But from such people who are not willing to submit to the power of the Holy Spirit, Paul tells Timothy, "turn away!"

> Sadly, those who are satisfied with an erroneous Bible but attempt to maintain an orthodox Christian faith are fighting a losing battle.

There have been discussions—sometimes arguments—over which elements of the early church our contemporary culture should copy. Issues of musical style and sacramental formats have been disputed. But Paul gives us the answer to those indisputable things that must be a priority in the church, and he confidently uses his own example as a model.

> But you have carefully followed my doctrine, manner of life, purpose,
> faith, longsuffering, love, perseverance, persecutions, afflictions,
> which happened to me at Antioch, at Iconium, at Lystra—
> what persecutions I endured.
> And out of them all the Lord delivered me.
> Yes, and all who desire to live godly in Christ Jesus will suffer persecution.
> But evil men and impostors will grow worse and worse,
> deceiving and being deceived.
> But you must continue in the things which
> you have learned and been assured of,
> knowing from whom you have learned them,
> and that from childhood you have known the Holy Scriptures,
> which are able to make you wise for salvation
> through faith which is in Christ Jesus. (2 Timothy 3:10–15)

All believers are to preserve all that is delivered to us in Scripture. This is the apostolic tradition—living a life that is rich enough to deserve persecution. And then, when persecuted, bearing it without failure.

Paul also delivers to Timothy what is perhaps the most succinct statement in the Bible about the veracity of its own words.

All Scripture is given by inspiration of God, and is profitable for doctrine,
for reproof, for correction, for instruction in righteousness,
that the man of God may be complete,
thoroughly equipped for every good work. (2 Timothy 3:16–17)

There may be no single issue that has become more divisive among believers than the accuracy of Scripture. Having committed my own life to the study and the teaching of the Word, I stand firmly on the Bible's inerrancy in its original revelation.

Why would I take this often-maligned position? Because the Bible itself claims it. If Holy Scripture is in error as inspired by the Holy Spirit, how can it be believed when it speaks of anything? And if it cannot be trusted with every word, who determines where the line is drawn again between truth and fiction?

If Holy Scripture is faulty and not thoroughly reliable, what does it say about the character of God? Sadly, those who are satisfied with an erroneous Bible but attempt to maintain an orthodox Christian faith are fighting a losing battle. Sooner or later, the same presuppositions that drew them away from the inerrancy of Scripture will pull them away from the fundamentals of the Christian faith. Paul agreed. So he warned Timothy to avoid stepping onto this slippery slope.

Paul's final charge to Timothy is absolute. These words clearly admonish not only Paul's young understudy, but everyone in ministry and church leadership: pastors, teachers, bishops/elders, and deacons.

I charge you therefore before God and the Lord Jesus Christ,
who will judge the living and the dead at His appearing and His kingdom:
Preach the word! Be ready in season and out of season.
Convince, rebuke, exhort, with all longsuffering and teaching.
For the time will come when they will not endure sound doctrine,
but according to their own desires, because they have itching ears,
they will heap up for themselves teachers;
and they will turn their ears away from the truth,
and be turned aside to fables.

But you be watchful in all things, endure afflictions,
do the work of an evangelist,
fulfill your ministry. (2 Timothy 4:1–5)

With the staccato-like rhythm of a good coach, Paul charges Timothy to preach the Word with all his might. He knows that there will be strong opposition: false teachers and counterfeit prophets. "Outlast them," Paul pleads. "You'll never out-market them. Their product is too sweet and shiny for many to resist. But be encouraged and continue to preach the Word to those who have ears to hear."

As Paul bids Timothy good-bye, he summarizes his life and calling.

I have fought the good fight, I have finished the race, I have kept the faith.
Finally, there is laid up for me the crown of righteousness,
which the Lord, the righteous Judge, will give to me on that Day,
and not to me only but also to all
who have loved His appearing. (2 Timothy 4:7–8)

Would that you and I could say this at the end of our pilgrimages on earth.

Not long after the letters reached Timothy, the sword of Nero fell on Paul's neck. Having passed the baton to his student, this powerful apostle had run the race and fallen, exhausted, into the arms of his Savior.

What emotion must have welled up in the heart of Timothy when he heard the news . . . the master of godly leadership had admonished him, encouraged him, instructed him, and then trusted him to carry on.

SUMMARY

▓ ROMANS

As the operations manual for our beliefs, Romans is the closest Paul comes to setting down a systematic theology of salvation. And, amazingly, it is relatively brief. Under the inspiration of the Spirit of God, Paul took enough time to distill the great themes of our belief system and put them into the sixteen concise chapters of Romans. Over the centuries, God has used Romans to bring revival to more churches than we could count. Saint Augustine, Charles Wesley, and Martin Luther are only a few of those who have been dramatically converted by the truths it contains.

Right from the top, Paul tells us what we need to know about living the Christian life. He tells us that we can't . . . without faith. Because we do not possess—and cannot achieve—the righteousness to be acceptable to a Holy God, we can find righteousness only as recipients of the gift of God's righteousness in Christ. Once we do receive this, then we *can* find the ability to live obediently . . . but again, only by the grace of God.

For those who ignore Him, God's judgment is often thought of as a consuming fire falling from heaven. But Paul introduces us to another, more devastating punishment. A Holy God's greatest punishment to sinful men is to turn them loose, separating Himself from their thinking and acting.

In the early chapters of Romans we are reminded of our sinfulness and rebellion. No one, even the elect, deserves His grace. The point is not in God's overlooking of some but in His mercy toward *anyone at all*.

■ 1 AND 2 CORINTHIANS

With a population of more than a half million people, Corinth was an international hub of commerce and entertainment. And it became known as a center for licentiousness and idol worship throughout the world. For the members of the church at Corinth, this pagan influence was apparently unavoidable.

Within the context of church discipline, "live and let live" has never been God's idea. However, one of the members of the Corinth church was sleeping with his stepmother. Not wanting to cause a stir, the church's leadership looked the other way. Paul scolded them for their lack of courage.

In civil matters, church members were suing fellow Christians, submitting themselves to pagan judges and bringing ridicule upon the name of Christ. So much for, "By this will all men know that you are My disciples, because of your love for each other."

At Corinth, people were using their spiritual gifts to impress one another rather than to edify one another. Their immaturity was most graphic in this area. Right in the middle of this discussion Paul delivered the great "Love Chapter." The primary motive for using spiritual gifts was to be one of love for one another, bearing with one another's weaknesses and strengths.

■ THE PRISON EPISTLES

The apostle Paul was in serious trouble. He had lived a life of passion—all the way from persecuting Christians with the infatuation of a zealot to defending the risen Savior with every fiber of his being. So, no one was neutral when it came to their opinions about him. From the accounts recorded in Scripture, we see that among Paul's persecutions for the cause of Christ, imprisonment was the most frequent. Some of these were overnight stays and some were longer, up to two years in Rome under house arrest.

It was during these involuntary confinements that Paul wrote four letters: Philippians, Colossians, Ephesians, and a brief note to Philemon.

■ 1 AND 2 TIMOTHY

One of the greatest joys I have had over the past several decades has been the chance to teach. This has especially been true when my students have been preparing for ministry. Being a teacher to future teachers and a clergyman to prospective clergymen has been a distinct privilege. And becoming a friend to my students has also been my delight.

As Timothy's tutor for ministry, Paul knew this joy as well. The church is in need of capable, trained, and mature people who have their own houses in order and are willing to take positions of leadership in God's house. The responsibility of governing the church cannot be relegated to one person. To have an impact on its members and the community that surrounds it, leadership must be portioned out to qualified, committed people.

The apostle Paul must have had a notion that these letters would be among his last. There is a sense in which they read like a last will and testament, so, as he says "good-bye," his words to his protégé are filled with tenderness, affection, encouragement, and kindhearted admonition.

Once this affirmation was complete, Paul went right to work. He admonished

Timothy—and others in leadership—to crack down on the corruption that was seeping into the church.

Remember, with this roster of terrible, horrible, very bad folks, Paul was not describing godless savages who knew no better than to act like this; he was talking about church people. And he was exhorting Timothy to go after such people, commanding them to change their ways or get out because their influence was affecting those around them.

Paul charges Timothy to preach the Word with all his might. He knows that there will be strong opposition: false teachers and counterfeit prophets. "Outlast them," Paul pleads. "You'll never outmarket them. Their product is too sweet and shiny for many to resist. But be encouraged and continue to preach the Word to those who have ears to hear."

Not long after the letters reached Timothy, the sword of Nero fell on Paul's neck. Having passed the baton to his student, this powerful apostle had run the race and fallen, exhausted, into the arms of his Savior.

CHAPTER SIXTEEN

HEBREWS AND THE GENERAL EPISTLES

.

- **Hebrews**
- James
- Other Epistles

It's interesting how our priorities line up under a severe crisis. For example, in most surveys of people who are asked what they would take first if their house were burning down, they say the family photo albums. Imagine running past all that expensive home theater equipment to save a few irreplaceable—which is the point—priceless pictures.

Well, if I encountered a "crisis," like my fishing boat sank and I were marooned on a secluded island, and I could have only one book, it would be the Bible. If I could have only one chapter, it would be Isaiah 6. If I could have only one verse, it would be:

> *And it came to pass,*
> *when the sun went down and it was dark,*
> *that behold, there appeared a smoking oven and a*
> *burning torch that passed between those pieces.* (Genesis 15:17)

But I have always said that if, for some reason, I could have only one book from the entire Bible, I would choose the book of Hebrews.

Why? The first reason is that Hebrews is a veritable gold mine of instruction, bringing together themes from the entire Scripture . . . like no other book of the Bible. The integration of the Old and the New Testaments is singular and strong. Second, the literary quality of Hebrews is greater than any other book in the New Testament. Among the other books, its form and structure stand alone—which raises a question of its authorship. As a writer, this unsolved mystery regarding who wrote the Hebrews also gives this book a sense of unique fascination to me.

But the most important reason why I love the book of Hebrews is how it emphasizes the supremacy of Jesus Christ over all things. The portrait of the Savior is one of Him exalted, glorified, and lifted up as "better than" any other figure in redemptive history.

When I was a kid in school, my teacher would write something on the blackboard and tell the class to "diagram this sentence." The goal was to identify the subject, the verb, the object of the verb, and the prepositional phrases. Fortunately, she never wrote the following. As a sixth grader, I may have been intimidated by its enormity.

> *God, who at various times and in various ways spoke in time past*
> *to the fathers by the prophets,*
> *has in these last days spoken to us by His Son,*
> *whom He has appointed heir of all things,*
> *through whom also He made the worlds;*
> *who being the brightness of His glory*
> *and the express image of His person,*
> *and upholding all things by the word of His power,*
> *when He had by Himself purged our sins,*
> *sat down at the right hand of the Majesty on high,*
> *having become so much better than the angels,*
> *as He has by inheritance obtained*
> *a more excellent name than they.* (Hebrews 1:1–4)

The subject and the verb of this sizable sentence, boiled down, summarize the totality of Holy Scripture.

God has spoken.

From the Genesis account of sovereign creation to the closing words of the Revelation, the story of the Bible is the written history of the voice of God. He has spoken "in various ways." The worlds were formed by the sound of God's utterance. A man named Abraham left his homeland and founded a great nation by the prompting of God's call. God spoke and nations rose and fell; prophets, priests, and kings were commissioned. By His word, people were condemned to die in their rebellion and sin. But in this sentence, the author of Hebrews reminds us that this time, God's gracious Voice was a *Person*. As the apostle John said, the Word became flesh.

God has spoken. And what did He say?

God said . . . "Jesus."

This takes my breath away.

The writer calls God's Son "the brightness of His glory." We have seen, throughout Scripture, how careful and extremely selective God has been in revealing His glory. It's not because He's stingy, but because we cannot bear to experience its awesome intensity. In these words, God's Son is called the brilliance of the brilliance of God's holiness. His perfection is beyond our comprehension.

The author of Hebrews wanted to be sure that we understood the magnitude of the person of Christ.

> From the Genesis account of sovereign creation to the closing words of the Revelation, the story of the Bible is the written history of the voice of God.

"BETTER THAN"

As he was writing to discouraged Jewish Christians who had survived extinction under Roman persecution, the author of Hebrews took the Old Covenant and the New Covenant and contrasted them with each other. He made it clear that the Old Testament is good, but the New Testament is better. The system that foreshadowed the full expression of God's redemptive will should never be seen as a failure. The old Law was fulfilled, and therefore replaced, through the Incarnation: the birth, life, death, and resurrection of Jesus.

Jesus is shown to be "better than" Moses, the mediator of the Old Covenant.

Moses also was faithful in all His house.
For this One has been counted worthy of more glory than Moses,
inasmuch as He who built the house has more honor than the house.
For every house is built by someone, but He who built all things is God.

And Moses indeed was faithful in all His house as a servant,
for a testimony of those things which would be spoken afterward,
but Christ as a Son over His own house, whose house we are
if we hold fast the confidence and the rejoicing
of the hope firm to the end. (Hebrews 3:2b–6)

This may have been a large pill for some Jews to swallow. But this writer does not mince his words. Moses presided over a house, but God built the house. Moses was the servant, but Jesus Christ is the Head.

> The author of Hebrews encourages his readers not to be satisfied with the surface teachings of Christianity, but to be willing to go deeper and develop a mature understanding of the things of God.

These words are reminiscent of God's chiding of a reluctant Moses at the burning bush, "Who made your mouth?" or His fiery reproach of a whining Job, "Where were *you* when I laid the foundations of the earth?" The Patriarchs were good, but Jesus is better. Period.

Jesus is also better than the priesthood. "How?" the readers of this book must have asked, "can *anyone* be better than a high priest?"

While the high priest made the sacrifice on behalf of the people on the Day of Atonement, that sacrifice was temporary. It had to be repeated. Jesus was better because His atonement was permanent.

And these sacrifices were symbolic; they were important based only on what they signified, not on their own merit. Jesus was better because what others' sacrifices could only symbolize, Jesus' sacrifice did in reality. The sacrifices of the priesthood pointed to Jesus' very sacrifice, confirming its superiority. Jesus is the perfect High Priest Who offered the superior sacrifice once and for all.

But this raised a technical question in the minds of those who first read Hebrews: "How could Jesus be a priest at all, not being from the tribe of Levi?"

Jesus was born into the family of Judah, from which kings were born, not from the priestly tribe of Levi. The author of Hebrews raised this question, then answered it, much like the apostle Paul did through dialecture. He introduces us to the ancient character of Melchizedek, an ancestor of Abraham.

And, as odd as this may sound to you and me, this was a convincing argument to a Jewish audience.

When someone tithed to someone else, the tither was inferior to the one receiving the tithe. Since Levi was a descendant of Abraham, and Abraham was a descendant of Melchizedek, then Melchizedek was superior to Levi. And since Jesus Christ, the Son of God, was greater than Melchizedek, His priesthood was not in conflict with tribal assignments.

The author of Hebrews encourages his readers not to be satisfied with the surface teachings of Christianity, but to be willing to go deeper and develop a mature understanding of the things of God. His argument is quite sobering: If God judged people from Old Testament times, who had limited knowledge of God, how much more will He judge those who have so much more information about salvation?

> Persecuted, rejected, and forgotten, the enemies of God would not have been worthy to host these precious heroes of the faith, much less persecute them.

If the writer of the Hebrews was comfortable admonishing his readers regarding their having access to more information concerning sin and redemption than their Old Testament ancestors had, imagine what he would say to you and me.

THE HALL OF FAITH

The author completes Hebrews by giving us a tour through the Hall of Faith.

> Now faith is the substance of things hoped for,
> the evidence of things not seen.
> For by it the elders obtained a good testimony.
> By faith we understand that the worlds were framed by the word of God,
> so that the things which are seen
> were not made of things which are visible. (Hebrews 11:1–3)

What a superior definition of *faith*—tangible "substance" in the place of intangible "hope," palpable "evidence" in place of invisible "things not seen."

And then, just in case the readers thought that the "better than" idea of

Jesus meant that the Old Testament faithful were inconsequential, the writer takes us on a walk down the corridor of time, past the portraits of the saints. As he pulls together the great themes of the Bible, the writer reminds us of something the apostle Paul mentioned in his letter to the Romans.

> *"Abraham believed God,*
> *and it was accounted to him for righteousness." . . .*
> *For the promise that he would be the heir of the world*
> *was not to Abraham or to his seed through the law,*
> *but through the righteousness of faith.* (Romans 4:3b, 13)

The faith of the Patriarchs was followed by their obedience. Centuries before the coming of the Savior, their faith in the Lord God was counted unto them as righteousness.

I can almost hear the sound of footsteps clicking on the polished floors of history's hallway. We stop momentarily as the author of Hebrews pauses to show us the faces of those faithful saints who have gone before: Abel, Enoch, Noah, Abraham, Sarah, Isaac, Jacob, Joseph, Moses, Joshua, Rahab, Gideon, Barak, Samson, Jephthah, David, and Samuel.

The second to last picture is a group shot. None of the faces are recognizable, but our tour guide stuns us with his description of who we're looking at.

> *Others were tortured, not accepting deliverance,*
> *that they might obtain a better resurrection.*
> *Still others had trial of mockings and scourgings,*
> *yes, and of chains and imprisonment.*
> *They were stoned, they were sawn in two,*
> *were tempted, were slain with the sword.*
> *They wandered about in sheepskins and goatskins,*
> *being destitute, afflicted, tormented—*
> *of whom the world was not worthy.* (Hebrews 11:35b–38a)

Even though we cannot name any of the people in this large portrait, the author of Hebrews tells us that these saints are giants. Persecuted, rejected, and forgotten, the enemies of God would not have been worthy to host these precious heroes of the faith, much less persecute them.

"WE ALSO"

The final portrait is actually not a portrait at all, but a mirror, polished to a glossy sheen.

> *Therefore we also, since we are surrounded*
> *by so great a cloud of witnesses,*
> *let us lay aside every weight,*
> *and the sin which so easily ensnares us,*
> *and let us run with endurance the race that is set before us,*
> *looking unto Jesus, the author and finisher of our faith,*
> *who for the joy that was set before Him endured the cross,*
> *despising the shame, and has sat down at the right hand of the throne of God.*
> *For consider Him who endured such hostility*
> *from sinners against Himself, lest you become*
> *weary and discouraged in your souls.* (Hebrews 12:1–3)

As we look into the mirror, our hearts are filled with a deep sense of gratitude and wonder. Because of God's mercy, we can receive the gift of faith and the gift of His grace.

The writer to the Hebrews tells us that those who have gone before are cheering us on. Their encouraging voices are heard above the things that distract us. Their example of faith gives us the courage to "set aside" the encumbrances that get in the way of our obedience. Their example of contrition gives us the strength to confess the sin that has overpowered us.

And the writer warns us that we do not know what lies ahead. We do not set the course for our race. No, this race is "set before us." Thankfully, he tells us that the ultimate task of the believer is simply this: Look unto Jesus, the author and finisher of our faith. We have "so great a salvation" because we have so great a Savior.

Now, do you understand why I love this book so much?

- Hebrews
- **James**
- Other Epistles

My entire life has been lived with a nickname. "R. C." is what everyone calls me, whether they are a brand-new acquaintance or a lifelong friend. Historians tell us that James, the writer of this powerful little book, had a nickname: "Ol' Camel Knees." I don't know about you, but for my money, I'm going to pay special attention to the writings of a man who was known for the extended time he spent in prayer.

James is a Wisdom Book of the New Testament—much like Psalms and Proverbs—in its style and format. While there is no unifying theme, James addresses practical and ethical concerns, deeply rooted in the common thoughts and ideas of first-century Judaism. In making his point, he often uses "antithetical parallelism," a distinctively Jewish approach.

> In God's economy, suffering is critical to our spiritual growth.

It's clear that a Jew named "James" wrote the book of James. The question is, Which James? I believe it was James the Just, the son of Mary and Joseph, the brother of Jesus . . . Ol' Camel Knees. And what makes the book special is that it was written by a man who would have known the Savior in a very intimate way . . . as only a brother could know Him.

Some have wondered why the author doesn't clearly identify himself. But James the Just presided over the council of Jerusalem (Acts 15), so it would make perfect sense that he would not have to identify himself by anything other than "James" for the community of believers to know which James.

Because this book is directed specifically to Jewish Christians who are being punished for following Jesus, James jumps right in with one of Scripture's most authoritative perspectives on suffering.

> *My brethren, count it all joy when you fall into various trials,*
> *knowing that the testing of your faith produces patience.*
> *But let patience have its perfect work,*

> *that you may be perfect and complete,*
> *lacking nothing.* (James 1:2–4)

In the world's economy, suffering is something to be avoided, a meaningless interruption, and a waste of time and energy. But in God's economy, suffering is critical to our spiritual growth. Because "perfection" and "completion" are desirable characteristics for all believers, suffering is not to be sidestepped; it's to be welcomed.

In fact, James calls suffering a "gift."

> *Every good gift and every perfect gift is from above,*
> *and comes down from the Father of lights,*
> *with whom there is no variation or shadow of turning.* (James 1:17)

Who doesn't love receiving "good" gifts—wrapped in happy paper and tied with colorful ribbons? But James tells us that the "perfect" (*telios*) gifts—the ones wrapped in suffering, growth, and completeness—are just as precious.

As a Jew, James was well versed in the writings of King Solomon. Filled with admonitions to follow wisdom, James begs the question, "But what if I'm only wise enough to know I need *more* wisdom?"

> *If any of you lacks wisdom, let him ask of God,*
> *who gives to all liberally and without reproach,*
> *and it will be given to him.*
> *But let him ask in faith, with no doubting,*
> *for he who doubts is like a wave of the sea driven and tossed by the wind.*
> *For let not that man suppose that he will receive anything from the Lord;*
> *he is a double-minded man,*
> *unstable in all his ways.* (James 1:5–8)

The motives of the believers are stiffly challenged. James cuts right to the chase . . . "So you want wisdom? Ask God for it, and really *want* it. Don't waste your time, or His." I really like this guy.

FAITH VERSUS WORKS

For centuries, scholars have debated the seeming conflict between the theologies of James and Paul. James talks about "works," and Paul talks about "faith." But this is a false dichotomy. James never says that doing good will save a man from his sin. He is, however, determined to communicate that faith will always reveal itself in a life of good works.

> Someone will say, "You have faith, and I have works."
> Show me your faith without your works,
> and I will show you my faith by my works.
> You believe that there is one God. You do well.
> Even the demons believe—and tremble!
> But do you want to know, O foolish man,
> that faith without works is dead?
> Was not Abraham our father justified by works
> when he offered Isaac his son on the altar?
> Do you see that faith was working together with his works,
> and by works faith was made perfect?
> And the Scripture was fulfilled which says,
> "Abraham believed God, and it was accounted to him for righteousness."
> And he was called the friend of God.
> You see then that a man is justified by works,
> and not by faith only. (James 2:18–24)

So is James contradicting the following statements made by Paul?

> For by grace you have been saved through faith. (Ephesians 2:8)

> We who are Jews by nature, and not sinners of the Gentiles,
> knowing that a man is not justified by the works of the law
> but by faith in Jesus Christ, even we have believed in Christ Jesus,
> that we might be justified by faith in Christ and not by the works of the law;
> for by the works of the law no flesh shall be justified. (Galatians 2:15–16)

I believe that James's use of the word *justify* indicates vindication before men and before God. In other words, "Man is vindicated for his improper behavior before others by good works and not by faith only." And, "Man is vindicated for his sin in the final judgment by the demonstration of his faith in good works."

In "faith," Paul is talking about the source of our righteousness, but in "works," James is talking about the demonstration of it.

When we consider the different audiences that these writers were addressing, we can see that Paul's Gentiles were bound up in legalism, and James's Jewish Christians believed that, in Jesus, they had been released from the Law to live without boundaries (antinomianism). Paul's audience needed the freedom of "grace," and James's audience needed the limitations of "obedience."

> Paul's audience needed the freedom of "grace," and James's audience needed the limitations of "obedience."

I believe that Paul and James were theological friends, not enemies. Although their messages were different, their thinking was compatible.

WATCH YOUR MOUTH

It's easy to believe that James was present when his sibling, Jesus the Messiah, delivered His magnum opus on the Mount of Olives (Matthew 5–7). He would have been very familiar with his big Brother's opinion regarding spoken words.

> *Let your "Yes" be "Yes," and your "No," "No."*
> *For whatever is more than these*
> *is from the evil one.* (Matthew 5:37)

Repeating Jesus' admonition almost word for word (James 5:12), James had some important things to say about the power of the things that come from our mouths.

> *For we all stumble in many things.*
> *If anyone does not stumble in word, he is a perfect man,*

able also to bridle the whole body.
Indeed, we put bits in horses' mouths that they may obey us,
and we turn their whole body.
Look also at ships: although they are so large and are driven by fierce winds,
they are turned by a very small rudder wherever the pilot desires.
Even so the tongue is a little member and boasts great things.
See how great a forest a little fire kindles!
And the tongue is a fire, a world of iniquity.
The tongue is so set among our members that it defiles the whole body,
and sets on fire the course of nature; and it is set on fire by hell.
For every kind of beast and bird,
or reptile and creature of the sea,
is tamed and has been tamed by mankind.
But no man can tame the tongue.
It is an unruly evil, full of deadly poison. (James 3:2–8)

Some may believe that James is exaggerating just a bit. "Certainly, the words we speak are important," they may say, "but isn't he overstating the case?" Not at all.

I can think of times in my life when I have spoken careless words that tore through the flesh of a priceless relationship, or times when I was the recipient of such thoughtlessness. The fallout from these words was unmistakable.

> Polluted words will discharge from a bad heart, and uncontaminated words will flow from a clean heart.

Or I think of Martin Luther, the dauntless monk who literally risked his life—and forever changed the course of religion—simply by the conviction of his heart and the daring words he spoke.

I'm also reminded of the little ditty that we used to chant when I was a kid: "Sticks and stones may break my bones, but words will never hurt me." James would have called this childish recitation a lie from the pit of hell.

Even more important than guarding our mouths, James makes it clear that what we speak comes from inside. Polluted words will discharge from a bad heart, and uncontaminated words will flow from a clean heart

Out of the same mouth proceed blessing and cursing.
My brethren, these things ought not to be so.
Does a spring send forth fresh water and bitter from the same opening?
Can a fig tree, my brethren, bear olives, or a grapevine bear figs?
Thus no spring yields both salt water and fresh. (James 3:10–12)

With a tender heart, James admonishes believers to be encouraged, have compassion, and pray for one another.

Is anyone among you suffering? Let him pray.
Is anyone cheerful? Let him sing psalms.
Is anyone among you sick? Let him call for the elders of the church,
and let them pray over him, anointing him with oil in the name of the Lord.
And the prayer of faith will save the sick, and the Lord will raise him up.
And if he has committed sins, he will be forgiven.
Confess your trespasses to one another, and pray for one another,
that you may be healed.
The effective, fervent prayer of a righteous man avails much. (James 5:13–16)

These words are filled with kindness and empathy. As the little brother of the Savior of the world, James had learned well.

- Hebrews
- James
- **Other Epistles**

---

1 AND 2 PETER

Like the first part of James's book, the epistles of Peter are filled with encouragement to Christians who were hurting. The root word for "suffering" is found sixteen times in these two short books. Peter knew believers who were being tortured for their faith. Today we may hear of Christians in Sudan or Indonesia who are suffering because of their love for Christ. Tomorrow it may be others who are living faithfully in a hostile environment. But Peter reassures them—and us.

> *Beloved, do not think it strange concerning the fiery trial which is to try you,*
> *as though some strange thing happened to you;*
> *but rejoice to the extent that you partake of Christ's sufferings,*
> *that when His glory is revealed,*
> *you may also be glad with exceeding joy.* (1 Peter 4:12–13)

Suffering is not God's great mistake; it is at the core of His plan for us.

Over the past several decades, something strange has crept into the church that radically contradicts these words: the prosperity, health, and wealth gospel. The essence of this teaching is that God wills nothing but blessing and happiness for His people. If you experience anything other than these perks, it's because of the sin of unbelief.

Proper training in the Scriptures would deliver us from this blasphemy.

The history of godly living is the repeated account of suffering, people living as exiles in a foreign land, those faithfully serving God in the midst of pain.

> Suffering is not God's great mistake; it is at the core of His plan for us.

The Scripture does not equivocate: We are refugees in a foreign land, serving God faithfully in the midst of struggle and pain. And this is not our burden, it's our privilege. The apostle Paul called it the "fellowship of His sufferings" (Philippians 3:10). Like someone who is about to share in a huge dividend on a venture, the word *fellowship* (*koinonia*) meant "partnership benefit." Suffering is not an impediment; it's an investment.

God is in the midst of the natural pain we face. But unlike earthly treasures and happiness, we have a treasure of true health and wealth waiting for us in heaven. We can rejoice in this hope right now, even though we may not possess it.

> *Blessed be the God and Father of our Lord Jesus Christ,*
> *who according to His abundant mercy has begotten us again to a living hope*
> *through the resurrection of Jesus Christ from the dead,*

to an inheritance incorruptible and undefiled, . . .
reserved in heaven for you, who are kept by the power of God
through faith for salvation ready to be revealed in this last time. (1 Peter 1:3–5)

These blessings are more valuable than anything prosperity could afford.

1, 2, AND 3 JOHN

The apostle John, the same man who wrote the gospel of John, wrote three brief letters that bear his name. Like James and Peter, John was an eyewitness to the entire ministry of Jesus. This was not hearsay. These words are filled with the exactness of an insider's experience.

That which was from the beginning,
which we have heard, which we have seen with our eyes,
which we have looked upon, and our hands have handled,
concerning the Word of life—the life was manifested,
and we have seen, and bear witness, and declare to you
that eternal life which was with the Father and was manifested to us—
that which we have seen and heard we declare to you,
that you also may have fellowship with us;
and truly our fellowship is with the Father
and with His Son Jesus Christ. (1 John 1:1–3)

In a tender and diplomatic way, John, the "disciple whom Jesus loved," addresses the faith versus works proposition that James and Paul addressed.

My little children, these things I write to you,
so that you may not sin.
And if anyone sins,
we have an Advocate with the Father,
Jesus Christ the righteous.
And He Himself is the propitiation for our sins,
and not for ours only but also for the whole world. (1 John 2:1–2)

Can you see it? John challenges his readers to "not sin"—the righteousness of *works*. But he makes the accommodation of "if anyone sins"—the gift of *faith* and of God's grace through Jesus, the Advocate, is available.

Then John delivers perhaps the most succinct summary of faith versus works in the entire Bible.

> *Now by this we know that we know Him,*
> *if we keep His commandments.*
> *He who says, "I know Him,"*
> *and does not keep His commandments,*
> *is a liar, and the truth is not in him.*
> *But whoever keeps His word,*
> *truly the love of God is perfected in him.*
> *By this we know that we are in Him.*
> *He who says he abides in Him*
> *ought himself also to walk just as He walked.* (1 John 2:3–6)

Which part of "by this we know that we are in Him" don't we understand? The godly person is constrained by God's love to live in obedience to His will. He is not compelled by obligation or threatened by reproof; he is strangely drawn to obedience and righteousness by the Savior's sacrificial affection. We should also be induced, by His example, to love others.

Like the other epistle writers, John encourages his audience to stand firm in the face of persecution, pain, and loneliness.

> *Do not marvel, my brethren, if the world hates you.*
> *We know that we have passed from death to life,*
> *because we love the brethren.*
> *He who does not love his brother abides in death.*
> *Whoever hates his brother is a murderer,*
> *and you know that no murderer has eternal life abiding in him.*
> *By this we know love,*
> *because [Jesus Christ] laid down His life for us.*
> *And we also ought to lay down our lives for the brethren.* (1 John 3:13–16)

John challenges believers to be discerning of whether a teacher is truly from God, filled with the Holy Spirit.

> *Beloved, do not believe every spirit, but test the spirits, whether they are of God;*
> *because many false prophets have gone out into the world.*
> *By this you know the Spirit of God:*
> *Every spirit that confesses that Jesus Christ has come in the flesh is of God,*
> *and every spirit that does not confess that Jesus Christ*
> *has come in the flesh is not of God.* (1 John 4:1–3a)

One of the heresies that was creeping into the early church was the denial of the humanity of Jesus. John lays this to rest with these words: "Jesus Christ *has* come in the flesh."

The other two brief letters from John are directed at resolving conflict and pointing out theological error. John, the loving disciple, adopts a posture of "tough love" in confronting these issues, laying down a framework for the church to properly conduct itself.

These letters—the Hebrews and the General Epistles—are a great gift to you and me. They provide us with truth concerning our faith that can be clearly understood and immediately applied.

SUMMARY
■ HEBREWS

Hebrews is a veritable gold mine of instruction, bringing together themes from the entire Scripture . . . like no other book of the Bible. The most important feature of the book of Hebrews is its emphasis on the supremacy of Jesus Christ over all things. The portrait of the Savior is one of Him exalted, glorified, and lifted up as "better than" any other figure in redemptive history.

As he is writing to discouraged Jewish Christians who had survived extinction under Roman persecution, the author of Hebrews takes the Old Covenant and the New Covenant and contrasts them with each other. He makes it clear that the Old Testament is good, but the New Testament is better. Jesus is shown to be "better than" Moses, the mediator of the Old Covenant.

This may have been a large pill for some Jews to swallow. But this writer does not mince his words. Moses presided over a house, but God built the house. Moses was the servant, but Jesus Christ is the Head.

While the high priest made the sacrifice on behalf of the people on the Day of Atonement, that sacrifice was temporary. It had to be repeated. Jesus was better because His atonement was permanent.

The author completes Hebrews by giving us a tour through the Hall of Faith. The faith of the Patriarchs and others was followed by their obedience. Centuries before the coming of the Savior, their faith in the Lord God was counted unto them as righteousness.

The final entry into the Hall of Faith includes us—you and me. Because of God's mercy, we can receive the gift of faith and the gift of His grace.

▪ JAMES

James is a Wisdom Book of the New Testament—much like Psalms and Proverbs—in its style and format. And what makes the book special is that it was written by a man who would have known the Savior in a very intimate way . . . as only a brother could know.

Because this book is directed specifically to Jewish Christians who are being punished for following Jesus, James jumps right in with one of Scripture's most authoritative perspectives on suffering.

In the world's economy, suffering is something to be avoided, a meaning-less interruption, and a waste of time and energy. But in God's economy, suffering is critical to our spiritual growth. Because "perfection" and "completion" are desirable characteristics for all believers, suffering is not to be sidestepped; it's to be welcomed.

For centuries, scholars have debated the seeming conflict between the the-ologies of James and Paul. James talks about "works," and Paul talks about "faith." But this is a false dichotomy. James never says that doing good will save a man from his sin. He is, however, determined to communicate that faith will always work itself out in a life of good works.

It's easy to believe that James was present when his sibling, Jesus the Messiah, delivered His magnum opus on the Mount of Olives. He would have been very familiar with his big Brother's opinion regarding spoken words. Repeating Jesus' admonition almost word for word (James 5:12), James had some important things to say about the power of the things that come from our mouths.

Finally, with a tender heart, James admonished believers to be encouraged, have compassion, and pray for one another.

1 AND 2 PETER

Like the first part of James's book, the epistles of Peter are filled with encouragement to Christians who are hurting. Peter knew believers who were being tortured for their faith. But Peter reassures them—and us. Suffering is not God's great mistake; it is at the core of His plan for us.

The history of godly living is the repeated account of suffering, people living as exiles in a foreign land, those faithfully serving God in the midst of pain. The Scripture does not equivocate: We are refugees in a foreign land, serving God faithfully in the midst of struggle and pain. And this is not our burden, it's our privilege.

1, 2, AND 3 JOHN

The apostle John, the same man who wrote the gospel of John, wrote three brief letters that bear his name. These words are filled with the exactness of an insider's experience.

In a tender and diplomatic way, John, the "disciple whom Jesus loved," addresses the faith versus works proposition that James and Paul addressed. John challenges his readers to "not sin"—the righteousness of *works*. But he makes the accommodation of "if anyone sins"—the gift of *faith* and of God's grace through Jesus, the Advocate, is available.

The godly person is constrained by God's love to live in obedience to His will. He is not compelled by obligation or threatened by reproof; he is strangely drawn to obedience and righteousness by the Savior's sacrificial affection. We should also be induced, by His example, to love others.

CHAPTER SEVENTEEN

GLORY

- **Background of Revelation**
- The Old and New Covenant Connections
- The Christ of Revelation
- The Glory of God

When I began this book, I said that the one-sentence Genesis summary of creation—"In the beginning God created the heavens and the earth"—was one of the most important statements in Holy Scripture. I also mentioned that it was one of the most controversial.

Isn't it interesting that the Bible begins with an idea that has been argued for centuries—how all things began? And the Bible *ends* with another, even more vociferous, argument over how all things will end. Of course, images of grocery store checkout tabloids do cloud our thinking:

> ## THE WORLD MAY END THIS YEAR!
> *Experts warn of meltdown soon.*

Perhaps the most important thing to remember about the book of Revelation is that, in spite of honest disagreement among scholars as to the sequence of events described, one thing is for certain: This is actually *not* a book about the end; it's the description of a new beginning.

When something starts, we say that it's commencing. Each spring, thousands of graduates around the world who have *finished* their studies celebrate "commencement." Actually, this ceremony is about two things: the *end* of classroom work and the *start* of something . . . the beginning of "real" life in the marketplace.

Revelation is this same kind of commencement: the description of the end of an era and the confident prediction of a new one.

THE AUTHOR AND HIS CIRCUMSTANCES

I, John, both your brother and companion in the tribulation
and kingdom and patience of Jesus Christ,
was on the island that is called Patmos for the word of God
and for the testimony of Jesus Christ. (Revelation 1:9)

There are several New Testament characters named "John," but the earliest, and most reliable, assumption was that the author of Revelation was the apostle John, the composer of the gospel of John and the three small General Epistles also bearing his name.

As we saw in the prison letters of the apostle Paul, it is interesting to look at John's situation while he wrote. Like Paul, John had been arrested for his courageous beliefs and his bold teaching concerning the Messiah. Roman authorities had had enough, so they banished the apostle to the tiny volcanic island of Patmos, located in the Aegean Sea, to live out the remainder of his life. We don't know what his exact physical surroundings were, but we know that John's neighbors on Patmos were convicted criminals and political prisoners. And whatever the specific setting, it must have been ripe for deep contemplation and wondrous imagination.

> A Bible student should be careful not to "shout" when God "whispers." And, when God "shouts," to pay careful attention. In Revelation, we find God both whispering and shouting.

Revelation contains some of the most glorious and yet most mysterious language concerning the last days, a literary form known as *apocalyptic* writing. This special subdivision of theology called *eschatology* focuses on the final consummation of God's work in the world. This is what John does in this significant book.

As I said in the first chapter regarding the "how" of creation, I have believed that a Bible student should be careful not to "shout" when God "whispers." And, when God "shouts," to pay careful attention. In Revelation, we find God both whispering and shouting.

FOUR DIFFERENT APPROACHES

As it concerns many of the issues regarding the end times, God chose to be sparing in His disclosures—to whisper. This is the reason why there has been so much sharp disagreement over what is going to happen—and what may have already happened. The safest way I have found in proceeding is to study the Revelation images as we find them in other books of the Bible. This gives us a sound starting point in our study of eschatology.

There are four basic approaches to the book of Revelation.

Preteristic

The person who views Revelation from this perspective believes that most—if not all—the events predicted in the book have already been fulfilled. The destruction of the city of Jerusalem, for example, which took place in A.D. 70, was John's primary end-times focus. I would consider myself a moderate preterist, believing that much of what is recorded in Revelation has taken place, not including the final judgment or final resurrection of believers.

Futuristic

Futurists see Revelation as a blueprint for a series of events that will precede the imminent return of Jesus Christ. According to this view, we wait for the fulfillment of the prophesied events of this book from Revelation chapter 6 onward. This is the perspective from which dispensationalism developed.

Historical

People who subscribe to this view see the first five chapters of Revelation as speaking to the early church. They believe that past chapter six, the book is a schematic description of the whole of church history. This viewpoint is taken by historical premillennialists.

Idealistic

Those who hold to this view see Revelation as a highly symbolic book. Not designed to give us a specific chronology of future events, John's writing describes the kinds of occurrences that have happened throughout church history. Revelation teaches a fundamental message of the triumph of God over Satan through seven different visions. This view is held by amillennialists or postmillennialists.[1]

After years of vacillation, I have personally settled on a postmillenial position.

While I hold to this position with conviction, I would also underscore my belief that God has, by and large, kept His volume down on these issues. So, in defending my conclusion, I will also use my own indoor voice.

The actual date of John's writing is also a topic of sincere disagreement.

The Revelation of Jesus Christ,
which God gave Him to show His servants—things which must shortly take place.
And He sent and signified it by His angel to His servant John,
who bore witness to the word of God,
and to the testimony of Jesus Christ,
to all things that he saw. (Revelation 1:1–2)

Some scholars place the writing of Revelation at the close of the first century, A.D. 95 to 106, decades after Jerusalem had been destroyed. But John's words make it clear that what he was predicting was about to happen soon—"shortly." The judgment that falls on Jerusalem is the most significant event that occurred around this time. And, John makes reference to an

> God wins, Satan loses . . .
> the end.

angel telling him to measure the Temple (chap. 11) in the present tense, something that could not be done if the Temple had already been laid to ruin. So many sources place the writing of Revelation at some time just before A.D. 70, the year Jerusalem fell.

The message of Revelation is deeply felt, even when many of the images it describes are not easily understood. All who have suffered affliction at the hands of the enemies of God have been blessed to read of how God is in control. He will eventually destroy His kingdom's foes and the enemies of the church of Jesus Christ. God wins, Satan loses . . . the end.

- Background of Revelation
- **The Old and New Covenant Connections**
- The Christ of Revelation
- The Glory of God

Reminiscent of accounts from the Old Testament, John is given the opportunity to peek behind the veil, into the workings of heaven.

Immediately I was in the Spirit;
and behold, a throne set in heaven, and One sat on the throne.
And He who sat there was like a jasper and a sardius stone in appearance;
and there was a rainbow around the throne, in appearance like an emerald.
Around the throne were twenty-four thrones,
and on the thrones I saw twenty-four elders sitting, clothed in white robes;
and they had crowns of gold on their heads.
And from the throne proceeded lightnings, thunderings, and voices.
Seven lamps of fire were burning before the throne,
which are the seven Spirits of God.
Before the throne there was a sea of glass, like crystal.
And in the midst of the throne, and around the throne,
were four living creatures full of eyes in front and in back.
The first living creature was like a lion,
the second living creature like a calf,
the third living creature had a face like a man,
and the fourth living creature was like a flying eagle.
The four living creatures, each having six wings,
were full of eyes around and within.
And they do not rest day or night, saying:
"Holy, holy, holy,
Lord God Almighty,
Who was and is and is to come!"
Whenever the living creatures give glory and honor and thanks
to Him who sits on the throne, who lives forever and ever,

the twenty-four elders fall down before Him
who sits on the throne and worship Him
who lives forever and ever, and cast their
crowns before the throne, saying:
"You are worthy, O Lord,
To receive glory and honor and power;
For You created all things,
And by Your will they exist and were created." (Revelation 4:2–11)

These words remind us of Ezekiel's vision of the wheel and Isaiah's account of the visit to the Temple. John's is a poignant rendering, a poetic description of the throne room of God. Isn't it dramatic? We hear the sound of the voices, the smell of the burning lamps, and we see the flashes of the lightning. We experience the rhythms of the bowing elders and their songs of praise—the same songs you and I will sing someday as we worship at His feet.

This is the way these scenes in Revelation are intended to be read . . . and experienced.

The scene unfolds in a way that ties together the Old and New Testaments.

And I saw in the right hand of Him who sat on the throne
a scroll written inside and on the back, sealed with seven seals.
Then I saw a strong angel proclaiming with a loud voice,
"Who is worthy to open the scroll and to loose its seals?"
And no one in heaven or on the earth or under the earth
was able to open the scroll, or to look at it.
So I wept much, because no one was found worthy to open and read the scroll,
or to look at it. (Revelation 5:1–4)

The Bible was originally written on scrolls. Unlike common writings, where both sides of the scroll were used, the biblical record was written on only one side. The sealed scroll that John described had writing on both sides, leading us to wonder, as was the case with the two-sided scroll in Ezekiel (2:10), if perhaps one side was God's promised blessings and the other His covenant cursings.

The drama in this scene is classical. The tension builds as God's emissary calls out, "Who is worthy to break the seals and open the scroll?"

All eyes look around, searching for one—*the* One—who can open the seals and reveal what is hidden inside. The beasts aren't worthy; the elders aren't worthy; who could it be? Apparently none were worthy.

> *But one of the elders said to me,*
> *"Do not weep. Behold, the Lion of the tribe of Judah,*
> *the Root of David, has prevailed to open the scroll*
> *and to loose its seven seals."*
> *And I looked, and behold, in the midst of the throne*
> *and of the four living creatures, and in the midst of the elders,*
> *stood a Lamb as though it had been slain,*
> *having seven horns and seven eyes,*
> *which are the seven Spirits of God sent out into all the earth.*
> *Then He came and took the scroll out of the right hand of Him*
> *who sat on the throne.* (Revelation 5:5–7)

Like the sword plunged into the stone from the legends of King Arthur, the scroll remained unopened; like the bow of Ulysses that remained unstrung, the scroll lies in wait for the Lamb. The audience is plunged into despair, with no hope of resolution. Then the Hero appears to fulfill His destiny.

- Background of Revelation
- The Old and New Covenant Connections
- **The Christ of Revelation**
- The Glory of God

Such is the tension portrayed here, as Jesus Christ comes forward to take the scroll—the lavish blessings of God and the eternal penalty for sinfulness—and break its seals. Finally, salvation comes to God's people, and they are overwhelmed with joy and gratitude. In the tradition of Moses, Deborah, and Mary, their voices are filled with song.

Then I looked, and I heard the voice of many angels around the throne,
the living creatures, and the elders;
and the number of them was ten thousand times ten thousand,
and thousands of thousands, saying with a loud voice:
"Worthy is the Lamb who was slain
To receive power and riches and wisdom,
And strength and honor and glory and blessing!"
And every creature which is in heaven and on the earth and under the earth
and such as are in the sea and all that are in them,
I heard saying:
"Blessing and honor and glory and power
Be to Him who sits on the throne,
And to the Lamb, forever and ever!"
Then the four living creatures said, "Amen!"
And the twenty-four elders fell down and worshiped Him
who lives forever and ever. (Revelation 5:11–14)

Jesus Christ, the Lamb of God, had fulfilled His calling. He had accomplished His mission. He was worthy to receive their worship.

It should come as no surprise that John is ready to lavish unbridled praise on Jesus. First, as a disciple, he knew the Savior. As he describes in his first epistle, John heard, saw, and literally touched God's Son. Next, as one of Jesus' closest friends, John caught a glimpse of His glory on the Mount of Transfiguration. Certainly, this was a moment John never forgot. Finally, as John opened the book of Revelation, he gives us the most breathtaking snapshot of the Messiah.

Then I turned to see the voice that spoke with me.
And having turned I saw seven golden lampstands,
and in the midst of the seven lampstands One like the Son of Man,
clothed with a garment down to the feet
and girded about the chest with a golden band.
His head and hair were white like wool, as white as snow,
and His eyes like a flame of fire;

His feet were like fine brass, as if refined in a furnace,
and His voice as the sound of many waters;
He had in His right hand seven stars,
out of His mouth went a sharp two-edged sword,
and His countenance was like the sun shining in its strength.
And when I saw Him, I fell at His feet as dead.
But He laid His right hand on me, saying to me,
"Do not be afraid; I am the First and the Last.
I am He who lives, and was dead, and behold,
I am alive forevermore. Amen." (Revelation 1:12–18a)

This certainly doesn't sound like the same Person who was birthed in a cattle stall, cast out of His hometown, ridiculed by the religious elite, abandoned by His closest friends, tried by a midnight kangaroo court, and executed like a common criminal. No, this sounds more like the apostle Paul's "highly exalted" Savior, the One Whose name is above every name, the King at Whose feet every knee will ultimately bow, the One Whom every tongue will praise . . . the Lamb Who alone is worthy.

It doesn't matter what interpretive grid we use to understand the mysteries of Revelation. On these issues, God's voice is barely audible. But the underlying message of Revelation can be heard at decibels to rival a vicious thunderstorm. Jesus Christ, the Lamb of God, is victorious.

- Background of Revelation
- The Old and New Covenant Connections
- The Christ of Revelation
- **The Glory of God**

Jonathan Edwards said that we tend to be like travelers who long to take a vacation in an exotic spot. But in order to get to our destinations, we must stop in a humble inn along the way. Edwards asks, "What person in their right mind would get to the inn and decide to spend all their vacation time there?"

Although no one would argue that it makes no sense to forgo the lavish resort in exchange for the lowly hostel, this is exactly how you and I are tempted to think about our pilgrimage on earth. We would rather "bear those ills we have," as Hamlet lamented, "than fly to others that we know not of."

Then what *is* the destiny of those whose hearts have been captured by Christ?

> *Now I saw a new heaven and a new earth,*
> *for the first heaven and the first earth had passed away.*
> *Also there was no more sea.*
> *Then I, John, saw the holy city, New Jerusalem,*
> *coming down out of heaven from God,*
> *prepared as a bride adorned for her husband.*
> *And I heard a loud voice from heaven saying,*
> *"Behold, the tabernacle of God is with men,*
> *and He will dwell with them, and they shall be His people.*
> *God Himself will be with them and be their God.*
> *And God will wipe away every tear from their eyes;*
> *there shall be no more death, nor sorrow, nor crying.*
> *There shall be no more pain,*
> *for the former things have passed away."* (Revelation 21:1–4)

It is a curious thing that, in the next world, there will be "no more sea." In Jewish culture, the sea was an unknown . . . a mysterious thing that conjured up deep feelings of foreboding and fear. Israel was never known for its navy, for deep in her cultural mind, she had a fear of large bodies of water. The stories Jewish parents told their children were of sea monsters. And going all the way back to the Exodus account of the demise of the Egyptian army, the stories of their enemies always ended in their being killed by the sea.

So this reference to no sea in the new heaven and new earth was a promise of safety.

> In heaven, we will be awash in God's glory. We will drink deeply of it. We will soak in it.

There is also a forthright promise of absolute relief from suffering. Since we always live under a death sentence, this pledge can be hard to believe. For people of every culture, it's just a matter of time until the threat of doom is carried out. But for those who trust in Christ, there will come a moment when death will forever die. In Jesus we have the testimony of the One Who defeated death and promised that those who believe in Him will never die.

When I was a little boy, I would play roughly. Of course, I would often fall down and get scraped up. The first words out of my mouth would be, "I want my mommy." I would make a dash for the kitchen, where I knew I'd find my mother. She would tenderly hug and kiss me, and take a clean spot on her apron and wipe away my tears.

My mother taught me well. I know what it means to love someone deeply as a father, pastor, or Christian friend. And I have had the honor of gently wiping away the tears of those who were suffering or mourning. But please hear this: While this human action soothes us for the moment, it is never permanent. The next day, I was back in the kitchen, getting more hugs and kisses from my mother. Yesterday's sympathy didn't suffice for today's struggles.

But Revelation teaches that when God wipes away our tears, He only needs to do it once. Suffering will be forever banished from His kingdom. He will make all things new.

This is what we are seeking—permanent redemption, the renewing, the perfecting of our lives. God, Who began a good work in His people, will be faithful to complete it, and that completion will be for His own glory and for our own good.

ONE FINAL REBUILDING OF THE CITY

John was told to carefully write down the next part of the vision so that people would be encouraged by these words of hope.

> *Then one of the seven angels who had the seven bowls filled with the seven last*
> *plagues came to me and talked with me, saying,*
> *"Come, I will show you the bride, the Lamb's wife."*
> *And he carried me away in the Spirit to a great and high mountain,*
> *and showed me the great city, the holy Jerusalem,*
> *descending out of heaven from God,*
> *having the glory of God.* (Revelation 21:9–11a)

The city of Jerusalem had been built, destroyed, and rebuilt many times in its long history. Each time it was restored, the people claimed that never again would the city be ravaged. But in renovating the walls, they used bricks and mud. Sooner or later, its enemies would demolish and trample the city again. But the Holy City, the *New* Jerusalem, will be built of materials that will never perish. No one—no enemies—will ever harm those who dwell within her precious walls.

These brilliant images are beyond spectacular, they taunt our mind's eye. But, as images, they are only shadows of the true nature of heaven—human images that inadequately describe eternal realities.

> *But I saw no temple in it.* (Revelation 21:22)

The Jewish reader would panic at this news. No temple? What would they do without a temple? In spite of all its glory, the temple was only a symbol that would be replaced by the manifest presence of a Holy God.

> *The city had no need of the sun*
> *or of the moon to shine in it, for the glory of God illuminated it.*
> *The Lamb is its light.* (Revelation 21:23)

No sun or moon? Why? Under the light of God's radiance, they will not be necessary. What a place heaven must be.

Moses tasted of God's glory. Isaiah caught a brief glimpse. Jacob and Ezekiel were visited by the wonder of *kabod* while they slept. The shepherds in the field who heard the angels speak of Jesus' birth tasted just a drop of the glory. Three disciples, standing on Transfiguration's mountaintop, were bathed in it for an instant. Saul was struck to the ground on the way to Damascus by an instantaneous strobe of glory's brilliance.

But in heaven, we will be awash in God's glory. We will drink deeply of it. We will soak in it.

> *And [the angel] showed me a pure river of water of life, clear as crystal,*
> *proceeding from the throne of God and of the Lamb.* (Revelation 22:1)

There will be a river flowing from under the throne of God to nourish the New Jerusalem. The very essence of a Sovereign God will sustain us. Even though this power is true now, it is not fully known. But in heaven, it will be delightfully clear.

> *And the Spirit and the bride say, "Come!"*
> *And let him who hears say, "Come!"*
> *And let him who thirsts come. Whoever desires,*
> *let him take the water of life freely.* (Revelation 22:17)

God has spoken. We can drink deeply of every word He has given us. And we can be filled with hope of the glory that awaits us.

SUMMARY

■ BACKGROUND OF REVELATION

Isn't it interesting that the Bible begins with an idea that has been argued for centuries—how all things began? And the Bible *ends* with another, even more vociferous, argument over how all things will end.

Perhaps the most important thing to remember about the book of Revelation is that, in spite of honest disagreement among scholars as to the sequence of events described, one thing is for certain. This is actually *not* a book about the end; it's the description of a new beginning.

Revelation contains some of the most glorious and yet most mysterious language concerning the last days, a literary form known as *apocalyptic* writing. Over the years, in my own study and teaching of Holy Scripture, I have believed that a Bible student should be careful not to "shout" when God "whispers." And, when God "shouts," to pay careful attention. In Revelation, we find God both whispering and shouting.

As it concerns many of the issues regarding the end times, God chose to be sparing in His disclosures—to whisper. This is the reason why there has been so much sharp disagreement over what is going to happen—and what may have already happened. The safest way I have found in proceeding is to study the Revelation images as we find them in other books of the Bible. This gives us a sound starting point in our study.

The message of Revelation is deeply felt, even when many of the images it describes are not easily understood. All who have suffered affliction at the hands of the enemies of God have been blessed to read of how God is in control. He will eventually destroy His kingdom's foes and the enemies of the church of Jesus Christ. God wins, Satan loses . . . the end.

■ THE OLD AND NEW COVENANT CONNECTIONS

Reminiscent of accounts from the Old Testament, John is given the opportunity to peek behind the veil, into the workings of heaven. The scene unfolds in a way that ties together the Old and New Testaments.

The Bible was originally written on scrolls. Unlike common writings, where both sides of the scroll were used, the biblical record was written on only one side. The sealed scroll that John described had writing on both sides, leading us to wonder, as was the case with the two-sided scroll in Ezekiel (2:10), if perhaps one side was God's promised blessings and the other His covenant cursings.

The drama in this scene is classical. The tension builds as God's emissary calls out, "Who is worthy to break the seals and open the scroll?"

All eyes look around, searching for one—*the* One—who can open the seals and reveal what is hidden inside. The beasts aren't worthy; the elders aren't worthy; who could it be? Apparently none are worthy.

Like the sword plunged into the stone from the legends of King Arthur, the scroll remains unopened; like the bow of Ulysses that remained unstrung, the scroll lies in wait for the Lamb. The audience is plunged into despair, with no hope of resolution. Then the hero appears to fulfill His destiny.

■ THE CHRIST OF REVELATION

Such is the tension portrayed here, as Jesus Christ comes forward to take the scroll—the lavish blessings of God and the eternal penalty for sinfulness—and breaks its seals. Finally, salvation comes to God's people, and they are overwhelmed with joy and gratitude. Jesus Christ, the Lamb of God, has fulfilled His calling. He has accomplished His mission. He is worthy to receive their worship.

This certainly doesn't sound like the same person who was birthed in a cattle stall, cast out of His hometown, ridiculed by the religious elite, abandoned by His closest friends, tried by a midnight kangaroo court, and executed like a common criminal. No, this sounds more like the apostle Paul's "highly exalted" Savior, the One Whose name is above every name, the King at Whose feet every knee will ultimately bow, the One Whom every tongue will praise . . . the Lamb Who alone is worthy.

It doesn't matter what interpretive grid we use to understand the mysteries of Revelation. On these issues, God's voice is barely audible. But the underlying message of Revelation can be heard at decibels to rival a vicious thunderstorm. Jesus Christ, the Lamb of God, is victorious.

■ THE GLORY OF GOD

I know what it means to love someone deeply as a father, pastor, or Christian friend. And I have had the honor of gently wiping away the tears of those who were suffering or mourning. But please hear this: While this human action soothes us for the moment, it is never permanent. Yesterday's sympathy doesn't suffice for today's struggles.

But Revelation teaches that when God wipes away our tears, He only needs to do it once. Suffering will be forever banished from His kingdom. He will make all things new.

This is what we are seeking—permanent redemption, the renewing, the perfecting of our lives. God, who began a good work in His people, will be faithful to complete it, and that completion will be for His own glory and for our own good.

In heaven, we will be awash in God's glory. We will drink deeply of it. We will soak in it. There will be a river that nourishes the New Jerusalem that flows from under the throne of God. The very essence of a Sovereign God will sustain us. Even though this power is true now, it is not fully known. But in heaven, it will be delightfully clear.

God has spoken. We can drink deeply of every word He has given us. And we can be filled with hope of the glory that awaits us.

1. In his book *Postmillennialism: An Eschatology of Hope*, Keith Mathison defines these terms:

MILLENNIAL DEFINITIONS

Historic Premillennialism: "Historic premillennialism teaches that at the end of the present age there will be the Great Tribulation, followed by the second coming of Christ. At Christ's coming, the Antichrist will be judged, the righteous will be resurrected, Satan will be bound, and Christ will establish His reign on earth, which will last for a thousand years and be a time of unprecedented blessing for the church. At the end of the Millennium, Satan will be released and will instigate a rebellion, which will be quickly crushed. The unrighteous will at this point be raised for judgment, after which the eternal state will begin."

Dispensational Premillennialism: "According to dispensationalism, the present church age will end with the rapture of the church, which, along with the appearance of the Antichrist, will indicate the beginning of the seven-year Great Tribulation on earth. The Tribulation will end with the Battle of Armageddon, in the midst of which Christ will return to destroy His enemies. The nations will then be gathered for judgment. Those who supported Israel will enter into Christ's millennial kingdom, and the rest will be cast into hades to await the Last Judgment. Christ will sit on the throne of David and rule the world from Jerusalem. Israel will be given the place of honor among the nations again. The temple will have been rebuilt and the temple sacrifices will be reinstituted as memorial sacrifices. At the end of the Millennium, Satan will be released and lead unbelievers in rebellion against Christ and the New Jerusalem. The rebellion will be crushed by fire from heaven, and Satan will be cast into the lake of fire. The wicked will be brought before the Great White Throne, judged, and cast into the lake of fire, and at this point the eternal state will commence."

Amillennialism: "Amillennialism sees Revelation 20 as a description of the spiritual reign of Christ with the saints throughout the entire present age, which is characterized by the parallel growth of good and evil. The present 'millennial' age will be followed by the second coming of Christ, the general resurrection, the Last Judgment, and the new heaven and the new earth."

Postmillennialism: "Like amillennialism, postmillennialism teaches that the 'thousand years' of Revelation 20 occurs prior to the Second Coming. Some postmillennialists teach that the millennial age is the entire period of time between Christ's first and second advents, while others teach that it is the last one thousand years of the present age. According to postmillennialism, in the present age the Holy Spirit will draw unprecedented multitudes to Christ through the faithful preaching of the gospel. Among the multitudes who will be converted are the ethnic Israelites who have thus far rejected the Messiah. At the end of the present age, Christ will return, there will be a general resurrection of the just and the unjust, and the final judgment will take place." (From Keith A. Mathison, *Postmillennialism: An Eschatology of Hope* [Phillipsburg, N.J.: P & R Publishing Co., 1999], 9–10.)

ABOUT THE AUTHORS

DR. R. C. SPROUL is chairman and president of Ligonier Ministries, an organization that provides biblical and theological training for laypeople. He has served as a professor at several seminaries and is currently senior pastor of preaching and teaching at St. Andrews Chapel in Sanford, Florida. The author of more than fifty books on philosophy and Christian doctrine, including the award-winning *The Holiness of God*, he also hosts the international radio program, "Renewing Your Mind," heard in over 120 countries.

ROBERT WOLGEMUTH is a popular lay Bible teacher, speaker, and best-selling author. His books include *She Calls Me Daddy*, *Men of the Bible*, and the notes to *The Devotional Bible for Dads*. A veteran publishing industry executive, he has taught the material in *What's in the Bible* to Sunday school classes for over thirty years.

Also Available from R.C. Sproul

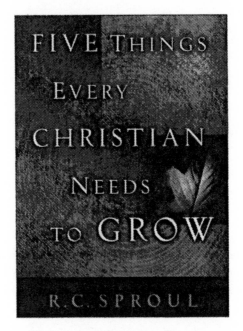

FIVE THINGS EVERY CHRISTIAN NEEDS TO GROW

In this book, veteran pastor and acclaimed theologian Dr. R.C. Sproul outlines for us the balanced diet that produces healthy spiritual growth. There are five things that every Christian needs to grow, according to Dr. Sproul. They are:

- BIBLE STUDY • WORSHIP • PRAYER
- SERVICE • STEWARDSHIP

Are you a brand-new child of God, eager to grow in His likeness? Are you a Christian whose spiritual growth has stagnated? You will be blessed by the practical tips Dr. Sproul offers to incorporate these five essentials into your life.

Also Available from R.C. Sproul

LOVED BY GOD

God is the embodiment of love. He created love. His character and His actions are defined by love. In *Loved by God*, acclaimed theologian R.C. Sproul explores the unrelenting love of God—a love demonstrated most fully through the Son. Sproul also delves into the perplexing aspects of God's divine nature, such as how divine Love coexists with God's holiness and sovereignty, and what the Bible means when it speaks of God's hatred. A compelling book for all who seek to fulfill their calling as Christians—to love as God loves.

CPSIA information can be obtained at www.ICGtesting.com
230289LV00007B/5/A